Food First

Food First

Beyond the Myth of Scarcity

Frances Moore Lappé and Joseph Collins
with Cary Fowler

Houghton Mifflin Company Boston

The authors are grateful for permission to quote from *We Don't Know How* by William and Elizabeth Paddock, © 1973 by Iowa State University Press, Ames, Iowa, reprinted by permission; and from *Eat Your Heart Out* by Jim Hightower, © 1975 by Jim Hightower, reprinted by permission of Crown Publishers, Inc.

Library of Congress Cataloging in Publication Data
Lappé, Frances Moore.   Food first.
Bibliography: p.   Includes index.
1. Food supply. 2. Underdeveloped areas — Food consumption. I. Collins, Joseph, 1945-   joint author.
II. Fowler, Cary, joint author. III. Title.
HD9000.6.L34   338.1'9   77-3733
ISBN 0-395-25347-0

Printed in the United States of America

V 10   9   8   7   6   5

Acknowledgments

During the years devoted to this book, one of our greatest satisfactions has been the discovery of a diverse network of good people everywhere, working hard on these difficult problems and willing to share their information and insights. We thank all of them. Their very existence underscores the fact that the great food awakening is widespread and very much alive.

We especially wish to thank three people whose contribution was so varied that it is impossible to detail but so invaluable that the book would have been impossible without them — Deborah Hepworth, Sue Kanor, and Judy Warneck.

We gratefully acknowledge the research assistance of Cary Fowler, particularly on land and people statistics and on Bangladesh and Food Power.

The book benefited greatly from the research assistance of Henry Frundt, Robert Olorenshaw, David Kinley, Erica Byrd, Connie Phillips, Clark Fisher, Sandra Callier, Peter Mann, and Tonia Heinrichs.

We are grateful to Kathe Flinker, Ann Nicols-Jones, Irene Rusnak, and Sonia Senkiwsky, who helped organize a library of thousands of documents from around the world on which this book draws. We are also grateful for the secretarial assistance of Jo Ann Isaacs, Ellen McAvoy, Jan Martin, Ina Moore, and Diane Spatz.

We also appreciate the help of Ruth Bua, John Callahan, Irene Fleming, Irene Gifford, Joan and Doreen Pietropaulo and Paul and Jeanette Lappé, who lovingly cared for Frances's children, Anthony and Anna, while this book was in progress.

We want to acknowledge those whose work we found especially

useful and whose advice we valued highly — Keith Abercrombie, Peter Adamson, Cynthia Hewitt de Alcántara, Silvio Almeida, George Anthan, Gonzalo Arroyo, Jun Atienza, George Baker, Solon Barraclough, David Baytleman, Fred Beck, Joe Belden, Alan Berg, Thierry Brun, Roger Burbach, The Center for Rural Affairs, Jacques Chonchol, Harry Cleaver, Robert Cohen, Barry Commoner, Kim Conroy, Kenneth Dahlberg, Susan DeMarco, Erik Eckholm, Richard Edwards, Richard Elsner, Ron Erickson, M. Taghi Farvar, Ernest Feder, Pat Flynn, Gil Friend, Isao Fujimoto, Johan Galtung, Susan George, Richard Gilmore, Ole Gjerstad, Harris Gleckman, Jerry Goldstein, Marcel Ganzin, Keith Griffin, Ross Hall, Merle Hansen, Jim Hightower, Anne-Marie Holenstein, Angus Hone, Michael Jacobson, Erich Jacoby, Brennon Jones, Jacques Kozub, Al Krebs, Ken Laidlaw, Robert Ledogar, Al Levinson, Cassio Luiselli, Arthur MacEwan, James McQuigg, Larry Minear, David Morris, Ingrid Palmer, Cheryl Payer, Andrew Pearse, Marco Quiñones, Christopher Robbins, Clodomir Santos de Morais, Susan Sechler, David Stohlberg, Colin Tudge, Liszt Aragon Vieira, Peter de Vries, Jean-Marc von de Weid, H. Garrison Wilkes, and Ben Wisner.

We want to express here our gratitude to all those who read all or part of the rough drafts, offering helpful comment — Ann Barnet, Richard Barnet, Erna Bennett, Richard Berliner, Roger Blobaum, Stephen Bossi, Michael Carder, Arthur Domike, Marion Gallis, Michael Gertler, Grace Goodell, Michael Henry, Marc Lappé, William Luttrell, Maureen MacKintosh, Harry Magdoff, Ali Manwar, Leah Margulies, John Moore, Fatemah Moyhadam, Vahid Nowshirvani, Ted Owens, Pascal de Pury, Marcus Raskin, Idrian Resnick, Mark Ritchie, Plinio Sampaio, Paul Sweezy in addition to many of those previously mentioned.

There are many whose general support and encouragement has been valuable to one or both of us — Eqbal Ahmad, Angus Archer, Sherry Barnes, Victoria Bawtree, Clifflyn Bromling, Diana Calafati, Dick Clark, William Sloane Coffin, Bettina Connor, Rusty Davenport, John Dillon, Frank Dobyns, Norman Faramelli, Edmundo Flores, Ramon Garcia, Nathan Gray, Ted Greiner, Joan Gussow, Steve Hayes, Jack Healey, B. Henderson, Nick Herman, Fred Just, Rich Killmer, Arthur Lincoln, Michael Locker, Ellen McAvoy, Brian MacCall, Julie Marshall, Eleanor McCallie, Mike McCoy, Dan McCurry, Michael Moffitt, Bill Moyer, Charles

Paolillo, Elliott Postol, Jim Ridgeway, Doug Ross, Emma Rothschild, Jacobo Schatan, Nevin Scrimshaw, Jay Steptoe, Milo Thornberry, Erica Thorne, Mark Vermillion, Stanley Weiss, Edie Wilson, and Debbie Wright.

We want to take this opportunity to thank our friends at World Hunger Year — Bill Ayres, Jeri Barr, Rory Bedell, Harry Chapin, Lyn Dobrin, Diane Feyler, and Wray MacKay.

We are grateful to Harry Chapin, Samuel Rubin (through the Transnational Institute), and Stanley Weiss for their much-needed financial assistance for parts of this project.

We want to thank Joan Raines, our literary agent, and Ronald Busch and George Walsh at Ballantine Books for their unwavering faith in this project and Robert Cowley at Houghton Mifflin for his supportive editorial contributions with the assistance of Dale Conway and Mandira Sen.

Finally, our thanks to Frances's brother, John Moore, Jr., for hitting upon *Food First* as just the right name for our book.

Contents

PART VI. The Trade Trap

PART VII. The Myth of Food Power

PART VIII. World Hunger as Big Business

PART IX. The Helping Handout: Aid for Whom?

PART X. Food First

PART I
Why This Book?

Why This Book?

WRITING A POSITIVE BOOK about world hunger sounds to most people like trying to make a joke about death — it just isn't in the material! This attitude comes home to us every time we are introduced to someone and attempt to describe what we are doing. A typical response is a sigh of sympathy overlaid with a look of bewilderment: "Why would any normal person choose to think all day and every day about starving people?" Sometimes we sense latent feelings of guilt because we inevitably appear as individuals who are "making a sacrifice."

We, too, feel uncomfortable. How can we explain in a few sentences that we are not dwelling only on the tragedy of hunger and deprivation? Instead, we are learning for the first time where our own self-interest lies. Rather than being a depressing subject to be avoided, the world food problem has become for us the most useful tool in making sense out of our complex world. But how can we explain that in a few sentences? We cannot — and that is why we decided to write a book.

To discover the positive message hidden in the apparent "hopelessness" of the world food problem we must first face the forces now pushing Americans into positions of guilt, fear, and ultimate despair. Given the threatening way that the global food problem is interpreted for us, is it surprising that most of us wish to shut it out most of the time? Everywhere newspaper headlines carry a clear message:

POPULATION BOMB AND FOOD SHORTAGE: WORLD LOSING FIGHT FOR VITAL BALANCE
New York Times, August 14, 1974

WORLD FOOD CRISIS: BASIC WAYS OF LIFE FACE UPHEAVAL FROM
CHRONIC SHORTAGES

New York Times, November 5, 1974

We are all in a life-and-death contest, we are told, between growing numbers of people and limited amounts of food. We are in a race and some must inevitably lose. The implicit message is that not everyone will have enough to eat. And how will we come out? According to C. W. Cook, retired chairman of General Foods, if we have "to compete with . . . an increasingly crowded and hungry world, providing adequate nutrition to millions of lower-income Americans could become an impossible dream." In *This Hungry World*, Ray Vicker warns: "If food shortages lead to starvation in Asia, Latin America or Africa, we may be affected directly too in inflation, in disease, in shortages and in forced changes in our American way of life."

Since there are *already* so many hungry people in the world, many think it obvious that even now we do not have sufficient food to go around. "Malthus has already been proved correct," declares the president of the Rockefeller Foundation, Dr. John Knowles. Another officer of the Rockefeller Foundation has likened the growth of the world's population to our most dreaded disease, cancer. Population growth was pronounced a "bomb" in the 1960s and a "human tidal wave" in the 1970s.

It is not, however, mere numbers that we are made to fear by these frightening images; the real issue we are supposed to take to heart is that of *whose* numbers are increasing. While describing the "race against hunger," President Nixon told us that "the frightening fact is that the poor are multiplying twice as fast as the rich."

Some writers threaten complete "catastrophe." They refer not just to starvation but to the amorphous specter of the submersion of our "civilized values" and the emergence of "thousands of desperadoes for every one now terrorizing the rich today." Thus not only our diet appears to be at stake, but the very fabric of our civilization is threatened by the hungry seeking our food.

To this dual threat our new, and potentially valuable, environmental awareness adds its own version of the apocalypse. Lester Brown warns that "new signs of agricultural stress on the earth's ecosystem appear almost daily as the exponentially rising food demand, fueled by population growth and rising incomes, presses the ecosystem's finite capacities. . . . There is no way to calculate the trade-off between increases in population and improvements in the quality of life — a choice we must now make as we press against the finite limits of our ecosystem." Such warnings lead people to believe that increases in food production will damage the environment and thereby threaten our future food supply. We are made to fear that there is no way out of scarcity without making our children pay the price.

These threats are sometimes accompanied by a more subtle but just as pervasive message. Americans, we are told, have a special role to play in staving off the apocalypse. We are made to feel that world hunger is our cross to bear. Again and again we read and we hear that the United States is the world's only remaining buffer against starvation. We see world food security defined strictly in terms of how much grain the United States can produce or hold as grain reserves. Inevitably the American consumer believes that food exports to the hungry are to blame for our rising food prices.

One intuitive response to such a burden on our national shoulders is to toughen up, to feel we are being unfairly put upon, to resist. "The United States is not under any moral obligation to feed the world. . . . The responsibility of America's leadership is to America's people," declared Anthony Harrigan of the United States Industrial Council.

Such a reaction to the frightening story of scarcity would be typical of even more Americans, if it were not for an equally deceptive and ultimately negative message pulling us in the opposite direction. Well-intended attempts to stir public action have shifted the world food crisis out of the political-economic arena onto the ground of individual morality. Our consumption is tirelessly contrasted with deprivation elsewhere; the message being that *our* consumption *causes their* suffering. We are told, for example, that the amount of fertilizer used on our lawns, golf courses, and cemeteries equals all of what India uses to grow food. We inevitably experience some shame, feeling our wastefulness must reflect a moral failing. Some find protection by pointing out, quite rightly, that eating one less hamburger a week will not mean that the grain saved will necessarily get to a hungry mouth. Yet with no understanding of how hunger is actually created, we

are defenseless against a diffuse but powerful sense of guilt —
guilt for just being American.

Thus the hungry are made into a powerful threat and, at the
same time, a burdensome responsibility. We are torn.

To resolve our conflict, one appealing answer has emerged:
"Lifeboat ethics" — the simple notion, popularized by scientist
Garrett Hardin, that the earth now constitutes a lifeboat in which
there is not enough food to go around. Isn't it then only logical
that food should go to those most likely to survive, that you do not
risk the safety of all by bringing new passengers on board? "What
happens if you share space in a lifeboat?" asks Dr. Hardin. "The
boat is swamped, and everyone drowns. Complete justice, complete catastrophe."

The remedy offered to ease the pain of our conflict is simple:
Stop feeling. We are told that the Judeo-Christian ethic is out-
moded in this new era of scarcity; that compassion is a luxury we
can no longer afford. A letter from a sociologist in *Science* magazine (March 21, 1975) tells us that our Christian do-gooderism is
the true root of the world's present predicament. "We Westerners
brought it on ourselves, by saving lives through medical skill and
humanitarian generosity. . . . The millions of lives saved by our
medical help became the hundreds of millions of lives that are due
to be lost in famines. . . ." In the same issue a letter from a group
of scientists continues in a similar vein: "The time is now to stop
responding emotionally to what all evidence indicates is an im-
pending disaster. The Judeo-Christian ethic cannot offer long-
term solutions." We are told we must learn a *new ethic*, the ethic
of detached reason; we must learn to let people die for the ultimate survival of the human race.

Such voices do offer one resolution of our conflicting feelings. In
the words of one writer, Peter Collier, they offer us "novocaine for
the uneasy soul." But must we take the novocaine? Do we have to
deaden our sensibilities in order to find some surcease for our anx-
ieties? Or can we transform what appears to be the most impossible problem of our generation — the world food crisis — into the
most useful and constructive tool for understanding the complex
forces that limit our own lives? Can we, moreover, on the strength
of that new insight, gain a sense of personal power over those
forces — forces that increasingly diminish our own freedom of
choice and our own well-being?

Why *Food First*? We met each other on the first national Food

Day in the spring of 1975 at Ann Arbor, Michigan. Frances had been invited as the author of *Diet for a Small Planet* and Joe, because of his work on *Global Reach*, a book on the impact of multinational corporations in underdeveloped countries, and his coauthorship of *World Hunger: Causes and Remedies*, a work countering the official United Nations world food assessment for the 1974 World Food Conference. Following our talks, the students asked us the same urgent questions we each had been asked many times before, and we tried to answer them. Yes, we did have some answers. But we were not satisfied. So afterward we talked and talked. Finally, we concluded that together we would throw all our energy into a search for answers to all the toughest questions that we ourselves had ever asked or that we had ever been asked by others about the causes of hunger. We would then put those answers together in a way we could share with other Americans.

As you read this book you will find that our title *Food First* takes on more than one meaning. In the first place it means that obviously food *must* come first. Until all the people of this earth are able to eat adequately, all other problems pale in significance. More concretely it means that no country can afford to think of its food resources as a *means* toward some other end — such as income from exports — until its people have fed themselves. This applies to the United States as much as it does to any other country in the world. Nor can anyone afford to look to a few countries as suppliers of food for the world. Every country can and must mobilize its own food resources to meet its own needs. Only then can trade serve to expand choices rather than to deprive people of their rightful resources.

As we studied, read, traveled, and interviewed people, we found that the media-repeated themes of scarcity, guilt, and fear are all based on myths. In fact, we had to learn that:

- There is no such thing today as absolute scarcity. *Every country in the world has the capacity to feed itself.*
- The malnourished abroad are *not* hungry because of the individual greed of the average American.
- The hungry are *not* our enemies.

Hunger, in fact, is not the problem at all. Hunger is the symptom of a disease, and we are its victims in much the same way as are the nomads in Mali or peasants in India.

Moreover, we came to see that no society setting out to put Food

First can tolerate the concentration of wealth and power that characterizes most nations today. The heaviest constraint on food production and distribution turns out to be the inequality generated by our type of economic system — the system now being exported to the underdeveloped countries as the supposed answer to their food problems. We are *not* saying merely that the solution to hunger lies in better distribution — getting the food to the hungry instead of the well-fed. We are saying something else: that food distribution only reflects the more fundamental issue of who controls and who participates in the production process. Thus to accept the challenge of Food First is to accept the challenge of confronting the basic assumptions of our present economic system.

But perhaps the greatest reward has been the discovery of realistic and self-liberating answers to the most urgent question: What can Americans do? We learned that Americans do not have to solve the world food problem. Hungry people do and can and will feed themselves, if they are allowed to do so. This qualifying phrase — "if they are allowed to do so" — is the heart of our answer to the question we previously could not adequately answer. Instead of "How can we feed the world?" we now ask an entirely different question: "What are we doing — and what is being done in our name and with our money — to prevent people from feeding themselves?" And "How should we work to remove those obstacles?"

The task of Americans now becomes clear. More important than food aid or designing some rural development project for the Third World is building a movement in this country that makes the connection between the way government, corporate, and landed elites continue to undermine food security both here and abroad. In underdeveloped countries, the forces cutting people out of the production process, and therefore out of consumption, are the same forces that have turned our food system into one of the most tightly controlled sectors of our economy. Fewer and fewer farms control a larger and larger portion of our food. We get more and more needless processing and less nutrition for higher prices. Thus, as we fight to democratize our food economy in this country, we are fighting directly against the very forces that contribute to hunger in other countries.

There is no other road to food security — for others or for us. Americans are made to believe that if justice becomes a priority, production will be sacrificed. We have found the opposite to be true. It is the land monopolizers, both the traditional landed elites and corporate agribusiness, that have proved themselves to be the most inefficient, unreliable, and destructive users of food resources. The *only* guarantee of long-term productivity and food security is for people to take control of food resources here and in other countries.

This is what Food First means to us. The first step, however, in implementing Food First is demystifying the problem of hunger. Maybe this is where we can help most. We did not start out as experts. We started out just as you might. We got interested. Food loomed as the greatest problem of our lifetime. So what could be more compelling? As we learned more and more, read what the "experts" read, traveled through our own country and abroad, we learned that the solution to world hunger is no mystery. It is not locked inside the germ plasm of a seed waiting for a brilliant young agricultural scientist to discover it. It is not spelled out in econometric studies of development planners. No. The only block to the solution to world hunger is the sense of powerlessness people are made to feel: that the enormity of the problem is outside their control, that it should be entrusted to others.

As you now read the questions and answers that follow, please remember that many of these questions are, or once were, our own. All are questions we have been asked over and over again by concerned Americans.

PART II

The Scarcity Scare

1

Standing Room Only? Too Many People?

Question: We now have less than one acre of cultivated land per person in the world and that will be cut in half within a generation even if population growth begins to level off. Aren't there already too many people in relation to our food and agricultural land base?

Our Response: One way to demonstrate that land and food scarcity is not the cause of hunger is to show that there is no scarcity of either. The second is to explain what really does cause hunger. In this book we will do both. But we will begin where this question begins: Are we running out of land and food?

Most people believe there is just not enough food to go around. Yet, despite the tremendous wastage of land — which we will document — and the "food crisis" of the 1970s, the world is producing each day two pounds of grain, or more than 3000 calories, for every man, woman, and child on earth.[1] 3000 calories is about what the average American consumes. And this estimate is minimal. It does not include the many other staples such as beans, potatoes, cassava, range-fed meat, much less fresh fruits and vegetables. Thus, on a global scale the idea that there is not enough food to go around just does not hold up.

Moreover, we have found "acre-to-person" comparisons to be poor measures of food scarcity. To many, the *size* of a plot of land is obviously the most important determinant of how many people it can feed. We have had to learn, however, that much more important than size are four other factors: First, the *level of human investments* made to improve productivity. As demographer Dr. Helen Ware notes, "soil fertility is not a gift of nature, determined once and for all, but dependent upon man's usage of the land." Most people associate the intensive use of the land with the loss of soil fertility, but, as Dr. Ware underscores, "fertility may indeed be the result of intensive methods of land utilization . . ."[2] The croplands of Japan were once inferior to those of northern India; today Japan's foodgrain yield per acre is five times that of India. The original soils of Western Europe, with the exception of the Po Valley and parts of France, were, in general, once of very poor quality yet today they are highly fertile. Centuries ago the soils of Finland were less productive than most of the nearby parts of Russia; today the Finnish croplands are far superior.[3] Thus using an acre as a fixed unit by which to measure the degree of overpopulation is not helpful. Depending on the human investments made, an acre might be capable of feeding five people or one — or none at all.

Second, how many people an acre can feed depends on whether the land is used to *feed people directly or to feed livestock*. In the Andean region of South America and in the Caribbean nearly four times as much land is used for extensive grazing of cattle as is devoted to crops. Cattle ranches often occupy the relatively flat land of the river valleys and coastal plains while food crops are relegated to poorer soils on erosion-prone slopes.[4] Moreover, in a world where many people are too poor to buy all the plant food being produced, livestock has been put into service to rid the economy of "surplus" grain that might drive down prices. Livestock consumes over one third of all the world's grain annually. The result is that the four billion human beings on earth, a figure many would use to measure the burden on our cropland, aren't four billion *equal* units at all. One person can represent a burden on agricultural resources many times greater than another. If a person consumes a largely plant-food diet in which the animal foods eaten are produced on waste materials and nonarable land, his or her "weight" on the cultivated farmland is relatively light. On the other hand, a person is a much greater user of cultivated farmland if he or she eats a diet of animal foods produced by shrinking annually 1800 pounds of grain into 250 pounds of meat, as the average American does. Again, a single acre can sustain a wide range in numbers of people. It depends in part on whether the land is cropped for food for human consumption or for animal feed.

Third, how many people a given measure of land can feed depends on whether it grows *luxury crops for export or food for the local people*. What Americans think of as "food-deficit areas" caused by the pressure of overpopulation are often "food-deficit areas" because much of the food produced goes to small urban elites or is exported. Worst of all, the exports are frequently made in the name of "development."

Here are some food paradoxes to ponder:

- Africa is a net *exporter* of barley, beans, peanuts, fresh vegetables, and cattle (not to mention luxury crop exports such as coffee and cocoa), yet it has a higher incidence of protein-calorie malnutrition among young children than any other continent.[5]
- In Mali, peanut exports to France increased notably during the years of drought while production of food for domestic consumption declined by 1974 to one quarter of what it had been in 1967.[6]
- Mexico now supplies the United States with over one half of its supply of several winter and early spring vegetables while infant deaths associated with poor nutrition are common.[7]
- Half of Central America's agricultural land produces food for export[8] while in several of its countries the poorest 50 percent of the population eat only half the necessary protein. (The richest 5 percent, on the other hand, consume two to three times more than is needed.)[9]

Fourth, agricultural land will, of course, *feed no one at all unless it is cultivated*. This fact seems too obvious to state, and yet many forget that in Africa and Latin America much good land is left unplanted by large landowners. A study of Colombia in 1960 showed that while farmers owning up to about thirteen acres farmed two thirds of their land, the largest farmers, controlling 70 percent of the agricultural surface, actually cultivated only 6 percent of their land.[10] Although Colombia is an extreme example, this pattern is found throughout Latin America. Only 14 percent of Ecuador's tillable land is cultivated.[11]

In addition, corporations often keep large tracts out of production or use them for open-pit mining and operations, such as tin dredging in Malaya, that destroy the topsoil, making land unfit for farming unless expensive reclamation is undertaken. Bauxite, copper, and oil companies decrease the potential food acreage by holding large areas of land thought to have reserves of those natural resources.

This widespread wastage of agricultural land, especially by largeholders, lends credence to the estimate, confirmed by several studies, that only about 44 percent of the world's potentially arable land is actually cultivated.[12]

The relationship of hunger to land turns out to be less a question of quantity than of *use*. We discover that the *amount* of land has less to do with hunger than who controls it.

2

But What About the Real Basketcases?

Question: Maybe in the world as a whole you are right, and there are, in principle, enough food-producing resources to go around. But don't we find the greatest hunger in the heavily populated countries with the fast-growing populations? Aren't there "basketcase" countries like Bangladesh that can't possibly feed themselves?

Our Response: One sees so many maps with the "hungry countries" colored in a darker shade and reads so many references to the "hungry world" that it is hard to escape thinking of hunger as a place — usually as a place "over there."

But think for a minute. Hungry people live in a country with the greatest food surpluses in history. Over 15 percent of all Americans are eligible for food stamps. Yet nutritionists have testified that even with food stamps it is impossible to buy a nutritionally adequate diet. Stanislaus County, California, in the heart of some of America's most productive farmland was nevertheless designated an official Hunger Disaster Area in 1969. Thousands of jobless and underpaid residents went hungry because they did not have money to buy the food they could actually see growing in the fields.

Is it true, that the most densely populated countries are also the hungriest countries? Surveys around the world show no such pattern. Some nations very dense in people per acre also have adequately nourished populations. Three comparisons come to mind. France has just about the same number of people for each cultivated acre as India.[1] Taiwan, where most are adequately nourished, feeds twice as many people per acre as famine-endangered Bangladesh.[2] And China, where starvation was eradicated in only twenty-five years, has twice as many people for each cropped acre than India.[3]

On the other hand, countries with relatively few people per cultivated acre nevertheless are often ones where most of the people are malnourished. In Africa, south of the Sahara, one of the worst famine areas in the world, there are almost two and one-half *cultivated* acres per inhabitant, more than in the United States or the Soviet Union and six to eight times more than in China. (And this estimate for Africa may represent as little as 12 percent of the region's potentially cultivable land.)[4]

Moreover the population in many parts of Africa is probably less dense than it was in the sixteenth century before the slave trade. Indeed, some economists have argued that certain African countries are *under*populated in terms of the labor force needed for agricultural development.

At the other extreme, a few African countries such as Ghana and Kenya have population-to-cultivated acre ratios approaching or greater than that of India. Yet these two countries do not hold the worst nutrition record in Africa. At present, that record is held by Zaire, a country with a smaller population per cultivated acre than most European and many Latin American countries. Zaire has the lowest protein per person intake in the world.[5]

Latin America, like Africa, is a region of overall low population density. With 16 percent of the world's cultivable land it has only 6 percent of the world's population yet proportionately more hungry people than in India, Pakistan, and Bangladesh. Here again there is no apparent relationship between the amount of agricultural land available per person and the extent of hunger. In a country like Bolivia, severe undernourishment is a daily reality for most of the population; yet Bolivia has well over one-half acre of cultivated land per person, significantly more than France (and a potential of over ten cultivable acres per person). Mexico, where most of the rural population is poorly fed, has more cultivated land per person than Cuba,[6] where now, virtually no one is underfed. Certainly there are countries in Latin America with both relatively high population density and widespread hunger — countries like Haiti and the Dominican Republic. But they are the exceptions.

As long as food is something bought and sold in a society with great income differences, the degree of hunger tells us nothing about the density of the population.

Bangladesh — A Basketcase?

Bangladesh is often singled out as the archetype of a country whose population has simply overwhelmed its resources. When our studies of countries around the world began to suggest that there is probably no country where local food resources are not sufficient for the population, we decided to focus on Bangladesh — the "basketcase." Frankly, we thought it might be an exception. It isn't.

Bangladesh probably now produces enough to keep all its people sufficiently fed. But the rich eat several times more grain than the poor. They consume 30 percent more calories than the poor and twice the protein. Even more revealing is the fact that food hoarders smuggle as much as one third of all Bangladesh's marketed grain across the border into India to be sold for much-valued rupees at prices twice as high as Bangladesh.[7] As in other countries, the poor do not eat no matter how much food there is. While many starved after the 1974 floods, an estimated 4 million tons of rice stacked up for want of buyers because, in the words of *National Geographic*, "the vast majority . . . were too poor to buy it." Much of this rice was grown by the very hungry who needed it. In order to pay off high-interest debts to moneylenders, they had to sell at harvest time when prices were at their lowest. Forced later to borrow again to buy at speculators' prices and in competition with higher-income city dwellers in India, they obviously faced increased chances of even greater hunger the following year.[8]

Bangladesh has twice the cultivated land per person as Taiwan. Moreover, its rich alluvial soils give it cropland second to none other in the world. Bangladesh has adequate potential water supplies even in the dry season, an ideal climate for year-round cultivation allowing for three harvests a year of rice, and inland fishery resources that, according to one Food and Agriculture Organization (FAO) research group, are "possibly the richest in the world."[9]

Why is the extraordinary food potential of Bangladesh unrealized? Not because there are too many people but because an elite few prevent the majority from having access to the country's resources. Without access to those resources, the majority of the people not only do not benefit from them but their initiative and energies do not go into making those resources more productive. Consider the vast inland fishing resources. At present the fishing areas are controlled by absentee owners who are satisfied to sell a small quantity of fish at high prices to a few well-off consumers. Their profits are so inflated that they find it unnecessary to invest in improving the fishing methods. The fishermen are mere hired hands who see no point in improving their fishing skills or the fish resources; they know they themselves would not benefit. In addition, the fishermen are, according to a confidential United Nations report,[10] severely exploited by the absentee owners, for the urban consumers pay about 500 to 600 percent more than what the fishermen receive — prices that keep fish out of reach of millions. Cooperative fishing by fishermen, who know that acquiring the knowledge to increase fish yields would benefit themselves, could provide employment to hundreds of thousands of landless families and an excellent protein source for millions. In this regard Bangladesh could well follow the example of Taiwan; through small-scale inland fisheries its fish production has increased eight times in only 25 years.

Then there is the pattern of landownership. About one quarter of Bangladesh's farmland is operated by sharecroppers who must take all the risks and give most of what they grow to the absentee landlords.[11] Only 7 percent of the country's farms take up 31 percent of the farmland.[12] Yet the larger landholdings tend to be less productive per acre and provide a livelihood for fewer people than those of small farmers. Moreover, the large landholders, whose farms are not, above all, a source of food for their families, frequently plant nonfood crops such as jute for export instead of rice. While the many go without rice, the few earn foreign exchange to pay for an imported life-style. Meanwhile, about two thirds of the rural population have no land at all or less than two and one half acres per household.[13] Those with little or no land must depend on meager wages for seasonal work on large farms. Controlling no food producing resources, they cannot store food and therefore are particularly vulnerable to adverse times: Precisely when floods and droughts deprive them of work altogether, speculative food prices due to hoarding shoot up from 200 to 500 percent.

Seasoned agricultural economist René Dumont reported during the 1974 famine that the richest landholders in Bangladesh stood in line all night at land registry offices in order to buy land that the hungry, mortgaged small farmers were selling as a last resort. As a 1974 report from the University of Dacca explained, "Fundamentally hoarding, blackmarketing and smuggling, although decried as 'anti-social,' are only rational behaviours of 'profit maximizers,' the heroes of private enterprise, in situations where ... the structure of command over scarce goods is unrelated to the structure of needs."[14] Competing with each other for the scarce resources not monopolized by the rich, millions of small farmers, sharecroppers, and landless laborers in Bangladesh are prevented from joining in collective self-help action to improve the country's food-growing resources. Yet only by such common effort could the people of Bangladesh build and maintain the irrigation and drainage canals and embankments necessary to convert water from the constant flood threat it now represents to the extraordinary resource it could be.

For such reasons, a 1975 FAO report on Bangladesh concludes, "A policy of really drastic land redistribution might promote *both production and equity*."[15] Cooperative farming structures could overcome the danger that redistribution would break up the land into units too small to be efficiently farmed. Greater production would result because for the first time the *entire* rural population would sense that the work necessary to unleash the land's great potential would benefit them and not the landlord or moneylender.

One measure of this untapped potential is that, even though one third to one half of the country's cultivated area could be irrigated at virtually no financial expense, only about 5 percent is actually irrigated.[16] Another measure is in crop yield potentials. Despite the basically prime natural conditions, current rice yields are only one half the world average and a mere 15 percent of what has been shown to be possible on experimental plots in Bangladesh itself.

Bangladesh, then, is not a hopeless basketcase. As we found in every other supposedly hopeless country, there is no insurmountable *natural* obstacle to its people feeding themselves. Their future need not be some combination of starvation and debilitating and degrading charity. The key obstacle is the present power of a few to postpone an urgent social reconstruction.

3

The Price Scare?

Question: Perhaps in specific countries you can make the case that the misappropriation of the land generates hunger. But how can you avoid seeing the *global* trend? Is not the rising price of food throughout the world proof that we have entered an age of scarcity? The time of cheap food appears to be over for good. The poor countries are placing greater demands on our food resources than ever before, not to mention the Russians. How can you say that these global trends are not, at least in large part, a reflection of a growing number of people on a limited agricultural base?

Our Response: As strange as it may sound, what we are taught to view as scarcity is actually a product of efforts to cope with the problem of *over*production in a world where most hungry people cannot buy the food that is produced.

This crisis of overproduction spawns scarcity-creating solutions: production cutbacks, the planting of nonfood and animal feed instead of food crops, and built-in inefficiencies in the use of what is produced. There *is* scarcity, but it is not a scarcity of food. The scarcity is of people who have either access to the means to grow their own food or the money to buy it.

Agricultural legislation in the United States going back to the 1930s reveals that historically the major farm problem has been overproduction. After the scourge of overproduction during the Depression toppled farm prices, the Agricultural Adjustment Act of 1933 established guaranteed minimum prices for crops. The allotment system (establishing limits to the acreage a farmer could plant with a particular crop), the Soil Bank (paying farmers to hold a certain number of acres out of production), and various other programs are some of the methods employed over the years to regulate and curtail the production capacity of America's farmers.

Approaching the 1970s, who would have thought that scarcity was around the corner? 1969 was called the year of the "Great Wheat Glut." An article in *Nation's Business*, in September 1969, entitled "Too Much of a Good Thing" and subtitled "America's Farm Problem Is Not How to Grow More Food but How to Grow Less" pictured a farmer standing on a tractor in the middle of a "field of plenty" waving the white flag of surrender. The article's conclusion: "There are too many farmers, working too many farms, with too vast a capacity to produce."

What Americans know as the "food crisis of rising prices," starting in 1972–1973, was largely the direct and intentional result of United States "Food Power" policies that hit upon scarcity as a way to increase both the volume and price of agricultural exports. As we will show in Part VII, Food Power was a strategy to create demand and raise prices so as to increase the foreign exchange earnings of the United States. The stage had already been set by acreage cutbacks in the late sixties and early seventies to deal with the mounting surplus of grain. The acreage allotment figure for 1970 was only 75 percent of that of 1967; less land was cultivated in 1970 than in 1948–1952.[1] In both 1969 and 1970 the amount of grain that could have been grown, but was not, on land held out of production amounted to over seventy million metric tons[2] — about double all the grain imported annually in the early seventies by the underdeveloped countries.

Against this backdrop, United States officials started to maneuver. By devaluing the dollar (thus making our grain cheaper abroad), by rescinding a law requiring that half of our grain going to the Soviet Union and Eastern Europe be carried by American ships, and by offering the Soviet Union financing for its grain purchases, the United States set the food bait. Other countries began to bite. The notorious Soviet grain deal was the first catch. Nineteen million tons of grain went not to feed the hungry but to feed Soviet livestock.

Nature cooperated, too, with a late monsoon in India, drought conditions in West Africa, China, Australia, and Argentina and a precipitous drop in the anchovy fish catch (used for feeding livestock). But United States strategists could not depend on the weather to create scarcity. Although they must have been aware of these adverse weather conditions in many parts of the world, President Nixon and Secretary of Agriculture Earl Butz took another five million acres of wheat land *out* of production in September 1972. This act marked the largest holdout of cropland in several years — equal in size to all the farmland in the United Kingdom. Then in early 1973, when export sales had started to cool down, the United States devalued the dollar for a second time — suddenly making American grain 15 percent cheaper for the Japanese. The Japanese jumped at the bait. A new cycle of scarcity was generated by the decisions of a few government policy makers.

The result was that world grain stocks that had stood at ninety five days worth of grain in 1961 were now down below thirty days. This planned and rapid depletion of grain reserves, more than any other single factor, contributed to the unprecedented increase and volatility in food prices. Scarcity, however, was *not* the problem; the world produced more grain per capita in the so-called scarcity year 1972–1973 — about 632 pounds — than it had in the year 1960, not considered a crisis year.

Yo-Yo Prices

The market system has built-in commodity cycles in which "years of glut" follow "years of want." The result? Yo-yo prices.

Do you remember that in 1973–1974 we were experiencing a rice "shortage"? By 1975 a Louisiana rice producer assessed the situation in this manner: "In my opinion there is just too much rice."[3] In the market system, a period of glut is the consequence of the previous period of scarcity. In the 1960s there was overproduction in relation to what people could buy. Prices fell as rice bags piled up. With low prices by 1970, investment in rice dropped and planting was cut back. The result: By 1973 the price of rice had doubled compared to the early 1960s. We then heard cries of scarcity. With prices up, of course, investment flowed in and production soared. By 1975, then, the rice growers grumbled about "the glut."

Chemical fertilizer is another dramatic example. New plants were constructed in the 1960s. Profits dipped as supply outdistanced buyers because most of the world's farmers are too poor to afford chemical fertilizer. The companies then cut back produc tion in hopes of increasing profits. As the world price of fertilizer climbed, the return on investment by the fertilizer industry jumped from 1.1 percent in 1971 to 39.6 percent in 1974.[4] Then, in less than a year, prices had soared so high that purchases again slowed down. In June, 1975, *Business Week* was covering the "fertilizer glut."

These alternating periods of glut and shortage occur because we have a food production system in which investment decisions are basically made only on assessments of *current* profitability. If prices are good now, farmers and livestock producers will plant or breed to take advantage of the prices. But since all other producers are following exactly the same cue, when the time comes to reap the harvest or slaughter the animal (in the case of cattle this may be thirty-two months from the initial decision to breed), there may well be a surplus, causing prices to drop. With prices down, farmers and cattlemen will be reluctant to plant or breed heavily; thus, there will be a future shortage, causing high prices. So the cycle begins anew.

Grain and livestock cycles are tightly interwoven. A good feedgrain harvest results in increased livestock production until the increase generates its own production cutback as livestock prices fall. Experts now expect the hog cycle to become more irregular; since grain reserves have been wiped out, the level of hog production will even more closely reflect each year's feedgrain harvest.

Americans are told that these price cycles represent the healthy balancing mechanism at the heart of a market system. The catch is that in a food processing and marketing system tightly controlled by a few corporations, consumer prices climb up in response to basic commodity cycles but often never come back down to where they were when the cycle began. Commodity price cycles then become a handy smoke screen for profit margin increases.

Chronic Surplus

The American people are being asked to believe that the age of scarcity is upon us. Yet, as long as food is bought and sold like any other commodity and as long as a large portion of people are too poor to buy the food they need, the major problem of agricultural economists will continue to be the threat of surplus, not scarcity.

Feeding over a third of the world's grain production to animals is one way enterprising profit-seekers have devised to reduce a price-deflating surplus and simultaneously to create a product for which the consumer will be willing to pay a high price. (Such a way of dealing with a chronic surplus situation makes it easy to forget that livestock *can* be produced with virtually no grain, as are the 250 million pigs in China!)

But feeding grain to livestock does not always so easily take care of the surplus. In 1975–1976 we were in the midst of a chronic world dairy surplus with stocks in Western markets heading toward an all-time peak — at least double those in most recent years. One way to deal with the surplus produced by livestock is to feed it right back to livestock. The European Economic Community (EEC) recently introduced a plan to get rid of its 400,000 tons of surplus powdered skim milk by requiring livestock producers to incorporate the milk into their feed rations.[5] This practice is nothing new. In 1973 the EEC used one million tons of skim milk powder as calf feed to produce high-cost veal.

The theory that we are now entering the age of inevitable scarcity because our numbers have surpassed some supposed threshold cannot be substantiated. In a world where food stocks are deliberately depleted so that United States grain exports might earn the greatest foreign exchange and where the major headache of hundreds of agricultural specialists around the world is how to *reduce* mountains of so-called surplus, the notion of scarcity is worse than a distortion. It shifts the blame for scarcity onto nameless masses of people and onto the "natural limits" of the earth. Seen this way, scarcity becomes a scare word before which we all feel powerless.

4

More People: A Thinner Slice for Everyone?

Question: As high birth rates eat up the economic growth of a country, won't its total production necessarily be divided up into smaller and smaller shares? And won't less economic growth mean that people will become poorer and less able to buy food?

Our Response: First, this question assumes that the growth rate of the economy of a country, as measured by standards such as Gross National Product (GNP), reflects the welfare of the people. But such measures become meaningless when one learns, for example, that Mexico in the early 1970s was declared "developed" because its per capita GNP had passed the magic $600 mark. At the same time, however, both the nutritional level and the real income of the rural majority in Mexico have been steadily declining.

Second, if this thesis is right, we would expect to find high birth rates correlated with low economic growth rates. What in fact do we find? One extensive study compares the population and economic growth rates of underdeveloped countries for the twenty-year period, 1950–1970.[1] The study shows, for example, that although Nicaragua has one of the fastest growing populations, its per capita national production grew faster than that of countries like Chile and Malawi whose populations are among the slower growing of underdeveloped countries. Examples of countries showing a *negative* growth in overall production per person could be found among those with both slower and faster growing populations. Simply put, there seems to be no clear relationship between national production per person and the growth rate of the population. *If anything*, the faster growing populations appear to have a slight edge.

It may seem to be self-evident that the more people there are, the less there is of everything for each person — until we remember that it is people who grow food and create all other goods.

5

Are People a Liability or a Resource?

Question: Certainly no one can deny that there are too many people in relation to the jobs available in underdeveloped countries. Economist Barbara Ward has likened the urban migration resulting from rural unemployment to a "tidal wave, a hurricane Camille of country people." For her, "it is not so much immigration as inundation." Robert McNamara, President of the World Bank, has described the growing number of unemployed as "'marginal men,' the wretched strugglers for survival on the fringes of farm and city."

Isn't the tragedy of unemployment-related hunger simply that a long-needed revolution in agricultural production is inevitably leaving behind an increasing number of unskilled, illiterate people? Haven't their numbers long surpassed what agriculture can constructively absorb? Aren't these modernizing countries condemned to growing numbers of surplus people left behind without jobs and thus without income for food?

Our Response: Terms like "tidal wave" and "inundation" can readily lead us to believe that we are witnessing a natural and inevitable process. Dramatic metaphors can jolt us by the very power of their imagery, but they can also lead us away from real understanding.

This question reflects several widely held beliefs that we have found to be myths.

MYTH ONE: *Agriculture in underdeveloped countries is held back because there are just too many people in the countryside to be productively put to work.*

If too many workers per acre really stood in the way of production, wouldn't countries that have a *more* productive agriculture have *fewer* workers per acre than their less successful neighbors? Yet, what do we find? Japan and Taiwan, both thought of as agriculturally successful, have more than twice as many agricultural workers per acre than the Philippines and India. The value of production per acre in Japan is seven times that of the Philippines and ten times that of India.[1] The overall trend, in fact, seems to show a *positive* relationship between the number of workers on a unit of land and the level of agricultural output on that unit of land. This may be hard for Americans to accept because we are taught to measure productivity in terms of how *few* people it takes to grow food. Such a measure makes no sense at all in underdeveloped countries with vast, untapped human labor resources.

Countries we think of as heavily overpopulated — countries that we assume could not use even one more farmer — are not necessarily overcrowded agriculturally. When China attempted to increase production utilizing its human labor potential, it found that it could gainfully triple or even quadruple the labor input per acre. Indeed, the World Bank has said that if countries like India could attain Japan's level of labor intensity — two workers per hectare (2.5 acres) — their agriculture could absorb all the labor force expected by 1985.[2] The significant difference, of course, is that countries like Japan, Taiwan, and China have developed labor-intensive farming that *productively* employs the additional labor; India and the Philippines have not.

Clearly, a large rural population is far from the handicap it is often perceived to be. In some countries a good case can even be made that there are *too few* agricultural workers. A recent survey of African rural development efforts concludes that many schemes had failed because of scarce agricultural labor. Focusing on the Ivory Coast, the survey noted a chronic shortage of unskilled labor in agriculture even to the point of having to import laborers from neighboring countries.[3] Large agricultural projects like the Gezira Scheme in Sudan were made possible only by importing labor from neighboring countries. Yet the migration of workers has frequently left regions to a large extent stripped of able-bodied manpower needed for local agricultural development.

MYTH TWO: *Since agriculture cannot absorb any more people, the overflow from rural areas must go to the cities where new jobs in industry must be created for them.*

It was exactly this analysis of the problem that prompted both the neglect of agriculture and the promotion of industrialization by development planners during the 1950s and 1960s. The result? A lot of capital investment but remarkably few new industrial jobs.

The percentage of workers employed in manufacturing dropped from 8.5 percent to 7.6 percent of the total labor force between 1900 and 1950 in underdeveloped countries.[4] This pattern holds even in countries like Brazil touted as "miracles" of industrial development. Between 1950 and 1964, the Indian government increased the capital invested in large-scale manufacturing fifteen-fold. Yet during the same period, the number of workers employed by such manufacturing only slightly more than doubled.[5] Foreign corporations with their labor-saving technologies from high labor-cost countries like the United States have aggravated the chronic "jobs crisis." Two hundred fifty-seven multinational corporations studied in Latin America employ less than one half the number of people per unit of sales as do local companies.[6] A corporation invariably claims its investment "created" so many hundred jobs. Many economists have come to recognize, however, that a new modern factory employing a couple hundred persons might well be putting thousands of local craftsmen out of business. Moreover, local savings borrowed by a foreign corporation to create a factory could have been used in entirely different ways that would have created many more jobs.

Efforts to solve the unemployment problem by creating jobs in centralized, urban areas are misplaced in any case. In underdeveloped countries agriculture and small-scale decentralized workshops serving the needs of local agriculture have the greater potential to absorb workers. China has been able to reduce the percentage of its workforce in full-time agricultural jobs to about 54 percent in contrast to the 70 to 85 percent in most underdeveloped countries. Likewise in Taiwan farm labor is now only 30 percent of the total. This was accomplished, not by creating urban industries, but by developing small factories and workshops throughout the countryside to make farm implements and basic consumer goods. China's large *rural,* but nonagricultural, popula-

tion also represents a sizable reserve labor force for agriculture —
on hand to deal with peak season farm labor bottlenecks that in
many countries are used to justify premature and costly mechanization.

MYTH THREE: *Population growth is a tremendous burden to the
struggling economies of the Third World countries since it
means having to scare up more jobs when 15 to 30 percent of the
population is already without work and much of the so-called
employed are really underemployed. The result is increasing
numbers of half-starved, marginal people living outside the
economy.*

In researching this book we began to understand that "marginal" people are not born. They are not caused by the inevitable
overflow of a limited land base or by the fixed capacity of an
economy to absorb workers. What, then, makes people appear
marginal and superfluous?

In sixteenth-century England and nineteenth-century Scotland
a shift in land use led directly to the appearance of "too many
people." The landed gentry had decided that sheep would be more
profitable than farming. Sheep, however, need a lot of land and
only a few shepherds. Land, therefore, was "enclosed" and
thousands of farming peasants were shut out. Many contempo-
rary commentators saw in the growing number of landless vag-
abonds a sure sign of "too many people" — a view that helped to
motivate overseas explorations. The overpopulation existed, of
course, only in relation to a sheep-based agricultural economy.
The total population of England in the sixteenth century was less
than in any one of several present-day English cities.[7]

Colonial powers similarly created such marginal people by reducing highly diversified agricultural systems to single crops —
monocultures on which the most profit could be made in foreign
markets. Converting whole countries into production sites for one
or two crops meant that planting and harvests were no longer
staggered throughout the year. Employment opportunities were
therefore limited to the cycle of the one or two main export crops.
Thus, in the predominantly sugar-plantation economy of Cuba
during the mid-fifties a half million sugar workers were employed
only for four months a year — at the time of the sugar harvest.[8]

Indeed, people are being made to appear marginal today by the
further transformation of agriculture taking place in most under-

developed countries. Once the livelihood of millions of self-provisioning farmers, agriculture is becoming the profit base of influential commercial entrepreneurs — traditional landed elites, city-based agricultural speculators, and foreign corporations. These new agricultural entrepreneurs use profits both to enlarge their landholdings at the expense of the small farmer and the landless and to mechanize production at the expense of the laborer's job. Some examples:

- Pakistan: A Pakistan Planning Commission official states that full mechanization on farms of twenty-five acres or more could displace 600,000 to 700,000 workers in fifteen years. The number of tractors in Pakistan has gone up from 3000 in 1960 to 20,000 in 1969.[9]
- Latin America: Each tractor displaces about three workers in Chile and about four in Colombia and Guatemala. A conservative estimate is that two and a half million laborers have been already displaced by tractor mechanization in Latin America. And less than a third of these will find other rural employment.[10]
- Central America: Coffee growers in Guatemala and Costa Rica have roughly halved their labor requirements by mechanization. The number of laborers needed per acre for banana production is now one quarter of what it was in 1930.[11] Sugar is a similar story.
- India: In the Punjab it is expected that by 1980 the demand for hired labor in field crop production will all but disappear.[12]

Displacing tenants and laborers with machines means a larger marketable harvest and more profit for the commercial cultivator — in addition to freedom from the "management problem" of a sizable underpaid labor force. Replacing people with machines in countries with immense untapped labor resources is not, of course, of social value. The value accrues only to the individual operator who can use machines to maximize the profit made on each laborer. As this process proceeds, however, all the outsider sees is more unemployment and therefore concludes that there are just too many people.

Both questions, on pages 27 and 29, reveal a lot about how we Americans are conditioned to regard people. We are made to think of people as an economic liability when, in reality, all the wealth of any country begins and ends with people — *with human labor*. The economic success of a nation does not depend so much on rich natural resources as on how effectively its people can be motivated and their labor utilized. People appear as a liability *only* in a certain type of economic system: one in which economic success is not measured by the well-being of all the people; one in which production is increasingly monopolized by a few; and one in which technology is used to exclude people from the production process so as to maximize the profit the landlord makes on each worker. People are not born marginal.

6

People Pressure on the Ecosystem?

Question: You have talked about the population problem in terms of the economic system. But what about the impact of increasing numbers of people on the ecosystem? The present high rates of population growth are putting tremendous pressures on the global environment that could have irreparable consequences for future food production. Perhaps *we* will not suffer but what about our children and their children?

Overgrazing, large-scale erosion, and encroaching deserts provide evidence of strain on the ecosystem, as the number of livestock and people increase. Increasing numbers of people are forcing agriculture onto marginal and vulnerable land. According to Lester Brown's *By Bread Alone*: "One consequence of the continuous growth in population is the spread of agriculture to land with thin mantles of topsoil that will not sustain continuous and intensive cultivation."[1] Surely you must recognize population pressures as the crucial factor in these ominous trends towards environmental decay.

Our Response: We share this concern about the long-term consequences of our present path. We, too, see signs of ecological destruction. The deterioration of our global ecosystem and its agricultural resources does coincide with an increase in the population of human beings and livestock. Yet is there a necessary causal link? We have had to conclude there is not.

Much of the current destruction of the ecosystem in underdeveloped countries began with colonialism. The plantations established by the colonial powers put a double burden on the land. First, they expropriated the best land for continuous cultivation of crops for export. Second, they usually pushed the local farmers onto marginal, often hilly, land not at all suitable for intensive farming. Land that otherwise might have served for grazing, forestry, or recreation soon became ravaged by erosion.

This double burden — cash cropping for export and squeezing the majority of farmers onto erosion-prone lands — is being reinforced today. Take a Central American country like El Salvador. The country is mostly steep hills and mountains. The most fertile and productive lands are the middle volcanic slopes, some scattered interior river basins, and the coastal plain. Beginning with the Spanish conquest, these prime lands have been owned by large estates devoted to exports: cotton, sugar, and coffee crops and cattle ranches. Less than one in a hundred farms in El Salvador has more than 250 acres; but those few that do, together take up *half* of the total farming area of the country, including all of the prime land.[2]

The land leftover, now mainly barren hills, is all that some 350,000 *campesinos* have on which to scratch out a subsistence living for their families. Much of the land they are forced to cultivate is so steep, it has to be planted with a stick. The erosion can be so devastating — one study concluded 77 percent of the nation's land is suffering from accelerated erosion[3] — that the *campesinos* must abandon a slope after a single year's meager yield. Where they will go in the future is not at all clear. Already the rapid soil depletion has set off a heavy migration of Salvadorians into neighboring Honduras. This land search by desperate Salvadorians helped precipitate a war between the two countries in 1969. And we were told that this was the first war in history caused by the population explosion.

It is tempting to look at an area such as the Caribbean, where semitropical forests have been destroyed and soil badly eroded, and simply diagnose the problem as too many people. Currently, local farms feed only one third of the Caribbean population and 70 percent of the children are malnourished.[4]

But before accepting "too many people" as the cause, consider some figures on Caribbean land use. Over half of all the arable land in the Caribbean is planted with cash crops for export: sugar cane, cocoa, bananas, tobacco, vegetables, and coffee. In individual countries the usurpation of the best land for export crops is even more dramatic. In Guadeloupe over 66 percent of the arable land is put to the plow for sugar cane, cocoa, and bananas. In Martinique over 70 percent is planted with sugar cane, cocoa, bananas, and coffee. In Barbados, 77 percent of the arable land grows sugar cane alone.[5]

"Haiti," comments environmentalist Erik Eckholm, "is among the few countries that already rival or perhaps surpass El Salvador in nationwide environmental destruction."[6] Not coincidentally, only a few people own the country's farmland. The best valley lands belong to a handful of elites and their foreign partners, who produce endless vistas of sugar cane, coffee trees, and cattle — all for export. We were particularly struck to see the miserable shacks of the landless along the edge of fertile irrigated fields growing feed for thousands of pigs that wind up as sausages for Chicago's Servbest Foods. Meanwhile the majority of Haitians are left to ravage the once-green mountain slopes in near futile efforts to grow food. In desperation thousands have fled to the United States, where they compete with the poorest paid Americans for minimum wage jobs.

The same pattern holds in South America. In Colombia the good level land, according to a World Bank study,[7] belongs to absentee landlords who frequently use it only for grazing cattle. We already noted that in 1960 rich landowners controlling 70 percent of all the country's agricultural land actually cultivated only 6 percent. Moreover, much of their land that once did grow staples like corn and wheat is now producing feed grain as well as carnations and other "ornamental crops" for export. The World Bank study found that at the same time "large numbers of farm families . . . try to eke out an existence on too little land, often on slopes of . . . 45 degrees or more. As a result, they exploit the land very severely, adding to erosion and other problems, and even so are not able to make a decent living."[8]

In Africa it is colonialism's cash crops and their continuing legacy, not the pressure of its population, that are destroying soil resources. Vast tracts of geologically old sediments perfectly suitable for permanent crops such as grazing grasses or trees have instead been torn up for planting cotton and peanuts. The soil becomes rapidly poor in humus and loses its cohesiveness. The wind, quite strong in the dry season, then easily erodes the soils. Soil deterioration leads to declining crop yields[9] and consequently to an expansion of cultivated land, often onto marginal soils.

In dramatic contrast to cash-cropping monoculture, the traditional self-provisioning agriculture that it replaces is often quite sound ecologically. It is a long-evolved adaptation to tropical soil and climate. It reflects a sophisticated understanding of the complex rhythms of the local ecosystem. The mixing of crops, sometimes of more than twenty different species, means harvests are staggered and provides maximum security against wholesale losses due to unseasonable weather, pests, or disease. Moreover, mixed cropping provides the soil with year-round protection from the sun and rain.

The problem of soil erosion *is* serious. We have discovered, however, that soil erosion occurs largely because fertile land is monopolized by a few, forcing the majority of farmers to overuse vulnerable soils. Moreover, soil impoverishment results, not from an effort to meet the basic food needs of expanding populations, but increasingly from the pressure to grow continuously nonfood and luxury export crops over large areas to the neglect of traditional techniques that once protected the soil.

Overgrazing: A Case Study in Land Misuse

Overgrazing is another sure way to ruin marginal lands. But to get at the cause one must ask, Who is overgrazing and why? And does it follow that marginal lands can never be suitable for livestock? Finally, since overgrazing means too many cattle on the land, must we conclude this reflects too many people?

Some outsiders see Africa's nomadic pastoralists as the culprits. We have come to learn, however, that nomadic pastoralists have traditionally made efficient use of vast stretches of semiarid land that otherwise would remain unproductive. While their migrations might look random to the outsider, they are, in reality, patterned to take advantage of variations in rainfall and vegetation. The nomads may herd their livestock over hundreds of miles from rainy season pastures to oases of perennial grasses in dry seasons. Pastoral nomadism, then, is a rational response to an environment characterized by the scarcity of water, seasonal drought, and widely scattered seasonal fodder resources. The nomads' tactics make use of resources that others would not even consider as resources.[10]

Another adaptation technique of traditional pastoralists is keeping a herd that consists of different types of livestock: camels, sheep, goats, donkeys, as well as cattle. A mixed herd can exploit a variety of ecological niches. Cattle and sheep graze on grasslands; camels graze but also browse on shrubs and high parts of trees; and goats browse on shrubs and low parts of trees. Valuable protein for human consumption is thus produced by plants that humans cannot eat. Different species also have different reproductive cycles; staggered breeding seasons ensure some type of milk throughout the year. The hardiness of goats and camels make them good animals to fall back on in times of drought when cattle die off. A varied herd also acts as a walking storehouse for food, either directly or in exchange for grain, during annual dry spells and periodic droughts.

Pastoralists traditionally produced enough meat and dairy products to exchange with farmers for grain. In addition, the pastoralists' herds annually manured the fallow fields of the farmers. The animals thus gained good grazing land and the fertility of the farmers' soil improved. This symbiotic relationship allowed for remarkably dense populations to comfortably inhabit seemingly inhospitable lands.[11]

If raising livestock has been and can be such an excellent way to make marginal lands productive, what has gone wrong? What is behind the many reports of overgrazing in regions, like the African Sahel, that vast stretch of semiarid land along the southern border of the Sahara?

To answer such questions we have to go back to the beginning of this century. The French colonial administration created arbitrary "national" borders (today enforced by the newly independent governments) without regard to the need of the nomads to migrate. Endless restrictions have made it increasingly difficult for the nomads to shift their herds in response to the short- and long-term cycles of nature.

The French also slapped a head tax on each nomad. The tax had to be paid in French francs even though most nomads lived within a barter economy. The nomads needed, therefore, to raise more livestock, so that some could be sold for cash. Over the years, their need for money has been compounded by the growing lure of imported consumer goods.

Higher market prices also prompted pastoralists to build up

their herds beyond the carrying capacity of the lands. Even the sedentary population began to keep small herds near their houses. These herds, kept in such a confined space, resulted in localized overgrazing.[12] Moreover, the urban and export demand for beef induced the pastoralists to upset the natural balance of a diversified herd in favor of cattle. Modern inoculations against disease also facilitated the build-up of herds beyond the carrying capacity of the grazing lands. Medicine that was meant to save these herds ultimately contributed to the death by starvation of tens of thousands of animals.

Aid agencies, including the United States Agency for International Development (AID), drilled deep water wells in the late 1950s and early 1960s. They ignored the reality that the only grazing pattern that would not overtax semiarid land is one relying on free migration over a wide area and that a year-round watering hole is an inadequate substitute, as experience would show. When the rains began to fail, the nomads started to move their cattle en masse to these wells. A well, however, acts as a false signal in the traditional culture's communication system. A well *appears* to be a good substitute for rain. Unlike rain, however, it does not make pasture grow. A seemingly continuous supply of water, usually the most fickle and limiting factor in their economy, convinced the nomads to keep on increasing the size of their herds.

Before long over six thousand head of cattle in the Sahel were milling about wells surrounded by grazing lands that at best could feed six hundred head. After the cattle ate out the areas around the wells and trampled down the soil, the caked earth could no longer even absorb the scarce rains. One eyewitness reported that each well "quickly became the center of its own little desert forty or fifty miles square."[13]

From 1955 to 1960, the number of cattle, goats, and sheep in Mali alone increased by 800,000. After 1960, when more boreholes were drilled, the total number of livestock shot up from five million to sixteen million, or more than three animals for every Malien. In the recent drought a large number of animals, crowded on the rapidly exhausted grazing lands around the wells, died, not of thirst, but of hunger.[14]

You probably have read that the plight of the pastoralists proves that these countries are overpopulated and have exhausted their resources. Does more cattle mean there are too many people? We think the answer is by now obvious: not necessarily. But there is no need to romanticize nomads. Undoubtedly they must come into a new ecological balance within the context of the rest of society. This will require some changes, such as regulation of herd composition and size. But it will also require even more fundamental changes in the larger society, for instance, the integration of agriculture and pastoralism, in part through equitable and *stable* values for the exchange of livestock and grain.

Outsiders especially urban-based government elites who have pronounced pastoralism an anachronism and an ecological disaster (perhaps principally because they cannot control the nomads) invariably advocate ranching as the "modern way." Commercial ranching with fenced-in grazing and grain feeding that squander's precious grain — geared largely to exporting beef — stands in dramatic contrast to the ecological sanity of traditional pastoralism that utilizes a full range of resources otherwise not available for human consumption. Ranching looms as a grave threat to Africa's semiarid lands and their traditional inhabitants.[15]

Moreover, commercial ranching overlooks the vast potential of game animals in Africa. Game, unlike cattle, are not affected by the tsetse fly that inhabits large areas of central and southern Africa. As strange as it may sound, some scientists suggest the tsetse fly may be a blessing in disguise.[16] If the flies were eradicated cattle ranching would probably lead to the extinction of game animals which, properly "cropped," represent an enormous meat potential for Africans. The noted ecologist Dr. Raymond F. Dasmann argues that game cropping "has the capacity in Africa, in many areas, of producing more meat per acre than can be obtained from the traditional domestic animals on the same land."

There is certainly a critical choice ahead for Africa. Commercial ranching would mean expensive, imported inputs with serious environmental risks, the extinction of many species of animals, and increased vulnerability to widely fluctuating foreign beef markets. The other alternative, the restoration of a balanced pastoral system and well-planned game "cropping" could realize Africa's enormous natural protein potential through the optimum utilization of vegetation.

The choice would seem obvious. But are the lure of foreign exchange, foreign loans for cattle projects, the foreign demand for beef, and the beef mystique of African urban elites all too irresistible to oppose before it's too late?

The Amazon

Like the wildlife areas of Africa, the Amazon River basin has long been seen as one of the world's few remaining great natural preserves. Recently the public has become vaguely aware that it too is being threatened. The Amazon basin *is* being "ravaged," but is the cause overpopulation?

Since the mid-1960s Brazil's largest government project is the "colonization" of this extraordinary region. The plans call for sweeping clean tens of millions of acres of tropical forest. Already legions of Caterpillar Tractors' gargantuan 35-ton D-9s, mounted with angle plows weighing 2500 pounds each are bulldozing the forest at 2700 yards an hour, uprooting everything in sight. In some areas the job calls for two D-9s with a heavy chain between them rolling a huge hollow steel ball eight feet in diameter and weighing 6000 pounds. As the tractors move forward, the chain jerks out the trees, destroying the extensive matted root system and exposing the thin tropical soil. Fires visible for miles devour the debris.[17] Such massive deforestation is, according to the President of the Brazilian Academy of Science, Warwick Kerr, "taking place at a faster pace than Brazil and perhaps the world has ever known before. The Amazon forest will disappear in 35 years if it continues to be destroyed at the present rate."[18]

Is it really Brazil's expanding population behind those unrelenting D-9 "Cats"? No, the truth is that Brazil with 2.3 acres of already cropped land per person hardly needs to invade its tropical forests in order to feed its people. The ratio of cultivated land to people is slightly better than what we enjoy in the United States. The Amazon forest is earmarked for destruction for two entirely different reasons.

Settlement or "colonization" schemes historically have been safety valves — primarily a way to sidestep the urgent need for land redistribution. In Brazil, a mere 1 percent of the farms take up over 43 percent of the country's total farmland, and the best land at that. In brutal contrast, 50 percent of the farms are left with less than 3 percent of the land. In addition, at least 7 million rural families own no land at all — in a country where, even without taking the Amazon region into consideration, there are potentially ten cultivable acres for every family. Four out of five rural families, even if they do find work on a large estate, earn less than $33 a month. Yet a family of three needs at least $65 a month to buy food alone. It all translates into a massive waste of human life. Almost 200 of every 1000 babies born in rural northeast Brazil die in their first year of life.[19]

To avoid provoking Brazil's most powerful families by dividing up the large, generally export-oriented estates, the military government announced an absurd solution: move the rural poor to the Amazon basin, a tropical region totally unsuited for intensive and continuous farming.[20] Thus the pressure on the Amazon forest comes *not* from Brazil's population growth but from a government's effort to diffuse pressures for a just redistribution of land.

Ten years after much self-serving fanfare, the government has resettled a mere 10,000 small farmers. Even then, despite enormous bureaucratic expenditures, many of these farms have been soon abandoned, since their tropical soils cannot support intensive cultivation. Far from being concerned, the government has added insult to injury. Only a few years after trumpeting that prosperity for the rural poor was just a thousand or so miles down a not yet completed road, the government opted for a different type of pioneer. Kingdom-sized concessions, none smaller than 125,000 acres, were the new order of the day — mainly for export-oriented ranching and pulpwood production.

The "pioneers" are some of Brazil's richest families, already among the country's largest landholders, a number of Brazilian corporations, and, for good measure, a few television stars. Also quick to find out what Brazil can do for them are many of the world's largest multinational corporations. These corporations include Anderson Clayton, Goodyear, Volkswagen, Nestlé, Liquigas, Borden, Mitsubishi, and Universe Tank Ship (a low profile giant chartered in Liberia for tax reasons but in fact belonging to the aged American multibillionaire, D. K. Ludwig). The "homesteads" of these pioneers run as large as 3.7 million acres, half the size of Holland.[21]

Never has a government given so much to so few for so little. A seemingly endless list of "fiscal encouragements" is offered. One such incentive allows a corporation to invest in the Amazon half the taxes it owes on its earnings in Brazil.

Additional special incentives are offered to beef export operations. The goal is to make Brazil the major supplier of beef to Europe and the United States. Belem, at the mouth of the Amazon, is virtually as close to Miami as it is to the most populous cities of Brazil and five days closer by ship to Europe than are the Argentine slaughter houses.

In 1975 a United States reconnaissance satellite's heat sensor detected a sudden and intense warming of the earth in the Amazon basin usually associated with an imminent volcanic eruption. A special alert mission was dispatched. And what did they find? A German multinational corporation burning down one million acres of tropical forest for a cattle ranch. Unlike the slash and burn of a few acres here and there by Cayapó tribes, the corporation's burning a million acres means the death of most local wildlife.

Several corporations like Ludwig's, Georgia-Pacific, and Bruyznell are actively stripping the forest (which contains over a sixth of the world's remaining timberland) of its valuable lumber resources. They are in reality mining the forests. The plan is to sweep clean the unwanted trees with more D-9 Caterpillars backed up by a legion of power saws and voracious fires. The next stage calls for planting a "homogeneous forest" of hundreds of thousands of gmelina trees uprooted from West Africa (who knows what environmental havoc this will cause?). The companies are betting the top soil will hold long enough to level these new trees with giant "tree munchers" for export as paper pulp. All this with government incentives and multimillions in profits, of course.

If you are wondering whether at least all this devastation will provide employment, the answer is that it won't. You could go out and do a head count of the total number to be employed. Like most mega-money corporations, the money invested goes mainly for machines, not to people. On his 3.7 million acres, Ludwig's cattle, pulp, and export-oriented rice operations expect to employ 1200 permanent workers and a relative handful of seasonal hired hands.[22]

Some justify the whole Amazon scheme as necessitated by

Brazil's or the world's population problem. In reality the scheme is a public relations fraud by the Brazilian government at the expense of the landless, a devastation of the country's natural resources to provide a fleeting profit for the rich. It is also, in the opinion of many noted environmental scientists, an ecological disaster in the making not only for Brazil but for the entire world. Many ecologists warn that such grand-scale tampering with the soil structure, drainage, and water evaporation rates might well set off chain reactions that could alter climates on a worldwide basis.

You may find yourself asking how it can be so utterly disastrous to clear a forest. After all, weren't the North American forests cleared to grow food? All forests, however, are not the same. In a temperate forest leaves decay relatively slowly, thereby creating an ever deeper accumulation of nutrient-rich topsoil. In a tropical forest, by contrast, the heat and humidity promote a rapid decomposition of vegetation. A leaf that may take eighteen *months* to fully decompose in England could be broken down in a matter of *hours* in the Amazon. Given such rapid decay, the organic matter for the most part is directly assimilated into new plant life. Tropical plant life, then, is virtually a closed cycle of growth and decay. The minute fraction that escapes this cycle becomes a thin, nutrient-poor topsoil that acts more as a mechanical support for plant life than a source of nutrients. If the multicanopied vegetation is stripped away, torrential rains, sometimes dumping six to eight inches in a single day, wash away the unshielded topsoil, and the equatorial sun bakes what remains into a bricklike wasteland.[23]

You might ask why such bleak prospects could ever attract a profit-oriented organization. Just consider that if the soil erodes on one holding of 100,000 acres, a corporation can always slash and burn a few more million trees nearby. But the heart of the matter is that, in part due to the government's "fiscal encouragements," the anticipated return on the little capital invested is extremely attractive. Investors, therefore, do not have to think beyond a five- to ten-year framework, let alone worry about future generations. They call it "making a killing."

Much of the destruction of the agricultural environment on examination turns out to be the result, not of the size of a country's population, but of other forces: land monopolizers who export non-food and luxury crops that force the majority of farmers to overuse marginal lands; colonial patterns of taxation and cash cropping that continue today; well-meant but unenlightened "aid" and other forms of outside intervention in traditionally well-adapted systems; and irresponsible profit-seeking by both local and foreign elites.

Cutting the world's population in half tomorrow would not stop any of these forces.

*   *   *

While taking credit for our tenacity and our considerable experience gained in manufacturing in 42 plants in 12 countries, Massey-Ferguson's success in Brazil certainly could not have been achieved without the enlightened policies of the Government since 1964 toward stability and development.

> "Massey-Ferguson in Brazil," statement by
> Albert A. Thornbrough, President 1975

I first visited Brazil over a decade ago. I was struck by the unbounded confidence and breadth of vision of the people I met. These reminded me of the moral strengths that marked the earlier generations that built the United States. And I could only conclude that your nation, like mine, was destined for greatness.

> Henry Kissinger in Brazil,
> February 1976

You can buy the land out there now for the same price as a couple of bottles of beer per acre. When you've got half a million acres and twenty thousand head of cattle, you can leave the lousy place and go live in Paris, Hawaii, Switzerland, or anywhere you choose.

> An American rancher who owns land in the
> Mato Grosso, as quoted in Robin Hanbury-Tenison,
> *A Question of Survival for the Indians of Brazil,*
> London, 1973

7

The Food versus Poison Trade-off?

Question: You may be right that the numbers of people are not the real threat to the adequacy of food resources — that the real issues are who controls the land and what it is used for. But you have totally neglected one very serious hazard encountered in trying to produce more food. We have all read and seen on television frightening accounts of the dangers of using pesticides and other chemicals to increase food production.

Perhaps we may have to live with these dangers since applying pesticides is one of the big reasons the United States can produce so much food. Perhaps our food surpluses might allow for some cutback in chemicals such as our recent ban on DDT. But what can you say about the underdeveloped countries where every bushel counts for survival? Granted those countries *could* increase their food production. But to do that, won't they need to use more pesticides? We feel trapped. Shouldn't food for starving people take precedence over all else? The choice seems to be between mass starvation and mass poisoning.

Our Response: We understand exactly the feeling of being trapped. Take, for example, the DDT issue. For us the campaign to ban DDT in the 1960s was a modest first victory for the burgeoning ecology movement. But what has the ban really amounted to? Despite the ban in most industrial countries, more DDT (over 150,000 metric tons) is annually deposited in the environment now than ten years ago.[1] One reason is that representatives of chemical corporations have succeeded in persuading Congress to exempt exports from every limitation or ban on the domestic use of DDT and other pesticides. In 1974, for example, one chemical corporation managed to have (at taxpayers' expense, of course) the Agency for International Development (AID) ship the insecticide Phosvel to Indonesia, even though it had been linked with massive damage to water buffalos in Egypt in 1972. Phosvel is not registered in the United States.[2]

Maybe, as the pesticide companies argue, the underdeveloped countries in their urgent struggle to produce enough food for their growing populations cannot afford to be concerned about the environmental consequences of pesticides. But what must be weighed in making such a judgment?

The decision on whether to favor such a desperate choice for the underdeveloped countries must first take into account the consequences for everyone. We, in this country, cannot escape the damage to our health and our environment from the poisons injected into the environment abroad. Our planet's ecosystem does not allow for the convenient quarantining of the underdeveloped countries. DDT, like all pesticides, just does not stay where it is put. Once applied to crops it works its way into lakes, streams, rivers, and oceans. Over one fourth of all DDT ever produced has wound up in our oceans. Fish are now almost universally contaminated.[3] DDT applied to cotton in Nicaragua showed up in the beef carcasses imported through Miami. Pesticides easily enter into the food chain and wind up in human tissue. Each young American adult already carries at least .003 of an ounce of pesticides permanently in his or her body fat.[4] In Guatemala DDT applied to cotton fields was detected at dangerous levels in nursing mothers' milk. In Egypt in 1972 six persons developed symptoms of neurotoxic poisoning several months after the pesticide Phosvel had been used on cotton fields miles away.[5]

The smallest amounts of pesticides can have devastating effects. Environmentalist Erik Eckholm notes that "as little as one part in ten billion of DDT in water severely cuts the growth rate of oysters, and two parts in ten billion can kill commercial species of shrimp and crabs."[6] Researchers have shown that as little as eight parts per million of DDT in an estuary off Texas prevents sea trout from spawning.

One can choose to *ignore* the effects but there is *no escaping* them. There is, however, an even more basic issue.

Are Pesticides Necessary?

In trying to decide how necessary pesticides are, the first eye openers for us came from uncovering a few basic facts about pesticide use in the United States. A great deal of pesticides are used in this country — about 1.2 billion pounds annually — six pounds of toxic chemicals for every American and over 30 percent of the world's total consumption. United States pesticide safety regulations are much more lenient than those of most other industrial countries, largely due to pressures exerted by the powerful chemical corporations.[7] According to a comprehensive study of international standards, if the United States applied Japan's standards governing toxicity levels, we would have to "do away with about half the organophosphate pesticides [the common substitute for DDT]." The study noted that the Soviet Union "also has tougher standards than we have."[8]

Such heavy use of pesticides would lead us to assume that the chemicals are applied to most of the nation's farmland and that our food growing productivity is in no small way thanks to liberal doses of pesticides. Wrong and wrong again.

- Fact one: Nearly half the pesticides used in the United States goes not to farmland but to golf courses, parks, and lawns.[9]
- Fact two: Only 5 percent of the nation's crop and pasture land is treated with insecticides, 15 percent with weedkillers, and 0.5 percent with fungicides.[10]
- Fact three: Nonfood crops account for over half of all insecticides used in United States agriculture. Cotton alone receives almost half (47 percent) of all insecticides used. It should be noted that even then half of the total cotton acreage receives no insecticides treatment at all.[11]
- Fact four: The Environmental Protection Agency (EPA) estimates that thirty years ago American farmers used 50 million pounds of pesticides and lost 7 percent of their crop before harvest. Today, farmers use twelve times more pesticides yet the percentage of the crop lost before harvest has almost doubled.[12]
- Fact five: Even if all pesticides were eliminated, crop loss due

to pests (insects, pathogens, weeds, mammals, and birds) would rise only about seven percentage points, from 33.6 to 40.7 percent.[13]

• Fact six: Several recent studies indicate the needless use of pesticides in agriculture. The EPA has shown that the waste on corn, sorghum, and apples alone is on the order of 16 million pounds annually.

Even before we could investigate possible alternatives to pesticides, the straightforward facts totally undermined our assumptions (and no doubt yours!) about the role of pesticides in American agriculture.

Do Pesticides Help the Hungry to Produce Food?

We put this question to the chief of the Plant Protection Service of the FAO. He estimates that annually 800 million pounds of pesticides are used in underdeveloped countries. The "vast majority," however, are for export crops, principally cotton and to a lesser extent "fruits and vegetables grown under plantation conditions for export."[14] This is not by chance. Imports such as pesticides encourage a focus on export crops in part to earn the foreign exchange to pay for them. An underdeveloped country easily gets locked into producing more and more export crops to pay for more and more imports. Pesticides lead to an agricultural environment requiring more pesticides. The diminishing financial returns per acre that result often step up the pressure to devote even more land to export crops. The entire process bypasses the need of local people for food.

Nor should the monetary cost to the individual farmer be overlooked. Pesticides, in economic terms, are just one more factor taking farming out of the hands of small, self-provisioning farmers.

Pesticides in underdeveloped countries are concentrated, then, in little export-oriented enclaves that functionally are mere extensions of the agricultural systems of the industrial countries. In these enclaves pesticides are often so intensively applied that environmental scientists have the "opportunity" to study the effects of extreme chemical farming. Such an opportunity came with the introduction of pesticides into the cotton fields of the Cañete Valley of Peru after World War II. By 1956 pests so overran the fields that production had to be suspended. Dr. Boza Barducci, the director of the region's agricultural experiment station notes, "In 1956 we concluded that it was nearly impossible, in practice, to obtain successful control of cotton pests by chemical methods, including the most efficient pesticides presently known." He further comments, "Such drastic losses as in the Cañete Valley disprove the worldwide belief in the theoretical efficiency of chemical products, an illusion created by the chemical industry."[15]

Insecticides introduced into Egyptian cotton fields in the mid-1950s were hailed as "a major triumph over nature." By 1961 yields began dropping by 35 percent a year. A similar pattern in northeastern Mexico brought a near halt to cotton production. In Malaysia and elsewhere, cocoa, palm oil, rubber, and other export crops have been devastated by pest attacks unleashed, ironically, by the introduction of pesticides.[16]

In Nicaragua cotton acreage was increased tenfold between 1950 and 1964. By the late 1950s the large growers acting on the advice of United States AID technicians scheduled insecticide applications an average of eight times per season as well as liberal fertilizer treatments. Yields increased. But by 1966 the growers found it necessary to apply insecticides twenty-eight to thirty times per season. Even then cotton yields began to drop: from 821 pounds per acre in 1965 to 621 pounds in 1968. Along the fertile Pacific coastal plain of Central America large cotton estates by the late 1960s had to schedule so many (45 to 50 a season) aerial sprays of a "cocktail" of pesticides (including DDT) that cotton production ceased to be profitable. By 1968 Nicaragua had the dubious distinction of holding the world's record for the number of applications of insecticides on a single crop.[17]

In spite of (or because of?) such heavy pesticide doses, food crops such as corn and beans, not themselves sprayed but merely located near the cotton fields, were for the first time heavily damaged by insects. Very little food could be harvested, according to an AID report.

In regions where pesticides have been intensively used mosquitoes have developed resistance. Malaria, once thought to have been "eradicated" by DDT, has broken out again in Central America and South Asia. In the Danli area of Honduras (population 32,000), only three years after the start of large-scale cotton production and pesticide sprayings, over one fourth of the population contracted malaria.[18] Similar outbreaks near cotton plantations using insecticides have been occurring throughout Central America.

What is happening? Why has everything seemingly gone wrong? In country after country there is a regular progression of events. For the first few years insects are controlled at reasonable cost and yields are higher than ever before. The growers, seeing the bugs literally drop from plants, feel the pesticides give them power over forces that have always been beyond their control. Gradually, however, the pest species develop resistant strains through a survival of the fittest selection.

A field is not just a battleground of pest versus plant. A closer look reveals a highly complex, interacting system of hundreds of different species of insects and other organisms occupying diverse ecological niches. It is not true that the only good bug is a dead bug. Some insects eat only very restricted parts of the crop plant, some are parasites or flesh-eating predators that live off selected insect species. The plant-eating species certainly do eat the crop plants. But studies show that the vast majority of species never cause sufficient damage to justify the cost of an insecticide treatment. Their numbers are restricted below economic injury levels by the action of parasites and predators. But when these natural controls are overthrown by the introduction of an insecticide that does not distinguish friend from foe, many ordinarily insignificant insects are able to multiply faster than their predators.

Because plant-eating pests generally are present in larger numbers than their predators, they statistically are more likely than their predators to contain a few individuals with inheritable resistance to the insecticide. As the few resistant pests gradually multiply, every application of the insecticide will kill more predators and fewer pests, thus compounding the damage to the crops.

Already by 1971 fifteen major pest species had developed resistance to the insecticides applied. The time taken to overcome susceptibility to an insecticide has ranged from four to fourteen years. The irony of nature is that the more effective an insecticide is in killing susceptible individuals of a pest population, the faster resistant individuals will evolve. Such is the case of several pest species (including the rice water weevil, the cabbage looper, the soybean looper, the banded cucumber beetle, the two-spotted spider mite, and the banded-wing whitefly) for which no new insecticide has been developed to buy a few more years' grace. Environmentalist Dr. M. Taghi Farvar notes the alarming possibility that the present pest control strategy in Central America may be leading to resistant populations of pests on a hemispheric scale.[19]

Only twenty-five years ago the spider mite was a minor pest. Repeated use of pesticides supposedly aimed at other pests have decimated the natural enemies and competitors of the mite. Today the mite is the pest most seriously threatening agriculture worldwide.[20] On Kenya's coffee plantations no one had ever paid much heed to the giant looper, not until, that is, someone started spraying insecticides to wipe out another relatively insignificant pest. They succeeded in wiping out that pest — but along with it the natural predator of the looper. Free at last of their enemy, giant loopers took over the plantations.

The Human Toll

Even after the American insecticide Phosvel had been associated with the crippling of some 1200 water buffalo in Egypt, the Velsicol Chemical Corporation in Texas continued to manufacture it. Phosvel was designed to attack the central nervous system of insects. Apparently it can do the same thing to humans. Former employees of Velsicol have brought a $12 million suit against the company for damage to their health, including muscle paralysis, nervous-system disorders, blurred vision, and speech and memory blocks. Raymond David, a former supervisor at the plant, reported that workers in the Phosvel section were dubbed "the Phosvel zombies" because of their obvious nervous disorders. "The company knew people were getting sick," said David. But the management tried to dismiss the problem. "They told me all those guys smoked marijuana. They said the guys were acid freaks," recalled David. In 1975 David quit, feeling that he could no longer take responsibility for the hazards his subordinates faced. But the Velsicol Corporation apparently did not share David's reservations. In 1976 the company attempted to get Phosvel licensed in the United States.[21]

Dr. Farvar reports, "In Central America thousands of highland Indians who annually emigrate to the estates on the Pacific Coast to pick the cotton crop are poisoned by insecticides and hundreds of documented cases of death are recorded per year."[22] In 1967–1968 in Nicaragua there were over 500 reported cases of human poisoning by insecticides with eighty deaths.[23] The United States Embassy in Mexico in 1974 reported 689 poisonings and seven deaths of agricultural workers due to insecticides manufactured by Shell and duPont.[24] The National Academy of Sciences Special Commission on Pesticides found that severe occupational injuries "might be seriously underestimated."[25]

In Asia pesticides are destroying an important protein source of the rural population — fish. In the flooded rice paddies peasants have traditionally cultivated fish as a cash crop as well as an excellent low-cost source of protein to fall back on in times of declining rice prices. But today the widespread use of pesticides is sharply reducing fish production on rice farms in the Philippines, Malaysia, and Indonesia. In Indonesia in 1969–1970, German and Japanese multinational corporations began spraying over two million acres of paddy with the same chemical that allegedly only a few years before had killed millions of fish in the Rhine. Water buffalo, an important source of labor and food to the peasant population of Indonesia, reportedly have died.[26] In Louisiana huge fish kills have occurred following the application of various insecticides to nearby cotton fields.

The Poison Business

Why is it that such destructive cycles get set in motion over and over again in different parts of the world? The simple answer is that the pesticide corporations are finished on Wall Street unless they maximize profits and expand at a steady clip sales that are now at well over $2.5 billion a year.

Basic environmental security, not to mention truly *effective* pest control, clearly points to the need to develop pesticides that are as *target-specific* as possible and to study fully the effects of each new pesticide on nontarget insects, other wildlife, and people; but a chemical corporation's interests propel us in exactly the opposite direction. In order to maximize profit margins and expand sales, a chemical company seeks to minimize research and marketing costs and to come up with pesticides that kill the broadest spectrum of pests.

Pesticide sales are further expanded by promoting "100 percent" pest elimination. Aiming for 100 percent eradication, however, is extremely expensive, unnecessary, often fails, is likely to be dangerous and can result in costly "overkills."

To maximize profits, the companies promote *scheduled* spraying, instead of spraying in response to a need. Scheduled spraying means greater and more predictable sales. It is easier for a chemical company manager to judge how much pesticide to produce and distribute to different outlets if he can simply multiply the number of acres his customers own by a given quantity per acre. That way he does not have to take into account predictions about how bad a particular pest really is going to be in a given year.

While agribusiness corporations are trying to promote "blind," scheduled spraying in underdeveloped countries such as India,[27] some farmers in the United States have realized that on top of environmental and health damage they were being just plain swindled. In Graham County, Arizona, cotton growers, working with scientists from the University of Arizona, proved they could save a lot of money by eliminating blind sprayings. Instead, they sent trained scouts out into the fields to measure pest levels. Pesticide expenditures dropped tenfold and so did pest damage. Even adding on fees paid to the "pest scouts," the total pest control costs were less than a fifth of what they had been with the scheduled approach. The chemical companies brought enormous pressure on the highest level of the university's administration to force the withdrawal of the scientists from the program.[28]

Similar experiments on forty-two cotton and thirty-nine citrus farms in California reduced pesticide expenditures by more than 60 percent.[29] A conservative estimate is that United States farmers could reduce insecticide use 35 to 50 percent with no effect on crop production, simply by treating only when necessary rather than by schedule.[30]

Much of the pesticides applied to cotton fields seem to have little if anything to do with yields or quality.[31] The naive observer of a cotton plant would not appreciate that the young plant sends out a considerable number of fruiting forms over and above the number it can possibly fill with cotton. Over the course of the season nearly two thirds of the young bolls fail to develop and thus fall off no matter how free of pests the plant might be. Insects devouring these excess fruiting forms may look alarming. Indeed it makes for the type of "before" photo that sells a lot of pesticides. In reality, however, the pests have little or no effect on the yield of cotton. Yet the grower, seeing the damaged immature bolls, is easily persuaded that he has already delayed too long in calling out the spray planes. The pesticide sprays, however, as mentioned earlier, kill not only some of the pests but also much of the predator population, thereby giving much freer reign to the pests early in the season. Once again, pesticides ensure the need for more pesticides.

Poison for Beauty

What we gain from pesticides turns out in many cases not to be higher yields or better eating quality. We pay a heavy price in pesticides for skin-deep beauty. Our notion of what an orange or apple should look like is largely the creation of millions of dollars spent on full-color ads depicting "perfect" fruit. In several Latin American countries the sharply increased use of dangerous and costly fungicides has nothing to do with efforts to grow more food for local people but with making sure that fruits and vegetables grown for export can pass the beauty standards of the United States.

In California citrus fields, tons of pesticides are applied several times each year in the war against the humble thrips.[32] The thrips is a minute pest that does not reduce yields, harm trees, or lower the nutritional value or eating quality of citrus fruits. Its only offense is that it can lightly scar the citrus skin. The intensive treatments backfire as usual. The thrips develop resistance. The growers pour on more and more deadly pesticides, significantly raising costs. Worse yet, other once innocuous pests such as red mites become real pests in the unnatural absence of their natural enemies. Farm workers become victims of chronic and acute illnesses due to exposure to parathion and other organophosphates used in place of DDT for thrips control.

Why do growers continue to release such deadly poisons into the environment and risk their own long-term welfare? Basically because advertising by giant grower associations such as Sunkist, Inc., have conditioned the buying public to expect their fresh fruit to be blemish-free. Growers get premium prices only for such fruit. (For example, in 1965 California growers received an average of $2.61 a box for navel oranges that passed the beauty standards but only 12 cents a box for navel oranges that were equally good inside but because of small skin blemishes were destined for processing into juice.) Growers naturally aim to maximize the percentage of their crop with the right complexion for the fruit market. This means ever more pesticides — and increased costs as well as damage to our food resources and the health of farm workers.

Any Alternatives?

We are happy — and relieved, we might add — to report that there are alternatives, many of which have been hastily discarded as old-fashioned. Now that the implications of tampering with complex natural systems are becoming clear, such alternatives can be viewed in a new light.

For decades crop rotation proved effective. Pests that attack corn were often controlled by alternating corn with a crop like soybeans in the same field. The corn rootworm will not eat the soybean plant so that when soybeans alternate with corn, the rootworm has nothing to survive on.[33] Some weed killers, now commonly used in corn cultivation in the United States, actually preclude this type of rotation because they remain in the soil and kill noncorn plants. Farmers who rely on pesticides thus must plant corn crop after corn crop on the same land, a practice that in itself tends to increase insects, disease, and weed problems. (Given such a vicious cycle, it is not surprising that corn accounts for almost half of the weed killers in United States agriculture.) By now the corn rootworm has developed almost total resistance to major pesticides.[34] In the end, corn farmers in the United States may be forced to return to that old-fashioned idea — crop rotation.

Mixed cropping patterns have been found to reduce the pest problem as compared to monoculture. Small cotton plots in Costa Rica, scattered among plots growing other crops, have less severe pest problems than cotton fields in Guatemala, often grouped in solid blocks, covering over 50,000 acres.[35]

In Egyptian cotton fields the tradition was to collect by hand the egg masses of the cotton leafworm. Then growers put their faith in insecticides. Yields declined disastrously.[36] Now progress means back to hand collection of the pest eggs.

Cleaning up fields after harvest (known as crop sanitation) can

remove the meal on which certain major pests feast. Burning ra-
toon cotton (what's left over after harvest) has proved more effective than pesticides.[37] In the United States in the thirties and
forties it was still common to plow corn stubble and stalks after
harvest as a measure to control the corn borer.[38]

Introducing populations of natural predators and parasites into
the fields is another nonchemical method with potential. After
the pesticide disaster in Peru's Cañete Valley, growers sought to
restore natural controls. They imported from California numerous beneficial insects including thirty million wasps and twenty
gallons of ladybugs to control leaf rollers, bollworms, and
aphids.[39]

In China the large-scale participation of rural communities in
agriculture makes it possible to control pests before they become
a serious problem. With the guidance of experienced agronomists,
young members of the production brigades organize themselves
into a pest early-warning system. In Shao-tung county in Honan
Province 10,000 youths patrol the fields and report any sign of
pathogenic change. These youth teams are appropriately called
the "barefoot doctors of agriculture." Their efforts have reduced
the damage caused by wheat rust and the riceborer to less than 1
percent and have brought under control the recurrent locust inva-
sions. Such a people-intensive technique has greatly reduced the
need for pesticides.[40]

Is spraying the only answer to weeds? An ordinary hoe or a corn
knife remains a realistic alternative to costly and often ineffective
herbicides. Even in the United States most weed control is still
accomplished by tillage. Hoeing and corn knifing require no
machinery and create opportunities for productive employment.
Mulching, the practice of putting organic or even inorganic material on top of the soil or incorporating it into the soil, can reduce
weeds without using herbicides. A study in Nigeria showed that
mulching reduced the competition from weeds to such an extent
that corn yields doubled.[41] Crop rotation can also keep weeds
under control.

The best news is that effective pest control methods do not require what underdeveloped countries and small farmers have
least of — money for imported pesticides. Rather, they create a
demand for what is most available — labor power — and thereby
involve more people in the production process.

In the United States, despite the danger of pesticides and the existence of real alternatives, Wall Street analysts predict that the market for chemical poisons will increase by 50 percent in the next eight years. Most farmers feel that no matter how much they question the safety or the sanity of pesticides they cannot risk being the first to stop using them. Thus Don Climer, a farmer in Nebraska, is convinced the only practical approach is to take dangerous chemicals off the market. If this happened, Climer doubts that many farmers would be upset. Even if some yields did drop, all farmers would be "in the same boat," notes Climer.

The Knowledge Monopoly

Governments and farmers throughout the world continue to fall into chemical traps in part because they lack information and advice about alternatives. The United Nations Food and Agriculture Organization (FAO) is supposed to offer a pool of independent experts discovering and disseminating plant protection information, including the proper uses of chemical pesticides and alternatives. In China experiments are being carried out, often by ordinary farmers, on nonchemical control of pests. Such research, publicly funded, is also going on in scattered centers in the United States and Europe. Will these advances be disseminated by the FAO?

Not likely. Already institutionalized *within* the FAO structure is direct collaboration with agribusiness corporations whose profits are directly threatened by any nonchemical alternatives. A prime example of this "industry cooperation" is the Pesticide Working Group, whose roster includes BASF, Bayer, Borden, British Petroleum, Ciba-Geigy, Cyanamid, FMC, Hoechst, Hoffman-LaRoche, Imperial Chemical, Liquigas, Merck, Phillips, Sandoz, Shell, Stauffer, and something called the Wellcome Foundation. More and more FAO technicians see themselves as "brokers" linking up a multinational agribusiness firm and an underdeveloped country. "So, your country has a corn rootworm problem? Let's see what advice we can get from our Pesticide Working Group."

The likely thrust of such advice — in case you could have any doubt — is clear from the action paper printed on United Nations letterhead at the official "Consultation with Agro-Industrial

Leaders" organized before the 1974 World Food Conference. Corporate executives stress how chemical pesticides are "necessary" to solve the hunger problem in underdeveloped countries. They argue for *shorter* delays in approval of new pesticides. Publicly funded international agencies should, according to them, carry out a long-range study of how much pesticides will be needed (read "marketed") in each region. Public funds should establish an international stockpile of "essential pesticides" (DDT included). Corporations should work more closely in training government technical staffs in pesticides use. (Some pesticide firms already work so closely with governments that the two must be indistinguishable to most peasants. In Tanzania, Hoechst has become the advisor to the government on insecticides and spraying equipment. Hoechst even uses government agricultural extension officers to supervise the spraying, for which they get a salary over and above the one they receive from the government. Hoechst has the power to fire a government extension officer who does not supervise "properly.")[42]

We hope you now see through the false threat that poisoning our environment will be necessary if the hungry are to eat. Clearly pesticides are not being used by or for the hungry and, as will be abundantly clear from this book, lack of pesticides is not what is keeping them hungry. The real threat is that pesticide technology is in the hands of a few corporations that will profit only if they can continue to make farmers and "concerned" people everywhere believe that our very survival depends on the increased use of their products.

The threat is even more ominous since some supposedly impartial bodies that could form a counter force to the power of multinational agribusiness have become, instead, their agents. Organizations such as the FAO, far from developing and disseminating suitable alternatives or even the knowledge of the appropriate use of pesticides, are becoming partners in promotion for the chemical corporations.

The first step to weaken the grip of agribusiness is to deflate the myth that chemical agriculture is "scientific," "modern," and the only way to high yields. Far from being the answer to hunger, increasing reliance on pesticides can actually lead to more hunger. And we will all bear the costs.

*   *   *

Hasty and punitive action in banning products [pesticides] does not protect the American consumer in any way, shape or form. At stake is a lot more than our ability to do business. We're not talking about regulating cigarettes, utilities, aircraft or autos. We're talking about the world food supply.

> Dr. W. P. Crawford, Vice-President and General
> Manager of Animal Health Products for the
> Agricultural Division of Pfizer, Inc.

[A] more important [difficulty in marketing products in India] is the mental attitude of the agriculturalist about killing. Pesticides spell killing, maybe small and perhaps invisible insects. But it is killing that they are used for. This killing is anathema to the majority of the agriculturalists, be they Hindu, Jain or others. By nature, the agriculturalist is generous, wanting to bestow on others what he reaps out of Mother Earth. He does not think that he alone should enjoy the fruit of his labour . . . to kill those unseen and unknown lives, though they were thriving on what Mother Earth yields, is foreign to his nature. Even when the crop is ripe, the farmer *drives* away the birds wanting to feed on the new grain. He does not *kill* any one of them. With pesticides, there is nothing but killing. It takes some time for the simple folk to get acclimatised to the very conception of killing tiny helpless and unarmed creatures.

> *Pesticides,* Journal of the Indian Pesticide Industry

Pollution control moves basically on a collision course with food production.

> National Academy of Sciences, 1974

8

Does Ignorance Breed Babies?

Question: You have said that overpopulation is not the cause of hunger, unemployment, economic stagnation, environmental deterioration, or chemical poisoning of the environment. Are you suggesting that rapid population growth is not a problem at all? Could the population growth rate be allowed to continue unchecked for an indefinite period? You may be right that overpopulation is not the most *direct* cause of these problems now, but won't you admit that it will be soon if we don't do something immediately to limit births?

People throughout the world have too many children because they do not know how to prevent unwanted births. Moreover, they cannot perceive that fewer children would be in their own best interests. If they could be helped to see that having more children makes them poorer and hungrier, then perhaps they would be willing to go to the trouble to use contraceptives. An urgent and prodigious educational job faces us — perhaps the greatest of all time — to convince all the world's citizens of the folly of uncontrolled population growth. Don't you agree?

Our Response: Because some might misinterpret our words, suggesting that we discount the problem of rapid population growth, we must be absolutely clear. We are *not* saying that the continuing expansion of the global population at the current rate is not a problem. We *are* saying that neither population growth nor the size of today's population is now the cause of hunger. Continuing to grow at current rates will certainly undercut the future well-being of all of us. That is self-evident. But this self-evident truth adds, for us, even *greater urgency* to our search for the *real* causes of rapid population growth.

The question suggests that the real cause of rapid population growth is ignorance — that people do not grasp that fewer children would be in their own best interest. We disagree. When sociologists go to the root causes of large family patterns among the poor in underdeveloped countries, time after time, they find that the poor are acting quite rationally. By having many children, poor peasants are fulfilling two absolute survival needs that the socioeconomic system fails to provide: the need for sufficient income and the need for security in their old age.

In many parts of the world, the birth rate is pushed up by the efforts of families to have several children, especially sons. As long as families are forced to compete with each other for food, the number of children in each family will largely determine its capacity to survive. For if the family is landless, its income depends on the number of children who can be hired out to work the fields of others. And if the family works as a sharecropper, the more children it has, the more land it will be able to work.

If a family owns only a small plot, one might suppose the desire for sons would be less due to the prospect of eventually having to divide up an already small plot among many sons. But, as one Indian farmer told population researcher Mahmood Mamdani, "Of course, I am worried about the fragmentation of land. But even before I worry about my land being divided up tomorrow, I must worry about making a living on it today."[1]

The rationale is very clear, inescapably logical. The same farmer commented: "Just look around; no one, without sons or brothers to help him, farms his land. He rents it out to others with large families. Without sons there is no living off the land. The more sons you have, the less labor you need to hire, and the more savings you can have." The poor farmer knows that he has to conserve his resources: "Why pay 2500 rupees for an extra hand? Why not have a son?" asks another farmer. "A rich man invests in his machines. We must invest in our children," states a peasant in northern India.

Demographer Dr. Helen Ware has observed a similar compelling rationale in African societies of the Sahel.[2] As early as age ten, notes Ware, a child may produce more than he or she consumes. Children, for example, can fetch water, carry wood, and herd animals.

But even where children are not a current economic asset, parents may need many children simply because they have no alternative security. In the African Sahel there are "no pension funds, no welfare benefits, no homes for the aged," observes Ware. Milkha Singh, a farmer in Manupur, a village in the Indian Punjab, put it this way: "You think I am poor because I have too many children." He laughed, "If I didn't have my sons . . . God knows what would happen to me and their mother when we are too old to work and earn."

In such societies, how can a family be sure to meet its need for a family labor force and for social security in old age? Not by having just one or two sons. In countries with high infant death rates, many children are necessary to ensure that some survive. Infant mortality appears to have a direct effect on the desired family size. A study in Egypt showed that women who had lost a child wanted more children than those who had not.[3] The belief of Indian peasants that many births are necessary to ensure that some sons survive is apparently valid. According to a computer simulation, an Indian couple would have to bear an average of 6.3 children to be confident (at a 95 percent level of probability) of the survival of one son.[4]

When more children are likely to survive, couples will feel less need for many children. Two doctors with extensive experience in Africa, conclude, therefore, that "the best birth control program is, simply, to feed the children."[5]

We have said that the fundamental problem is *not* ignorance. Large families are in many social systems the only *rational* option for survival. Impoverished peasants *do* plan their families — only they need to plan for large ones. "Preaching population control to peasants is like preaching thrift to the moneyless," observes one Indian scholar.[6]

Rapid population growth is not the cause of hunger. Both hunger and rapid population growth turn out to be *symptoms* of the same disease. Fixating on symptoms is fruitless; it is a tragic diversion we cannot afford. If we are really serious about eventually balancing this planet's population and resources, we must now address the disease that causes both hunger and high birth rates: the insecurity and poverty of the majority that results when a minority controls a country's productive resources.

9

Sophisticated Fatalism?

Question: The poor people in the hungry countries seem to be multiplying at higher rates than ever, totally oblivious to the industrial countries' preoccupation with the "population problem." As long as so many people are kept poor, is there any hope for population limitation? Poverty is not about to be eliminated everywhere in the world. Aren't your arguments, then, just a sophisticated form of fatalism?

Our Response: Because of the way the population bomb has been thrown into the public's consciousness, one is convinced that the poor are multiplying faster than ever. In reality, at least eleven underdeveloped countries are undergoing an even more precipitous decline in their birth rates than did any of the now industrial countries, including the United States, during their "demographic transition" of the nineteenth and early twentieth centuries.[1] Seventy-two out of 82 underdeveloped countries showed a decrease in birth rates between 1960 and 1970. Seventeen of these declines were quite significant — at least ten fewer births per thousand.[2]

These trends, added to the slowing rate of population growth in certain industrial countries, mean that the annual increment in world population has dropped in the last few years. In 1970 the growth in world population, that is, the excess of births over deaths, was 69 million. By 1975 the increase was probably closer to 64 million. When one considers that the number of people of reproductive age is still getting larger each year, this drop in the annual increment is impressive. The rate of world population growth appears to have reached an all time high around 1970 and has since begun to subside.[3]

Such generalizations do not tell us a great deal — except that they do effectively deflate the "explosion" myth. More useful is to look at which countries have declining birth rates and to contrast them with countries that do not. The lowering of the population growth rate is apparently *not* related to the growth rate of the Gross National Product (GNP) or even to the *level* of per capita income but to a trend toward *equal distribution* of income and services such as health care.[4]

Let us take two countries that have made distinctly different progress toward stabilizing their populations. The birth rate in Taiwan started coming down in the late 1950s even while per capita GNP was extremely low — not more than $150. In the Philippines, however, the birth rate continued to be high. Why? Partly because even when the per capita figures for both countries were roughly the same in the 1960s, the bottom 20 percent of the population in Taiwan was about twice as well-off as its Philippine counterpart. Moreover, in Taiwan income distribution has improved over time while in the Philippines it has become more and more concentrated in the upper classes.[5] These social differences are dramatically reflected in the birth rates of the two countries. Twenty-five years ago both Taiwan and the Philippines had a birth rate of approximately 40 per 1000. But by 1974 the Taiwanese rate had declined to 23 per 1000. In the Philippines, however, the birth rate is still almost 40 per 1000.

Taiwan's birth rate began declining well before the introduction of family planning programs, which became sizable only in 1966. Several population experts have linked Taiwan's declining birth rates instead to the land reform introduced as early as 1902–1903 by Japanese rulers. This reform, plus many other measures reinforcing the security of tenure of small farmers, has created a viable small-farm agriculture so unlike other Asian countries that have faster growing populations.[6]

Similar contrasts can be drawn between countries where birth rates are declining such as Sri Lanka, Singapore, Hong Kong, Egypt, China, Argentina, Uruguay, Costa Rica, and Cuba — most of which do have, or once had, some national policies favoring the low-income groups — and countries such as Brazil, Venezuela, and Mexico where the welfare of low-income groups is diminishing and birth rates are not declining significantly.[7] In countries where the decline in birth rate has been significant, the causal factors do not appear to be direct birth control programs so much as a shift in resources toward the poorest groups.

Welfare is not measured in income alone. Other factors besides income distribution per se seem to correlate with declining birth rates. Two Asian examples of declining birth rates — the state of Kerala in India and China — illustrate this. In Kerala, statistics show that the population is poorer than in many other Indian states, but there are critical social and political differences that may well contribute to Kerala's declining birth rate. Alan Berg, a World Bank nutritionist, has noted that of all the states of India, Kerala has the highest literacy rate (it is the only state where the majority of women are educated); the highest per capita consumption of nutritionally important foods; the lowest infant mortality rate; and a death rate lower than that of West Germany or Great Britain.[8]

The average Indian birth rate has fallen from 41 to 37.2 per 1000 over the last twenty years. By contrast, Kerala's birth rate has dropped from 37 to 27 per 1000 during only a ten-year period.

China has the most comprehensive approach to providing what seem to be social and economic prerequisites to population limitation. After retirement workers receive 50 to 75 percent of their earnings while most other benefits, notably health care, continue. In the countryside, the commune maintains a welfare fund to provide for those unable to work. In both city and countryside the collective working group ensures that no family's income falls below a certain minimal level.[9]

In addition, you will recall from our previous response that families competing against other families, must have their own labor supply for survival. But when labor and production is shared beyond the family through group ownership and work, as it is in China, then the need to raise one's own family work force disappears.

China demonstrates the capacity of people to change their rate of reproduction with impressive rapidity once basic security needs have been met. China's birth rate has declined at perhaps unprecedented speed — down from 32 per 1000 in 1970 to between 20 and 25 per 1000 five years later.[10] Since the Chinese people constitute one fifth of humanity, their efforts to lower their birth rate have significantly lowered world figures.

To those of us in the industrial West, the people in the countries experiencing real declines in their birth rates may still seem "poor" — some with per capita incomes not much over $200 per year — but in most of these countries the lives of the poor are changing in critical ways. Viable income and old age security needs that had previously been met only by bearing many children are beginning to be met by social and political reform: by more secure land tenure, by more reliable food supply, by better health care, and by old age security. Do we need still more studies to prove that people will limit the number of their offspring only when the social and economic context makes such a decision rational and feasible?

10

Controlling Births or Controlling the Population?

Question: By focusing on socioeconomic factors, aren't you ignoring the right of everyone to have access to birth control information and contraceptive devices? You may be right about the need for family labor and old age security, but many people in the poor countries *want* to limit their family size. High rates of abortion in underdeveloped countries (most of them self-induced and carried out at great danger to the woman) are proof of this. Although you talk about China, you overlook the fact that China has one of the most extensive birth control programs in the world. In most countries the rich already have access to birth control; isn't it only fair we do everything possible to provide the same for the poor who want it?

Our Response: No one could fault the goal of providing every couple access to the tools necessary to choose the size of their family. A crucial distinction, however, must be drawn. Family planning programs that *purport to alleviate the problem of hunger* by limiting population growth carry the message that poor people are themselves to blame for hunger. Family planning as a valuable social service to facilitate individual self-determination is entirely another matter. It can be a legitimate way to increase people's real options. What we have been saying, however, is that birth control programs simply are not effective — short of an Orwellian authoritarianism — unless social and economic conditions make it possible for people to take the option of fewer children.

Harvard University and the Government of India cosponsored the Khanna program, which lasted six years and cost one million dollars. At its completion, the directors had to conclude that "although the birth rate of the test group had fallen, the birth rate in the control group (which had no family planning program) had also fallen at almost exactly the same rate. Both declines were mainly attributable to a rise in the average age of marriage that had nothing whatever to do with the Khanna programme."[1] Although small (a sample of 8000 Indian peasants), this study has become a classic illustration of the general observation so well stated by James Kocher in a study for the Population Council:

> I am aware of no evidence of sustained fertility decline — either spontaneous or induced through a family planning program — ever having taken place in the absence of significant socioeconomic development and modernization that considerably altered the lives of most of the population.[2]

Stressing individual self-determination as the legitimate goal of birth control programs does not preclude a national policy in which birth control *also* serves the end of population stabilization because of a limited land base. China did make this decision. But in China the reconstruction of the social order was already providing all the people with the material security necessary to make birth control a *rational* option. Their birth control program can then make fewer children a *feasible* option as well.

Those who argue, as we have, that social and economic change must precede a fall in the population growth rate are often accused of being too mechanistic. Such critics believe that we are saying that once the social and economic preconditions have been met, the problem of rapid population growth will automatically "take care of itself." China's extensive birth control programs testify, they say, to the need for positive action through family planning programs.

What China illustrates to us, however, is that if the majority of people participate in the process of development, then they themselves will come to recognize the need for population limitation — if indeed the need exists.

Advocating birth control programs in underdeveloped countries can represent more than a benign misunderstanding of the root causes of hunger. Where people do not have control of resources nor even the minimum necessities for survival, birth control programs are not only ineffective, they also divert funds that could be going to improve the welfare of the poor through basic agrarian reconstruction.

Some governments are going even farther. India is seriously considering legislation to directly punish people for having children. Rural areas that do not have successful sterilization programs would have low priority for getting drinking and irrigation water. The Indian state of West Bengal is framing legislation that would fine or imprison a spouse if he or she is not sterilized after having more than two children. Such legislation is not surprising when you consider that it comes from an elite-controlled government that has chosen to penalize the people instead of jeopardizing the status quo by re-ordering control over resources. India's approach brings to mind Barry Commoner's words in *The Closing Circle*: "War is . . . a means of solving a social issue, not by social means but by a biological process — death. The same is true, I believe, of enforced population control."[3]

Already with the few facts we have presented in this first section of our book, it should become clear that "too many people" is not the cause of hunger. "Too many people" is an illusion growing out of increasingly concentrated control over resources. The specter of overpopulation arises as more and more people are severed from control over and participation in the production process. Thus they appear as superabundant. Often the very people who prefer to blame the poor themselves — and their breeding — for deplorable social conditions are those who stand to lose by the redistribution of power over productive resources that for the first time would give people the real option to limit their family size.

Every time we read or hear about the size of the population as the cause of hunger and population control as the solution, we must train ourselves to ask: Why focus on rapid population growth — a mere symptom — when we can point to root causes? Even if family planning measures *were* able to reduce population growth, without a gain in control over productive resources by the poor majority, would the hungry be better fed?

PART III
Colonial Inheritance

11

Why Can't People Feed Themselves?

Question: You have said that the hunger problem is not the result of overpopulation. But you have not yet answered the most basic and simple question of all: Why can't people feed themselves? As Senator Daniel P. Moynihan put it bluntly, when addressing himself to the Third World, "Food growing is the first thing you do when you come down out of the trees. The question is, how come the United States can grow food and you can't?"

Our Response: In the very first speech I, Frances, ever gave after writing *Diet for a Small Planet*, I tried to take my audience along the path that I had taken in attempting to understand why so many are hungry in this world. Here is the gist of that talk that was, in truth, a turning point in my life:

When I started I saw a world divided into two parts: a *minority* of nations that had "taken off" through their agricultural and industrial revolutions to reach a level of unparalleled material abundance and a *majority* that remained behind in a primitive, traditional, undeveloped state. This lagging behind of the majority of the world's peoples must be due, I thought, to some internal deficiency or even to several of them. It seemed obvious that the underdeveloped countries must be deficient in natural resources — particularly good land and climate — and in cultural development, including modern attitudes conducive to work and progress.

But when looking for the historical roots of the predicament, I learned that my picture of these two separate worlds was quite false. My "two separate worlds" were really just different sides of the same coin. One side was on top largely because the other side was on the bottom. Could this be true? How were these separate worlds related?

Colonialism appeared to me to be the link. Colonialism destroyed the cultural patterns of production and exchange by which traditional societies in "underdeveloped" countries previously had met the needs of the people. Many precolonial social structures, while dominated by exploitative elites, had evolved a system of mutual obligations among the classes that helped to ensure at least a minimal diet for all. A friend of mine once said, "Precolonial village existence in subsistence agriculture was a limited life indeed, but it's certainly not Calcutta." The misery of starvation in the streets of Calcutta can only be understood as the end-point of a long historical process — one that has destroyed a traditional social system.

"Underdeveloped," instead of being an adjective that evokes the picture of a static society, became for me a verb (to "underdevelop") meaning the *process* by which the minority of the world has transformed — indeed often robbed and degraded — the majority.

That was 1972. I clearly recall my thoughts on my return home. I had stated publicly for the first time a world view that had taken me years of study to grasp. The sense of relief was tremendous. For me the breakthrough lay in realizing that today's "hunger crisis" could not be described in static, descriptive terms. Hunger and underdevelopment must always be thought of as a *process*.

To answer the question "why hunger?" it is counterproductive to simply *describe* the conditions in an underdeveloped country today. For these conditions, whether they be the degree of malnutrition, the levels of agricultural production, or even the country's ecological endowment, are not static facts — they are not "givens." They are rather the *results* of an ongoing historical process. As we dug ever deeper into that historical process for the preparation of this book, we began to discover the existence of scarcity-creating mechanisms that we had only vaguely intuited before.

We have gotten great satisfaction from probing into the past since we recognized it is the only way to approach a solution to hunger today. We have come to see that it is the *force* creating the condition, not the condition itself, that must be the target of change. Otherwise we might change the condition today, only to find tomorrow that it has been recreated — with a vengeance.

Asking the question "Why can't people feed themselves?" carries a sense of bewilderment that there are so many people in the world not able to feed themselves adequately. What astonished us, however, is that there are not *more* people in the world who are hungry — considering the weight of the centuries of effort by the few to undermine the capacity of the majority to feed themselves. No, we are not crying "conspiracy!" If these forces were entirely conspiratorial, they would be easier to detect and many more people would by now have risen up to resist. We are talking about something more subtle and insidious; a heritage of a colonial order in which people with the advantage of considerable power sought their own self-interest, often arrogantly believing they were acting in the interest of the people whose lives they were destroying.

The Colonial Mind

The colonizer viewed agriculture in the subjugated lands as primitive and backward. Yet such a view contrasts sharply with documents from the colonial period now coming to light. For example, A. J. Voelker, a British agricultural scientist assigned to India during the 1890s, wrote

> Nowhere would one find better instances of keeping land scrupulously clean from weeds, of ingenuity in device of water-raising appliances, of knowledge of soils and their capabilities, as well as of the exact time to sow and reap, as one would find in Indian agriculture. It is wonderful, too, how much is known of rotation, the system of "mixed crops" and of fallowing. . . . I, at least, have never seen a more perfect picture of cultivation."[1]

None the less, viewing the agriculture of the vanquished as primitive and backward reinforced the colonizer's rationale for destroying it. To the colonizers of Africa, Asia, and Latin America, agriculture became merely a means to extract wealth — much as gold from a mine — on behalf of the colonizing power. Agriculture was no longer seen as a source of food for the local population, nor even as their livelihood. Indeed the English economist John Stuart Mill reasoned that colonies should not be thought of as civilizations or countries at all but as "agricultural establishments" whose sole purpose was to supply the "larger community to which they belong." The colonized society's agriculture was only a subdivision of the agricultural system of the metropolitan country. As Mill acknowledged, "Our West India colonies, for example, cannot be regarded as countries. . . . The West Indies are the place where England *finds it convenient* to carry on the production of sugar, coffee and a few other tropical commodities."[2]

Prior to European intervention, Africans practiced a diversified agriculture that included the introduction of new food plants of Asian or American origin. But colonial rule simplified this diversified production to single cash crops — often to the exclusion of staple foods — and in the process sowed the seeds of famine.[3] Rice farming once had been common in Gambia. But with colonial rule so much of the best land was taken over by peanuts (grown for the European market) that rice had to be imported to counter the mounting prospect of famine. Northern Ghana, once famous for its yams and other foodstuffs, was forced to concentrate solely on cocoa. Most of the Gold Coast thus became dependent on cocoa. Liberia was turned into a virtual plantation subsidiary of Firestone Tire and Rubber. Food production in Dahomey and southeast Nigeria was all but abandoned in favor of palm oil; Tanganyika (now Tanzania) was forced to focus on sisal and Uganda on cotton.

The same happened in Indochina. About the time of the American Civil War the French decided that the Mekong Delta in Vietnam would be ideal for producing rice for export. Through a production system based on enriching the large landowners, Vietnam became the world's third largest exporter of rice by the 1930s; yet many landless Vietnamese went hungry.[4]

Rather than helping the peasants, colonialism's public works programs only reinforced export crop production. British irrigation works built in nineteenth-century India did help increase production, but the expansion was for spring export crops at the expense of millets and legumes grown in the fall as the basic local food crops.

Because people living on the land do not easily go against their natural and adaptive drive to grow food for themselves, colonial powers had to force the production of cash crops. The first strategy was to use physical or economic force to get the local population to grow cash crops instead of food on their own plots and then turn them over to the colonizer for export. The second strategy was the direct takeover of the land by large-scale plantations growing crops for export.

Forced Peasant Production

As Walter Rodney recounts in *How Europe Underdeveloped Africa*, cash crops were often grown literally under threat of guns and whips.[5] One visitor to the Sahel commented in 1928: "Cotton is an artificial crop and one the value of which is not entirely clear to the natives . . ." He wryly noted the "enforced enthusiasm with which the natives . . . have thrown themselves into . . . planting cotton."[6] The forced cultivation of cotton was a major grievance leading to the Maji Maji wars in Tanzania (then Tanganyika) and behind the nationalist revolt in Angola as late as 1960.[7]

Although raw force was used, taxation was the preferred colonial technique to force Africans to grow cash crops. The colonial administrations simply levied taxes on cattle, land, houses, and even the people themselves. Since the tax had to be paid in the coin of the realm, the peasants had either to grow crops to sell or to work on the plantations or in the mines of the Europeans.[8] Taxation was both an effective tool to "stimulate" cash cropping and a source of revenue that the colonial bureaucracy needed to enforce the system. To expand their production of export crops to pay the mounting taxes, peasant producers were forced to neglect the farming of food crops. In 1830, the Dutch administration in Java made the peasants an offer they could not refuse; if they would grow government-owned export crops on one fifth of their land, the Dutch would remit their land taxes.[9] If they refused and thus could not pay the taxes, they lost their land.

Marketing boards emerged in Africa in the 1930s as another technique for getting the profit from cash crop production by native producers into the hands of the colonial government and international firms. Purchases by the marketing boards were well below the world market price. Peanuts bought by the boards from peasant cultivators in West Africa were sold in Britain for more than *seven times* what the peasants received.[10]

The marketing board concept was born with the "cocoa hold-up" in the Gold Coast in 1937. Small cocoa farmers refused to sell to the large cocoa concerns like United Africa Company (a subsidiary of the Anglo-Dutch firm, Unilever — which we know as Lever Brothers) and Cadbury until they got a higher price. When the British government stepped in and agreed to buy the cocoa directly in place of the big business concerns, the smallholders must have thought they had scored at least a minor victory. But had they really? The following year the British formally set up the West African Cocoa Control Board. Theoretically, its purpose was to pay the peasants a reasonable price for their crops. In practice, however, the board, as sole purchaser, was able to hold down the prices paid the peasants for their crops when the world prices were rising. Rodney sums up the real "victory":

> None of the benefits went to Africans, but rather to the British government itself and to the private companies . . . Big companies like the United Africa Company and John Holt were given . . . quotas to fulfill on behalf of the boards. As agents of the government, they were no longer exposed to direct attack, and their profits were secure.[11]

These marketing boards, set up for most export crops, were actually controlled by the companies. The chairman of the Cocoa Board was none other than John Cadbury of Cadbury Brothers (ever had a Cadbury chocolate bar?) who was part of a buying pool exploiting West African cocoa farmers.

The marketing boards funneled part of the profits from the exploitation of peasant producers indirectly into the royal treasury. While the Cocoa Board sold to the British Food Ministry at low prices, the ministry upped the price for British manufacturers, thus netting a profit as high as 11 million pounds in some years.[12]

These marketing boards of Africa were only the institutionalized rendition of what is the essence of colonialism — the extraction of wealth. While profits continued to accrue to foreign interests and local elites, prices received by those actually growing the commodities remained low.

Plantations

A second approach was direct takeover of the land either by the colonizing government or by private foreign interests. Previously self-provisioning farmers were forced to cultivate the plantation fields through either enslavement or economic coercion.

After the conquest of the Kandyan Kingdom (in present day Sri Lanka), in 1815, the British designated all the vast central part of the island as crown land. When it was determined that coffee, a profitable export crop, could be grown there, the Kandyan lands were sold off to British investors and planters at a mere five shillings per acre, the government even defraying the cost of surveying and road building.[13]

Java is also a prime example of a colonial government seizing territory and then putting it into private foreign hands. In 1870, the Dutch declared all uncultivated land — called waste land — property of the state for lease to Dutch plantation enterprises. In addition, the Agrarian Land Law of 1870 authorized foreign companies to lease village-owned land. The peasants, in chronic need of ready cash for taxes and foreign consumer goods, were only too willing to lease their land to the foreign companies for very modest sums and under terms dictated by the firms. Where land was still held communally, the village headman was tempted by high cash commissions offered by plantation companies. He would lease the village land even more cheaply than would the individual peasant or, as was frequently the case, sell out the entire village to the company.[14]

The introduction of the plantation meant the divorce of agriculture from nourishment, as the notion of food value was lost to the overriding claim of "market value" in international trade. Crops such as sugar, tobacco, and coffee were selected, not on the basis of how well they feed people, but for their high price value relative to their weight and bulk so that profit margins could be maintained even after the costs of shipping to Europe.

Suppressing Peasant Farming

The stagnation and impoverishment of the peasant food-producing sector was not the mere by-product of benign neglect, that is, the unintended consequence of an overemphasis on export production. Plantations — just like modern "agroindustrial complexes" — needed an abundant and readily available supply of low-wage agricultural workers. Colonial administrations thus devised a variety of tactics, all to undercut self-provisioning agriculture and thus make rural populations dependent on plantation wages. Government services and even the most minimal infrastructure (access to water, roads, seeds, credit, pest and disease control information, and so on) were systematically denied. Plantations usurped most of the good land, either making much of the rural population landless or pushing them onto marginal soils. (Yet the plantations have often held much of their land idle simply to prevent the peasants from using it — even to this day. Del Monte owns 57,000 acres of Guatemala but plants only 9000. The rest lies idle except for a few thousand head of grazing cattle.)[15]

In some cases a colonial administration would go even further to guarantee itself a labor supply. In at least twelve countries in the eastern and southern parts of Africa the exploitation of mineral wealth (gold, diamonds, and copper) and the establishment of cash-crop plantations demanded a continuous supply of low-cost labor. To assure this labor supply, colonial administrations simply expropriated the land of the African communities by violence and drove the people into small reserves.[16] With neither adequate land for their traditional slash-and-burn methods nor access to the means — tools, water, and fertilizer — to make continuous farming of such limited areas viable, the indigenous population could scarcely meet subsistence needs, much less produce surplus to sell in order to cover the colonial taxes. Hundreds of thousands of Africans were forced to become the cheap labor source so "needed" by the colonial plantations. Only by laboring on plantations and in the mines could they hope to pay the colonial taxes.

The tax scheme to produce reserves of cheap plantation and mining labor was particularly effective when the Great Depression hit and the bottom dropped out of cash crop economies. In 1929 the cotton market collapsed, leaving peasant cotton producers, such as those in Upper Volta, unable to pay their colonial taxes. More and more young people, in some years as many as 80,000, were thus forced to migrate to the Gold Coast to compete with each other for low-wage jobs on cocoa plantations.[17]

The forced migration of Africa's most able-bodied workers — stripping village food farming of needed hands — was a recurring feature of colonialism. As late as 1973 the Portuguese "exported" 400,000 Mozambican peasants to work in South Africa in exchange for gold deposited in the Lisbon treasury.

The many techniques of colonialism to undercut self-provisioning agriculture in order to ensure a cheap labor supply are no better illustrated than by the story of how, in the mid-nineteenth century, sugar plantation owners in British Guiana coped with the double blow of the emancipation of slaves and the crash in the world sugar market. The story is graphically recounted by Alan Adamson in *Sugar without Slaves*.[18]

Would the ex-slaves be allowed to take over the plantation land and grow the food they needed? The planters, many ruined by the sugar slump, were determined they would not. The planter-dominated government devised several schemes for thwarting food self-sufficiency. The price of crown land was kept artificially high, and the purchase of land in parcels smaller than 100 acres was outlawed — two measures guaranteeing that newly organized ex-slave cooperatives could not hope to gain access to much land. The government also prohibited cultivation on as much as 400,000 acres — on the grounds of "uncertain property titles." Moreover, although many planters held part of their land out of sugar production due to the depressed world price, they would not allow any alternative production on them. They feared that once the ex-slaves started growing food it would be difficult to return them to sugar production when world market prices began to recover. In addition, the government taxed peasant production, then turned around and used the funds to subsidize the immigration of laborers from India and Malaysia to replace the freed slaves, thereby making sugar production again profitable for the planters. Finally, the government neglected the infrastructure for subsistence agriculture and denied credit for small farmers.

Perhaps the most insidious tactic to "lure" the peasant away from food production — and the one with profound historical consequences — was a policy of keeping the price of imported food low through the removal of tariffs and subsidies. The policy was double-edged: first, peasants were told they need not grow food because they could always buy it cheaply with their plantation wages; second, cheap food imports destroyed the market for domestic food and thereby impoverished local food producers.

Adamson relates how both the Governor of British Guiana and the Secretary for the Colonies Earl Grey favored low duties on imports in order to erode local food production and thereby release labor for the plantations. In 1851 the governor rushed through a reduction of the duty on cereals in order to "divert" labor to the sugar estates. As Adamson comments, "Without realizing it, he [the governor] had put his finger on the most mordant feature of monoculture: . . . its convulsive need to destroy any other sector of the economy which might compete for 'its' labor."[19]

Many colonial governments succeeded in establishing dependence on imported foodstuffs. In 1647 an observer in the West Indies wrote to Governor Winthrop of Massachusetts: "Men are so intent upon planting sugar that they had rather buy foode at very deare rates than produce it by labour, so infinite is the profitt of sugar workes. . . ."[20] By 1770, the West Indies were importing most of the continental colonies' exports of dried fish, grain, beans, and vegetables. A dependence on imported food made the West Indian colonies vulnerable to any disruption in supply. This dependence on imported food stuffs spelled disaster when the thirteen continental colonies gained independence and food exports from the continent to the West Indies were interrupted. With no diversified food system to fall back on, 15,000 plantation workers died of famine between 1780 and 1787 in Jamaica alone.[21] The dependence of the West Indies on imported food persists to this day.

Suppressing Peasant Competition

We have talked about the techniques by which indigenous populations were forced to cultivate cash crops. In some countries with large plantations, however, colonial governments found it necessary to *prevent* peasants from independently growing cash crops not out of concern for their welfare, but so that they would not compete with colonial interests growing the same crop. For peasant farmers, given a modicum of opportunity, proved themselves capable of outproducing the large plantations not only in terms of output per unit of land but, more important, in terms of capital cost per unit produced.

In the Dutch East Indies (Indonesia and Dutch New Guinea) colonial policy in the middle of the nineteenth century forbade the sugar refineries to buy sugar cane from indigenous growers and imposed a discriminatory tax on rubber produced by native smallholders.[22] A recent unpublished United Nations study of agricultural development in Africa concluded that large-scale agricultural operations owned and controlled by foreign commercial interests (such as the rubber plantations of Liberia, the sisal estates of Tanganyika [Tanzania], and the coffee estates of Angola) only survived the competition of peasant producers because "the authorities actively supported them by suppressing indigenous rural development."[23]

The suppression of indigenous agricultural development served the interests of the colonizing powers in two ways. Not only did it prevent direct competition from more efficient native producers of the same crops, but it also guaranteed a labor force to work on the foreign-owned estates. Planters and foreign investors were not unaware that peasants who could survive economically by their own production would be under less pressure to sell their labor cheaply to the large estates.

The answer to the question, then, "Why can't people feed themselves?" must begin with an understanding of how colonialism actively prevented people from doing just that. Colonialism

- forced peasants to replace food crops with cash crops that were then expropriated at very low rates;
- took over the best agricultural land for export crop plantations and then forced the most able-bodied workers to leave the village fields to work as slaves or for very low wages on plantations;
- encouraged a dependence on imported food;
- blocked native peasant cash crop production from competing with cash crops produced by settlers or foreign firms.

These are concrete examples of the development of underdevelopment that we should have perceived as such even as we read our history schoolbooks. Why didn't we? Somehow our schoolbooks always seemed to make the flow of history appear to have its own logic — as if it could not have been any other way. I, Frances, recall, in particular, a grade-school, social studies pamphlet on the idyllic life of Pedro, a nine-year-old boy on a coffee plantation in South America. The drawings of lush vegetation and "exotic" huts made his life seem romantic indeed. Wasn't it natural and proper that South America should have plantations to supply my mother and father with coffee? Isn't that the way it was *meant* to be?

12

Isn't Colonialism Dead?

Question: It may be true that colonialism impaired people's ability to feed themselves. But most of the underdeveloped countries have been independent for ten to twenty years, or even longer. If colonialism is dead, why can't people now feed themselves?

Our Response: Colonialism may be dead. But it left an indelible imprint on every society it touched. The effects of colonialism could not be wiped clean simply by a proclamation of independence.

The colonial enforcement of export agriculture handicapped future development by orienting indigenous production and trade patterns to serve narrow export interests. Internal trade that might have served as the means for autonomous development was disrupted or even destroyed in the wake of all-encompassing colonial cash crop systems geared to the needs of foreign interests. Thriving industries serving indigenous markets were destroyed. The onslaught of low-priced textiles from the mills of the colonizing countries ruined skilled village spinners and weavers in India and Africa.

Whole countries became synonymous with only one city — the capital — or, if it was inland, the capital and its port. Internal communications and trade never developed. Latin American Eduardo Galeano writes poignantly:

> Brazil has no permanent land connections with three of its neighbors; Colombia, Peru and Venezuela. . . . Each Latin American country still identifies itself with its own port — a negation of its roots and real identity — to such an extent that almost all intraregional trade goes by sea: Inland transport is virtually nonexistent.[1]

Colonialism stunted indigenous agriculture by directing agricultural research only to export crops. Moreover, slavery severely limited the impetus for improved agricultural techniques. As Rodney points out: "People can be forced to perform simple manual labour, but very little else. This was proven when Africans were used as slaves in the West Indies and America. Slaves damaged tools and carried out sabotage, which could only be controlled by extra supervision and by keeping tools and productive processes very elementary."[2] As another writer observed, the African peasant "went into colonialism with a hoe and came out with a hoe."[3]

The most ignored but perhaps pervasive effects of colonial plantation culture are these: A narrowing of the experience of agriculture to plantation work, especially with tree crops, has over generations robbed entire populations of basic peasant farming skills. Moreover, it is more difficult today for people to return to growing the food they need, because farming has come to be associated in their minds with misery and degradation.

From 1650 to 1850, when the populations of other continents increased many times, greatly stimulating development, the slave trade caused Africa's population to stagnate.[4] Moreover, the slave trade depleted Africa of its most able-bodied workers.

The transfer of people of one race and culture to work plantations in a foreign land was a basic strategy of colonialism in all parts of the world. People of different racial and cultural backgrounds were thrown together in conditions of extreme hardship. Racial differences and antagonisms among laborers were ways for colonizers to control the labor force.[5] Is it at all surprising that this forced mixing of races and cultures has left a legacy of social tensions that make cooperation and economic unity almost impossible? By the forced migration of people, the pitting of race against race for the crumbs from the colonial table, colonialism undermined development based on mutual cooperation.

Colonialism also undercut the moral substratum of traditional societies. Traditional societies appear to many as totally autocratic with the chief, the warlord, or the village headman having unlimited power. But while the peasants were obliged to serve their rulers in most traditional societies, the privileged elite were also under obligation to protect and provide for the welfare of the peasant majority. Because of this principle of reciprocity, such societies did have a degree of trust and compassion in human relationships. Hard times were shared to some degree.[6] In Vietnam before the French, for example, the rulers allowed communal land to be used to ensure that each family had at least a minimal food supply.

But colonialism destroyed the basis for this traditional moral system. First, the traditional rulers lost much of their authority in the eyes of the peasants when they proved unable to defend their country against the colonial invader. With the introduction of a commercialized production system, traditional obligations were replaced by money-based ties. The belief that ruler and ruled were responsible for each other was replaced by the notion that a growing GNP would provide for all. Most important, while colonialism undermined the traditional respect for the elite class, it invested that class with greater real power. In eighteenth-century Bengal, India, for example, the British made the traditional elites — previously responsible only for fiscal and administrative duties — into landed proprietors, now responsible for collecting revenue from the tenant-cultivators for the crown. These *zamindars*, as they were called, used their power to acquire vast holdings of land for themselves.[7]

Before the British ruled India, debt was commonplace but the moneylender was not powerful. Part of the reason was that land was not owned privately. Without private ownership it was impossible to lose land through indebtedness. But once the British had established private ownership to facilitate tax collection, the position of the smallholders, as most were, became precarious. Rain or drought, good harvest or bad — the taxes had to be paid in cash. With private ownership, land became the collateral for loans with which to pay one's taxes in bad times. If hard times continued, cultivators lost their land as the colonial legal system put its weight behind foreclosures.

When colonial policy tried to stem this transfer of land to nonagriculturalist moneylenders, many moneylenders simply became landlords themselves. Also larger landholders took on the role of moneylending. They were hardly sorry to see their debtors fail since foreclosure meant they could add to their property. Here we find some of the origins of present-day India's mushrooming landless laborer class.[8]

In Java, before the Dutch, the peasants had substantial economic strength. But the Dutch introduced a system similar to the British one of indirect rule through an existing elite. Peasants unable to pay their taxes to the Dutch could only turn to the local Chinese moneylenders. When the peasants could not repay a loan, they in effect became tenants on their own land, forced to grow crops chosen by the creditors for a below-market price determined by the creditors.[9]

In these two examples we see how colonialism, in its need to extract wealth from the colony, introduced a money economy and put its power behind the already well-placed. Colonialism thus promoted the increasing concentration of landholding by the few and the increasing landlessness of the many. It is this trend, set in motion centuries ago, that forms such a great obstacle to true agricultural development today.

But colonialism did more than simply reinforce the emergence of one class over another. Colonialism exacerbated regional inequalities. And, as colonial policy focused on the rapid development of the most potentially profitable regions, the less obviously well endowed were left behind. A few urban areas became the seats of colonial power. These imbalances still plague development efforts.

We have seen how colonialism stifled and distorted traditional agriculture to extract wealth in the form of luxury cash crops; how colonialism enslaved or forced the migration of the agriculturally productive population in search of wage labor to pay colonial taxes; how colonialism laid the foundation for racial and social strife as disparate cultures were thrown together in competition for survival; and how colonialism exacerbated inequalities in the countryside, ending land-tenure security, a security that is now recognized as the first prerequisite of agricultural progress.

Our knowledge of the past is fundamental to our understanding of the present. The history of the colonial period should be familiar to any of us, its outcome predictable by any of us: declining food production and greater food imports, increasing impoverishment, growing vulnerability to the constant fluctuations in the international market, and internally uneven growth.

But it has not been so familiar. In the 1960s as college students we read the latest textbooks on "international development" that described these economies as "dualistic" — meaning that one sector, the commercial export sector — had potential for dynamic growth as part of an expanding international economy while the other sector, the traditional sector, was hopelessly mired in the past. According to this analysis, the task of development was to give the subsistence sector a big shove into the modern world, into the international market economy.

But dualism describes a condition while ignoring a process. If, however, we describe underdevelopment as a *process* and understand its colonial roots, we know that the traditional and the modern sectors do not stand side by side by mere chance. This history of underdevelopment shows that the economic decline of the backward sector was the direct product of the formation of the other, commercial sector, tied into the international economy. Once colonialism has raked over a country, there is no such thing as a "traditional" culture left for economic planners to push into the present.

The irony is that development "experts" see the answer to underdevelopment in thrusting Third World economies wholesale into the very international market system that was initially structured to keep them in submission (see Part VI).

PART IV

Blaming Nature

13

Haven't There Always Been Famines?

Question: Haven't there always been famines due to droughts and floods? Wouldn't we now be somewhat immodest to expect that we can eliminate all famines everywhere in the world? After all, we cannot control the weather.

Our Response: No, we cannot control the weather. And since everyone associates famines with weather disasters, we too once felt the world must resign itself to periodic famine. What we have learned, however, is that famine is a social fact, not a natural one; the result of human arrangements, not an act of God. Invariably the problem is *not* the weather. The problem is *not* a drought or a flood. The problem is the failure of a social system to meet the challenges of nature.

This is true not only today but perhaps throughout much more of history than we ever realized. We were struck by the words of a French historian: "The great french famines and food shortages of the Middle Ages occurred during periods when foodstuffs were not lacking; they were indeed produced in great quantity and exported. The social system and structure were largely responsible for these deficiencies."[1]

Most people believe famines in India have been constant phenomena related to a poor climate. But the frequency of famine in India has not been constant. Famine intensified under colonialism, especially during the second half of the nineteenth century, even though food production kept pace with population growth. After the opening of the Suez Canal in 1870, India became a major exporter of wheat to England, other Western countries, and Egypt. As Sir George Watt wrote in 1908, ". . . the better classes of the community were exporting the surplus stocks that formerly were stored against times of scarcity and famine."[2]

Let us take a closer look at one of the most "famous" famines of this century, that of Bengal, India, in the 1940s. By 1944, an official government report conservatively estimated that one and a half million lives had been lost by famine.

What caused such loss of life?

The immediate food crisis was precipitated by the exigencies of war. In 1943, Churchill ordered the Indians and the thousands of British military in India to "live off their own stocks" when the Japanese conquest of Burma had cut off a main outside source of rice for Bengal and all of India. A drought in 1942 translated into a poor winter rice harvest. But despite all this, the colonial government allowed rice to flow out of Bengal (185,000 tons was exported in the first seven months of 1942).[3] The food went where the money was and great profits were registered along the way. Similarly in a severe famine of 1876–1877 India exported record quantities of food grains. In 1943, The Royal Famine Commission — the twelfth such commission during the two centuries of British rule — commented:

> We have referred to the atmosphere of fear and greed which, in the absence of controls, was one of the causes of the rapid rise in the price level. Enormous profits were made out of this calamity, and in the circumstances, profits for some meant death for others. A large part of the community lived in plenty while others starved, and there was much indifference in the face of suffering. Corruption was widespread throughout the province. . . .[4]

The failure was one of the social and economic system, not merely of the rains.

The underlying causes of the Bengal famine are rooted in the long-term stagnation of Indian agricultural production under the two centuries of British rule. What few investments in agriculture the British did make were for nonfood crops. From the mid-1890s to the time of the Bengal famine, production of nonfood commercial crops (such as cotton and rape seed) increased by 85 percent, while food production declined by 7 percent. During the same period in eastern India, including Bengal, food (rice) production declined even more markedly, by 38 percent per capita between 1901 and 1941.[5] The result was that by the early 1940s nonfood production equaled almost one third of total production.[6]

How should we react, then, the next time we see the Bengal famine referred to by writers such as Lester Brown as "the last great famine due to the vicissitudes of weather?"[7]

Land of Famine?

As a child were you admonished not to leave any food on your plate because people were starving in China? Even if the connection wasn't clear, there was good reason for your parents to associate China and famine. According to Walter Mallory's 1928 book, *China: Land of Famine*,[8] China experienced famine in some province nearly every year and had done so for over a thousand years. A 1929 American Red Cross report estimated that 3 million deaths a year could be attributed to starvation. The same report commented on the affluence of the elite.[9]

Official dynastic histories going back over 2000 years record a total of 1621 floods and 1392 droughts — confirming Mallory's estimate of more than one disaster a year![10] Certainly, the "vicissitudes of weather" in China have not changed. The North Plain, potentially the most productive area of the country, has undergone a drought, a flood, or both every year, for the past several years.

If the weather has not changed, what has? The *effect* of the weather on both the land and the people of China has changed and changed dramatically. In 1972–1973 when eighteen nations, containing one third of the world's people were being hit by droughts, when western India was facing famine and herds of cattle were dying in the Sahel in Africa, China was also facing its third year of drought, the worst in three decades. But, China had no famine. In fact the provinces *most affected* reaped three years of record harvests.[11] What made the difference?

In China food now comes first. The focus has not been simply on production and distribution but on the creation of an agricultural system that is less vulnerable to weather change. Traditionally, areas devastated by drought are just as likely to be vulnerable to floods next season, as is the case in Bangladesh. But a system of water control can make one season's flood into a blessing for the next.

The harnessing of the Hai River in Hopei province near Peking was one major effort at water control. In just eight years several hundred thousand men and women improved 1700 miles of the riverbed, digging 200 new tributaries and 12,000 channels and building 50,000 bridges and tunnels, in addition to over 800 other major and medium construction works. In all, thirty-five large and medium-sized reservoirs in the mountains were built to store over 106 billion cubic meters of water.[12]

Complementing the water control projects were mobilizations to tap underground water resources. Under the slogan, "We'll exchange sweat for water and water for grain," the people of Hopei, Honan, and Shantung provinces organized themselves to sink hundreds of wells, sometimes working with picks and shovels or with labor-saving rigs they devised themselves. These three provinces now benefit from some 700,000 pump wells. During one year of the drought in Peking's Hopei province alone, this work expanded the irrigated land by over 850,000 acres.[13]

Just as important, all these projects were carried out with low capital expenditures. Instead of the usual huge sums spent on machinery, it was possible to mobilize the work power of millions of peasants because they knew *they* would be the beneficiaries — never again to experience famine. China, without a single World Bank or a United States Agency for International Development (AID) loan, has become the country with one third of the world's irrigated cropland.[14] Wind destruction and erosion have been controlled by widespread tree planting programs. In the area around Peking alone, eleven million trees are being planted each year.[15]

The Chinese people have prepared not only the land but also themselves. Each family in the Tachai commune in Hopei has two below-ground rooms, one of which is commonly used as a storeroom for stockpiling ground maize, millet, and some wheat flour.[16]

So what has made the difference in China? The answer is clearly that the Chinese are developing a system that *assumes* the weather is going to be less than ideal. The people have built, largely by hand, an agricultural system that mitigates the negative impact of bad weather on production. But there is another factor — an economic system that mitigates the impact of weather on any given individual. In China even if there were a decline in total grain output, it would be shared more or less equally by all. No one feasts while others starve. In India, by contrast, the impact of drought falls almost entirely on the area affected and largely on the poorest. As the price rises in response to the drop in supply, it is the landless laborers, the unemployed, and the urban poor who suffer disproportionately.

We human beings have been on this planet long enough to know that adverse weather changes are to be *expected*. The evolution of human civilization can largely be defined as the process of working out many ingenious ways of protecting ourselves against the vagaries of nature. Therefore, when we hear of a widespread famine the first question we should ask is not "What terrible natural event caused it?" but "Why wasn't that society able to cope with the bad fortune? Why is it that one country can suffer natural disasters and have no deaths and another have a million deaths?"

*　　*　　*

China quite literally cannot feed more people . . . the greatest tragedy that China could suffer, at the present time would be a reduction in her death rate . . . millions are going to die. There can be no way out. These men and women, boys and girls, must starve as tragic sacrifices, on the twin alters of uncontrolled reproduction and uncontrolled abuse of the land and resources.

William Vogt, *Road to Survival,* 1948

14

Can We Hold Back the Desert?

Question: Are there not important exceptions? What can we really do, for example, about the expansion of deserts? We have all seen pictures of the barren, parched land of the Sahel, that vast tract cutting through several countries bordering the Sahara. Obviously, it cannot support life. Do you really believe that in this case the deteriorating climate and encroaching desert has not been the cause of hunger?

Our Response: We have seen many references to an AID study[1] in which the Sahara is supposedly taking giant steps south at rates of up to thirty miles a year. On examination, however, it turns out to be merely based on hearsay collections of travelers' impressions. More scientific attempts to measure desert movements have reached different conclusions. Although there is evidence of some southward "movement," the rate appears to be more like one-half mile a year (or 100 miles over the last two centuries) — hardly thirty miles per year![2] We do not wish, however, to argue over how fast or how slow the desert is supposedly advancing and thus reinforce the notion of the desert as an independent, unstoppable force. Such debates only cloud the *social origins* of the problem.

Many falsely assume that the Sahelian drought beginning in 1969 was *the* Sahelian drought. But climatologists consider drought to be an "integral part" of the climate of the region.[3] Most of the older inhabitants of the Sahel believe that the drought years of 1910–1913 were more severe than the recent, much more publicized ones and the figures bear them out.[4] Rainfall, lake, and river levels were not as low in 1969–1973 as they were during the earlier drought. By studying the retardation in the growth of tree-rings scientists have detected that there have been severe droughts several times over the past three centuries and numerous dry spells from time to time. The most recent study we know of concluded "there is no indication of any long continued upward or downward trend in rainfall nor is there any obvious cycle." Thus the expansion of the desert cannot be attributed to any long-term climatic change.[5]

In any case, desertification is not a one-way process. Deserts *can* be reclaimed — and without great financial expense — if great reserves of labor power are invested. For example, Algeria is today the site of a massive and successful reforestation program. The goal over the next twenty years is to plant six million trees in a 1000 mile belt across the northern fringe of the Sahara.[6] Between 1965 and 1970, 160 acres were reclaimed at the Saharan village of Bou Saadu in Algeria, through planting acacia and eucalyptus trees. These gave protection from sandstorms and increased surface humidity. According to one report, "Soon grasses and shrubs sprang up and later [farmers cultivated] citrus fruits, olives, figs and pomegranates, grain, tomatoes, potatoes, peas, beans and onions.

The experience of China further confirms that deserts can be reclaimed. More than one tenth of China is made up of deserts. Thirty years ago Western observers wrote of "encroaching sand covering fertile fields forcing the people to flee." Since the Revolution the Chinese people have transformed the deserts by planting trees and grasses, building wind-and-sand breaks, and developing water conservation projects. Tens of thousands of acres of desert have been brought under cultivation and many more have become pastures.[7]

The Sahel

In Part II we discussed the many adaptive techniques of the pastoral nomads to the climate of the Sahel. We showed how colonial intervention and commercial interests led to the breakdown of the traditional system of the nomads, making them vulnerable to drought. Now we'll look at the other half of the story — the transformation of the lives of the small farmers who inhabit the southern region of the Sahel. Over the centuries they also had developed a profound understanding of their environment. They knew the necessity of letting land lie fallow for up to twenty years and they cultivated a wide variety of crops, each adapted to a different microenvironment and yet offering nutritional complementarity. Nomads and cultivators often developed a mutually beneficial relationship. The cultivators offered the nomads lands for pasture in the dry season and grain in exchange for milk, manure for the fields, and donkeys for plowing.

Sahelian Mali was once known as the breadbasket of Africa. It could always be counted upon to trade grain in times of neighbors' needs. The Sahelian precolonial custom was to construct small farming and village granaries for storing millet for flour and in some cases for even more years of consumption, knowing full well that small-harvest years should be expected. One United Nations study arguing against the idea that the Sahel is overpopulated noted that, if the traditional storage practices were followed, the "carrying capacity" of the land in people and animals would be that of the average years and not that of the poorest years.[8]

What happened to a system that was adapted over centuries to deal with periodic drought? First, even before the French conquest in the late nineteenth and early twentieth centuries these civilizations had already been severely undermined by two centuries of forced depopulation as millions of the youngest and strongest were taken as slaves to the New World. Then came the French and years of bloody fighting. After conquering the Sahel, the French decided that the southern region was ideal for exporting cotton (at a time when England controlled most other sources for textile mills) and peanuts (to provide a cheap substitute for walnut oil). Forced cash crop production under colonialism undermined self-provisioning agriculture, as we have already seen.

The techniques of colonialism and their devastating impact on the land and its people are hardly realities only of the past. While the Sahelian countries achieved formal independence in 1960, the successor governments have often outdone the French in forcing export crop production. Taxes that farmers can pay only by producing crops for export have been increased. In Mali in 1929 the French levied a tax that required each adult over fifteen to grow between five and ten kilos of cotton to pay it. By 1960, the last year of French rule, the tax had risen to the equivalent of forty kilos. By 1970, during the drought, the successor government forced each adult peasant to grow at least forty-eight kilos of cotton just to pay taxes.[9]

Higher taxes, as well as falling export prices, force the peasants to increase the production of export crops. But since colonial times, up to and including the recent drought years, these increases are mainly achieved by destructive methods of cultivation. Ever deeper plowing for planting cotton in Senegal and northern Cameroon has eroded vast areas. With even less humus to retain water, it appears as though there is less rain. Larger and larger tracts are cultivated (more accurately, "mined") against the norms of traditional wisdom on soil maintenance. Expanding export crop production means that lands once allowed to lie fallow for a number of years and to be manured by the pastoralists' herds, get forced into virtually uninterrupted cultivation.[10]

The circle is vicious. Continual cultivation rapidly depletes the soil, necessitating still further expansion of export cropping at the expense of food crops and pasture land. Chemical fertilizers that once raised yields of some export crops, making the expansion of cultivation less pressing, are now so costly that the peasants in the end are obliged to bring still more land under cash cropping. Moreover, as the farmers grow less grain, they have had little or none to exchange for milk with the pastoralists. The result, as you can imagine, is hunger for farmers and pastoralists alike, starvation for thousands of animals — and an "encroaching desert."

Recent studies confirm the hunger impact of export cropping. The Yatenga villagers of Upper Volta have found that the soil that once grew cotton is impoverished as now evidenced by the low yield of food crops. The villagers doubly complained, for they found their cotton earnings could not buy enough millet (at inflated drought prices) to cover their grain shortfall.[11] A detailed study in Niger concluded that the peasant families in villages that emphasized peanut production earned a smaller income and ate less well than those in villages in the same province where farmers gave priority to food crops rather than peanuts.[12]

Exports from Famine

How do those who blame drought and an encroaching desert for famine in the Sahel explain the vast amounts of agricultural goods sent out of the region, even during the worst years of drought? Ships in the Dakar port bringing in "relief" food departed with stores of peanuts, cotton, vegetables, and meat. Of the hundreds of millions of dollars worth of agricultural goods the Sahel exported during the drought, over 60 percent went to consumers in Europe and North America and the rest to the elites in other African countries, principally in the Ivory Coast and Nigeria.[13] Marketing control — and profits — are still by and large in the hands of foreign, primarily French, corporations.

During the drought many exports from the Sahel actually increased, some attaining record levels. Cattle exports from the Sahel during 1971, the first year of full drought, totaled over 200 million pounds, up 41 percent compared to 1968. The annual export of chilled or frozen beef tripled compared with a typical year before the drought. In addition, 56 million pounds of fish and 32 million pounds of vegetables were exported from the famine-striken Sahel in 1971 alone.[14]

Mali was one of the countries most affected by the drought and a principal recipient of emergency shipments of food. During the early 1970s production of food crops for local consumption dropped sharply. Corn production, for example, fell by more than one-third between 1969 and 1971, and millet, the basic staple needed to take up the slack, showed no increases. During the same period, Mali's export crops reached new highs. During the year 1971–1972, cottonseed production hit 68,000 metric tons, more than a 400 percent increase over the six years previous with normal rainfall. Peanut production totaled more than 150,000 tons, an increase of nearly 70 percent over a four-year period. More than one third of Mali's cropped area was planted with peanuts. Rice production, *also largely for export*, reached a record high in 1972 of 174,000 tons.[15]

Immediately before and during the drought Chad carried out a major program (with fertilizer subsidized by the European Common Market countries) to increase cotton production. Two thirds of a million acres of the best of Chad's scarce resources are devoted not to food but to cotton. This increase in cotton production throughout the Sahel prompted one French nutritionist to observe, "If people were starving it was not for want of cotton."[16]

Governments and international agencies continue to subsidize export operations. Roads and railways are laid out exclusively to transport exportable commodities from the interior to the principal ports. (A current major United Nations proposal to "help the hungry" in the Sahel — and one with strong United States backing — is a $250 million Trans-Sahelian highway.) Improved internal distribution of food would require, by contrast, a more extensive but less expensive network of village roads. Governments plan irrigation schemes, based on abundant underground water and the Sahel's major rivers, to assure water for export crop areas. During the drought an irrigation scheme in the Segou and Mopti areas made record rice production possible. Almost all of it was exported! Finally, government credit, research, and extension services, as well as fertilizers, pesticides, and improved seeds, are directed primarily toward export crops. With such support for exports at the expense of domestic food production, it comes as no surprise that *even before the drought* food production was seriously deteriorating while export crops were booming.[17]

How are the peasant farmers reacting? Abba Sidick, Secretary General of the National Liberation Front of Chad, a peasant-based movement that has seized control of large areas of Chad, told us in an interview that growing food crops before cotton is a goal of the liberation movement. In certain regions of Senegal peasants have refused to plant more peanuts.[18] In the face of the resistance of the peasants and a drop in world market prices, the Senegalese Government is taking — in the words of the World Bank — "drastic measures" to "stimulate" peanut output. Promoting "modern, labor-saving production methods on the biggest farms" means less dependence on peasants who might always decide they prefer the security of food in the ground.[19] As peasants are pushed off the land, doubtlessly we will hear more and more about the "overpopulated" Sahel. Yet, in Niger, to cite but one example, a country almost twice as large as Texas, there are only four million inhabitants.

Why is it that the Sahelian governments push export crops?

To earn foreign exchange. That is the answer everyone gives. But for what is the foreign exchange used? Much of it is used to enable government bureaucrats and other better-off urban workers to live an imported life-style — refrigerators, air conditioners, cars, and television sets. In 1974, 23 percent of the foreign exchange earned by Senegal went for just such items. The peanut exports annually account for one third of the national budget of Senegal — but 47.2 percent of the budget goes for the salaries of the government bureaucrats.[20] Between 1961 and the worst drought year, 1971, Niger, a country with marked malnutrition and a life expectancy of only thirty-eight years, quadrupled its cotton production and tripled that of peanuts. Together these two exports in 1971 earned about $18 million. But $20 million in foreign exchange was then used up importing clothing, over nine times the amount earned by exporting raw cotton. Over $1 million went for private cars and over $4 million for gasoline and tires. In only three years, 1967–1970, the number of private cars increased by over 50 percent, most of them driven by the miniscule elite in the capital. Over $1 million was spent to import alcoholic beverages and tobacco products.[21] On a visit to the capital city, Niamey, we found that the local elites were shopping in a well-stocked supermarket right out of Paris — complete with frozen ice cream cones from a shop on the Champs-Elysées.

Even when part of the export earnings is used to import food, it generally does not reach those who labor in the fields but is consumed by the better-off urban classes. More than half of the foreign exchange Senegal earned exporting peanuts in 1974 was spent to import wheat for French-owned bread factories that turned out European-style white bread for urban dwellers.[22]

Fattening on Famine

Even more shocking than the pushing of export crops in the face of declining food production is the fact that *every Sahelian country, with the possible exception of mineral-rich Mauritania, actually produced enough grain to feed its total population, even during the worst drought year.*[23] Why then did so many go hungry?

Most farmers who grow cash crops find themselves without enough money or food reserves to meet their families' needs from one marketing season to the next. In order to survive what they call the "hungry" season — the months of particularly arduous work right before harvest — they are forced to take out loans in cash or millet at usurious interest rates from the local merchants. Local merchants have the grain because they buy it from farmers during harvest time when abundant supply makes for low prices and when farmers must sell to pay their debts and taxes. When we visited the Tensobentenga region of Upper Volta, we found that even during the normal rainfall year of 1976 the price of grain virtually doubled between the time of harvest and only seven months later. The merchants can sell the hoarded grain during the hungry season at two or three times the price originally paid and even export it to higher income markets in neighboring countries. An AID officer in Ouagadougou, Upper Volta, shocked us with his "conservative estimate" that two thirds of the grain that merchants obtain from peasants in payment of debts gets exported to the Ivory Coast and Ghana. In such societies where speculation in food is "normal," adequate production can still result in scarcity for many — even for the producers.

For farmers made vulnerable by the vicious cycle of indebtedness, drought *does* precipitate famine. Victimized by profiteers, farmers cannot afford to improve the quality of their land and are often forced to exhaust the soil and even to forfeit their land altogether. But clearly, hunger and the seeming expansion of the desert are the products not of drought but of a parasitic class of usurers and grain-hoarding speculators.

The Sahel: A Potential Breadbasket?

Far from being a forsaken waste land, there are those who see the Sahel as a potential breadbasket. They point to the region's exceptionally large underground lake basin and three major river systems, including the Niger, the world's twelfth largest river. With this potential for irrigation and the region's gift of a tropical sun, they estimate the Sahel could produce at least six times more grain than at present, as well as startling quantities of meat, vegetables, and fruit for the lucrative European and Middle Eastern markets. On a recent visit to Upper Volta we found a German agribusiness firm experimenting with the use of a blimp to "lift" vegetables and fruits from outlying villages to the Ouagadougou airport so that they could be airfreighted to Frankfurt.

Anyone who knows the Sahel knows that there is no doubt that much more could be produced. But if the majority of the people are not in control of that production, what chance is there that they will benefit?

The recent hard times actually were good times for the already better-off minority. An FAO report concludes that the overall collective structure that helped the people to adapt to crises is rapidly disappearing. Once this process of individual gain-seeking had begun, a few years of scarce rain greatly increased the polarization of ownership of resources. As a recent United Nations report on the Sahel states, "All it now takes is a year or two of short rains and what is left lands in the hands of a few individuals."[24]

This process has already driven many pastoralists and peasants off the land. A French research team even suggests that the drought has acted as a modern enclosure movement, paving the way for large-scale, mechanized, irrigated agricultural enterprises.[25] The now landless peasants would at best be available for seasonal, low-wage work on the commercial complexes. The rural majority's impoverishment in the midst of an agricultural boom would ensure that the bulk of production would be exported to the continued enrichment of the same old elites and their foreign partners. We will examine an example of a California-based agribusiness corporation already "rolling back the desert" in Senegal on pages 259–260.

An analysis of famine that puts the blame on an "encroaching desert" will never come to grips with the inequalities in power at the root of the problem. Solutions proposed will inevitably be limited to the technical and administrative aspects — irrigation programs, modern mechanization, new seed varieties, foreign investment, grain reserve banks, and so on. Such an analysis allows no reflection upon the political and economic arrangements that, far more than changes in rainfall or even climate, are at the root of low productivity and human deprivation. Until all the people in a country control their nation's resources, such "solutions" can only work against the interest of the majority.

We have seen that drought cannot be considered the cause of famine. Drought is a natural phenomenon. Famine is a human phenomenon. Any link that does exist is precisely through the economic and political order of a society that can either minimize the human consequences of drought or exacerbate them. And while a people cannot change the weather, they can change the political and economic order.

*   *   *

The recurrent drought of the past few years has made clear that the desert is encroaching on a large scale and that food production capacity in western Africa is seriously threatened. . . . What is now needed is a comprehensive international program that, rather than ease the effects of the drought, will help roll back the desert.

Henry Kissinger, 1976

Above all, the Sahelian situation calls for the immediate launching of a major effort to slow and stabilize population growth in the region. Such a long-term cooperative international program will have to be comparable in scope to the program that launched the Green Revolution in the late sixties.

Lester R. Brown, *By Bread Alone*, 1975

PART V

Modernizing Hunger

15

Isn't Production the Problem?

Question: The Third World countries clearly lag far behind in food production. Only four decades ago the average grain yields in both the industrial countries and the underdeveloped countries were about the same. Now the grain yields in the industrial countries outstrip those of the underdeveloped countries by over 200 percent. India and the United States have about the same crop acreage, but look what India produces. If India's yield per acre equaled that of the United States, its cereal production would be three times what it is.

By 1985 it is estimated that the underdeveloped countries will fall short of the food they require by 85 million tons annually. Don't all other questions fade before the most urgent one of how to produce more food?

Our Response: Who wouldn't agree? If people are hungry, everyone assumes there must not be enough food. Indeed, for at least thirty years the central question of every War on Hunger has been: How can more food be produced? We learn of supposed answers almost daily in what we call the "news release" approach to hunger, one new breakthrough after another — protein from petroleum, harvests of kelp, extracts from alfalfa — all to expand the food supply.

In the view of many, the production approach is working. Today more food is, in fact, being produced. The "Green Revolution" now adds an estimated 20 million tons annually to the grain larders of Asia (not including China). In Mexico wheat yields tripled in only two decades.

But wait. There are also more hungry people than ever before.

Since in country after country there is more food than ever before, we can draw two alternative conclusions:

Either the production focus was correct but soaring numbers of people simply overran even these dramatic production gains;

or, the diagnosis was incorrect. Scarcity is not the cause of hunger. A production increase, no matter how great, can never in itself solve the problem.

The simple facts of world food production make clear that the overpopulation-scarcity diagnosis is, in fact, incorrect. Present world grain production alone could provide every person on earth with more than 3000 calories a day. Even more to the point, between 1952 and 1972, 86 percent of the total population living in underdeveloped countries lived where food production kept pace with or exceeded the rate of population growth.[1]

Indeed, as ironic as it may sound, the narrow focus on increasing production has actually *compounded* the problem of hunger. Because this startling conclusion goes against the popular wisdom, we have found ourselves wanting to verify and re-verify it in country after country.

Most useful to us in understanding just why and how a narrow focus on production undercuts the welfare of the poor majority has been our examination of the Mexican origins of the Green Revolution, the most highly publicized attempt to increase production. Before we began our research we assumed that the Green Revolution (the campaign to breed "miracle seeds" and to provide the "ideal conditions" — the fertilizers, irrigation, insect-and-weed killers they depend on) was introduced into countries like Mexico in order to bring new hope to people trapped by backward, stagnating agricultures. We found we were wrong.

Agrarian Reconstruction under Lázaro Cárdenas

In 1910, 2 percent of the Mexican population owned 97 percent of the land while in most states 95 percent of the rural population had no land at all. During the bloody revolutionary war between 1910 and 1917, well over one million peasants died fighting for land. Theoretically the revolutionaries were victorious. But for seventeen years the country's peasant majority saw less than revolutionary changes. Then, in 1934, Lázaro Cárdenas, a rural-born general in the revolutionary army, was elected president. His administration immediately enacted the country's most sweeping agrarian reform law. For the first time much of the country's better land was appropriated for distribution to the landless, some to be farmed individually and some cooperatively. By 1940, near the end of Cárdenas's term, 42 percent of the entire agricultural population benefited from the distribution of over 78 million acres.[2] Together these small farmers owned 47 percent of all farmland and produced an impressive 52 percent of the value of the nations' farm output.[3]

One reason for such productivity was that a newly created national bank channeled credit and technical assistance specifically to the now numerous land reform beneficiaries. The provision of peasant-oriented services — literacy programs, health services, farm-relevant schooling, and modest rural communications — injected new life into the countryside. Often the results were immediate. In the Laguna area, to cite but one example, the real income of land reform beneficiaries quadrupled between 1935 and 1938.[4]

The Cárdenas administration also invested in scientific research. The purpose, however, was not to "modernize" agriculture in imitation of United States agriculture but to improve on traditional farming methods. Researchers began to develop improved varieties of wheat and especially corn, the main staple of the rural population, always concentrating on what could be utilized by small farmers who had little money and less than ideal farm conditions.

Social and economic progress was being achieved not through dependence on foreign expertise or costly imported agricultural inputs but rather with the abundant, underutilized resources of local peasants. While production increases were seen as important, the goal was to achieve them through helping every peasant to be productive, for only then would the rural majority benefit from the production increases. Freed from the fear of landlords, bosses, and moneylenders, peasants were motivated to produce, knowing that at last they would benefit from their own labor. Power was perceptibly shifting to agrarian reform organizations controlled by those who worked the fields.

The Green Revolution as Counter Revolution: Agriculture to Serve Industrialists

You will probably not be surprised to learn that by the end of his administration in 1940, Cárdenas had made powerful enemies. First were those who had seen their haciendas expropriated. Next were the urban-based monied groups, alarmed by the Cárdenas model of cooperative ownership of land and public ownership of certain industries. Instead of rural services and collective enterprises, they wanted the state to pay for electric power, highways, dams, airports, telecommunications, and urban services that would serve privately owned, commercial agriculture and urban industrialization — from which they would profit.

Not the least of the enemies of Cárdenas were United States policy makers. Land redistribution with cooperative ownership, as well as Cárdenas's nationalization of the Rockefeller Standard Oil subsidiary and foreign-owned railroads, caused "concern" in Washington and on Wall Street. United States corporate investment dropped by about 40 percent between the mid-thirties and the early 1940s.[5]

By 1942, these enemies of Cárdenas's rural reconstruction succeeded in seizing the balance of power within the administration of Cárdenas's successor Avila Camacho. The significance of this shift for the future of Mexican agriculture was immediately clear. President Avila Camacho's first agricultural plan stated that agriculture was now to serve as the basis for the "founding of industrial greatness."[6] Agricultural progress was no longer to be measured first and foremost in terms of the well-being of the rural majority but in how well it served growth elsewhere in the economy.

United States policy only reinforced this fundamental shift. United States policy makers identified American interests with the stability of the Avila Camacho administration and with Mexico's ability to produce manufactured goods to support the war effort. Getting more food out of the rural areas and into the cities was seen as critical. More food in the urban areas meant lower food prices, an essential ingredient for quieting urban unrest and keeping industrial wages low. Low wages would ensure industrial profits high enough to attract investors, both local and foreign.

It was in this historical context that the Green Revolution was born. The Avila Camacho administration welcomed the Rockefeller Foundation to Mexico, and in 1943 the Foundation joined with the new administration to initiate an agricultural research program. The result on one level was in the much-heralded technical package later to be publicized as the Green Revolution. On another level, it served to reverse the entire thrust of the Cárdenas rural reconstruction.

The field director of the Rockefeller Foundation in Mexico became head of a new office *within* the Mexican Ministry of Agriculture. His job was to oversee a scientific revolution that would transport Mexican agriculture into the modern era. Policy choices systematically discarded research alternatives oriented toward the nonirrigated, subsistence sector of Mexican agriculture. Instead, all effort went to the development of a capital-intensive technology applicable only to the relatively best-endowed areas or those that could be created by massive irrigation projects. The focus was on how to make seeds, not people, more productive. Agricultural modernization came to substitute for rural development.

Rapid urban-centered industrialization, so profitable for a few, simply could not coexist with the type of rural development promoted by the Cárdenas administration. First, true rural development based on making each rural family productive and better-off would have meant that the rural majority itself would have eaten much of any increment in food production. This increment was exactly what the ascendant urban interests counted on taking *out* of the countryside to feed an industrial work force. Second, genuine improvement in rural life would have sharply diminished the steady exodus to the towns and cities. But it was just this ongoing influx of rural refugees that was so "needed" to perpetuate low industrial wages.

Thus, only one type of agricultural policy would serve the ends of the urban and industrial interests — one that willfully neglected the problems of the land reform communities created by Cárdenas while lavishing public funds on increasing the production of a few large commercial growers in producing for outside the rural areas. In the words of a United Nations study,

The burden of transforming the frontier of Sonora into a vast agricultural emporium was . . . borne to a great extent by the federal treasury; but most of the fruits of the effort remained firmly under the control of the private landowning elite. . . .[7]

The Mexican government subsidized imports of agricultural machinery. In addition, between 1941 and 1952, 18 percent of Mexico's federal budget and 92 percent of its agricultural budget was spent on large irrigation projects to create vast new stretches of rich farmland in the North. This valuable land was then sold at low prices, not primarily to the landless poor, but to politically powerful families of businessmen and bureaucrats. Although by law no one in Mexico can own more than 250 irrigated acres, today the average farm in the Mexican Green Revolution area of Hermosillo, has grown to 2000 irrigated acres[8] with some holdings running much larger.[9] Not surprisingly, about 3 percent of all farms accounted for 80 percent of the production increase during the 1950s.

Here we have the model of agricultural development that has been actively exported to virtually all the underdeveloped countries within the sphere of influence of the United States.

Betting on a Winner

Ignoring overwhelming evidence from around the world* that small, carefully farmed plots are more productive per acre than large estates and use fewer costly inputs, governments, international lending-agencies and foreign assistance programs have invariably passed over small farmers (not to mention the landless). The French agronomist René Dumont describes a Ford Foundation mission of thirteen North American agronomists to India in 1959. The mission argued that it was practically impossible to make simultaneous headway in all of India's 550,000 villages. So they advised subsidization of technical inputs in those areas that were well-irrigated — thereby leaving over half of the nation's farms totally out of the national agricultural development program. It appeared easier to help a small number of large farmers increase wheat production by 50 percent within just a few years than to mobilize the productive potential of 50 to 60 million farm

*See Question 21.

families. Thus in the mid-sixties, India's New Agricultural Strategy to promote the improved seed varieties ended up concentrating on merely one tenth of the cultivable land and to a great extent on only one crop, wheat.[10]

Everywhere the large farmer has been directly favored. A study of Gapan, Nueva Ecija, in the Philippines, in 1966, showed that the first seeds produced by the Rockefeller-funded International Rice Research Institute were distributed only to landholders owning 25 acres of rice paddy or more.[11] No seeds were sold directly to sharecroppers or tenants.

The Tunisian agriculture program provided credit only to those owning a certain minimum acreage — usually 125 acres, a largeholding indeed in that country. Moreover, subsidies to dairy farmers went only to those producing more than 525 quarts of milk a day. Subsidies for purchasing combine harvesters benefited only the largeholder, the only one in a position to even consider such a purchase.

Once selected as the focus of government help, the large farmers have taken full advantage of their head start. Frequently the wealthiest landowning families have reaped additional profits by monopolizing distribution of fertilizers, pesticides, and machinery needed to make the new seeds respond. Associations of large commercial farmers like those in Mexico have been able to make considerable extra earnings by exporting the Green Revolution, selling thousands of tons of the new seeds annually to Asia and Africa.

Focusing on production totals has transformed rural development into a technical problem — one of getting the "right," usually foreign-made, inputs to the "progressive," invariably better-off, farmers. We refer to this production focus as *narrow* precisely because it ignores the social reality of hunger — the problem of releasing the vast untapped human potential of local people developing local resources and skills. Reducing the problem of agriculture to one simply of production increasingly divorces agricultural progress from basic rural development. Such a mirage of rural development undercuts the interests of those within the rural community in order to serve those outside — landowning elites, moneylenders, industrialists, bureaucrats, and foreign investors.

The influx of public funds for the purpose of increasing production has turned farming into a place to make money, sometimes big money. But to take part, one has needed some combination of land, money, access to credit, and political influence. That alone has eliminated most of the world's rural majority.

16

But Isn't Nature Neutral?

Question: You see the Green Revolution as a prime example of the production approach that has given the upper hand to the larger landholders. But isn't the essence of the Green Revolution the new, high-yielding seeds? Why shouldn't they grow as well for the poor farmer as for the rich farmer? Nature, after all, is less partial than are governments beholden to the vested interests of the wealthy. Once the poor obtain the high-yielding varieties, can't they improve their positions too? Even though the gap between rich and poor may still exist, won't all farmers improve their yields, their livelihood, and their nutritional status?

Our Response: The term "high-yielding varieties" — HYV's as they are called in the Green Revolution literature — is, in fact, a misnomer. Understanding why the term is a misnomer is the key to grasping why the new seeds might not be as neutral as the question suggests.

As part of a fifteen-nation study of the impact of the new seeds conducted by the United Nations Research Institute for Social Development, Dr. Ingrid Palmer concludes that the term "high-yielding varieties" is a misnomer because it implies that the new seeds are high-yielding *in and of themselves.*[1] The distinguishing feature of the seeds, however, is that they are highly *responsive* to certain key inputs such as irrigation and fertilizer. Following Palmer's lead we have chosen to use the term "high-response varieties" (HRV's) as much more revealing of the true character of the seeds. The Green Revolution is obviously more complicated than just sticking new varieties of seeds into the ground. Unless the poor farmers can afford to ensure the ideal conditions that

will make these new seeds respond (in which case they wouldn't
be poor!), their new seeds are just not going to grow as well as the
ones planted by better-off farmers. The new seeds prefer the "better neighborhoods."

Just as significant for the majority of the world's farmers is that
the new seeds show a greater yield variation than the seeds they
displace.[2] The HRV's are more sensitive to drought and flood than
their traditional predecessors. They are particularly prone to
water stress — the inability to assimilate nutrients when not
enough water is getting to the plant roots, especially at certain
stages in their growth cycles. Under these conditions it is often no
more profitable to apply fertilizers to the new seeds than to the
previous ones.[3] In 1968–1969 in Pakistan, for example, yields of
Mexican dwarf wheat declined by about 20 percent because of a
two-thirds reduction in average rainfall and higher than normal
temperatures. The locally adapted varieties, however, were not
adversely affected by the weather changes. Instead their yields
increased 11 percent.[4] The new sorghums now being planted in
Upper Volta in Africa are also less drought-resistant than their
local cousins.[5] The HRV's can also be more vulnerable to too much
water. Being shorter, the HRV's of rice cannot tolerate the higher
flood levels that indigenous varieties can endure.

Since the HRV's are more sensitive to both too much and too
little water, they need, not mere irrigation, but sophisticated
water management. The significance of this need becomes clear in
India's Punjab. Higher yields from the new seeds depend on a
tubewell for a controlled water supply. But a tubewell is well beyond the means of the small farmer.

Taking advantage of the HRV's has required farmers to double
or even triple their indebtedness. Since small farmers are already
in debt for preharvest consumption and for other family needs —
often at very high rates of interest — most will not be able to take
on this heavy new burden.

HRV's are often less resistant to disease and pests. Vulnerability results from transplanting a variety that "evolved" over a
short period in one climate (with a little help from agronomists) to
an entirely different climate, thus supplanting varieties that had
evolved over centuries in response to a long history of natural
threats in that environment. A small farmer, whose family's very
survival depends on each and every harvest, cannot afford to risk
crop failure. For the large farmer that risk is minimized. The dif-

ference is not just that the large farmer can better withstand a crop failure. Large farmers have also managed in many instances to protect themselves against disease-prone seeds. In Mexico, for example, associations of large farmers have, since the early days of the Green Revolution, kept in constant touch with government seed agencies and have, therefore, been warned of any disease likely to attack a particular new plant variety. By way of contrast, when the agency to which the land-reform beneficiaries were tied was notified that its seeds had become susceptible to disease, it was reluctant to throw them out and often continued to sell them. To a large extent this accounts for the disastrous yields in the Mexican land-reform sector during the late 1950s and early 1960s.[6]

In addition, the new seeds have been restricted to well rainfed and irrigated regions. It is not coincidental that these favored regions are inhabited by the more affluent farmers. Almost all of the HRV increases in wheat cultivation in India have taken place in the states of Punjab and Haryana, largely because the soil is alluvial and a canal system assures a year-round water supply.[7]

Nyle C. Brady, Director of the International Rice Research Institute, where many of the new strains have been developed, estimates that the "new rice varieties may be suitable for only 25 percent of the world's acreage, largely those areas with water for irrigation."[8] Because the new varieties are less resistant to flooding, there are many parts of Thailand, Bangladesh, and South Vietnam in which they cannot be used.[9] None of the new seeds are successful in areas of constant high temperatures and rainfall, limited sun, and thin, badly leached soils.

Knowing the biological requirements of the seeds, we should not be surprised that as late as 1972–1973 the HRV's covered a very small percentage — only about *15* percent of the total world area excluding the socialist countries.[10] Furthermore, they are highly concentrated: 81 percent of the HRV wheat grows in a small area in India and in Pakistan; and four countries (India, the Philippines, Indonesia, and Bangladesh) account for 83 percent of the HRV rice.[11]

The seeds, due to their need for ideal conditions, are restricted to certain favored areas. They therefore have reinforced income disparities between geographic regions, just as they have exacerbated the inequalities between social classes.

Two other factors contribute to making the new seeds less than neutral. First, hybrids of corn and sorghum do not remain genetically pure year after year. To maintain high yields new hybrid seeds must be purchased each year. This requirement alone gives the edge to the wealthier farmer and to the farmer more closely linked to seed distributors and other credit sources. The many farmers with only enough land to grow the food their families need will never have the cash to purchase hybrid seeds.

Second, the new seeds, because they require special knowledge to be used effectively, are inherently biased in favor of those who have access to government agricultural extension agents and instruction literature. In many countries the large landowners have been able to monopolize the services of the extension agencies. They have also been able, as in the Mexican state of Sonora, to hire private agricultural and pest experts to solve their technical problems.[12] A study in Uttar Pradesh, India, showed that, since 70 percent of the family heads were completely illiterate, "access to literature is thus primarily the prerogative of the better educated, wealthier landowners." Nonwritten material was no more successful in overcoming the problem: the village headman regarded the radio as his private property and invited only his friends to listen.[13]

The bias can be quite subtle. As one student of the Green Revolution so aptly put it: "The new technology puts a relative handicap on those whose assets include traditional knowledge of the local idiosyncrasies of soil and climate and whose energies are absorbed by the labors of husbandry. . . . It gives the advantage to those skilled in manipulating influence."[14]

Still the idea that a seed, the product of impartial scientific research, must be neutral, without built-in bias, is deeply rooted in most of us. Most assume it will just be a matter of time before the new seeds spread out to the poor and bring the standard of living up for all farmers. But the dependence of HRV's on *optimal* conditions make that impossible in most areas today. Both the rich and the poor farmer certainly can plant the seed, but who can feed the plants the optimal diet of nutrients and water and protect them from disease and pests? Can the family who depends for their food on what they grow afford to gamble with the less dependable seeds?

The only way that such seeds can be neutral is if the society prepares the way — giving equal access to the necessary inputs to all farmers. If this means redistribution of control over all food-producing resources, including land redistribution, it can work. In Cuba, for example, between 75 and 90 percent of the rice acreage is planted with the high-response seeds.[15] In Taiwan, also a country of fairly equal land distribution, the use of improved seeds is over 90 percent. But where "equalizing access" has merely meant credit programs it has rarely worked.

Any notion of equalizing access to a new technology without altering the basic social structure overlooks the only truly workable approach — the farmers themselves becoming the innovators. Then the issue of dissemination of new seeds or new skills evaporates as a problem. And, as you might guess, the kinds of seeds developed are not those demanding ideal conditions.

As early as 1961 the Chinese were breeding seeds for less favorable climes. Chinese farmers have successfully developed seeds that are both higher yielding and *more* able to withstand bad weather and other dangers, such as barley strains adapted to high altitudes and cold-resistant strains of wheat.[16] Moreover, the production of the new seeds does not take place in central experimental stations but is handled by ordinary families themselves.[17] Most communes have their own laboratories for locally developing new varieties. Spreading the new technology is therefore not a problem.

Once it is manipulated by people, nature loses its neutrality. Elite research institutes will produce new seeds that work perfectly well for a privileged class of commercial farmers. Genetic research that involves ordinary farmers themselves will produce seeds that are useful to them. A new seed, then, is like any other technological development; its contribution to social progress depends entirely on who develops it and who controls it.

17

Hasn't the Green Revolution
"Bought Us Time"?

Question: You say that the narrow focus on increased production has benefited the prosperous farmer. But why is that so terrible? More food at least has been produced. How could this hurt the poor? They need food more than anything else. You seem to expect the strategies to increase production, such as the Green Revolution, also to solve *social* problems. How could they? Increasing production is a scientific and a technological problem. Norman Borlaug, father of the Green Revolution, has said that the most the Green Revolution could do is to "buy us time" while we slow population growth and work on economic problems. Hasn't the Green Revolution accomplished all one could reasonably expect? Isn't progress with disruption better than no progress at all?

Our Response: To answer this question we had to look systematically at just what happens once the solution to hunger is sought in a big technological push to increase production. This search has revealed a powerful dynamic by which the better off have "progressed" *at the expense* of the majority. Around the world we find a strikingly consistent pattern. Although the question implies that the impact of the Green Revolution is limited to underdeveloped countries, it is not. (Part VII will demonstrate a similar transformation of agriculture going on in the United States.)

More Grain: Who Gains?

For many outsiders looking at hunger in underdeveloped countries, the fact that greater production can bring cheaper grain appears as part of the solution. The mistake is in forgetting two points: First, many of the poor are also producers whose livelihood depends on selling their grain. Second, for those unable to take part in the new technology, yields have often *not* increased. With overall greater availability, however, and the failure of government policies to maintain prices, the poor farmers with the unimproved yields are in a worse plight than ever.

In Greece the agricultural credit corporations pressure farmers to sow foreign-bred HRV wheats. In the lowland areas occupied by large farms the result has been higher yields, thus increasing total Greek output. But in the mountains the HRV seeds yielded less than the varieties that had been grown for generations by the mountain people. As the national (and world) yields increased, wheat prices fell. The large commercial farms in the plains could withstand the price drop because their volume of production was large and increasing. But for the poorer farm on the mountain slopes the fall in income resulting from lower yields was often the final blow leading to the desertion of many mountain villages, as well as the loss to the world of wheat varieties unconsciously selected, over centuries, to thrive in more difficult conditions.[1]

Rents Go Up

Landlords in many countries have found they can transfer part of the burden of increased production costs onto the tenants or sharecroppers, in effect, forcing the tenants to pay for the new technology. For instance, with the introduction of the new technology, the cash rents tenants must pay have gone up by about one-third to one-half. Crop share rents are changing from the traditional 50-50 division between the landlord and the tenant to 70-30 in favor of the landlord,[2] effectively cutting the tenant out of the production gains. In one area of India where the sharecropper used to get half the harvest, he now gets only one-third; another third goes to the landlord and the remaining third goes to pay off the debt for the tubewell the landlord purchased (it will, of course, go to the landlord once the tubewell is paid for).[3] In one area of Malaysia tenants now have to provide 100 percent of the fertilizer costs.[4]

Traditional landlords once had very clearcut, reciprocal obligations to tenants or sharecroppers. The landlord would have never considered passing on his obligations to the tenants. But now that more and more landlords are absentee city dwellers, traditional face-to-face dealings are being replaced by impersonal, money-based relationships. Landlords increasingly demand cash payment of rent instead of payment in kind. In the northern states of Malaysia cash payments are required at the *beginning* of the season. The tenant has to come up with rent at just the time he is least likely to have it. He therefore has to borrow at high rates of interest — thus reducing his total income. Moreover, if the crops fail, the tenant still has to come up with the rent.

By the same token, many landlords now prefer to pay in money wages rather than in farm produce. In times of inflating food prices, however, it is much better for the tenant-farmer to have part of the harvest than money. We learned of one district in India where landlords now pay only money wages, preferring to hoard and sell the rice later for enormous profit. In 1974, India's *Economic and Political Weekly* reported that in Thanjavur, Tamil Nadu, "hordes of the police were stationed in the paddy fields to quell disturbances arising out of the landlords' refusal to pay even a part of the wages in kind."[5]

Land Values Soar

In countries where food-resources are still allowed to be held for private gain, the inpouring of government funds in the form of irrigation works and subsidies for fertilizers and machinery have combined with the higher potential yields of the new seeds to turn farming into the world's hottest growth industry. Instead of a way of livelihood for millions of small, self-provisioning farmers, agriculture is increasingly seen as a lucrative opportunity by a new class of "farmers" with the money or influence to get in on the action — moneylenders, military officers, bureaucrats, city-based speculators, and foreign corporations. In those areas targeted by the "production strategy" land values have gone up three-, four-, or even fivefold as these so-called farmers compete for the land that they believe, often rightly, will make them a fortune.[6]

Here is development economist Wolf Ladejinsky's well-known account of how nonfarmers in India buy up land for speculation:

> The buyers are a motley group: some connected with land through family ties, some altogether new to agriculture. A few have unemployed rupees acquired through undeclared earnings, and most of them look

upon farming as a tax-haven, which it is, and as a source of earning tax-free supplementary income. The medical doctor from Jullundur who turned part-time farmer is sitting pretty. The 15 acres purchased four years ago have tripled in value. To listen to him, he is in farming "for the good of the country." . . . His only vexation is whether or not he will succeed in buying another 10 acres he has his eyes on — and what a disappointed man he will be if they escape him! As we watched him supervise the threshing, he was anything but a "gentleman farmer."[7]

Nonfarmers are taking over agriculture not only because governments have made investments attractive, but because increasingly only the wealthier urban dwellers can obtain credit or afford to buy the higher-priced land and the necessary inputs. As the price of land rises, purchase by the smallholder or tenant, if unlikely before, becomes completely out of the question. In countries where security of tenure is legally guaranteed after the tenant has continuously cultivated a given plot for a certain number of years, some landlords maneuver to ensure that their tenants are never given legal title to the land, now that land is more valuable. In Tanjore, India, landlords shift sharecroppers from one plot to another each year to successfully dodge such tenure regulations.[8]

Moreover, as the market value of land increases, taxes increase. In Colombia wealthy potential buyers of small plots persuade tax authorities to revalue the land in order to put pressure on the small farmers. Peasants who cannot afford to plant the new varieties of coffee find that they cannot pay the higher tax bill and are forced to sell to larger landholders who usually can evade the tax by paying a bribe.[9]

Fewer People Control More Land

Fewer and fewer people control more and more of farm production. A pattern of increasing monopolization of agricultural land moves ahead in India, Bangladesh, Mexico, the Philippines, Colombia — in virtually all countries where officially subsidized "modernization" now means that high returns stem from the sheer amount of land one can control, not from how well one farms.

In the area of Tamesis, Colombia, the better-off coffee growers able to adopt the new seed varieties increased the average size of their holdings by 76 percent between 1963 and 1970.[10] Similarly, in the government-subsidized irrigated zones of Morocco land concentration is increasing. In just five years, from 1965 to 1970 the average size of modern, Moroccan-owned farms in one irrigated area increased 30 percent.[11] In the Indian Punjab, between the fifties and the mid-sixties, the amount of land owned by the largest farmers (those with 100–150 acres) increased at a rate four to ten times greater than that of the smaller-sized farms.[12]

Another sign of increasing concentration of land ownership is that the smallest farmers are selling their land. In both 1969–1970 and 1972–1973 farmers in Bangladesh who owned less than one acre (accounting for about a quarter of all farmers) sold well over half of their land.[13]

To some, the decline of the small farmer appears unfortunate, but, alas, inevitable. But the tightening of control over agricultural production is not inevitable. It results from the actions and even the planning of people. In the early 1950s, large farmers in the Mexican state of Sonora saw that land values were about to go up because of massive government irrigation plans for the area. They began to contrive to take over cheaply the land owned by thousands of smallholders. They turned to their friends within the National Agricultural Credit Bank — the government agency on which smallholders in the area depended for survival. The bank began to delay crop credit for smallholders. In some cases they received credit so late that their wheat, to take but one example, had to be planted out of season and thus failed during several years. The bank also began to provide sacks of wheat seed that some say turned to dust between their fingers and fertilizer which they are sure was nothing more than white powder. The smallholders' expenses soared. They had several disastrous years. Then came the final blow: The government foreclosed on all properties with outstanding debts to federal agencies. The large farmers had succeeded. The majority of the smallholders in one devastated settlement ended up selling their land for about one ninth of the market price to two of the largest and most politically influential landowners in the state.[14]

Where much land has traditionally been communally worked, as in Africa, the new agricultural entrepreneurs might have an even easier time expanding commercial operations. Without private property rights and a small farm tradition that exists in Asia, little if anything stands in the way of tribal chieftains and foreign corporations who want to appropriate communal land for their private gain.

The Making of the Landless

In certain areas landlords are moving to push their tenants off the land. The landlords see several advantages. For instance, they are freed from tenants who might conceivably claim land under a land-to-the-tiller reform movement. Moreover, the large landowner finds it more profitable to mechanize production or take advantage of part-time laborers who have no claim on the land or on the harvest. A study for the World Bank on the size of farms in the Indian Punjab during the 1960s concluded that farms that had been mechanized grew by an average of 240 percent over a three-year period, primarily because the landlords decided to cultivate land they had previously rented out.[15] The landlord's gain — higher cash income — was society's loss, as a substantial number of tenants could no longer rent the land they needed to support themselves. In India, in 1969, there were 40,000 eviction suits against sharecroppers in Bihar alone and 80,000 in Karnatika (Mysore).[16]

As the control of land tightens and more tenants are evicted, the number of landless laborers mounts. In all nonsocialist underdeveloped countries 30 to 60 percent of rural adult males are now landless. In Mexico between 1950 and 1960 the number of landless laborers increased much faster than the general population, from 2.3 to 3.3 million.[17] In the state of Sonora, where Mexico first concentrated its Green Revolution production push in the 1940s, landless laborers represented 57 percent of the agricultural work force. By 1960, the proportion had grown to 62 percent and in 1970, it was roughly 75 percent.[18] Between 1964 and 1970 the number of landless families in Colombia more than doubled.[19] During the fifteen years beginning in 1951, the number of landless laborers in Bangladesh has increased by two and a quarter times.[20] In India, between 1961 and 1971, the number of agricultural laborers increased by over 20 million (by 75 percent). In the same period the number of cultivators decreased by 15 million (by 16 percent). None of these startling figures includes the millions of landless refugees who, finding no farm work, join an often hopeless search for work in the urban areas.

So the number of landless mounts while the number of rural jobs shrinks. Traditionally in many countries even the poorest landless peasant had access to part of the harvest. In India, Bangladesh, Pakistan, and Indonesia the large landowner once felt obligated to permit all who wished to participate in the harvest to retain one sixth of what they harvested. Thus even the most impoverished were assured of work for a few bags of grain. Now, with the increased likelihood of profitable sales, the new agricultural entrepreneurs are rejecting the traditional obligations of the landowner to the poor. It is now common for landowners to sell the standing crop to an outside contractor before harvest. The outsider, with no local obligations, can seek the cheapest labor, even bringing in workers from neighboring areas.[21]

In Java landless laborers were once permitted to squat on dry land in the off season to grow cassava and vegetables. With the new rice seeds, landlords are now interested in irrigating the land for year-round production for commercial markets. Squatters are no longer welcome.[22]

In addition, the introduction of large-scale mechanization is a double-edged sword for the rural poor. Large landowners say that the only way they can make their new machines pay off is to reduce per acre cost by expanding their acreage. As we have already seen, expansion by the largeholders forces more and more tenants and small farmers off the land, thereby creating greater numbers of landless in search of farm work. Simultaneously, however, the machines drastically decrease the number and length of jobs available. A tractor cuts to a fifth the number of workers needed to prepare the same field with a bullock-drawn plow. The same is true of a mechanical reaper compared to a hand scythe.[23]

The net result in the Pakistani Punjab, for example, is that the amount of human labor required in the fields is 50 percent less than in the premechanization period only a few years ago. An analysis of the trend in India concluded that "the introduction of mechanical harvesting will eventually result in an overall decrease of about 90 million man-days of employment in the Punjab, most of it for day laborers."[24]

During Mexico's rapid mechanization, when the number of landless laborers rapidly rose, the average number of days worked by each laborer fell from 194 to 100. The larger the number looking for work, the easier it is for the large landholders to keep wages low and thereby, ironically, to offset the operating costs of machinery (often already heavily subsidized). The incomes of landless laborers around the world, incredibly low to begin with, are steadily declining. In the same period in Mexico, the decade of the 1950s, the *annual* income of landless rural workers declined from $68 to $56, while per capita national income increased from $308 to $405.[25]

The production strategy we have been describing often offers the poor the illusion of rural employment. One of the best documented cases is the Mexican state of Sonora. There, the clearing of new land and vast irrigation projects executed with public funds attracted workers to Sonora during the fifties and sixties. By 1971, when these projects had been completed, the laborers still needed jobs but, with the land now run as large highly mechanized operations, they could at best hope for six months' work a year.[26] Thus those who actually had labored to make it possible for Sonora to become Mexico's production showcase were largely cut out of its bounty.

We have seen that with the introduction of new technologies into societies where small groups can monopolize agricultural resources, the price of land and therefore land rents go up and tenants are displaced from the land and laborers from their jobs. It is not surprising, therefore, to find peasants in these countries invariably sinking deeper into debt to stay alive. Cheap credit schemes often only worsen the predicament of the poor. In Malaysia, for example, landlords commonly obtain loans from rural banks by using their land as collateral. (The banks are reluctant to issue low-interest loans to tenants because they have no collateral.) The money obtained by the landlord is then re-lent to tenants at interest rates left to the landlord's own discretion. The result is the reinforcement of debt bondage, making the peasant permanently so indebted that he is obliged to accept wages for his labor at a rate 30 to 50 percent below the going market rate.

When More Food Means More Hunger

We have now arrived at the endpoint of the tragic decline of the rural majority. In country after country, where agricultural resources are allowed to be sources of private wealth, the drive to increase food production has made even worse the lives of the poor majority, despite per capita production increases. We have seen how:

- Land values go up, forcing tenants and small farmers off the land.
- Rents increase.
- Payments in money become the rule, yet money buys less food.
- The control of farmland becomes concentrated in fewer hands, many of whom are speculative entrepreneurs, not farmers.
- Even communal lands (as in many African villages or land-reform areas) are appropriated by powerful individuals such as chieftains or caciques for their private gain at the expense of the welfare of the community.
- Corporate control, often foreign, extends further into production.
- Peasants are trapped into debt bondage.
- Poverty and inequality deepen.
- Production totals, not the participation of the rural population in the production process (livelihood and nourishment), become the measure of success for agricultural planners.
- Quantity and market value, not nutritive value, become the goal of agricultural planning.

The net result? Hunger tightens its hold on the rural majority.

A series of major studies now being completed by the International Labor Organization (ILO) documents that in the seven South Asian countries comprising 70 percent of the rural population of the nonsocialist underdeveloped world, the rural poor have become worse off than they were ten or twenty years ago. The summary study notes that ironically *"the increase in poverty has been associated not with a fall but with a rise in cereal production per head, the main component of the diet of the poor."* Here are typical examples:

- The Philippines: Despite the fact that agricultural production increased by 3 to 4 percent per year during the last fifteen to twenty years, about one fifth of the rural households experienced a dramatic and *absolute* decline in living standards, which accelerated during the early seventies. By 1974 daily real wages in agriculture fell to almost one third of what they were in 1965.[27]

- Bangladesh: Between 1963 and 1975, the proportion of rural households classified as absolutely poor increased by more than a third and that of those classified as extremely poor increased five times. Yet about 15 percent of the rural households in Bangladesh had significantly higher real incomes in 1975.[28]
- West Malaysia: By 1970 the bottom 20 percent of rural households had experienced a fall of over 40 percent in their average income since 1957, while the average income of the next 20 percent fell 16 percent. By contrast, the top 20 percent of rural households increased their mean income 21 percent.[29]
- Sri Lanka: Despite a rise in per capita income between 1963 and 1973, actual rice consumption *fell* for all except the highest income class. All workers experienced a fall in real wages, except for those in industry and commerce whose real wages remained static.[30]

Part of the reason that most people have not been able to perceive this tragic retrogression is what we have come to call the "language of deception" — terms that obfuscate reality. One such term is "per capita." As these examples show, per capita production and income have been going up in the very countries where often the majority of the people have become worse off with each succeeding year. It is, of course, precisely the kind of development policy that measures itself in per capita terms that results in the absolute decline of the majority.

Bought Us Time?

Many view the Green Revolution as a technical innovation and feel that, as such, it should not be expected to solve social problems. But what we have found is that there can be no separation between technical innovation and social change. Whether promotion of the wealthier class of farmers is deliberate government policy or not, inserting any profitable technology into a society shot through with power inequalities (money, landownership, privilege, access to credit) sets off the disastrous retrogression of the less powerful majority. The better off and powerful in a society further enrich themselves at the expense of the national treasury and the rural poor. As those initially better off gain even greater control over the production process, the majority of people are made marginal, in fact, totally irrelevant, to the process of agricultural production. In such societies the reserves of landless and jobless function only to keep wages down for those who do find jobs. Excluded from contributing to the agricultural economy, the poor majority are no longer its beneficiaries, for being excluded from production means being excluded from consumption. A thirty-six-cents-a-day laborer in Bihar, India, knows this truth well: "If you don't own any land, you never get enough to eat," he says, "even if the land is producing well."[31]

The Green Revolution has *not* "bought us time" as the question suggests. "Modernization" overlaid on oppressive social structures entrenches the ownership classes who are now even better positioned and less willing to part with their new-found wealth. Thus, defining the problem of hunger as one of production is not merely incorrect. To focus only on raising production, without first confronting the issue of who controls and who participates in the production process, actually compounds the problem. It leaves the majority of people worse off than before. In a very real sense the idea that we are progressing is our greatest handicap. We cannot move forward — we cannot take the first step toward helping improve the welfare of the vast majority of the world's people — until we can see clearly that we are now moving backward.

*   *   *

In most of the developing nations, rural people have traditionally had little faith in the national governments. Governments' policies were usually regarded with suspicion and perhaps with good reason. . . . The rural people are beginning to regard this government with more trust and confidence, to feel to some degree at least, that it is their government. In this way, the Green Revolution can also be said to be contributing constructively towards political stability.

George Harrar, President of the Rockefeller
Foundation in his *Review and
Annual Report,* 1970

18

Where Has All the Production Gone?

Question: A while back you said that in many countries huge capital investments made in the modernization approach to production did boost the yields of many better-off farmers. So at least there is more food. Yet if people are still hungry, in fact hungrier than before, what has happened to that extra production? Certainly the increased production is helping somebody. Whom has it helped? Where has it gone?

Our Response: You are right. If the way chosen in many countries to produce more food has actually reduced the chances of many to eat, then we should ask what happens to the increased production. Here is what we have discovered from studies around the world:

· Some of it goes to urban middle- and upper-income groups.

In countries like the Philippines and Mexico increased production has benefited emerging industrialists and their foreign partners who want to have cheap food for workers in urban industries in order to keep wage demands low. Total production increases have also helped government elites who fear urban unrest — such as the food riots in Mexican cities during the 1940s — if not enough food could be extracted from the rural areas.

· Some of it gets reduced into luxury products the poor cannot afford.

The governments of the United States and Pakistan collaborated with the New Jersey-based Corn Products Corporation to improve yields of Pakistani corn — traditionally a staple food grown by the rural poor. Hybrid seeds and other inputs did increase yields. The corn, however, is now a cash crop grown by relatively few large farmers for manufacturing a corn-based sweetener used in such things as soft drinks.

 • Some of it gets fed to livestock to create meat that the majority of the local population cannot afford.

In 1971, an FAO report advised Third World countries on the problem of how to dispose of "surplus" grain resulting from the success of the Green Revolution production campaigns. The FAO suggested using a greater proportion of wheat for animal feed or shifting to cultivation of coarse grains more suitable for livestock than wheat and rice. Could they be serious? FAO was advising countries with the most serious undernutrition problems in the world to deal with the so-called surplus problem by stepped up livestock feeding!

In 1973 two thirds of Colombia's Green Revolution rice was being fed to livestock or going into the production of beer. Increased yields of corn provided the raw material for starting up a chicken feed industry. Did this mean Colombia's undernourished would be eating chicken? For over a quarter of the country's families, buying just two pounds of chicken or a dozen eggs would require an entire week's earnings or more. Much of the increased egg production goes into processed foods such as snacks and mayonnaise sold by multinational food companies to elite urban groups.[1]

Even though in many countries per capita grain production totals are higher, they do not result, as one would think, in a decline in prices. The "demand" for grain by cattle and chickens keeps grain prices up.

And what has happened to the fruits of our own Green Revolution? Although the United States succeeded in increasing corn yields almost three times over, it has not meant the elimination of hunger in America. The increased corn production has gone to livestock — doubling the meat consumption of many Americans who already were taking in more protein than their bodies could use.

With a good deal of help, then, from food processors and animals, food for many can be converted — and sold for higher profits — into food for a few.

 • Some of the increased production gets exported.

Where the majority of people are kept too poor to constitute a domestic market and agriculture is made to rely on imported inputs like fertilizers and machines, the colonial pattern of production for export is reinforced in the search for a paying market and the foreign exchange needed to pay for imported inputs. India exports such excellent staples as potatoes to countries like Sweden and the Soviet Union yet the amount of potatoes available to the Indian people has been reduced by 12 percent between 1972 and 1974.[2] Central America exports between one third and one half of its beef to the United States alone.

   • Some of the increased production simply gets dumped.

Fruits and vegetables produced in Central America for export to the United States frequently either are shut out from an over-supplied market or fail to meet United States "quality" standards — size, color, smoothness. Since the local population, mostly landless, is too poor to buy anything, fully 65 percent of the fruits and vegetables produced, according to one study, "must be literally dumped or, where possible, fed to livestock" (which in turn are exported).[3]

Neglect of rural reform and concentration instead on the production advances of commercial growers have determined where the production goes. Since any increase in production is not met by a similarly enlarged buying public, no matter how much food is produced it will end up going to an urban elite, to an export market, or to make livestock products that can only be purchased by the well-off.

*   *   *

Mexico exported 10 percent of its grain crop between 1965 and 1969, but the production gains were overwhelmed by one of the world's fastest population growth rates. . . . By the mid-seventies, Mexico was importing one-fifth of its grain needs. . . . . The problem is not that agriculture did not advance in Mexico and the Philippines, but rather that the advances were simply eaten up by the relentless growth in population.

Lester R. Brown, *The Global Politics of Food: Role
and Responsibility of North America*, 1975

19

Wasn't the Green Revolution a Vital Scientific Breakthrough?

Question: You may criticize the impact of the Green Revolution, but didn't the Green Revolution at least provide us with critical knowledge that we wouldn't have gotten any other way? Now that farmland can't be expanded in many parts of the world, what could be more important than plant research to improve yields?

Our Response: To assume, as this question does, that breakthroughs in knowledge of plant genetics would never have been made without the Rockefeller Foundation's research institutes is an acute form of cultural myopia. The attempt to improve yields genetically is hardly a new departure. Since the early 1950s, improved indigenous rice seeds, referred to now as "locally improved varieties," have been independently produced in several Asian countries — specifically Japan, Taiwan, Malaysia, Indonesia, Sri Lanka, and China. Such efforts in India and Egypt go back at least half a century.

Even before the introduction of the new seeds from the International Rice Research Institute during the 1960s, locally improved varieties occupied 34 percent of the rice area in India.[1] Sri Lanka has been so successful in developing improved indigenous seeds that it has avoided dependency on foreign seed varieties almost entirely.[2] In fact, the portion of Sri Lanka's croplands growing improved seeds from foreign sources, only 4.4 percent in 1970–1971, was cut in half by 1972–1973.[3] Sri Lanka decided to concentrate on its own improved seeds when the imported variety, pushed for years by international agencies, was virtually wiped out one year by disease.[4]

Several other countries have significantly large areas planted with locally improved varieties. In the 1969–1970 season 69 percent of Brazil's rain-fed wheatlands was planted with seeds selected and improved locally. Egypt uses local varieties suitable for rain-fed conditions on 45 percent of its wheatlands. Significantly, the locally improved varieties are grown without irrigation, a condition that the more sensitive foreign-bred seeds, as discussed earlier, cannot tolerate.[5] United Nations researcher Dr. Ingrid Palmer reports that in Iran and Iraq improved local types may do better than imported seeds. This is also true of wheat in Tunisia and of rice in Brazil and Sri Lanka.[6]

During a recent trip to China, American agricultural scientists were surprised to find high-response dwarf rice varieties similar to the "miracle" rice developed by the International Rice Research Institute in the Philippines.[7] But they should not have been surprised. A seed improvement program has long been underway in China. Between 1952 and 1964, 1200 major kinds of improved-grain seeds were introduced and put into general use. Indeed, if, as reported by the Chinese Academy of Science, one half of China's cultivated land was planted with improved seeds in 1965, then China was far ahead of the rest of the agrarian countries in the world.[8]

Now that the initial flurry of attention to *the* Green Revolution has begun to wane, some areas are returning to the locally improved varieties, better suited both to the local ecology and the local taste.

A Little Better Farming

The question also suggests that *genetic* research is the most important contribution to improving agricultural production now that land area is limited. But higher yields do not come only from seeds better able to utilize the sun and water and resist pest infestation. Higher yields have historically come from that old-fashioned idea — better farming practices: How the seeds are planted, how the land is plowed, how the plants are protected and how the fields weeded. An American wheat expert who helped farmers in Turkey double their wheat yields admits, "There are no miracle seeds involved. . . . It is just farming a little better." The key element was the retention of moisture in the soil during the fallow period achieved by using careful plowing and harrowing techniques and eliminating weeds.[9]

In some areas of the world, improved seeds are hardly the appropriate place to start when the soil structure is the limiting factor. In her work on Africa, Dr. Palmer concluded that ". . . the main problem in the foreseeable future is not raising responses or yields of plants, but improving the soil." Until this is accomplished, she feels the local seed varieties would probably do better than the imported varieties.[10] In parts of Africa the soil structure is so poor that it cannot even absorb the nitrogen fertilizer on which the new seeds depend. The first step would not be introducing new seeds, but crop rotation, including grasses and legumes, and adding organic matter to rebuild the soil structure.

In areas of Africa such as Togo and Upper Volta improved farming techniques could certainly increase yields without "miracle" seeds. Donkey and ox power, now virtually unknown, could double a family's production. Sowing in lines could enable about 80 percent more seed to be sown. Foot-high dykes in shallow valleys would be enough to hold rain so that flood rice could be grown, which in itself could double production.

Turning worldwide attention via Nobel prizes and newspaper coverage to the miracles occuring under the ideal conditions of research test fields makes it easy to ignore proven traditional practices that could still be improved upon to use the soil better. For example, a proper cropping sequence can restore nutrients taken out by one crop with those put in by another — thus providing one alternative to imported chemical fertilizers.

Why is crop sequence so important? Some crops (like corn and wheat) are heavy consumers of nitrogen, while crops of the pulse family (peas, beans, and lentils), because they house nitrogen-fixing bacteria, actually take nitrogen from the air and put it back into the depleted soil. Even now with the heavy emphasis on chemical fertilizers, pulses contribute about as much nitrogen to the soil of India as manufactured fertilizers. Moreover, the contribution of pulses could probably be increased. For example, the large area of irrigated wheatlands left fallow in India during the off-season could be replenishing its nitrogen by being planted with pulses. Besides, pulses are excellent foods.

We have already noted how the Green Revolution's focus on monoculture displaces interest in the advantages of the opposite approach — mixed cropping. It has become fashionable to view mixed cropping, the planting of several crops in one field, as primitive and less scientific. When local farmers suggested planting beans and corn in the same field, the technical advisors to the

United States AID-sponsored Puebla project in Mexico dismissed the idea. Finally, after a number of years, the "experts" discovered that the mixed-field approach gave better yields. Putting the two crops in one field had the same effect as alternating legume crops with grains. Mixed cropping can have multiple advantages including the maximum use of the land and the most efficient use of labor because of staggered planting and harvesting times. It is a technique that is profitable and suitable to local labor and land conditions. In an area of northern Nigeria over three quarters of the cropland is planted with more than one crop and sometimes as many as six, including pulses, starchy roots, tubers, and vegetables. Such sensible farming is threatened by the Green Revolution's introduction of single-stand crops, best suited to large-scale mechanized commercial operations, not the peasant farmer.

Divorcing Agriculture and Nutrition

Concentrating narrowly on yields makes it easy to forget to ask *what* is being produced. In Mexico, 60 percent of the people eat corn as a staple. Yet corn has been the neglected stepchild of the Green Revolution. Between 1940 and 1960, Mexico's large entrepreneur farmers often shifted out of corn to plant more lucrative commercial crops such as wheat, cotton, and feedgrains.[11]

The focus on a few cereal grains has shifted the traditional diet of several Third World countries away from the balanced consumption of grains (like corn or rice) in combination with legumes (like beans or lentils). The wisdom of the traditional mix has only recently been appreciated by nutritionists in "developed" countries.

When I, Frances, first started the work that eventually became *Diet for a Small Planet*, I was fascinated by the discovery that diets evolving independently in different parts of the world had a common, nutritionally sound base. Combining corn and beans in Mexico, or rice and lentils in India, or rice and soybean products in Japan, was no accident. These combinations created more biologically usable protein than if the diet centered on only one food. When eaten together, the two foods, because of contrasting amino acid patterns (the building blocks of protein), make up for each other's weaknesses. Thus, if Green Revolution grain displaces legumes in the traditional diet, not only does the overall protein intake fall, since legumes have two to four times the protein content of grain, but just as critical, the *balanced combination* of grains and legumes that improves the biological usability of protein is also undercut.

Yet cropland planted in legumes continues to shrink. Since the early 1960s the legume acreage in India alone has declined by two and a half million acres.[12] This drop is reflected in the Indian diet. Between 1956 and 1971 the average daily consumption in India of legumes declined by about 31 percent. On Java the cultivation of soybeans, virtually the highest protein plant food in the world, is giving way to the government's promotion of Green Revolution rice and its enforcement of mandatory sugar quotas.[13]

The Green Revolution Imperative

The question implies both that genetic research is the most valuable contribution to agricultural progress and that the knowledge embodied in the Green Revolution would never have been discovered without the sponsorship of research by the Ford and Rockefeller foundations. Neither is true, as we have just seen. Many think of the Green Revolution as an imperative. We think of it as a choice.

It was a choice to come up with seeds that produce high yields under optimum conditions. It was a choice *not* to start by developing seeds better able to withstand drought or pests. It was a choice *not* to concentrate on improving traditional methods of increasing yields, such as mixed cropping. It was a choice *not* to develop technology that was productive, labor-intensive, and independent of foreign input supply. It was a choice *not* to concentrate on reinforcing the balanced, traditional diets of grains plus legumes.

Moreover, in light of all these "paths not taken," we must ask ourselves: In our eagerness to embrace the new, in our rush to extend the scope of human knowledge and control, do we forget to work on *applying* the collected wisdom already handed down to us? Has our fascination with science prevented us from tackling the incomparably more difficult problems of social organization and the agricultural practices of real farmers?

For the majority who are hungry, "miracle" seeds are meaningless without secure access to land, water, tools, storage, and a market. What the Green Revolution has taught us is that the problem of world hunger will not be solved in any research institute.

20

Don't They Need Our Machines?

Question: In your discussion of the Green Revolution you always seem to include mechanization as one of the problems. But isn't mechanization part of the solution to hunger? Are you sure that in your eagerness to empathize with the poor peasant in underdeveloped countries, you are not running the risk of romanticizing misery? Wouldn't a poor agricultural laborer in India be glad to be relieved of backbreaking work by a more efficient machine?

Our Response: This question is the subject of much heated debate. For many people concerned about the environment, "technology" is a red flag. Machines are seen simply as fuelguzzlers that damage and ravage the earth. For others, agricultural technology is our last, best hope. Questioning the appropriateness of transferring highly mechanized farming to agrarian societies becomes tantamount, in their eyes, to condemning poor peasants to lives of dreary, backbreaking toil.

This debate dismayed us, too. We certainly did not want to condemn the mass of humanity to stagnate in the fields just because we might find a hoe more aesthetically pleasing than a tractor! We did not want to jump on the antimachine bandwagon simply because it had become fashionable to proclaim that "small is beautiful." Would it be possible, we asked ourselves, to arrive at a position that was not a reflection of our possible prejudices but would speak to the real needs of both the farmer and all the hungry?

We now believe that it *is* possible. We simply asked ourselves two questions about the introduction of large-scale agricultural machinery into the Third World: Is it realistic? . . . Is it necessary?

The answers to these questions are not so elusive as we had thought.

First, is it *realistic* to think of modern fuel-consuming technology as the answer to agricultural stagnation in poor countries? We think not. For most countries, agricultural machines mean imported machines plus imported fuel and parts. Often poor countries just do not have foreign exchange for these imports. During 1974 in the Indian Punjab, the area that supplies most of India's marketed wheat, tractors and irrigation pumps stood idle due to a lack of foreign exchange to pay for the increasingly costly imported fuel. This situation is not likely to get better but worse. By 1975 the gross foreign debt of the governments of the nonindustrial countries had grown to over $150 billion. New loans of foreign exchange are not of much help. Annual payments on old loans already eat up over 40 percent of the total new aid from the industrial countries (see Part IX).

In any case, making a nation's food production dependent on imported machinery that requires foreign exchange can be self-defeating. In a real sense, the machines tend to determine what is to be grown. In order to import agricultural technology, a country has to sell something else to get the foreign exchange to pay for it. Thus, the more tractors and harvesters imported, the more peanuts, vegetables, cotton, meat, palm oil, or cocoa are likely to be produced for export to pay for them. Relying on imported agricultural technology can thus reduce the domestic food supply simply because land that might be growing food is forced to "grow" foreign exchange to pay for the machines.

Even more fundamentally, agriculture heavily dependent on fossil fuel cannot be the long-term solution for any of us. Professor David Pimentel, one of the most respected analysts of our long-term energy options in agriculture, points out:

> To feed a world population of 4 billion while employing modern intensive agriculture would require an energy equivalent of 1.2 billion gallons of fuel per day. If petroleum were the only source of fossil energy and if all petroleum reserves were used to feed the world population using intensive agriculture, known reserves would last a mere 29 years.[1]

Georg Borgstrom, a man who has spent much of his professional life studying these questions, makes a similar estimate: "A global food system with the degree of energy expenditure of the U.S. food system would require 80 percent of the world's current energy account."[2]

Professor Pimentel and Dr. Borgstrom are certainly not starry-eyed members of a back-to-the-land generation romanticizing old-fashioned ways. Yet they seriously question whether or not it is realistic to think of spreading high-energy agricultural technology around the world.

But even if it were possible, we have just seen that the cost would be very high: the diversion of land use away from food production for local consumption to foreign exchange–earning crops. Also to be considered is the loss of independence that comes with heavy indebtedness and reliance on imports and foreign firms. Since no one can debate that the cost is high, it seemed logical next to ask ourselves:

Is Large-Scale Mechanization Necessary to Increase Production?

Small farms, even very small farms of less than an acre, have proved to be more productive per acre than larger farms in every part of the world, as documented in the response to Question 21 (p. 156). Since we know that these small farms are less mechanized than the larger ones, we have to conclude that mechanization in itself does not lead to greater production per acre.

Mechanization will, of course, increase productivity per field worker. We say per *field* worker deliberately because highly mechanized agriculture requires many workers who are not in the field. Indeed, one out of every seven in the civilian work force in the United States is employed in the production of farm machinery or fertilizer or in food processing or marketing. (The next time you hear that one American feeds 45 people remember that a more accurate estimate would be closer to 16 — taking into account all of these hidden workers).[3]

The most important point, however, *is* that there is one useful way to measure productivity. Agricultural consultant Roger Blobaum suggests that productivity should always be measured in terms of the *scarcest* resource: the level of output per unit of energy consumed, for example, would be the most important efficiency indicator in a nation running out of fossil fuel. In countries with an abundant potential labor supply but limited land, productivity per *acre* is what counts. And increasing productivity per acre is often not a matter of a "modern" machine but of intensive and careful farming by people who have a living stake in the production. According to an International Rice Research Institute (IRRI) study of lowland rice farming, there is no significant difference in yields between farms using a tractor and those using a buffalo. Even more striking was the conclusion that in Japan, in 1960, highly mechanized farms had no higher yields than those farmed with a hoe. (And no one has ever accused the IRRI of romanticizing the hoe!) The striking rise in rice yields in agarian-reform Japan before 1960 was not due to mechanization but in part to the small farmers' use of improved seeds, fertilizer, water pumps, better animal-drawn plows and harrows, and simple revolving weeders and pedal threshers. This is hardly high technology — but it worked.[4]

Proponents of large-scale mechanization have one case, however, that they feel is airtight. The faster growing seeds of the Green Revolution make it possible for two and sometimes more crops to be grown successively in the same field in one year. Those promoting tractors and harvesters claim there is often a labor bottleneck during planting and harvesting time due to the extra work required to get each crop planted and harvested quickly so that the next one can be planted.

But, we must ask, who is defining the term "bottleneck"? A bottleneck to a landlord may mean that time of year when he has to pay higher wages because the greater demand for labor gives laborers some bargaining power. The same period the landlord calls a bottleneck may be the time of year the laborer depends on to earn the extra rupees or pesos to survive throughout the rest of the year, when jobs are scarce and wages even lower.

In any case, large-scale mechanization is not the only solution to the problem of peak periods of labor needs. Small-scale improved techniques can help, as we will show below. Moreover, the need for labor can be spread more evenly throughout the year by, for instance, improving irrigation facilities to make planting less dependent on weather and staggering harvests by using seed varieties and crops of varying maturation periods.[5]

There is still another aspect that rarely (never) enters the heads of planners in industrial countries for whom city and country are distant and unrelated. Light industry and services can be integrated into the life of the countryside, an approach that has been successful in countries as different as Egypt and China. In many Chinese rural communes as much as 30 percent of the population is not directly employed in agriculture but in local small-scale industry. This group represents a critical reserve labor force to help plant or harvest a crop. On the other hand, once the peak work is over, these workers are not unemployed but return to their factories and service industries. Such a plan works in China because most people no longer look down on farming and nearly everyone has practical experience in the fields.

What must be kept in mind in all discussions of mechanization is that "labor-saving" to the rural entrepreneur means displacing laborers from their jobs, thereby saving on his labor costs. Labor-saving mechanization, however, is good for the society at large only when it means saving workers from unnecessarily arduous labor and when a genuine economic evolution ensures employment for everyone in other sectors of the economy.

Finally, we Americans assume large-scale mechanization is necessary to increase production in underdeveloped countries because that is exactly what we have been taught about the introduction of mechanization in the United States. But has this been true in every case? At least two cases — the mechanization of tobacco and of cotton — show that it has not. One thing is obvious to anyone who has ever seen a mechanical harvester sweep through a cotton or tobacco field. The machines were certainly not invented to increase yields. A harvester actually reduces the amount taken out of the fields by picking less cotton or tobacco than a human being. One estimate is that mechanical tobacco harvesters reduce the harvest per acre by 15 percent.[6] Moreover, the tobacco harvester lowers the grade and quality of the harvest because it cannot discriminate in picking the leaves. The attraction is that they cut down on the wages per bushel as well as the need to deal with workers. The tobacco harvester certainly is "laborsaving"; a recent Department of Agriculture estimate is that the introduction of tobacco harvesters will eliminate 350,000 jobs in the Carolinas and Virginia.[7]

If Not American-Style Machines, Then What?

Clearly large-scale mechanization is not necessary to increase production. On the other hand, technological improvements are possible that can increase production per acre, make work easier, and yet do not displace laborers as do U.S.-style machines. Contrast, for example, a 100 horsepower tractor and a 10 horsepower rotary cultivator. A rotary cultivator is affordable and usable by small farmers; a tractor is not. While a 100 horsepower tractor *replaces* human labor, a rotary cultivator *complements* human labor.

In the response to Question 5, we pointed out that agriculture in most underdeveloped countries could use many more workers than are presently employed. Indeed, the more successful agricultural systems were shown to have a *greater* number of workers per cultivated acre. What is needed, then, are machines that both make work less arduous and increase the need for human labor instead of replacing it.

What is needed in agrarian countries today is not a different level of technology but a different kind of technology. One with a different purpose. One that raises production while usefully involving *more* people in the production process.

The irony is that the Green Revolution seeds could have been part of such an approach. The new seeds and their need for greater care and greater application of fertilizer have the potential to create more jobs. But in most countries the forces that started the Green Revolution also initiated a process of mechanization that reduced employment. In Colombia an estimate was made of the labor requirements of modernization using high response seeds, more fertilizer, greater care in planting, and so on. *Without* mechanization these improvements would require 45 percent more human labor per acre. With mechanization, 34 percent *less* labor would be required.[8]

The potential for greater employment with the High Response Varieties (HRVs) is due to several factors. We have already noted that the generally faster-maturing varieties allow farmers to plant more than one crop each year — thereby increasing the need for human labor and the need to speed up all operations. But speeding up operations would not have to mean large-scale mechanization. Reducing seed bed preparation time can be accomplished by a moldboard plow (a simple wedge-shaped instrument) and a modern harrow (an implement for breaking up the earth resembling a giant comb), which do the job in one-fifteenth the time needed using the traditional plow and plank method.[9] Threshing by hand may take too long to accommodate multiple cropping. Large-scale machines, however, are not required. A simple thresher can reduce the job from a month to only several days, making double cropping possible. (Machines do not always speed things up. On some rice fields, Chinese farmers have discovered they can squeeze in three crops if an entire team joins in to plant intensively by hand rather than relying on the slower-going rice-planting machines.)

In addition to the possibilities for more frequent planting afforded by small-scale technology, the introduction of certain simple machines can actually increase labor input. The rotary weeder is an example. The new seeds, with their high-response potential, make weeding even more worthwhile. And, precisely because the rotary weeder is more efficient, it makes more sense to put more labor into weeding with it.[10]

We do not want to give you the impression that we are talking about techniques recently dreamed up in some alternative technology research center. Pascal de Pury, an indefatigable agronomist with years of experience in Africa and now working with the World Council of Churches on appropriate technology, told us that often such technology turns out to be rediscoveries of a people's traditional practices that Western arrogance caused them to be ashamed of. Over and over again he finds peasant cultures that had refined and adapted techniques over centuries to be losing them in our times. What stands to be irretrievably lost is not the quaintness of "cultural diversity" but successful, productive techniques uniquely suited to local conditions and, by definition, controllable by the people. They will be lost if elites in these countries are allowed, indeed encouraged by foreign aid, to import machines in order to increase their profit margins.

The hallmark of techniques that grow out of the experience of the people is that they can be made by the people themselves. There is simply no need to depend on the transfer of technology. These basic agricultural techniques are not of complicated design.

Tubewells, simple diesel engines, animal-powered plows and seed drills can all be manufactured at the local level by workers without the need for heavy capital equipment. For example, in the city of Daska, in the Pakistani Punjab, more than 100 small factories produce diesel engines principally from local materials.[11] In Pakistan, as in most other underdeveloped countries, this is the exception. In China it is the rule. As mentioned earlier, each commune houses some light industry, often more like a workshop than a factory, to service agriculture. One example is the low cost pump, locally invented in 1962 through the stimulus of the *withdrawal* of Soviet technicians. It costs one-eighth as much as the Russian equipment previously used and is manufactured in thousands of rural communes.

In China, most significantly, designs for new machines come from those who work in the fields. Agricultural researcher and China visitor Roger Blobaum tells of a new Chinese tractor that "isn't much to look at." But he adds, "the factory manager emphasized that it was designed by engineers who spend their summers out on the communes, is just what the peasants ordered, and will be redesigned anytime they decide they want something else."[12]

What Are the Forces Behind Large-Scale Mechanization?

If large-scale foreign technology is not necessary to increase production, why is it being increasingly imported into underdeveloped countries? To answer that question we first have to understand who is introducing the machines. Mechanization is fully the business of the large landholders. The 4 percent of Indian farmers with holdings of more than 25 acres make up 96 percent of tractor owners in India.[13] With the breakdown of the traditional ties that have held agrarian societies together, large landholders are eager to be rid of all tenants so that they might retain a greater share of the profits. Mechanization gives them the way. Rhetoric about the efficiency of mechanization gives them the rationale.

Large landholders have seen mechanization as a way to escape minimum wage requirements, such as the Agricultural Minimum Wages Act in Kerala, India. Studies of agricultural modernization in India reveal a major reason for rapid "tractorization" in the late 1960s was not increased efficiency but the opportunity to get rid of laborers. Getting rid of tenants is attractive to a landlord threatened by land-reform legislation that would give land to those who till it, that is, to his tenants.

Mechanization makes it possible for wealthier farmers to increase further their cultivated holdings. As long as a farm relies on laborers, there are limits to the size of the holding that a landowner can efficiently oversee. But machines can make it possible to farm land of virtually any size. Moreover, machines are more easily controlled than human beings. Landlords do not have to worry about rice being taken out of the fields to feed the hungry family of a tractor.

Who else gains from the spread of large-scale technology around the world? The people who manufacture it, of course. As Green Revolution commentator Lester Brown put it in *Seeds of Change*, "the multi-national corporation has a vested interest in the agricultural revolution along with the poor countries themselves."[14] The thought has not been wasted on multinational agribusiness, as we found on our visits to such Green Revolution areas as northwest Mexico.

The giant agribusiness firms, their markets at home becoming saturated, began to push in the 1960s for new markets, especially in the underdeveloped countries. During the period 1968 to 1975, International Harvester built up its sales outside North America from less than one fifth to almost one third of total sales and John Deere's sales overseas jumped from 16 percent to 23 percent of its total. Massey-Ferguson, a farm machinery giant with headquarters in Canada, was first to see the real growth potential abroad; 70 percent of its sales are now outside North America.[15]

This rapid expansion has not been without the help of powerful friends. The governments of industrial countries, directly and through international lending agencies such as the World Bank, provide foreign agricultural assistance mostly in the form of credits to import machinery.

Both the United States Agency for International Development (AID) and the World Bank have given large loans to Pakistan for farm mechanization. The Bank has given similar loans to India, the Philippines, and Sri Lanka. In 1966, when a World Bank loan to the Philippines made cheap credit available for farm mechanization, tractor sales soared.[16] Although the Bank, observes development economist Keith Griffin, claims to be "having second thoughts about this policy . . . the Agricultural Projects Department of the Bank remains firmly pro-tractor."[17]

As with the problems of protecting plants from pests, the United Nations Food and Agriculture Organization, rather than help develop appropriate alternatives, is becoming a broker between underdeveloped countries and multinational farm machinery firms. Its advisory Farm Mechanization Working Group includes Caterpillar Tractor, John Deere, Fiat, FMC, Massey-Ferguson, Mitsui, British Petroleum, and Shell. The FAO has joined with Massey-Ferguson to set up in Colombia the School of Agricultural Mechanization for all of Spanish-speaking Latin America. It will not take a conscious conspiracy for such a prestigious institution to overdose Latin America's rural societies with machines.

In many underdeveloped countries the value of domestic currency in relation to foreign currency is kept artificially high to promote certain imports. Agricultural machinery brought from abroad is thus often "cheaper" than it otherwise might be. This policy and other forms of subsidization in countries like Pakistan ended up making the same tractor cost one half of what it would in Iowa, calculated in terms of wheat. In the late 1960s, the Indian government subsidized mechanization so heavily through cheap credit that in the Ludhiana district of the Punjab farmers with even less than 15 acres were encouraged to buy tractors. This was in spite of the fact that even the principal suppliers of farm machinery thought that at least 25 to 30 acres were needed to make the tractors economical.[18] The government of Iran encouraged large, mechanized farming by exempting those farms that mechanized from the Land Reform Act.[19]

Transfer of Technology or Transfer of Assumptions?

To most Americans the release of human beings from labor in the fields is equated with efficiency and progress. (How could anyone but the most "pathologically anti-technological" person see it any other way?)[20] Who would not prefer to help people escape a backbreaking life in the fields for an easier life of the city? In most cases, however, the introduction of large-scale, high-energy agricultural technology does not suddenly give the agricultural workers the option to leave. It gives them rather no other option *but* to leave. Indeed the same may be said of small farmers in America today. We cannot look at technology in agriculture as freeing people from labor when productive work is what people need and want more than anything else.

Although large-scale mechanization is not necessary for increased production, Americans have a hard time believing it. Why? In part because we tend to think that machines are necessary for doing all the big jobs in life. Our notions are based on our own self-conceptions. Most of us accomplish very little with our bodies. Maybe our arms and hands shift a gear; our fingers push a button. But we know little of what our bodies are capable of creating. Naturally we come to assume big machines are necessary.

A most impressive and visible example that counters this assumption is the transformation of eroded valleys in China into a series of fertile, terraced fields — almost all accomplished *without* machinery. H. V. Henle's FAO study of China recounts the logical way the Chinese people put gravity to work for them. Large dams were built mainly by hand in the eroded and barren valleys. Slowly they silted up to what eventually became a new terraced field, then, another dam was built a little higher in the valley. Gradually, a series of terraced steps was created.[21]

Perhaps another reason Americans tend to assume that large machines are essential is that we live in a society where we are made to feel isolated from and competitive with our neighbors. The potential of collective action, therefore, is seldom even considered and virtually never experienced.

Who's Doing the Mechanizing?

Those who promote mechanization as the answer for underdeveloped countries like to throw out this challenge: "Look at China," they say. "Chinese agriculture is now starting to mechanize in a big way. Isn't this a lesson for the rest of the Third World?"

This view is correct in one sense: There is an important lesson here for the rest of the world. It is not, however, that large-scale mechanization is the answer for underdeveloped agriculture. The lesson is that mechanization is itself not the issue at all. The issue is *who* owns the machines.

Where the workers themselves own the machines, as in China, mechanization will proceed because the workers naturally wish to lighten the backbreaking toil of field labor. In China the goal is to eliminate the "three bendings" — pulling weeds, transplanting seedlings, and harvesting. The result of mechanization will be a better life for the farmers, not unemployment. In China farm mechanization is a high priority because labor is needed in other labor-intensive efforts such as building and maintaining water-control systems, running factories that produce cement from local sources, and operating decentralized fertilizer plants. Farm mechanization that frees labor for other such vital work contributes to Chinese society *as a whole*, not to private gain.

Similarly Cuba now has the greatest tractor density of any country in Latin America. Yet there is employment for everyone. The story of loading sugar freighters is instructive. Traditionally Cuban raw sugar was loaded into freighters by laborers lugging a sack at a time on their backs up a gangplank and into the hold. It took over a month to fill a ship. The sugar companies tried to mechanize the operation (with conveyor belts) but they were continually thwarted by organized workers who knew that their very lives depended on keeping the machines out. But once the Cuban government expanded other sectors of the economy and guaranteed everyone a productive job, the sugar terminals were quickly mechanized. Now a ship is loaded in a little over 24 hours! Nobody objected when the conveyor belts came in; no one ever *wanted* a life of carrying sugar sacks up and down a gangplank. Now Cuba is rapidly mechanizing the cutting of sugar cane, one of the most grueling of all agricultural jobs. Rather than creating masses of unemployed, it will speed the development of Cuba by releasing workers for other sectors of the economy.

Just as we cannot say that all large-scale mechanization is necessarily bad, neither can we say that appropriate technology is necessarily the answer. Even the "right" technology cannot be imposed nor can it do much good in the "wrong" society. The truly right technology, whether it be capital- or labor-intensive, can only be the product of a profound social restructuring in which those who work the fields decide what is right for them.

Focusing on the so-called technology gap continues to frame the problem of hunger in terms of how to increase production. And, as we have already seen, a narrow production focus only serves to put more profit and more food into the hands of an elite while further undermining the position of the majority.

Hunger cannot be solved simply by developing better seeds. Neither can hunger be solved by building better machines. Hunger is not a technical problem.

*　　*　　*

We need redistribution not of wealth but of the technology possessed by the industrial world. . . . The receiver of technology must be willing to change his way of life, and like it or not, he may have to cooperate closely with the donor of that technology during a transition training period of years. Some Third Worlders may term this "neocolonialism," and they are welcome to their opinions. Others might call it "mutually beneficial cooperation."

> Ray Vicker, *Wall St. Journal* bureau chief, in
> *This Hungry World*

In Telukpinang, 60 miles south of Jakarta, as in other parts of Indonesia, the mill has taken over work traditionally done by women by hand — the threshing and hulling of rice stalks. Rice mills are estimated to have eliminated a million or more jobs in the fields of Java alone, the principal Indonesian island.

He [the landlord] recalled that he used to employ two women, sometimes three or four, giving them two liters of rice for every 10 they produced. But now, he said, he keeps the entire crop, paying those who help him the equivalent of about 60 cents a day plus lunch.

The mill is owned by a major general in the Indonesian army who lives in a Jakarta suburb. The villagers asked that his name not be disclosed since they fear his power.

> *New York Times*, November 30, 1975

Some past attempts to apply mechanization have also found resistance in less developed countries — especially in areas with high unemployment and a seemingly unlimited supply of low-cost labor. . . . These have been temporary setbacks.

> Arthur J. Olsen, Vice-President, FMC Corporation,
> speech at "Feeding the World's Hungry"
> Conference, 1974

21

Isn't the Backwardness of Small Farmers to Blame?

Question: You seem to think the small farmer is the savior of the hungry world. But isn't one basic reason for low production levels in the poor countries that so much land is in farms too small to be efficient? Aren't most small farmers just too backward and tradition-bound to respond to development programs?

Another point to keep in mind is expressed well by Ray Vicker in his book *This Hungry World*: ". . . the big farmer may be big because he has the intelligence, the capital, and the management talent to stay big." Moreover, a big farmer is more willing to take risks. Isn't this the kind of farmer that we need now more than ever? Maybe we have just reached the point where we cannot afford equality — if we are also going to eat.

Our Response: Whether the "little guy" is necessarily less efficient and less productive than the "big guy" is of critical importance in assessing the production potential of the underdeveloped countries, since about 80 percent of the rural producers are the so-called little guys who cultivate less than twelve acres of land.

So we asked: Well, does smallness equal low levels of production? To answer that question we looked at studies from all over the world and everywhere the verdict is the same: Contrary to our previous assumption, the small farmer in most cases produces more per unit of land than the large farmer. Here are just a few examples:

- The value of output per acre in India is more than one-third higher on the smallest farms than on the larger farms.[1]
- In Thailand plots of two to four acres produce almost 60 percent more rice per acre than farms of 140 acres and more.[2]

- In Taiwan net income per acre of farms with less than one and a quarter acres is nearly twice that of farms over five acres.[3]
- The World Bank reports an analysis of the differences in the value of output on large and small farms in Argentina, Brazil, Chile, Colombia, Ecuador, and Guatemala. The conclusion? The small farms were three to fourteen times more productive per acre than the large farms.[4]

Consider now the significance of such comparisons in explaining the low productivity of agriculture in underdeveloped countries. Based on a study of 83 countries, *slightly more than 3 percent of all landholders, those with 124 acres or more, control almost 80 percent of all farmland.*[5] An extreme example is Bihar, the poorest state in India, where 90 percent of the 53 million inhabitants live off the land and three quarters of the cultivators owned less than 1 percent of the land. In other words, the largest landholders control most of the farmland, yet studies from all over the world show that they are the *least* productive.

To explain the higher productivity of the small farmer, one need not romanticize the peasant. Peasant farmers get more out of their land precisely because they need to survive on the meager resources allowed to them. Studies show that smallholders plant more closely than a machine would, mix and rotate complementary crops, choose a combination of cultivation and livestock that is labor-intensive and, above all, work their perceptibly limited resources to the fullest. Farming for the peasant family is not an abstract calculation of profit to be weighed against other investments. It is a matter of life and death.

What About Small Farmer Efficiency in the United States?

Every single study ever made by the United States Department of Agriculture (USDA) has found that the most efficient farm, measured in terms of cost per unit of output, is the mechanized one- or two-farmer unit, not the large corporate operation. Any savings associated with sheer size (and there are remarkably few) are quickly offset by the higher management, supervisory, and labor costs of the large farms.[6]

To test this finding we looked at net income per acre by farm size in the United States from 1960 through 1973. We found that in all those fourteen years there were only two in which the biggest farms realized a net income per acre greater than the family farm.[7] The very pattern of greater production by small farmers that so struck us in our study of underdeveloped countries is found right here in America.

But, turning back to the underdeveloped countries, a big question remains: If smallholders are not inherently unproductive and most of the farms in the underdeveloped world are small, why do national production levels there remain so low?

The Small Pay More

First, of course, while small farmers may constitute the majority of farmers, they certainly do not own most of the land, as we have seen. Moreover, compared to largeholders, small peasant producers do not have equal access to land and agricultural inputs, such as water, fertilizer, and tools. As Green Revolution pioneer Norman Borlaug himself expressed it:

> I have a lot of respect for the small farmer. . . . Almost invariably when you look at what he's doing with his land, you find he's producing the maximum under the situation he has to work with. The thing is that he usually doesn't have much to work with.[8]

Agricultural inputs such as fertilizer and water do not reach small farmers because they have neither the cash nor the credit to buy them. Quite often loans from government agencies stipulate a minimum holding that cuts out the small farmer. In Pakistan, for example, to get a loan for a tubewell from the Agricultural Development Bank a peasant must have at least 12.5 acres. This single stipulation excludes over 80 percent of Pakistan's farmers.[9] One estimate is that only about 5 percent of Africa's farmers have access to institutional credit — and it is not hard to guess which 5 percent![10]

Sudhir Sen, an Indian commentator on the Green Revolution, has estimated that roughly one half of India's small farmers lack any recorded right to the land, without which they are unable to obtain crop loans from credit institutions.[11] (Even where there are exceptions, the tenant is still penalized. In Tamil Nadu, India, the tenant is allowed only 60 percent of the amount of credit per acre advanced to landowners.)[12] Perhaps, even more important, small farmers are reluctant to use their land for loan collateral anyway. Poor farmers quite sensibly decide that they do not want to risk losing their land.

Largely excluded from institutional credit, smallholders are left dependent on private moneylenders and merchants who charge usurious rates of interest. We have seen estimates of interest rates ranging from 50 percent to 200 percent! Agricultural economist Keith Griffin relates how in one area of the Philippines 15 percent of the borrowers paid an interest rate of over 200 percent while 20 percent of the borrowers paid only 16 percent. Moreover, merchant-creditors can increase the interest by underpricing harvest repayments and overpricing the goods that debtors buy from them.[13] By contrast, the large operator may pay no interest, or even come out ahead by borrowing money. When the nominal rates of interest on credit available to large operators from commercial institutions are adjusted for inflation, the real rate of interest is often negative.[14]

Obligations to Moneylenders and Landlords

Earlier we described the debt bondage that keeps so many peasant farmers in a form of perpetual vassalage. As Keith Griffin so aptly puts it, "the *campesinos* of Latin America have suffered not from insecurity of tenure but from excessively secure tenure." Debt bondage, he points out, has been used to tie peasants to the land to assure landowners that labor would be available, particularly in labor-scarce economies in Latin America.[15] What is the impact on production? Inevitably, motivation to increase production is stifled because the trapped peasants know that higher yields will never benefit them, only the landowner or moneylender. Debt bondage can mean that the peasant farmer must work off the debt by tending the fields of the creditor. The peasant's own farm then suffers neglect. Unable to work his land adequately, the peasant farmer often has no choice but to give it up.

The question suggests that one of the main problems facing poor countries is the backwardness of their small farmers. But are the poor farmers truly backward or does their performance simply reflect a realistic assessment of their options?

Consider sharecroppers who represent a significant portion of the rural population in many of the underdeveloped countries. Although in many cases they must provide all of the inputs, they get to keep only a portion of the crop. If much of their crop is taken away, why make the investments necessary to increase production? Likewise, insecure tenancies result in inefficiency. Tenants, in constant indebtedness and unsure of whether or not they will even be on the same plot next year, can hardly be expected to protect soil fertility by rotating crops and leaving fields fallow to restore the soil.

Without a certain minimum landholding, a security of tenure, credit at a reasonable rate and control over what is produced, a peasant simply makes a realistic and rational assessment that it is not worth it to buy inputs to increase production or to take steps to preserve soil fertility. Peasants generally do not spurn fertilizers or any other input or improvements out of so-called backwardness but out of hard economic sense.

Is Bigger Better?

The notion that those at the top are there because they are better at whatever they are doing is deeply imbedded in most of us. But this is a false assumption. What must come to replace it is the new understanding so well stated by Erich and Charlotte Jacoby in their classic, *Man and Land*:

> Landlords, moneylenders and traders, the chief components of any rural hierarchy, did not attain their strong economic position because they increased agricultural production through improved farm management or reasonable investment, but merely because they were able to take advantage of the economic opportunities arising from the weak bargaining power and social helplessness of the peasants.[16]

We have already seen how largeholders gain preferential access to credit and government-subsidized technology, not because of a proven record of efficient production, but because they have the assets and the influence to be creditworthy. Having this access to credit makes it possible to finance farm improvements that can generate still more income. As of 1968 a small minority of Pakistani farmers, those with more than 13 acres, had installed 96 percent of the tubewells in Pakistan. Studies suggest that a tubewell alone, even without improved seeds and fertilizer, can increase net farm revenue by 35 percent. Now, all the outsider sees is that the production of the larger farmer increases and that perhaps his farm grows too. But is this due to the individual farmer's intelligence and talent or to a social factor: the unequal access of the larger landowner to credit that enabled him to buy the tubewell?[17]

Large farmers also benefit because of the inability of the small peasant producer to meet institutional credit terms. Large commercial farmers in Mexico, for example, were only too happy to buy on the black market at a discount the inputs — seeds, fertilizer, or pesticides — that poor farmers had received as government loans but were too poor to make productive enough to pay back.[18] The same process was reported in Tunisia during the Green Revolution campaign of 1970–1971.

In addition, large landowners are able to obtain higher prices than small farmers through devices that in no way reflect greater efficiency in their farming operation. In Mexico during the late 1940s and early 1950s the large landlords formed exclusive producer associations. Often with the help of government credit these associations invested in warehouses and silos that enabled them to bargain collectively, thus freeing them from dependence on the official price of grain. The small farmers who had received land through the earlier land reform could not, however, follow the same path. They were bound by the terms of the official credit on which they were dependent. They had to sell their crops to the government credit banks that, in order to fight inflation, kept the prices paid to these small farmers low.[19]

Furthermore, price supports, often justified as a way to help the poor farmer, have actually helped concentrate the profits from agriculture in the hands of the rural elite. Turkey supports its wheat at a level 63 percent above the world market price; in India and Pakistan the support was 100 percent above the world price during the early Green Revolution years. But who benefits? Mostly traders and wholesalers. The higher price hardly ever reaches the peasant producer. The "constantly indebted peasant is virtually bound by contract to sell his produce at prices set by the private moneylender-cum-trader, as no effective marketing cooperatives exist to safeguard his interests," the Jacobys explain. "In many underdeveloped countries, rigid tenancy systems prevent the tenant cultivator from placing even his own share of the crop on the market and force him to accept a price set by land-lords and moneylenders who hoard the crop until the market offers the best prices."[20]

The Risk-Taking Large Farmer?

The question suggests land redistribution might hurt those large landowners who are innovative and willing to take risks. But if this picture of the large landowner is accurate how can one explain the slowness with which large landowners in Mexico adopted the new varieties of wheat? The reason is that powerful large landowners found they could continue to increase their profit *without* increasing yields. After 1954 they bargained successfully to keep the guaranteed price of wheat so high that they could reap fortunes without making use of the new Green Revolution inputs. Green Revolution analyst Cynthia Hewitt de Alcántara tersely comments:

> If one felt it necessary to make more money from wheat, the logical path to follow was to lobby in Mexico for a still-higher wheat price, and only secondarily to master the subtler requirements of the new technology.[21]

Second, without seriously attempting to increase yields, large commercial Mexican growers during the 1950s and early 1960s found they could raise their profits enormously by expanding their operations, often taking over the fields of nearby small-holders and land-reform beneficiaries.

With their ability both to lobby for higher prices and acquire more land, many large landowners scoffed at the idea of improved seeds for years after the much higher-yield potential of the new seeds had been demonstrated. When they did begin to consider change, it was only when *all risk was removed* by a federal investment program that poured billions of pesos into irrigation works, roads, storage facilities, electricity, railroads, long-term agricultural credit, and ultimately, into a guaranteed price for wheat. Even so, it took the private wheat growers in Sonora fourteen years to reach the level of production found in the Green Revolution test plots.[22] So much for the myth of the innovative, risk-taking big guy.

The Waste of Wealth

Continuing to pin hopes for genuine development on the contribution of the large landowners overlooks another critical question: What happens to the profit made by the large landowner? Is this profit as likely to be productively invested in agriculture as would the same profit spread among many smaller farmers or collectively controlled?

What we have found is that many of the large landowners, those who some would say demonstrate management talent merely by becoming large, in fact squander their new wealth. Concentrating the profits from agricultural modernization into a few hands has meant that much of what might have been returned to agricultural development goes instead for luxury items to satisfy the conspicuous consumption impulse of the rural nouveaux riches. Around the world the new agricultural entrepreneurs can also be found "investing" surplus profits in tourist resorts, bars, taxi fleets, and travel agencies.

In studying Mexico we were astonished to find that the very landed elite, so pampered for 30 years by the Mexican government, was by the 1970s on the verge of bankruptcy. By 1971, reports Hewitt de Alcántara,

> An estimated 80 percent of the large agricultural enterprises of the Hermosillo Coast [Mexico] were operating year after year in the red, and the situation was little better in the Yaqui Valley. One large farmer after another filed for bankruptcy.[23]

The financial collapse of the overextended commercial farmers was not a consequence solely of overinvestment in farm technology. On our research visits we found obvious frivolous expenditures by a few amid the equally obvious poverty of the majority: tasteless, sprawling ranch-style houses, multiple imported luxury automobiles, periodic shopping sprees across the border, Las Vegas junkets, swimming pools, private planes, and children in American boarding schools.

Large farmers are the *least* reliable credit recipients. The World Bank reports that large farmers actually have *poorer* repayment records than small farmers in countries as diverse as

Bangladesh, Colombia, Costa Rica, and Ethiopia.[24] Similarly, the USDA tells us that rates of delinquency and foreclosure in the United States are greater on big loans for large-scale farm units than on smaller loans for family farms.[25]

A final factor to weigh is the literal waste of valuable land by large landholding interests. Plantations have always been noted for acquiring more land than they would ever use. But a recent study of land use in Central America tells us that the historic pattern holds true today: farmers who own up to 10 acres cultivate 72 percent of their land, but farmers with over 86 acres cultivate only 14 percent of their land. They use 49 percent for pasture, and leave 37 percent idle.[26] Similarly a 1968 study of Ecuador showed that farmers with less than 25 acres farmed about 80 percent of their land while the largest farmers with more than 2500 acres cultivated little more than a quarter of their land.[27] Since large landowners are the *most* wasteful of the land, what makes people now believe that they are the last best hope for agricultural development?

The Inefficiency of Inequality

The motivation and willingness of people to cooperate toward a common goal are ultimately what all development depends upon. But a social system that gives preferential access to land, agricultural inputs, and government programs to a few undercuts any possibility for cooperation and shared learning. It was thought, for example, that focusing the new seeds and other inputs on the large farmer would have such a powerful "demonstration effect" that all the smaller producers would seek to emulate the large landholder. But small farmers have more savvy than that. Rural development authority Dr. Ingrid Palmer neatly sums up the perspective of the small farmer:

> It must be obvious to the small farmers that the successful farmers learned of the goodies first, were pals with the purveyors of same, and did all manner of string pulling for inputs. Since the whole deal is not open to public gaze, the small farmers see it as another example of the charmed circle excluding them, and if they are ever approached by technical authorities to do the same, they are damn sure it won't be on the same terms offered the large farmers.[28]

And such an intuition is ordinarily correct. The much-touted demonstration effect has thus been just the opposite of that intended. The simple fact that the large landowner is successful with the new approach is often enough to convince the smallholder that he himself could *not* be.

Finally, the suggestion that we simply cannot afford greater equality if we want to increase production ignores the most fundamental brake on production within a market system: the lack of buyers with the cash to pay for the increased production. One too often forgets that hunger alone is not enough to stimulate production in a market system. Only paying customers stimulate production and in most market economies today, their number is growing very slowly, if at all.

The question implies that "a little inequality is a good thing" or at least a necessary evil. In times of supposed scarcity it becomes even easier to accept the idea that we should turn to those who are "on top." The facts have, however, forced us to conclude that this is exactly the wrong approach. We have learned that the very power of the large landowners makes them less compelled to try to increase production, especially of locally needed food; that they divert resources out of agriculture into unnecessary consumption and unproductive investments; that they underutilize the land; and finally, that the constraints poverty places on motivation and consumption are the greatest blocks to increased production. Economic justice and economic progress are inseparable.

Our conclusion is buttressed by the actual experience of societies that have deliberately reduced rural inequality. The Chinese people decided not merely to end favoritism to the better-endowed farms but to compensate for inequalities so that all farmers would move forward together. As Sterling Wortman, a vice-president of the Rockefeller Foundation, stated after returning from China, "Locally, there's no such thing as a good or bad farmer. Various farming regions may differ, but within a given locality the productivity on all lands has been raised to the same standard of excellence."[29]

In his *Report on China's Agriculture*, H. V. Henle of the FAO writes of Huadong Commune. Before the Revolution, Huadong was among the poorest in the region. Between 1933 and 1949 about 3600 people died of hunger, 4620 children were sold as slaves and 4400 fled. The poor peasants, representing 84 percent of the population, owned only 9 percent of the land. Today, now that basic inequality and its inefficiencies have been eradicated, this commune so successfully produces rice, oilseeds, peanuts and other food crops that no one is hungry and a third of its inhabitants do not need to be employed in agriculture.[30]

China's national production figures show that greater productivity does result from greater equality. By the mid-seventies China was producing close to 2000 pounds of grain per acre — double the corresponding per acre production in India and Pakistan and almost double the yield per acre before the Revolution.[31] As Cornell's China watcher Dr. Benedict Stavis told us, China feeds 50 percent more people, 20 percent better (comparing per capita figures for grains and pulses) with 30 percent less cultivated land. Moreover, precisely because of China's far greater equality of access to productive resources, its per capita statistics much more accurately reflect the reality of food distribution.

Is Small Always Beautiful?

Although small farmers, working under the extreme handicaps we have outlined, often prove to be more productive than largeholders, agricultural progress is *not* a task of simply channeling more credit, equipment, seeds, fertilizers, and irrigation to them. First of all, 30 to 60 percent of those employed in agriculture in underdeveloped countries are landless. Just shifting inputs in the direction of small farmers could never, therefore, initiate a development momentum for the entire population.

Neither should one make the mistake of believing that the small farm is inherently more productive than the large. We have found that the *size* of the parcel of land matters less than the *relationship* of the people to it. We have seen that small farms can be very productive — as in Japan — where the people working the land know that the productivity will benefit them. And we have seen exactly the opposite: small farms with low productivity when credit, debt, and tenancy arrangements deny those who work the fields the fruits of their labors.

Likewise with large farming units. We have just documented the inefficiencies of privately owned, large landowner operations. Exchange these private landowners for antidemocratic bureaucrats and productivity will still remain low, as developments in

Soviet agriculture have demonstrated. The Chinese people have developed a different system — one that takes advantage of larger farming units while putting the people who work the land directly in control. In China the ownership of land is vested in the production brigade, equal to one large village or several smaller ones. In practice the production brigade turns over the land for cultivation to the village labor force, called the production team. Except where large tractors or combine harvesters are involved, the village production team is responsible for its own field management and accounting. Income is distributed according to an agreed upon work-point system, with everyone being assured of the basic foodgrains and other essential items.[32]

Thus, in China those who work the fields directly control both the land and the necessary inputs. They themselves determine how the income is to be divided up. The central government, rather than demanding a fixed amount, leaving the localities to get by with what is left over, demands a small percentage of total production as taxes. The tax is usually only 1 to 7 percent.[33] Even when production increases considerably, the central government does not necessarily increase the tax rate. Greater production, therefore, directly benefits those who work the field. We have already noted the result: Food production in China has climbed consistently and there has been no famine since at least the early 1960s.

We have stressed that greater equality through land redistribution has been associated with increased production — in countries as different as Japan, China, Taiwan, Egypt, Cuba, and Vietnam. But, while the redistribution of land and other agricultural resources, even if partial, can stimulate production, redistribution per se will not instigate a genuine development momentum.

If the program is carried out by a state bureaucracy in which the people are mere passive recipients of government favors, the old dependency pattern continues. The only change is that the group now in power is acting benevolently. Since the development of any social structure is based entirely on the development of the individuals within it, the reduction of inequality must break this dependency pattern. It must involve a process of the people themselves taking more and more control over their own lives. The *process* of land reform is therefore as important as the reform itself.

The people must together deliberate and decide how they want to distribute the land and resolve any conflicting claims that arise. The experience of land reform will then be one of a valuable social education, training the people for the new task of collective administration. Such is the conclusion of a group of Asian rural economists reflecting upon what the Chinese experience has to teach. Their report observes: "Land reform through mass . . . action also gives an opportunity for other dominance-dependence relations to be shaken up: women and youth, the low castes, even the children, will be in the thick of this experience which will shock them emotionally and help remove deep-seated inhibitions in their minds as well."[34]

Thus, achieving greater equality through the initiative of the people is the only path to individual and social self-reliance and self-respect. Without these, there can be no development.

*   *   *

Today, some sociologists view the large landowner with horror, arguing that the task of development should be to level incomes within particular countries, and this means concentrating on the small rather than the large landowner. This brings us once more to that question: Are we aiming at obtaining more food to feed a world with an exploding population? Or are we aiming at redistribution of incomes. I don't think we can do both.

Ray Vicker, *This Hungry World*

Under any circumstances, agrarian reform subverts the productive process.

Magalhaes Chacel, Brazilian economist speaking
at a government-sponsored conference,
New York Times, August 16, 1976

22

Hasn't the Green Revolution Strengthened Food Security?

Question: You choose to see only failure. You fail to recognize the real contribution of the Green Revolution. The *New York Times* has reported that the improved seed varieties are adding 20 million tons of grain annually to production in Asia and Southeast Asia.

You are undoubtedly right that certain groups have benefited more than others. But just where would we be today if the new seeds had not been introduced? In the early 1970s we were faced with unusually bad weather. International reserves dropped dramatically, but somehow we squeezed by. At least the situation was not as desperate as it would have been if the Green Revolution had not increased world grain output in the previous decade. Hasn't the Green Revolution at least provided some level of global food security?

Our Response: As important as anything else we have learned in our study is that genuine food security cannot be evaluated in mere production figures but only by answering this question: How vulnerable is a food production system to forces outside the control of the food producers themselves?

How Reliable Are the Producers?

Opting to make agricultural progress synonymous with the promotion of large commercial growers means taking agriculture out of the hands of self-provisioning farmers who have a personal stake in producing food and entrusting it to entrepreneurs whose only concern is making money. The result is decreased food security.

Here is what we mean: If farm businessmen in Colombia find they can make more money growing livestock feed for processors like Ralston Purina than a staple like beans, they will grow feed. When a Mexican commercial grower in Sinaloa discovers he can make almost twenty times more raising tomatoes of export quality than raising wheat, he is likely to switch to tomatoes. If large operators in Central and South America find they can make more money growing flowers for export rather than corn for local people, they will plant flowers.

On a research trip to northwest Mexico, we came upon several distilleries newly built to produce brandy from grapes to be grown on thousands of irrigated acres, land on which local people could grow nutritious food. The next day the head of cereal research at a nearby government-sponsored research center explained to us that a farmer in the area makes a profit of almost $500 per acre growing grapes — four times more than with wheat.

In a country like Mexico, where early childhood death due to malnutrition has gone up 10 percent over the last ten years, acreage devoted to basic food crops — corn, wheat, beans and rice — actually declined 25 percent over the same period. Not surprisingly, in the last three years Mexico has had to import 15 percent of its corn, 25 percent of its wheat, and 45 percent of its soybeans.

Mexico is a prime example of a country that has gone far down the path of entrusting its agricultural resources to large commercial growers. The result? The government has had to practically bribe the "modernized" growers to keep them producing basic staples for the national market; the Mexican government had to hike price guarantees by 112 percent between 1970 and 1975 and even then the proportion of land growing basic foods has declined. Because of the tight control of the commercial farming sector over production, the large commercial growers have been able to use threats of production cutbacks to get higher government-supported prices. At times they have carried out the threats — switching to feedgrains or export crops — until the support offered by the government for growing a basic food was raised high enough. The food security of a country in which large commercial growers virtually control food production is forever in jeopardy for yet another reason: The large growers can withhold food from the market in periods of rising prices in expectation of higher profits later.

Entrusting a country's food supply to a pampered elite turns out to be a dangerous and costly choice indeed.

How Vulnerable Is an Agricultural System to Natural Hazards?

Can we measure food security in production totals if the agricultural base that produced the gains is itself threatened?

Consider these apparently isolated events:

- Indonesia, 1974–1975: At least 500,000 acres of riceland planted with the new variety was devastated by a viral disease spread by plagues of brown leaf hoppers.[1] (Indonesia has since inaugurated a program aimed at replacing HRV rice with its own locally improved varieties.)
- Philippines, 1970–1972: Tungro rice virus reached epidemic levels in the Green Revolution rice fields.[2]
- Zambia, 1970s: Disaster in the form of a newly identified mold called *fusarium* has struck new hybrid corn strains grown by the commercial farmers while the traditional corn crops of the villagers appear free from attack.[3]

What do these examples of crop loss from disease and pests reveal?

Green Revolution fields are often more vulnerable to attack than fields planted in traditional ways with locally evolved seeds. Why? Part of the reason is simply that the denser stands in Green Revolution fields provide a more abundant diet for pests. Multiple cropping allowed by the faster-maturing new seeds also provides pests with a more even year-round food supply. Moreover, the new seeds were bred with the highest priority on the greatest yield possible, not on resistance to disease or pests.

The danger of crop loss is compounded because, while the new seeds present novel opportunities for disease and pests, effective traditional practices for dealing with these problems are becoming casualties of the Green Revolution. Historically, wet rice farming involved flooding the fields for several weeks each year, thus drowning many pests. Unfortunately, the rigorous timing of the new seeds often does not accommodate this practice. Alternating the cultivation of a food crop with a soil-building crop (called green manuring) is a proven traditional way to control pests by eliminating their hosts for a season. This practice was widespread even in the United States until recently. But, with increasing use of chemical fertilizers, green manuring has become passé. Puddling is yet another practice on the way out. (In case you are wondering, puddling means using water buffaloes to plod through the fields in order to aerate the soil, increase water retention, trample the weeds, and eliminate insects.)[4]

Finally, the genetic uniformity of the new seeds planted over large areas means that they are more vulnerable to epidemics. A few years ago, the United States had a glimpse of what this could mean. In 1970, the great southern corn leaf blight wiped out 50 percent or more of the crop in many of the Gulf Coast states (15 to 20 percent of the total domestic corn crop). A more tragic example is the Irish potato blight in which over 1 million people died during the 1840s. Scientists now believe that the underlying problem was the lack of genetic diversity of the potato crop.

Today all the Green Revolution dwarf wheats* (now 20 percent of all wheat grown) trace themselves to a *single* parent plant. The same is true of dwarf-rice varieties. Should the genes that those parents have for dwarfness ever be linked to one conferring susceptibility to a plant disease such as glume botch, root rot, or Karnal smut (real names!), the Green Revolution could turn black overnight.

Because of their denser stands, multiple cropping, and genetic uniformity, the new seeds can be more vulnerable to attack. Current plant research is therefore placing greater emphasis on breeding for resistance. But the issue is much more complex than simply finding a seed that is resistant to today's diseases. Nature is not static. Pests and diseases are constantly adapting.

Scientists such as Dr. H. Garrison Wilkes, a specialist in corn genetics at the University of Massachusetts, believe that it is only a matter of time before a mutation of an existing disease will take place, permitting it to attack a new seed strain. Wilkes states that "In their wilderness state, both plants and diseases which attack them are forever adapting to each other through the evolutionary process. The diseases mutate new forms of attack, the plants new forms of resistance." But, he warns, "Under modern agriculture plants no longer mutate but are grown from new seeds each year for continuous high yields. *The mutation of diseases, however, cannot be stopped.*"[5]

---

*"Dwarf" refers to characteristic shortness of the plants that prevents their tipping over even when more abundant yields makes their tops heavier.

This inevitability would not be so serious if we could always rush back to the lab to produce a new strain — keeping one step ahead of nature and losing at most one crop. But it takes time to develop a resistant strain. Could the world wait as many as ten to twenty generations of seeds, that is, four to five years, for a resistant hybrid?[6] Clearly the answer is no.

Moreover, this scenario presumes that the material will continue to exist from which plant breeders can always come up with a new resistant strain. But will it? We have talked here in Part V about the social and economic transformation of agriculture. But what of the transformation of world agriculture in terms of the plants themselves? What happens when commercialized, standardized agriculture penetrates almost every corner of the globe?

The human race historically cultivated over 3000 species of plants for food, about half of them in sufficient quantity to enter into commerce. Today, in stark contrast, only fifteen species including rice, corn, wheat, sorghum, barley, sugar cane, sugar beets, potato, sweet potato, cassava, the common bean, soybean, peanut, coconut, and banana actually feed the entire world, providing 85–90 percent of all human energy. Of these, only *three* plants, wheat, rice, and corn now supply 66 percent of the world's seed crop.[7]

Especially since there are now so *few* plants on which we all depend, the maintenance of genetic diversity within these species is absolutely critical. Genetic diversity, as we have already seen, is necessary to prevent the wholesale wiping out of a crop in which all the plants are vulnerable to the same pathogen and it is also crucial as the storehouse of material from which to breed new resistant strains. The heritage of genetic diversity has not been evenly spread over the earth. In the 1920s, the Russian plant geneticist N. I. Vavilov discovered eight major and three minor centers of extreme plant gene diversity, all located in underdeveloped countries (along the Tropic of Cancer and the Tropic of Capricorn), in mountainous regions isolated by steep terrain or other natural barriers. These centers represent only one fortieth of the world's land area but have been the source of almost all our food plants. From these reservoirs have come many of the most valuable strains and genes used by plant geneticists in the last fifty years.[8]

Until now scientists have returned to these areas of diversity for new germ plasm with which to breed resistance. But this diversity has never been adequately protected. Collections of genetic material were often lost when scientists discarded them after hitting upon the genes that would serve their immediate purpose. Suddenly in the 1970s the problem worsened dramatically. As plant geneticist Wilkes puts it: "We are discovering Mexican farmers are planting hybrid corn seed from a Midwestern seed firm, that Tibetan farmers are planting barley from a Scandinavian plant breeding station, and that Turkish farmers are planting wheat from the Mexican Wheat Program." He concludes, "Each of these classic areas of genetic diversity is rapidly becoming an area of seed uniformity."[9]

Once foreign strains are introduced, the native varieties can become extinct in a single year if their seeds are consumed and not kept. Dr. Wilkes states, "Quite literally, the genetic heritage of a millennium in a particular valley can disappear in a single bowl of porridge."[10]

Some argue that our security against genetic "wipe outs" will lie in establishing seed banks that would be treasuries of genetic diversity. Unfortunately, seed banks, too, are vulnerable. A major Peruvian collection of corn germ plasm, one of South America's largest, was irretrievably lost when the compressors for the refrigerators in which it was stored failed! And, the corn research center in Mexico that produced the original Green Revolution seeds inadvertently lost some of its irreplaceable corn germ plasm collected during the 1940s.[11] Bangladesh still has some 1200 different traditional varieties of rice and Indonesia has 600. How effectively can that genetic diversity be protected once it is removed from the field for cold storage in a seed bank? One alternative to seed banks proposed by many scientists is carefully selected natural preserves throughout the world that could maintain living collections in the field.

As long as such research is primarily the domain of a few corporations one wonders what protective measures will be taken. Already Pioneer Hy-Bred International, Inc. and DeKalb Ag Research supply 55 percent of the hybrid corn market. These two, plus six others, dominate virtually all hybrid development and marketing.[12] Can such firms be expected to help maintain living treasuries of genetic diversity in which all countries might participate? Or will they guard their genetic research against competitors and promote only the currently most salable variety?

How Self-Contained Is the Agricultural System?

This is the third measure of true food security. To measure how self-contained an agricultural system is one must first know who controls the farm inputs necessary to make the land productive. Take, for example, the new hybrid corn seeds. Since these seeds do not reproduce themselves perfectly, farmers who save seeds from one crop for the next planting find their yields and quality greatly diminished. The farmer — once he is hooked into the hybrid seed system — is dependent, therefore, on a new supply of seeds season after season. These seeds now come primarily from private companies able to produce them through controlled pollination. The USDA has just developed seeds called "apomictic" hybrids that the farmers would be able to use year after year without new purchases from seed companies.[13] It is unlikely, we are told, that this development will be pursued by the big seed companies since their whole sales system would be threatened.

Obviously reliance on imported chemical fertilizers runs counter to the maintenance of a secure, self-contained agricultural system. Nevertheless, corporations and institutions based in the industrial countries are exporting the myth that chemical fertilizers are the best way to achieve production gains. This road to increased yields is a model most Americans take for granted. From 1942 to 1967 chemical fertilizer use in the United States expanded tenfold — not because it was the only path to production gains but for other reasons. For one thing, chemical fertilizers became dirt-cheap. The cost of nitrogen fertilizer dropped to one half and in some cases one quarter of what it was immediately after World War II. The greater demand for nitrogen fertilizer can also be linked to the rapid promotion of meat consumption. (It takes about sixteen times more nitrogen to produce grain-fed meat than it does to produce plant protein.)

Even more significantly, chemical fertilizer use is accelerating in order to compensate for soil nutrient depletion due to the nitrogen lost by bad cultivation practices and resultant erosion. One estimate places the loss of soil nitrogen in rich Midwest soils at 40 percent in the last century.[14] It is estimated that fifteen to twenty years of returning organic matter — manure, crop residues, sewage sludge, and so on — would be necessary to restore the organic content and the nitrogen of American soils. Such soil depletion reveals much about American agriculture. Careful husbandry necessary to maintain fragile soils or enrich poor soils never evolved here because until now it simply did not seem necessary.

The critical importance of careful land husbandry came home to us recently. A Soil Conservation Service official in Iowa explained how, depending on the way the land is cared for, top soil might last only thirty-six years or for an indefinite period. If the soil is plowed up and downhill in the fall and corn is planted year after year with no crop residue left, the entire six to eight remaining inches of Iowa's top soil will be lost from land with even a very slight slope. If, by contrast, no-till farming and contour terracing are practiced and crop residue is left on all year, the eight inches of top soil could last indefinitely since new top soil would always be in formation. Yet, as of today, only one third of Iowa's agricultural land is protected by the kind of conservation practices needed to protect the top soil.[15]

Is this American record — neglect of soil maintenance and reliance on chemical fertilizers — a useful model for underdeveloped countries today?

Underdeveloped countries now import 55 percent of their nitrogen fertilizer,[16] making them highly vulnerable to skyrocketing fertilizer prices. World fertilizer prices jumped threefold between 1970 and 1974. Crop production fell in many underdeveloped countries simply because they had become hooked on chemical fertilizers and yet could no longer afford to import them. But even if it *were* possible to rely on imported chemical fertilizer to increase food production, is this the place for underdeveloped countries to start?

Chemical fertilizers can increase yields but they cannot maintain or enhance the soil's organic matter. Organic matter, however, is the ultimate key to fertility; it maintains the porous soil structure, providing superior waterholding capacity (critical during droughts) and allowing oxygen to penetrate for use by soil organisms that break down manure, crop residues, and other organic matter. Relying primarily on chemical fertilizers can be self-defeating in the long-term. The more one relies on chemical fertilizers instead of manure, compost, crop rotation, and green manure, the more the organic matter declines, the less able plants are to absorb inorganic nitrogen in chemical fertilizers.

Chemical fertilizer must, therefore, never be thought of as a *substitute* for organic sources. First, all sources of organic matter should be mobilized and returned to the soil. Then, for countries like China and Algeria with petroleum available to produce chemical fertilizer, developing and using that potential can make sense. (Furthermore, even though China is making a big push to utilize its petroleum for fertilizer, 70 percent of its fertilizer is still from organic sources, enough to guarantee sufficient food production.)

Even if there are no local resources for chemical fertilizer production (and this is the case for most underdeveloped countries), yield gains can be achieved by mobilizing the now wasted potential of organic matter. Conservatively estimated, waste material from animals, plants, and humans in underdeveloped countries could supply *six to eight times* more nutrients than these countries obtained during 1970-1971 from the use of chemical fertilizers. In 1973, the economic value of such organic wastes in underdeveloped countries was estimated at over $16 billion. Using labor-intensive methods, urban waste in India could be processed into fertilizers at one-third the cost of imported chemical fertilizers.[17] Yet virtually none of this potential has been tapped.

Most measures of food security fixate on global statistics of agricultural production. But food security simply cannot exist in a market system where food is a business. Commercial growers cannot be relied upon to keep growing food for hungry people when they can make more money growing luxury crops for the minority who can always pay more. Moreover, we have seen that much of the increased production has been at the price of increased vulnerability, *and unnecessarily so*. Increased production approached as a mere technical problem has completely re-shaped agriculture itself, reducing a very complex, self-contained system into a highly simplified and dependent one. The Green Revolution approach converts a recycling, self-contained system into a linear production formula: pick the "best" seeds, plant uniformly over the largest area possible, and dose with chemical fertilizer. The reduction of agriculture to this simple formula leaves crops open to attack and soils highly vulnerable to deterioration.

Such reductionist agriculture turns chemical fertilizers and pesticides into necessities to cover for its built-in vulnerabilities. True food security is further undermined as production is made increasingly dependent on external sources of supply over which there is no local control. We are all exposed repeatedly to catchy corporate ads that attempt to scare us into believing that the corporate-marketed inputs are the only safeguards against hunger. Yet the increasing capital costs of this way of producing food exclude ever larger numbers of rural people abroad as well as in the United States from a livelihood and push the price of food beyond the means of those who most need it.

This system of agriculture has been in operation no more than twenty-five years in the industrial countries, yet it is being exported as the sure, indeed, the only, answer for the entire world. That is an incredibly risky proposition, however you look at it.

We have learned that real food security simply cannot be measured in production figures. It must be measured in how reliable, how resilient, and how self-contained the agricultural system is. On each of those counts the Green Revolution approach means less food security for us all.

PART VI

The Trade Trap

23

What About Their Natural Advantage?

Question: You have brought to light the food-producing potential of the underdeveloped countries. Yet there is another issue: Why is it necessary for these countries to grow all of their own food? Aren't certain regions better suited than others for growing particular crops? Underdeveloped countries cannot support themselves by exporting industrial goods. They just do not have the industry. It is only logical that these countries do what they can do best. If that turns out to be growing coffee, tea, or cocoa — why not let them exploit this natural advantage?

Our Response: The "natural advantage" argument does sound like common sense. But an apparently natural state of affairs may look that way simply because the economic forces molding our reality have been operating such a long time. When we enjoy a morning cup of coffee or snack on a chocolate candy bar, we assume that the sources of these treats are practically God-ordained. Americans have come to think of certain countries as regions of uniform climate, destined to grow coffee, cocoa, rubber, and banana trees to supply the rest of the world with such nonessential "essentials." (At least to many people that morning cup of coffee seems pretty essential.) We must begin, however, to erase the notion that there is anything "given" about the way the poor countries now use their land. Land use represents a choice by people, not by nature.

One of the most oppressive food myths is that many of these countries can grow only "tropical crops." In reality they can grow an incredible diversity of crops — grains, high-protein legumes, vegetables, and fruits. "Banana-republic" terminology has made it easy to forget that Latin America got along quite well without a single banana tree until the late 1830s. (The first banana did not arrive in the United States until 1866.) What United Brands, Standard Fruit (Dole), and Del Monte call "prime banana land" turns out to be first-class agricultural land — flat, deep soil, well-watered, suitable for a full range of food crops. In fact, when United Brands and Standard Fruit abandoned their larger banana plantations in Honduras' Rio Aguan valley (for "production consolidation reasons"), landless peasants settled in and grew corn, rice, and beans. When World War II restricted the coffee market, many coffee trees in Brazil were uprooted so that food crops could be planted on what was some of the country's best land.[1]

We repeat: There is nothing "natural" about the underdeveloped countries' concentration on a few, largely nonnutritious crops. And, as we shall see, there's no "advantage" either.

Most underdeveloped countries now depend for 50 to 90 percent of their export earnings on only one or two crops. Bananas in the period 1970—1972 accounted for 58 percent of the total export earnings of Panama, 48 percent of Honduras, and 31 percent of Somalia's.[2] Coffee has become crucially important for eleven countries that depend on it for 25 percent or more of their foreign earnings. In 1972, coffee brought in 53 percent of Colombia's foreign exchange; 78 percent of Burundi's; 50 percent of Rwanda's; 50 percent of Ethiopia's; and 61 percent of Uganda's.[3]

Concentration on a limited number of crops creates the vulnerability that is the hallmark of the economic and political position of underdeveloped countries. Vulnerability means an inability to control one's own destiny. Is there a more apt definition of underdevelopment itself?

In addition to the vulnerability to market changes inherent in being dependent on very few crops, there is the larger question of the overall decline in the value of the agricultural commodities most underdeveloped countries export. In fact, the total loss of foreign exchange earnings to Africa due to falling prices, particularly in agricultural products, in the two decades following World War II *exceeded* all foreign funds invested, loaned, or granted to Africa during the same period.[4]

Bananas, the most important fresh fruit in international trade, serve as a good illustration of what this means. The price of bananas has fallen about 30 percent in the last twenty years while the price of manufactured goods has gone up. In 1960, three tons of bananas could buy a tractor. In 1970, that same tractor costs the equivalent of eleven tons of bananas.[5] (It is quite a treadmill if you have run almost four times as fast just to stay in the same place!)

A Roller Coaster Ride to Development?

But as much as the declining export income hurts the economies of underdeveloped countries, fluctuations in price are the real nemesis of economic planning. The high prices of one year can lure economic planners and farmers into continued reliance on a given crop, even to expand production. Wild price swings then wreak havoc with long-term development plans. Not only can prices fluctuate sharply from year to year but from week to week and even from day to day.

The colonizing powers chose those crops, you will recall from Part III, that did not require frequent planting. That was all well and good for the colonizer who wanted to minimize dependence on labor. But for those former colonies that now have their entire economies locked into coffee, palm oil, or bananas, the results can be disastrous. A coffee tree takes five years to mature; palm oil trees require three to four years. Likewise, you can't just go in and out of banana production in response to price changes, as an American farmer might with wheat and oats. A banana tree does not reach its full potential until two years after planting and even then the payoff, if any, comes over its next five to twenty years of yields. With cocoa trees you have to sit tight for a decade or more before your first harvest.

What happens then if you are encouraged by high current prices to rush into new coffee planting? By the time your first harvest of such crops is ready you might find the bottom has dropped out of the market. And it probably will have, since producers in your country and others will also have planted to meet the demand at the same time you did. The likely result is overproduction once the new trees begin to bear more than the consumers are willing to buy even with a drop in price. (Remember a ten cent drop in the retail price that General Foods charges you for Maxwell House is likely to represent a far greater price drop

for the grower. And still, you probably won't drink more coffee.)
There have been several coffee busts. In the Depression coffee
prices fell by 80 percent. The Brazilian government tried unsuc-
cessfully to bolster prices by burning 80 million bags (weighing
132 lbs. each!), or the equivalent of two years' total world consumption.[6]

Speculative activities are a major cause of extreme fluctuations
in price. Take the case of cocoa. Most of the raw cocoa exported
(about four fifths of the total production is exported raw) is sold
through dealers and specialized firms in New York, London,
Paris, Amsterdam, and Hamburg on the basis of prices determined by bids and offers on the cocoa futures markets. What
causes price swings on the cocoa futures market? Perhaps a meeting of cocoa producers has been called. That alone might be taken
as bullish by the hard-core cocoa traders, thus inflating cocoa
prices for a period as short as a day or as long as a month.[7]
Rumors of a political change in the government of a major cocoa
producer or a single report of some obscure cocoa pest can have
the same instantaneous effect.

The point is that the range of price fluctuations due, say, to
weather-caused variations in supply, are greatly magnified by a
small number of people who usually have nothing to do with
growing the crop. Their "business" is gambling. Their interest is
in an actively fluctuating fast-changing market, since by playing
it correctly one can make money whether prices go up or down. As
an official of the Chicago Board of Trade told an agribusiness
executives seminar in 1975, "Stability, gentlemen, is the only
thing we can't deal with." Unlike fluctuations in stock market
quotes that have no impact on the earnings of the corporations
traded, speculation on the futures market directly hits the producers' earnings and the *predictability* of earnings.

Speculation also introduces an element of uncertainty that in
itself can dampen sales prospects for producers. For instance,
manufacturers of candy bars seek to reduce their profit risks by
reducing the use of ingredients that fluctuate widely in price. A
speculative commodity like cocoa is likely to be used less and less
and to be eventually replaced by a more reliable synthetic substitute. If you flip through the advertisements of such publications
as *Food Engineering* and *Food Technology*, you will discover that
companies like Monsanto Chemical are already bragging to

candy manufacturers that their chemical chocolate — Monodoad — is better than the real thing.

"All Your Eggs in Two Baskets"

What can a national planner in Ghana do given that over half of his country's arable land is now planted with cocoa trees? In the late 1950s when cocoa prices were high, Ghana decided to double its production. Development plans were drawn that counted on the increased foreign exchange earnings. But, as the prices that Ghana had to pay for its imports rose steadily, the price it could get for cocoa seesawed. Up to about $1000 per ton one year and down to less than $400 another; up to $1000 again and down to less than $600 later.[8] The overall decline from the mid-fifties peak has been estimated at 80 percent.[9] You can imagine what became of Ghana's development scheme. Income from sisal has been no more reliable. Tanzania's first five-year plan anticipated a minimum world sisal price of 90 pounds. Soon after, the price dropped to 60 pounds. In late 1976, Cuba announced that the sudden collapse of sugar prices (from 64 cents to 6 cents a pound in eighteen months) would make it necessary to revamp its five-year development plan.

Several years ago the government of Malaysia, in one of the most ambitious settlement schemes ever undertaken in Asia, transformed hundreds of thousands of acres of jungle into new settlements growing oil palm and rubber for export. It seemed to work. The settlers were able to improve their homes, buy some consumer items, and even save for their children's education. Then, in 1974, the entire picture changed. Recession in the industrial countries sent the price of rubber and palm oil plummeting. With no alternative crop to rely on, settlers' incomes also dropped sharply. Today none of the newly cleared land is being settled. A member of the Malaysian parliament observed that: "All our land-development eggs have been put in two baskets — rubber and palm oil. There is no diversification, we grow too little of our own food. Everything is for cash, and when the world prices that we do not control drop, it is our people who suffer."[10]

In addition to the vulnerability built into reliance on slow-maturing crops with highly unstable prices, the choice of crops handed down by the original colonizers contains another limitation. Many are commodities that appear to be reaching the saturation point among consumers. No matter how affluent the consumers or how low the prices drop, consumers seem to eat or drink only so much of products like cocoa, coffee, and bananas.

The "Rewards" of Export Agriculture

So what has export agriculture done for the underdeveloped countries?

Over half of the 40 countries on the United Nations list of those most seriously affected by the food crisis of the 1970s depend on agricultural exports for at least 80 percent of their export earnings.[11] That alone should tell us something.

The revenue from their agricultural exports has simply not kept pace with the cost of their mounting food imports from the industrial countries — in grain alone, up now to over 50 million tons a year. Ironically, the prices of the crops sold predominantly by the industrial countries, crops like grains and soybeans, have risen much faster than the prices of the commodities exported by the underdeveloped countries. The *agricultural* export earnings of the industrial countries have, therefore, increased more than twice as fast as those of the underdeveloped countries. The share of the underdeveloped countries in world agricultural trade revenue dropped from 40 percent in 1961–1963 to 30 percent in 1970–1972.[12] Moreover, two thirds of the benefits of the most recent increases in prices of agricultural exports accrued to the industrial countries.[13] It is they, not the underdeveloped countries, that have definitely won the battle for agricultural export revenue.

The reward for relying on agricultural trade as the main stimulus for growth has meant no growth. Almost half of the people in the underdeveloped countries experienced no increase in per capita income in the last four years. Of course this average really means that a few have gained while the majority are worse off than they were four years ago.

Why shouldn't the underdeveloped countries exploit their "natural advantage" in producing a few tropical crops? We have had to conclude that there is nothing natural about it and there is no advantage in it. We have learned that the development of export agriculture was not natural, that it was built on crops deliberately chosen by colonizing interests. And we have seen how the prices for colonial inheritance crops have declined, in some cases absolutely, and in every case relative to the industrial products they buy abroad; how price swings make development planning a nightmare; and how saturation of the consumer market in industrial countries makes the long and winding road a dead end.

What was originally designed as a system to transfer wealth out of subjugated countries is still promoted by many as the only road to development for those very same countries. Oddly enough, most observers do not see or do not wish to see a contradiction. To us, the contradiction is undeniable. Today export agriculture, dominating the economies of underdeveloped countries, serves foreign interests in the same way it has for hundreds of years. As such, how could it ever be thought of as the basis for self-determined development?

24

Don't the Rich Countries Need Their Products?

Question: But don't the industrial countries *need* the tropical products from the underdeveloped countries that they are unable to grow themselves? Doesn't this give the underdeveloped countries a strong bargaining position?

Our Response: While agricultural exports of underdeveloped countries come to assume life and death importance for their economies, their exports are of secondary significance to the industrial countries. Thus, the industrial countries can afford to take a "ho-hum" attitude toward any effort by the underdeveloped countries to get higher prices for their commodities. A price increase always runs the risk of an informal but devastating consumption cutback. Americans responded to the coffee price hike in 1954 with a permanent change in their coffee drinking habits. They began to stretch a pound of coffee in order to make sixty cups in contrast to the previous forty.

In the few cases in which the imported commodity is critical to the economy of the industrial countries, such as rubber or jute, the industrial countries can develop substitutes. Indeed, the industrial countries spend at least $1 billion a year to do just that.[1] Natural rubber, jute, and hard fibers are the most vulnerable. Synthetic substitutes for coffee, tea, cocoa, and spices already exist. Can the artificial banana ("guaranteed not to rot") be far off?

All in all, the bargaining position of the underdeveloped countries is hardly airtight.

The Myth of Free Trade

Through tariffs and quotas on imports, on the one hand, and subsidization of their own agricultural products, on the other, industrial countries can always prevent underdeveloped countries from realizing any comparative advantage they might have. Since the Kennedy Round of trade negotiations in the 1960s, the average duty on imports from underdeveloped countries has been twice that on imports from all countries together.

In addition, duties of the industrial countries on imports increase according to the degree the product has been processed; thus duties on finished products (like chocolate bars) are five times higher than duties on raw materials (like cocoa beans). Half-processed items (like cocoa powder) fall somewhere in between.[2] Japan typically levies no duty on cocoa beans, 30 percent on cocoa powder, and 35 percent on chocolate. Such tariff laws have effectively dampened the underdeveloped countries' possibilities of (and even interest in) graduating from the export of raw commodities to export of processed products. Since much of the potential for profit and for developing an integrated, self-sufficient economy lies in the processing of raw materials, this is certainly a serious handicap.

In the mid-sixties, the Brazilian government decided to promote the creation of an instant coffee industry (not necessarily to be owned by Brazilian firms and, when possible, marketed in the United States through an American firm such as Hills Brothers Coffee). Since Brazil-processed coffee was price competitive, in less than two years it captured 14 percent of the United States market. United States coffee processors, led by the giant General Foods, retaliated by getting the State Department to put pressure on Brazil to tax its own processed coffee exports to such an extent that they would no longer be competitive with Brazilian coffee processed in the United States.

The most direct tactic industrial countries use to limit imports is simply to levy import quotas. Quotas work in several ways. The importing country can say, in effect, it will import such and such a commodity from any country until a certain level has been reached. Then, no more. It is easy to imagine the discouraging and disruptive effect this system must have on countries that never know, even after they have invested in production for export, if the product will be allowed to enter foreign markets. In 1975, the outcry of California and Texas growers against the wholesale import of strawberries and vegetables from Mexico prompted United States authorities to turn back millions of pounds, many of which were subsequently dumped.

Then there is the allotment of a quota to each exporting country, based on their past export levels. Newcomers clearly lose out. And motivation to improve production methods is stifled.[3]

The threat of the imposition of quotas by the industrial countries continually hangs over the heads of would-be Third World suppliers. Since the demise in 1974 of the U.S. sugar-quota system, policy makers in several underdeveloped countries (Senegal and the Sudan, in particular) have expanded their sugar production, eager to take advantage of their competitive position in the new open ballgame. But what will happen to these countries if the United States Congress, responding to pressures from American farmers, decides again to slap on a highly restrictive import quota? They could simply be left holding the (sugar) bag.

But quotas and tariffs are only part of the story of how the industrial countries keep out products from the poor countries. Sometimes small changes in an industrial country's regulations governing a domestic industry can completely undermine an underdeveloped country's exports. Cotton bales in the United States used to be bundled up with those brown, heavy-fibered covers with the cotton popping through, as you will probably recall from old movies of plantations and riverboats. These coverings had been made almost exclusively from jute, the major (and almost only) export of Bangladesh. The adoption of net-weight trading regulations in 1971, however, created an incentive for the industry to find less expensive, lighter-weight coverings.[4] Synthetic covers have now entered the market and are being sold even below cost by chemical companies trying to capture the market and drive jute out for good.

Of course, those in power in the underdeveloped countries have not stood by placidly as the industrial countries impose tariffs and quotas. They have actively lobbied for "preference schemes," that is, trading rules that would give them preferential entry over other exporters. With great reluctance (the United States being the most reluctant) these schemes have been introduced by a number of Western countries. It should come as no surprise, however, that the products granted preferential treatment are those in which the industrial countries already enjoy such a substantial lead in terms of price, quality, design, marketing channels, and know-how and not the agricultural commodities that are the exports of the underdeveloped countries. The reduction of tariffs will not, therefore, shift the balance much, if at all.[5] Any items that might have posed a real threat became "exceptions" to the preferential treatment. When after years of delay the United States decided to join the preference system, it reserved for itself the right to exclude several items thereby making the concessionary value of the scheme almost a joke. The 1974 Trade Act excludes textiles, footwear, steel, watches, as well as any items subject to "import relief" (threatening a domestic industry) or national security rulings (like petroleum).[6]

The industrial countries have written into preference schemes clauses that allow them to suspend the tariff reductions if the imports begin to "endanger domestic jobs" (read reduce sales and profits of domestic corporations). In addition, United States trade law specifies that whenever a country's exports of an item during one calendar year exceeds a value of $25 million or 50 percent of total United States imports of that item, preferential treatment will be suspended for that item.[7] What all this means is that the industrial countries are *not* about to hand over on a platter called "preference schemes" the advantages that they have built up and guarded over centuries.

We have brought out the multifaceted vulnerability of the underdeveloped countries in international trade only to make one point: Even if export agriculture were a sound development base (and we believe that it is not), it could never work because of powerful discriminatory forces originating in the industrial countries.

25

Don't They Have Cartels Now?

Question: Aren't some underdeveloped countries organizing producer associations, a polite term for cartels, to get a better price for their products? What is stopping the banana producers, the cocoa producers, and the tea producers from forming their own little "OPECs"?

Our Response: First of all, bananas are not oil. People in the industrial countries can get along much more easily without bananas, cocoa, and tea than they can without oil. Furthermore, most producing countries are pitted against each other for a share in stagnating markets dominated by a few buyers. Angola competes with Brazil for the coffee market. (This is a direct colonial inheritance. In the mid-twenties and again immediately after World War II, Britain, France, and Portugal encouraged the cultivation of coffee in their African colonies in a direct effort to break Brazil's dominance.) Ghana tries to stay on top of Cameroon in selling cocoa. Bangladesh desperately seeks an edge over India's jute. Jute from India and Bangladesh compete with kenaf from Thailand.

The industrial countries can also keep producing countries divided by punishing those who join producer associations. The United States inserted into its Trade Act of 1974 a clause denying trade preferences to any country that joined a producer's association for any commodity.

The Corporate Cartel

Most important, however, the governments of producing countries have been pre-empted: How can an underdeveloped country hope to organize an effective producers' cartel when the corporate cartels are already in charge? We hope that in our response to Question 23 we did not leave you with the impression that the price gyrations of agricultural commodities are just a matter of bad harvests, political unrest, and speculation. When a few corporations control the access to markets, there is very little to prevent them from manipulating the market to maximize profits, forcing prices down to buy up cheap from producers and then up so as to unload at a nice profit.

Cocoa serves as a good illustration of the contrast between the fortunes of the producing countries and those of the multinational corporate cartels that really control the production and marketing of most commodities. Cocoa processing, dominated by a small number of large firms in the industrial countries, remains one of the most profitable industries in the world. In 1967 the gross profit margin earned in chocolate production was 38 percent above the average margin for comparable food processing industries.[1] But how profitable is it for the producing countries?

According to a Ghanaian journal, in 1970-1971 Ghana lost $50 million because of manipulation of the cocoa market by the world's few large cocoa houses. One multinational corporation, Gill and Duffus, controls 40 percent of world cocoa trade. They manufacture chocolate, hedge and speculate in the cocoa futures market, and publish the *Cocoa Market News*. As the journal observes, "there are no checks and balances which can prevent Gill and Duffus from manipulating the market to maximize its profits.[2]

Palm oil is a similar story. We heard about a producers' entente for palm oil and looked into it to see how it might help underdeveloped countries that export palm oil. We discovered that the producers' entente was, in effect, none other than Unilever, one of the first corporations profiting on tropical agriculture. Unilever now controls 80 percent of the international oil seed market. The producers' entente has six members, but Zaire-Palm, an arm of Unilever in Zaire, exports over 80 percent of the group's total. We learned, too, that when the world market price for palm oil dips, the local government and the peasant producers suffer, not Unilever. The company simply "slows down their activities when the price goes down and appeals to the State for multiple exemptions."[3] Unilever thus buffers itself from the vagaries of the international palm oil market. A nice arrangement — for Unilever.

Coffee is not as tightly controlled as palm oil — yet. But Nestlé and General Foods already together control 30 to 40 percent of the world coffee trade.[4] Tight control over supplies gives corporations like General Foods, Nestlé, Coca-Cola, and Proctor and Gamble who process and market coffee a twofold method for increasing profits: lowering the return to the producers in the underdeveloped countries while increasing the price charged to consumers in the industrial countries. Take the price trends for Brazilian coffee in the 1960s. In 1968 American companies paid 30 percent less for Brazilian coffee than in 1964. But the coffee drinker in America paid more — 13 percent more. The processors and distributors thus increased their cut by 43 percent! During this same period the return to the Brazilian producers was sliced in half.[5]

The governments of the industrial countries cash in, too. As the Latin American writer Eduardo Galeano complains, coffee "puts more wealth into European state coffers than it leaves in the hands of the producing countries." In 1960 and 1961, the total import taxes on Latin American coffee netted the European Common Market $100 million more than the supplier countries received.[6]

Bananas exemplify the same points. A United Nations investigative report on how the final retail banana dollar is divided up concluded that the producing countries get only an average of 11 cents out of every dollar we pay for bananas. Thus from the retail sale of a box of bananas in the United States at $5.93, the producers in Honduras would get a gross return of roughly 66 cents. The chain supermarkets, controlling 99.8 percent of retail banana sales in the United States, gross approximately $1.90 on the same box.[7] No one has yet calculated what minute fraction of the price we pay goes to the plantation workers who labor to grow the bananas.

Like the cocoa industry, the $2 billion plus banana industry is dominated by a few giant corporations — in this case really only three — United Brands (formerly United Fruit, with 35 percent of the world market), Castle and Cook (Dole, with 25 percent), and Del Monte (a newcomer, with 10 percent).[8] We can appreciate the significance of this degree of corporate market power by looking at what happened when the banana-producing countries attempted to hold onto a larger share of the revenue earned from their products.

In 1974, the governments of five banana-producing countries organized for joint action and formed the Union of Banana Exporting Countries (UBEC). They decided on a uniform increase in export taxes on every box of bananas leaving their countries. But the corporations' market control made it easy for them to fight the tax. One corporation simply refused to export bananas; 145,000 boxes of bananas were lost. The corporation was large enough to absorb this loss. (Food-producing countries, unlike the OPEC countries, cannot opt to sit on their product for a while. Bananas have a lifespan of only twenty-one days from the time of cutting to the retail shelf.) After Hurricane Fiji in 1974, Castle and Cook threatened not to replant their banana plantations if the export tax was not lowered. United Brands tried bribery. They admittedly offered Honduran officials $1.25 million to lower the tax. It worked. The bribe succeeded in getting the tax of 50 cents a box cut to 25 cents. Thus an outlay of $1.25 million saved United Brands $7.5 million in taxes. At this writing, only three of the five members of the banana producers' association have succeeded in levying any tax at all (ranging from 25 cents to 40 cents per box).[9]

The victors in the "banana war" were clearly not the five members of the banana producers' association but United Brands, Castle and Cook, and Del Monte. In 1973, these corporations were making a profit of 20 cents on each box of bananas. But when the producers put on the tax and the corporations retaliated by cutting back purchases, the world price of bananas increased by 40 percent. The corporations were able to blame that "awful Third World cartel" for the price increase, while pocketing a profit of nearly 70 cents per box — more than three times their earlier profit. As *Newsweek* commented, "all of which goes to prove that sometimes organizing a cartel is just plain bananas!"[10]

Thus whether a producer's association will raise the export revenues of the participating countries hangs in serious doubt. In addition to the nonessential nature of the commodities, there is the competition among the producing countries. How do you get full cooperation among all producers when the one producer who refuses to join the association will attract all the buyers? For a country desperate for foreign exchange, staying outside the association may just be too great a temptation. For example,

Ecuador, producing about 30 percent of all bananas exported from Latin America, has refused to join the banana association.

*   *   *

Banana trees are like money trees. I wish we had more of them.

Alfred Eames, Jr., Chairman, Del Monte Corporation,
Forbes, December 15, 1970

26

Doesn't Export Income Help the Hungry?

Question: Although the problems are indeed great, doesn't the income that underdeveloped countries receive from their agricultural exports ultimately help the hungry?

Our Response: On the contrary, some researchers have found that often when a country's earnings from export agriculture decrease, the well-being of the majority of the people in that country increases. Andre Gunder Frank, a well-known student of the process of underdevelopment in Latin America, writes:

> When commercial agriculture's good times decline, as they did during the 1930s, this brings along a period of "good times" for subsistence agriculture. Thus, during that decade the trend toward land concentration was temporarily reversed as large owners sold off parts of their holdings to increase their liquid capital. In such circumstances, tenants are better able to enforce their demands for land and for permission to raise subsistence crops; and the "non-commercial" sector in general grows. But when the demand for one or more commercial crops expands, small owners begin to find themselves squeezed and bought out.[1]

A slight increase in income, if any, that peasant farmers in underdeveloped countries might acquire from a rising world price for their commodity has to be weighed against the increased threat of displacement by land-grabbing commercial farmers or corporations that see the higher prices as new grounds for profit.

The peasant producers or laborers have little to gain from increased export earnings of their country, partly because so little of the export price reaches them to begin with. Typically, in

Guatemala, where 75 percent of all children under the age of five are underfed, migrant workers on the coffee plantations earn approximately $1 a day.[2] Like many other commodities, coffee boomed in 1973. Brazil's earnings shot up to $1,343,048,000. How much of that went to the actual worker on a typical coffee estate? About $58 a month. (Yet in "coffeeland" itself it takes $1.66 to buy a single pound of roasted coffee.) In 1975, Sri Lanka's tea exports amounted to $860 million and were produced by 650,000 workers on recently nationalized plantations. The maximum a male worker could earn was $14 a month; a woman, $11.40.[3]

In Mali, peasants are contracted to grow peanuts by a French multinational firm. They contribute the land and their labor and yet receive only the same amount per pound of peanuts as the profit per pound made by the corporation that merely sells the peanuts abroad.[4] The same pattern exists for peasants growing peanuts in Senegal. One Senegalese official reported that the net profit to the state exceeds the total amount the state cooperatives pay to the producers of peanuts.

Increases in the world price for a commodity may not translate into an increase in the price paid to peasant producers. A recent United Nations report on the "least developed countries" notes that while international coffee prices have advanced 58 percent from 1968 to 1973, producer prices in Rwanda have remained fixed.[5]

In fact, an increase in the world price for a commodity might actually mean less income for the plantation worker or the peasant producer. When the world price for peanuts went up in 1968–1969, the Senegalese government's price to farmers actually fell.[6] In the Ivory Coast the pattern is the same: between 1960 and 1971 the export price rose 11 percent while the price paid to producers dropped 6 percent.[7] When the price of sugar on the world market increased several fold a few years ago, the real wage of a cane cutter in the Dominican Republic fell to less than it was 10 years earlier; even more significantly, it was not enough to buy an adequate amount of food.

Government policy makers everywhere push for greater production whenever the world price for an exported commodity goes up. What at first surprised us, however, is that some government marketing boards in Africa do so by paying peasant producers *less* for each unit produced. The reasoning is that the peasants will then have to produce even more just to maintain their incomes at the same level.

Thus we have to erase from our minds the automatic connection between a poor country's rising export income and an improvement in the welfare of the majority of its people. We have found, moreover, that export crop production often directly undermines the local food supply. Not only does it monopolize the best land, but the demands of export crop production can interfere with the cultivation of food.

In Kenya, for instance, much effort was put into the production of a more productive variety of cotton. The seed strain finally developed was more productive but unfortunately less hardy. Food crops could no longer be planted in the same field with cotton, as was the tradition; the new cotton could not take the competition. So while cotton exports have gone up, we wonder what has been the impact on the diets of the people. In Upper Volta's drier regions the planting season is short. Where farmers are obliged by the government to grow a certain acreage of cotton, they have to find a crop that can be planted later but can still be squeezed into the planting season. Sorghum and millet, the traditional food crops, just cannot fit this schedule; but cassava, a much less nutritious food, will. Low-nutrition cassava is also taking the place of more nutritious food crops in Tanzania because of the need for labor in tobacco production during certain seasons; cassava requires less labor than other food crops.[8] Agricultural economist Ingrid Palmer has also noted an alarming increase in per capita cassava output in Latin America.[9]

World Bank rural economist Uma Lele writes of the substantial substitution of food crops with cash crops such as cotton, tea, and tobacco in Kenya and Tanzania. In one decade the acreage per family planted in tea increased more than two and a half times in Kenya. In Tanzania cotton acreage per family increased fivefold. Government resources allocated to developing agricultural extension techniques and incentive systems for cash crops have rarely been transferred to the production of traditional food crops. And the drop in food production in the cash-crop areas of these countries has not been matched by expansion elsewhere of food crops.[10]

In an effort to make Brazil a leading soybean exporter, soya production there has massively displaced the cultivation of black beans, the traditional staple of the people. By October 1976, stores serving Rio de Janeiro's poor simply ran out of black beans. In desperation the poor rioted, only to be suppressed by the police. Scarce black beans were available only on the black market. To buy one pound, however, would require a half day's labor at the minimum wage.[11] Doubly tragic is that now Brazil has begun to import black beans from Chile, where the government is also willing to sacrifice the nutritional well-being of the local people in order to earn foreign exchange.

As governments have put the pursuit of foreign exchange above the interest of the masses, more and more peasants have been forced into the position of having to sell cash crops, often highly nutritious, to obtain the money to buy empty calories just to keep their families alive. As one writer summed up the tragic reality of so many underdeveloped countries, "the small farmer sells the nitrogen, phosphorus, potassium and trace minerals from his soil in the form of tobacco or cotton and in return buys polished rice or noodles from the little . . . store down the road, thus selling the life-blood of his soil to buy starch and carbohydrates."[12]

Finally, giving priority to cash cropping means that a farming family's very survival through the year depends on the cash received only once or twice a year at harvest time. But such lump sum payments turn peasants into open targets for predatory merchants peddling gadgets and costly packaged foods. Diversified food cropping is the only guarantee of year-round food security for the rural family. In self-reliant China it is said that when peasants step outside their front door they see from where their next meal is coming.

Hungry people cannot eat that which is exported. Nor are they likely to eat from export earnings or benefit from the so-called development achieved through these export earnings. People will escape from hunger only when policies are pursued that allow them to grow food and to eat the food they grow.

27

If It's So Bad, Why Does It Continue?

Question: You have documented the devastating impact on the Third World of a heavy dependence on export agriculture. But if it has been as bad as you say, the underdeveloped countries would certainly not have continued along this path. Why haven't they realized the trap they are in?

Our Response: The pervasive use of shorthand terms like "Third World," "poor world," "hungry world," makes us think of uniformly hungry masses in which all the people are equally affected by poverty and malnutrition — all with equal interest in eliminating hunger. It just is not so.

The fixation on export agriculture continues simply because, while harmful to most, it is highly advantageous to a few. The first beneficiaries are large producers and plantation owners. In Guatemala, for instance, the large coffee growers and merchants have formed a National Coffee Association to which anyone producing more than 40 bags of coffee per year is required to belong. This private organization (which nevertheless receives public funds) provides technical assistance and assigns quotas to producers. Since these services and decisions are in the hands of the large growers, the smallholders are almost completely shut out.[1]

The second group to benefit is the small class of better-off urban dwellers because much of the foreign exchange earned ultimately gets spent on their food and consumer "needs." Zaire is a typical case. There, export agriculture has led to the decline of food production to such an extent that 30 percent of Zaire's foreign exchange now goes to buy imported foodstuffs. The staple foods of the people are in very short supply, but imported meat is still available for those who can pay. It comes from South Africa for the Zaire elite.[2] The Dominican Republic is another case in point. In 1974, the very year that the world price of its export commodity, sugar, soared 400 percent, the Dominican Republic came close to a trade deficit because export earnings from sugar were squandered on luxury import items for the small urban elite.

Finally, export agriculture benefits those associated with the multinational corporations in their country and government officials who get paid for managing the export system.

By rewarding these elite groups, a small fraction of the entire population, export agriculture compounds the inequalities in wealth and well-being. A recent report from the United Nations confirms that

> Gains from foreign trade . . . and particularly from sharply increased export prices frequently tend to be concentrated among upper income groups to a much greater extent than is income from domestic production.[3]

Tending the Goose

If a government becomes convinced that export earnings are the sine qua non of development, export industries, whether domestic or foreign, appear as the salvation of the country. As political economist Cheryl Payer points out, the government will certainly refrain from "killing the goose that lays the golden eggs" and will tend the goose with a great deal of care.[4] But looking at their country with the interests of the goose in mind is hardly the same as keeping the interests of the people foremost; for what export agriculture most needs is cheap and docile labor and the control over large tracts of land with no requirement to invest in their conservation.

The myth that export agriculture is the *only* path to development makes it possible for plantation owners, multinational corporations, and state marketing boards in underdeveloped countries to claim that they must keep wages of agricultural laborers low so that their products can compete in the international market. In 1973 the disclosure by British television of the appalling living conditions of Sri Lanka's tea estate workers met with protests from the government and the foreign estate owners (including Lipton's, the Unilever subsidiary, which markets over

50 percent of the tea sold in the United States). Improving the living conditions of the 650,000 workers and increasing their meager wages ranging from 36 to 48 cents a day would, they claimed, price Sri Lanka tea out of the market.[5]

Making similar excuses, governments have excluded large landowners from land-reform schemes. They argue that dividing up the large, cash-crop–producing estates would endanger the country's trade and monetary position. In the Philippines, for example, any land growing export crops, including over seven million acres with such crops as sugar and coconut, was exempted from land-reform legislation.[6] Government officials who make such decisions are themselves, of course, often large landowners.

Export Crops Expand

Given that multinational agribusiness and local elites benefit by the continuation of a focus on export agriculture and that export agriculture continues to be reinforced by international lending agencies, it is not surprising that export crop production is growing at a much faster rate than food crop production.

From the mid-fifties to the mid-sixties, the growth rate of export crops was 2.2 times faster than the total agricultural growth rate in the underdeveloped countries. In specific countries this trend was even more marked. From 1940 to 1962, Mexico's production of cotton and coffee grew almost three times faster than the production of rice and corn.[7] Coffee production in Africa has increased more than fourfold in the last twenty years, tea production sixfold, sugar cane production has trebled, while cocoa and cotton production have doubled.[8] Between 1952 and 1967, the cotton acreage in Nicaragua increased fourfold while the area in basic grains was cut in half.[9]

Elite-controlled governments have encouraged this trend. In Colombia in 1965, 90 percent of all agricultural credit went to cash crops — coffee, cotton, and sugar.[10] As we found in the Sahel, many governments continue to use the techniques of past colonial regimes to enforce the production of cash crops. In East Java the government requires that as much as 30 percent of the land grow sugar cane.[11] Even in countries like Tanzania that have directed a large proportion of their resources to rural development and have talked of self-reliance, colonial laws have been reactivated specifying minimum acreages for export crops. The rhetoric of many development planners about diversification of agriculture becomes in reality diversification among export crops.[12]

"Hooked" on Exports

Once set out along the export agriculture path, it does indeed *appear* next to impossible to get off. In *Diet for a Small Planet*, I, Frances, likened the "export crop trap" to drug addiction. It seemed to me the only apt analogy. Once "hooked," it is terribly painful to get off. But at that time I did not understand the role that debt plays in maintaining this addiction, both for the individual farmer and for the nation.[13] Farmers growing export crops might want to compensate for sharply reduced income from falling crop prices by shifting to food crops for their families, but if they have gone into debt to obtain the inputs to grow export crops, they may no longer have that choice. They may be obliged to earn a cash income to repay their debts or face the possibility of losing their lands to a creditor.

Similarly, on a national level, when an underdeveloped country receives "aid" from abroad, even if the borrowed money does help to increase the country's production capacity, the debt cannot be paid back until the country has exported enough to earn the needed foreign exchange. Pesos and rupees do not help. Most so-called aid has to be repaid in the same currency in which it was given. The country is likely to be on a treadmill. If exports are not sufficient to acquire the needed foreign currency to pay back debts and to pay for necessary imports, the only immediate solution appears to be to seek yet another loan. This, of course, means only a greater push for export crops to pay back an even greater debt!

What we must remember is that this pattern continues not because the governments of the underdeveloped countries do not *understand* the nature of their trap. It continues because, as we have seen, export agriculture serves the interests of the elite landholding and consumer groups in underdeveloped countries and the interests of multinational agribusiness and international lending agencies like the World Bank.

Thus, promoting trade justice must not lend credence to the idea that export agriculture can be the foundation for development. To do so would be to equate the country's balance of payments and its economic growth with the welfare of the people. Until fundamental restructuring occurs within the underdeveloped nations, higher prices and better export deals for their commodities are likely to work against the interests of the poor majority.

28

Isolationism or Self-Reliance?

Question: You seem to be saying that underdeveloped countries are faced with a choice between continued dependence and isolationism. Isn't isolationism always a step backward?

Our Response: We are not talking about isolationism. What we are saying is that constructive interdependence can only come from a position of strength and security. Basic food self-reliance is the sine qua non of that security; without it, "interdependence" becomes a smokescreen for food control of one country by another. One example will explain more fully what we mean.

The history of Cuba during the last twenty years, particularly in contrast to a country such as the Dominican Republic, reveals that, once the basic food needs of the people are being met, trade need not work against the welfare of the majority. At the beginning of the Cuban Revolution, the revulsion against the elite-controlled sugar economy was so strong that not only were food crops promoted but sugar production was actively neglected. In time, however, the Cuban people learned that they could produce food for local consumption and still earn considerable foreign exchange by exporting sugar.

In 1969, the National Agrarian Reform Institute developed a decentralization policy that combined intensive cultivation of export crops alongside local production of varied food staples for local self-sufficiency. In other words, one area might concentrate on sugar cane, citrus fruits, or livestock with the farmers cooperating according to an overall national plan that they help formulate. This local specialization increased production and marketing efficiency. But next to these areas of commercial crops were farms growing vegetables and other foods for local consumption.[1]

As a result of such policies, advances in local food production in Cuba continue. During the period 1971–1975 nonsugar agricultural production increased by 38 percent. In the same period vegetable production for the local population more than doubled and fruit production increased by over 60 percent. Egg production amounts to 1.7 billion, over six times that in 1958. Poultry production has increased four times since 1963. Pork production is threefold the 1963 figure and sugar cane waste products and food wastes have been increasingly used in feeding pigs.[2]

Cuba today remains by far the world's largest exporter of sugar. Yet sugar exports from Cuba do not work against the food well-being of the people.

In Cuba little malnutrition remains, as evidenced by the rapid decline in infant death rates associated with poor nutrition during the last decade. Between 1971 and 1974, food consumption increased 20 percent. Moreover, there has been virtually no increase in food prices in the last ten years.[3]

When thinking of food-dependent and impoverished people, one supposes that, at best, feeding everyone instead of only the elite minority would require using every single acre for local food consumption. The last twenty years of Cuban history have proved that this need not be true. Even though over 40 percent of all cropland under public control in Cuba grows sugar,[4] dramatic food production increases are produced to ensure a nutritious diet for every Cuban.

How different is the fate of the people of the Dominican Republic whose food well-being is sacrificed to the country's "sugarization." A rapidly expanding amount of land is planted with sugar to enhance the profits of such multinational conglomerates as Gulf and Western, while food production per person declines sharply.

Additional contrasts can be drawn as to the effects of sugar exports on the welfare of the people of these two countries. They illustrate that, once basic food security is achieved, neither sugar nor trade need be the "enemy." Trade by whom and for whom are the real questions. First, the foreign exchange earnings from exports of sugar play a very different role in the economy of a nation like Cuba than in the Dominican Republic. In Cuba, the earnings from sugar exports help import a broad range of goods for productive, job-producing industries. In the Dominican Republic foreign exchange earnings are squandered on luxury imports, as we noted earlier, or wasted on such investment projects as Gulf and Western's resort enclave.

A second contrast can be drawn on the question of the employment impact of sugar. The Dominican Republic suffers from a 30 to 40 percent unemployment rate. Seventy-five percent of all farmers have less than 135 workdays a year.[5] In addition, Dominican workers' interests are further jeopardized by the sugar growers' importation of Haitian laborers, who now make up over half of the cane-cutting work force. The intensive seasonal labor demand of sugar cane (which spoils if not cut and milled within a short period of time) has created high population densities in cane monoculture areas and yet few year-round jobs.

With mechanization of cane harvesting, unemployment in the Dominican Republic deepens still further. Mechanization of the Cuban sugar harvest, expected to be a reality for the entire crop by 1985, will not mean unemployment, as we pointed out earlier, instead farm mechanization in Cuba releases human labor from the backbreaking job of cane cutting for guaranteed jobs in other vital areas of the economy.

Finally, Cuba's sugar exports are within an altogether different trading framework than the Dominican Republic's. Cuba's sugar production is no longer controlled by private corporations. Thus planning for the welfare of the country as a whole is possible. The greater part of Cuban sugar exports is now handled through inter-governmental economic agreements, with both socialist and capitalist countries.

Thus when sugar prices slump, as they did in mid-1976, Cuba's development plans were adversely affected but the basic welfare of the people has not been jeopardized. No one in Cuba will starve because the bottom dropped out of the world market. The Cuban people do not plan to make the mistake of relying on this export income to import food needed for the basic well-being of the people. The major food imports by Cuba today are rice, milk products, and wheat — and local production of the first two items is increasing dramatically.[6]

Perhaps Cuba is successful at using agricultural exports to earn income for development in part because it has avoided extrcmc price swings due to an assured market for its sugar in the Soviet Union and Eastern European countries. Other underdeveloped countries may not be in a similar position and thus might need to become even less dependent on trade than Cuba to provide for local needs. Cuba, therefore, may not be a model that is totally applicable. But the central point remains: The impact of export agriculture depends on whether or not food for local consumption has been made the first priority and whether the export income earned contributes to a better life for all. Neither of these conditions has been met in any of the countries in which people are hungry today.

PART VII

The Myth of Food Power

29

Don't They Need Our Food?

Question: You have made a good case for why the development efforts of the poor countries should not hinge on export crops. But doesn't the United States have the best soils and the best climate in the world for growing grain? We are one of the very few countries in the world with a surplus to export. Shouldn't we export it to the world's hungry? Our unique endowment gives us a special obligation.

Our Response: Perhaps my first real surprise when I, Frances, began the research that eventually led to *Diet for a Small Planet* was the discovery that America's role in world food trade was not to feed the hungry but to sell to the rich.

The idea that the United States is the world's breadbasket is so deeply ingrained that we think of America solely as an exporter. The usual impression from the news media is that the United States exports large volumes of food under aid programs. But there are three gaping holes in this national self-image:

- First, what food we *do* export on an aid basis (that is, with long-term, low-interest financing) is only a tiny fraction of our commercial exports (6 percent in 1975).
- Second, over 56 percent of our agricultural exports go to the industrial countries, not to the underdeveloped.
- Third, although it is true we are the world's leading food exporter, we are also one of the world's top food importers.

We have found these facts amazingly hard to keep in mind. Everything one hears or reads seems to give exactly the opposite impression.

In the fiscal year 1975, the top four recipients of our agricultural exports were Japan, the Netherlands, West Germany, and Canada. Contrast our exports to these countries with our exports to the underdeveloped countries listed by the United Nations as "most seriously affected" (MSA) by the food and oil price increases of the seventies.[1] The United States exported no agricultural products to nine of the forty MSA nations in either 1973 or 1974. Thirty-six of the forty MSA's export food and other agricultural products to us, including three that receive no agricultural exports from the United States.

To give you some idea of how little our trade has to do with feeding people in need, here is another example. In both 1973 and 1974, United States agricultural exports to Canada, itself a grain exporter, were greater in value than to all the MSA countries combined or to the entire continent of Africa. In fact, in 1973, such exports to Canada were almost twice as large as those to Africa. Our agricultural exports during the drought years 1973 and 1974 to four African Sahel nations — Mauritania, Mali, Niger, and Chad — were less than half (in terms of value) of those to *either* Sweden or Norway or Denmark.

When we consider the per capita quantities of our food going to poor countries versus those going to rich countries the picture detracts even more from our "country bountiful" image of America. In 1974, the United States exported 114.5 pounds of wheat per person to Japan but only 7.5 pounds per person to India. Per person, Pakistan received only 18 percent as much wheat from us as did the Netherlands.[2]

We tend to pay much more attention to our food exports than our imports. Contrary to popular notions, the industrial countries are the major food importers; not the underdeveloped countries. In 1974, the United States ranked third among the world's leading food importers, close behind Japan and West Germany. And over two thirds of our imports come from underdeveloped countries.[3]

While we think of America as the world's beef capital, the United States is in reality the world's leading beef importer. The United States imports over 40 percent of all beef in world trade. In 1973 the United States imported almost two billion pounds of meat. Often it is stressed that this is but a small amount since it represents only about 7 percent of our own production. The amount, however, is hardly small in relation to the needs of most other countries. It also means that a considerable portion of the food-producing resources in several countries with many hungry people go into producing beef for Americans. In international trade more meat flows from underdeveloped to industrial countries than the other way around.[4]

The United States is the world's principal importer of food from the sea. With only 6 percent of the world's population, the United States imported more than one quarter of the fish and one third of the shellfish in world trade.[5] In addition, the United States is a net importer of milk products.[6]

The next time you hear or read an article in which the author talks about how much the hungry "depend on" our exports and how we are the "breadbasket" of the world, recall some of these facts.

Who are the *real* food donors? They are many of the world's hungriest people.

30

Food Power to Save the Economy?

Question: You have said that the United States uses its food exports to make money and not to be charitable. That is certainly true. But isn't it absolutely necessary? Our oil import bill is so high because of the outrageous prices imposed upon us by OPEC (the Organization of Petroleum Exporting Countries) that we must rely on food to balance our international payments. Since we have to export *something* in order to pay for the oil we need, isn't food our best bet? The days of cheap food in America may be over, but in the long run, might it not be in our best interest?

Our Response: This question suggests that our ability to pay for oil imports depends on increasing our food exports. Indeed, we Americans are being made to believe that not only our monetary strength but also our diplomatic strength and even our moral persuasiveness hinge on our new-found Food Power.

We are told by an official of USDA that food exports are necessary to pay for "the imported petroleum and other goods we must import to maintain our standard of living."[1] We were told by President Ford that "our agricultural abundance helped open the door to 800 million people on the mainland of China. . . . It helped improve relations with the Soviets. It helped to build bridges to the developing world."[2]

We are told that our food will not only alleviate hunger but will even turn hungry people toward democracy. The past president of the Colorado Cattle Feeders Association hopes that by our improving diets abroad "nations will change their political feelings and move away from Communism to a more democratic form of government."[3] All in all, we are made to believe Food Power saves! The message is clear: For all these rewards we should be willing to tighten our belts.

The question expresses the feelings of many Americans who are willing to do just that: to make the best of an unavoidable situation. It disturbs us that the genuine good will of most Americans is being manipulated so that they do not see that the food export strategy of the seventies was not a necessary development but a promotion of certain interests at the expense of most of us.

Just what are the underlying reasons behind the American Food Power strategy in the seventies?

For many Americans the concept of Food Power was born during the 1974 World Food Conference in Rome during which many delegates and observers accused Earl Butz, then Secretary of Agriculture, of playing politics with the lives of the starving. Butz himself declared that food is "one of the principal tools in our negotiating kit."[4] In reality, however, it was several years before the Food Conference that high government officials worked out a United States Food Power strategy.

The Origins of Food Power: The Payments Crisis

By the late sixties, administration officials had decided that something had to be done about the nation's balance of payments deficits. To most Americans the balance of payments has no understandable link with their everyday well-being — certainly no connection with the price of food or the fate of the family farmer. The balance of payments is something bureaucrats have to worry about, not ordinary people. Yet, in researching this book, we have been forced to learn the fundamental truth that the less ordinary citizens make themselves aware of an area of government policy making, the more manipulation goes on for narrow, even personal, gain and the more often the majority of Americans pay the costs.

What is the balance of payments problem and what caused it? How *does* it relate to the question about the need for food exports?

The meaning of a balance of payments deficit is really no great mystery. Quite simply, a country has a deficit, an unfavorable balance, when more money goes out than comes in. The balancing up takes into account government, corporate, and even individual transactions.

For years the United States government had been spending billions upon billions as the standing military force of the anti-socialist world. Vietnam alone cost the United States well over a half trillion dollars. In addition, United States-based corporations, beginning in the late fifties and throughout the sixties, made large capital investments in Western Europe and to a lesser extent in Latin America and Asia. The outflow was so great by 1965 that President Johnson decreed a Voluntary Capital Export Restraint Act that after a year of dismal ineffectiveness became the Mandatory Capital Export Restraint Act. Subsequent government studies, however, showed that even mandatory controls were ineffectual in the face of the sophisticated accounting and financial techniques of the multinational corporations. Moreover, federal tax laws encouraged these corporations to keep their considerable earnings outside the United States since profits were not taxable until actually repatriated, that is, returned to the United States.

Many multinational corporations exacerbated the negative balance of trade. Their "runaway plants" turned cheap-labor, low-tax countries like Mexico, Taiwan, and Singapore into "platforms" for exporting back to the United States consumer goods such as transistors, television sets, cameras, and textiles. Ironically, then, the United States was sending dollars abroad to import products made by U.S.-based corporations. In the late 1960s many European and Japanese firms also went global and began exporting to the United States, often from low-tax, low-wage plants side by side with competing subsidiaries of American multinational corporations. By 1970, therefore, the United States was importing an alarming $5.5 billion more in manufactured goods than it exported.[5] U.S.-based multinational corporations accounted for 42 percent of all imports, often "buying" from their own overseas subsidiaries.[6]

United States corporations had also become increasingly dependent on foreign sources of critical raw materials. The United States was importing more than 90 percent of eight basic raw materials. By 1970, the trade deficit in raw materials was $3.4 billion.[7]

In 1971, as a result of all these capital drains, the United States experienced the first balance of payments deficit in the private sector (corporations and individuals) in a century. Thus, it was well *before* the price of imported oil increased that the balance of payments crisis developed.

The Myth of Oil Dependency

Most Americans have been made to believe that oil is the root of our international economic problems. We have accepted the idea that we have become dependent on imported oil because the United States is running out of domestic sources; in fact, such an idea does not fit the facts at all. In his *Poverty of Power*, Barry Commoner argues that after 1957, United States oil companies made less and less effort to look for domestic oil. Commoner notes that "exploratory expenditures per barrel of oil produced fell by some 25 percent in the next ten years."[8] According to a mammoth study by the American Association of Petroleum Geologists (with funds from the industry's National Petroleum Council), "none of the 11 regions [in the U.S.] has been adequately explored."[9] This study concludes that the United States has about 320 billion barrels yet to be discovered — *three* times more than has already been consumed.

It was not, therefore, that the United States started to run out of oil but that the oil companies had concentrated their efforts in countries where profits looked even better. Between 1956 and 1974, the profitability of foreign oil almost doubled while the profitability of domestic oil remained about the same.[10] A Chase Manhattan Bank study of the early sixties computed the cost of producing a barrel of Middle East oil at 16 cents, as compared with $1.73 a barrel for United States oil.[11] Thus, while imported oil covered only 14 percent of domestic demand in 1954, by November of 1974 it had jumped to 40 percent.[12]

Commoner concludes that the United States has sufficient untapped oil reserves to get through a gradual transition period until we have developed renewable energy sources, such as solar radiation (No matter how big the reserves, fossil fuel is a *finite* resource.) The problem has been, not the lack of energy resources, but the lack of a national political will that could have countered the narrow profit-seeking of a few oil corporations, making us increasingly dependent on foreign and finite oil. With this historical context in mind, it becomes hard to accept the simplistic Food Power rationale that it is the lack of domestic energy resources that necessitates food exports to pay for imported oil.

The Birth of Food Power

By the late 1960s, the United States had approached the international equivalent of having its credit cards recalled. In the two decades following World War II, countries everywhere accepted dollars as if they were gold, in part because the United States claimed it could always redeem them for gold. This arrangement proved handy for underwriting United States military operations overseas, promoting exports of American goods, and U.S. corporate purchases of foreign companies. But by the late sixties, other countries began to get uneasy about honoring dollars, as it was less certain whether they could always be converted. Foreign countries, furthermore, began to react to the takeover of their key industries by United States corporations using the power of good-as-gold dollars. Foreign treasuries, therefore, started demanding gold instead of paper in settling balance of payments deficits. American gold reserves began to shrink. By 1970, United States reserves had been reduced to less than one half of what they were in 1950. How could the United States shift its balance of payments into the black?

One way would have been to cut drastically the outflows of money from the country, as we discussed above. It could be done but not without going against the most powerful vested interests in the country — not a course of action President Nixon would consider. He knew that he had to balance United States international payments *without* reducing U.S. military expenditures abroad, *without* limiting the free control of capital by multinational corporations, and *without* confronting the corporations that were making the country ever more import-dependent.

For the Nixon administration, then, the only possible question was: What exports from the United States could be stepped up in a really major way to compensate for the mounting import bill? In 1970, Nixon appointed a commission composed of corporation executives and their lawyers to come up with an answer. This Commission on International Trade and Investment Policy, now known as the Williams Commission, concluded that there were only two trade categories that could earn the huge sums of foreign exchange needed to balance United States payments: high technology products and agricultural commodities.

One type of high technology thought easy to push abroad was armaments. The Vietnam War had produced new "generations" of arms and every country just *had* to acquire the latest. American military attachés and corporate hustlers around the world doubled their efforts (and often their bribes) to compete with French and British armaments manufacturers. Vast credits were extended to underdeveloped countries. All went "well"; soon annual sales reached the multibillions. By 1975, armament sales were contributing $4.8 billion to the balance of payments. Moreover, boosting arms sales had no awkward domestic repercussions for the administration.

But the second recommendation of the Williams Commission — boosting agricultural exports — was another matter. How could American farmers and consumers be made to go along with a plan to vastly increase agricultural exports?

It was then that the broad outline of a Food Power strategy was concocted. Food Power would have to be "sold" to the American people as an absolute necessity. A lot of questions had to be dealt with. Just how do you get other countries to import enough American food to balance all the import expenditures that the United States was not willing to reduce? Equally crucial, how do you push up prices so that every bushel sold will do the most to help the United States balance of payments? And how do you accomplish this in countries that want to protect the livelihood of their own farmers?

It was not easy. The Nixon administration, however, thought that there was one gameplan that just might work: First, tempt potential buyers by making their initial purchases of grain cheap and by providing ample financing. Then, persuade other countries to lower their protection against U.S. grain exports by offering, under the banner of free trade, to abolish domestic price supports for American farm products. To ensure that prices go up, direct the secretary of agriculture to order cutbacks in United States crop acreage; then the final touch needed to raise grain prices would be bad weather in the major grain-producing countries. The Nixon-Butz gameplan was conceived heedless of the fact that it was tampering with the livelihood of millions and the lives of millions more — people for whom food is not a balance of payments problem but a balance of survival problem.

Now let us look at the steps by which the Food Power strategy was actually implemented. Keep in mind that the first goal was to make exports as attractive as possible. Devaluing the dollar would make United States products less costly to foreign buyers. And devalue is what Nixon did: first 11 percent in December 1971 and then a further 6 percent in early 1973. (Underdeveloped countries that had been encouraged to hold their reserves in dollars and to fix their currency to dollar values, lost hundreds of millions overnight.)

A second way to make United States commodities more attractive would be simply to offer convenient financing, and that is what Nixon and Butz did. In July 1972, the United States announced a $750 million credit through the government's Commodity Credit Corporation to help the Soviets purchase our grain. Nixon had already courted the Soviets by rescinding the requirement that at least half of any grain sold to the Soviet Union or any Eastern European country be carried in American flag ships. And the Soviets were ready to buy. Although their grain production, somewhat exceeding that of the United States, was sufficient for direct consumption, many Soviet citizens clamored for more meat in their diets. Producing it quickly would require more livestock feed. Kremlin domestic strategists decided that 19 million tons of cheap United States grain on such fine terms was the solution. Bad weather, which cut their harvest by a third, further convinced them.

The next step was to get prices to shoot up. The quickest way was simply to cut production back. Butz ordered another five million acres of wheat lands taken out of production in September 1972. This put the total acreage kept out of production at 62 million, an amount equal in size to all the cultivated land in Great Britain. With the Soviets buying, the dollar devalued, and acute weather problems worldwide, this acreage cutback was enough to guarantee shortages, depleted reserves, and higher prices for any additional foreign sales.

Food Power and the "Free" Market

Still one question remained for the Nixon administration: How to make the strategy stick? The Williams Commission had concluded that the only way would be to negotiate a "free trade" policy that would open up protected European and Japanese markets to American farm products. The free trade doctrine thus became the strong arm of Food Power. You cannot, the commission said, have one without the other. It was left to Peter Flanigan, Nixon's assistant for International Economic Affairs, to spell out the specifics of a free trade strategy to put Food Power into high gear. In 1972, he requested that the Department of Agriculture develop a strategy for the upcoming international trade negotiations. The resulting "Flanigan Report" was leaked to Congress, despite the administration's efforts to suppress it.

The Flanigan Report was clear on one point: the United States could best increase agricultural exports by capitalizing on its "comparative advantage" in grain and livestock feed. That in turn could best be accomplished under free market or laissez faire conditions. This meant that government-financed minimum price supports, acreage allotments, and other programs to regulate farm income and productive capacity would have to be dropped. The administration calculated it was a good moment to get previously reluctant farmers to support just such a move: The Soviet grain purchase had significantly reduced world grain reserves and weather conditions in many areas of the world were poor; it all added up to a very bullish market for U.S. farm products.

It was easy, therefore, to pursuade Congress that the agricultural support programs were unnecessary. The 1973 farm bill virtually ended payments for land held out of production; established such low target prices (i.e., the market price below which the government would step in to help the farmer) as to be meaningless in protecting the small farmer; and, in effect, abolished government-held grain reserves. After the previous cutbacks designed to create scarcity prices, farmers were now being told to "plant it all" on the assurance that the government would arrange an ever-climbing foreign demand. This bill meant that the United States government was releasing its agriculture — a significant part of the world food economy — to the speculative market where a small change in supply, indeed even a threat of such change, can set off huge price swings.

Drumming Up Customers

Between fiscal years 1970 and 1974, the quantity of American wheat exports increased about 90 percent while the *value* increased almost 400 percent![13] The pattern was almost as striking for feedgrains. But what would happen if widespread good harvests increased the worldwide availability of grain? To keep prices up, it was necessary to find some new customers.

In 1974, the Foreign Agricultural Service (FAS) spent over $10 million developing markets for American exports. In a recent issue of its periodical, *Foreign Agriculture*, FAS was conspicuously proud to explain how it is furthering an "aggressive foreign market development" to beat out the "stiff competition" in the race for increased agricultural exports.[14] An arm of the USDA, FAS is also the leading wedge for agribusiness penetration into the markets of other countries. FAS's "cooperation" with food export industries falls into three categories called "market intelligence," "trade servicing," and "product promotion."

If an American corporation wants to know whether it would be profitable to enter a certain market, it turns to its friend in FAS — one of the 96 U.S. agricultural attachés or officers in foreign countries — who jumps into action. First: Does the product meet the foreign government's import entry requirements? Second: Is it acceptable to local tastes? (Call in the "professional taste panel"!) If the company's product makes it past steps one and two, FAS helps sponsor a market test. In addition, FAS sponsors exhibits around the world for the benefit of U.S. producers. One favorite exhibit is a lifelike reproduction of an American supermarket.

FAS has sponsored a beef campaign in Japan, noting that it is "aimed at better-class hotels and restaurants catering to the tourist trade."[15] Its efforts there have also helped to account for the success of fast-food outlets like McDonald's — 90 percent of whose ingredients are imported. Although American-style fast-food outlets only began operating in Japan in 1970, FAS predicts that by 1979 these chains will have taken 70 percent of all such sales, displacing the traditional rice, fish, and noodle bars.[16]

FAS helped sponsor a "Wash Your Hands with Soap" campaign in Japan to promote the sales of United States tallow, a by-product of livestock production. Part of the promotion was a "magic fountain" — basically a giant basin of soapy bubbles in a Japanese department store. Since the United States exports 44 percent of all the wheat in world trade, FAS also helps sponsor schools to teach people how to cook with wheat in areas of the world where wheat is not a traditional food.

Our Food Power strategy thus rests, not on shipping our food to a world of hungry people, but on molding the tastes and habits of a certain class of people to make them dependent on products and styles that they had never wanted before. American policy makers are encouraging other countries to become more and more food dependent on the United States and the United States itself is becoming more and more economically dependent on food exports. Reading the FAS material, one would think that the survival of our nation rested on its success in creating one more hamburger lover in the world.

The question suggests that Food Power was born as the only possible response to the rising cost of oil imports and that it was a good response because United States could at the same time meet the real food needs of people overseas. But, the Food Power strategy predated the oil price increase and, as we demonstrated in our answer to Question 29, most American food exports do not go to the hungry. Furthermore, Food Power was not the *only* possible response but the choice of policy makers who wanted to protect the economic status quo. Food Power, you will recall, was born out of the need to pay for the military drain of the Vietnam War, the overseas expansion of American corporations importing cheap-labor manufactured goods back into the United States, growing corporate dependence on foreign raw materials, and United States petroleum corporations' decision to import massive quantities of oil.

Today Food Power continues as a way to buttress our balance of payments. Military expenditures are less of a foreign exchange drain now, in part because of increased arms sales abroad. But imports of consumer goods, largely by U.S. multinational corporations, continue as the single most important balance of payments drain after oil and industrial raw material imports. In 1973, the United States imported $9.5 billion in manufactured products from foreign plants owned by American corporations.[17] (This figure would be significantly higher, if we included other United States foreign investments with minority or licensing control.) In addition, the United States now spends over $10 billion for agricultural imports. Thus, while officials talk only of how our agricultural exports bring in over $20 billion in foreign exchange, close to half of every dollar gained in agricultural exports is spent on agricultural *imports*! Ironically, about two thirds of these agricultural imports are commodities that the United States can and does produce — meat, sugar, vegetable oil, vegetables, to-bacco, wine, and dairy products. Less than one-third are items — like coffee and bananas — the United States does not grow.[18]

Thus the notion that Food Power is necessary to save the economy from collapse and Americans from deprivation just does not hold up. Even assuming that we had to rely on imported oil (and we have documented the deliberately neglected potential for domestic energy self-sufficiency), a balance of payments deficit is not inevitable. Because of American multinational corporations' ability to run away to wherever labor and other resources are cheapest, the United States imports consumer and agricultural goods that could well be produced at home. The cost of these imports approaches what the United States pays for imported oil.

31

At Least Food Power Works?

Question: But Food Power at least *works* in earning foreign exchange: $22 billion in agricultural export earnings exceeds even the Flanigan Report's expectations. Won't we expect the high earnings from our agricultural exports to continue?

Our Response: In judging whether Food Power can work, even by the narrow measure of sustained high levels of export income, we must ask: Can the United States continue to underprice and outsell other countries that have cheaper land and labor costs, especially when U.S.-based corporations can profit by promoting exports from the very countries competing with U.S. domestic producers?

Take soybeans, the central pinion of the structure of the Flanigan strategy. It is true that the United States does have an excellent climate for growing soybeans. But as the USDA's Clayton Yeutter himself pointed out, while the analogy between the Food Power of the United States and the Oil Power of the Middle East is often drawn, there is a big difference. "Food is not oil," declared Yeutter. "The market is noncompetitive on fuel and competitive on food."[1] This applies to soybeans as well as to grain exports on which the United States export strategy is based.

Forbes has called soybeans our "chief trump card." Dwayne Andreas, Chairman of Archer Daniels Midland, the largest soybean-processing firm, is even more adamant: "The soybean will be the saviour of the dollar." *Forbes* went on to point out that there were no trade barriers to soybeans in any country in the world. "If we had 200 million bushels more, we could sell every one of them. That alone would make a $1 billion dent in our payments deficit."[2] Soybeans became America's second cash crop after wheat. The administration was so insistent on the future of the United States as a soybean producer that in 1973 it was paying farmers in the Corn Belt 15 cents a bushel just to plant soybeans on land that might have grown corn.[3]

Such optimistic projections came in 1973 and 1974. By 1975, the picture looked a little different. Suddenly the soybean business was no longer a seller's market. In 1975, exports of soybean meal for livestock feed were down a million tons from 1974. The reasons are clear: poor profit margins for livestock producers in inflation-ridden Western Europe dampened United States sales there, and competition from foreign producers increased. It turns out, too, that our unique climatic advantage is not so unique. The long summer days in southern Brazil are just what soybeans thrive on. A few years ago Brazil's share of world soybean exports was only 1 percent. By 1975, Brazil had captured 30 percent of the world market, to become the world's third ranking soybean exporter. A coffee frost that killed many coffee trees only accelerated Brazil's movement into soybeans.

Ironically, among the greatest promoters of Brazil's soybean success are United States corporations. They are investing in Brazilian soybean production and processing for the very same customers to whom the United States has been selling. Anderson Clayton is doubling its current soybean processing capacity in Brazil. Cargill and Central Soya are also involved, and the agricultural loan office of the Chase Manhattan told us the bank couldn't invest enough.

And who would have thought that Paraguay would compete with U.S. soybean exports? It probably would not, without the help of United States corporations. The Florida Peach Corporation of America has put $12 million into a soya-processing plant there as only the first phase of a huge agribusiness complex. Gulf and Western has just purchased over 100 thousand acres of land in Paraguay to begin soy production.[4] In 1971, the Overseas Private Investment Corporation (OPIC), which is a quasi-official government agency, approached Cargill, the giant American grain corporation, to encourage it to take out a loan for a new soybean-crushing plant in Brazil. The next year they concluded a loan for $2.5 million.[5] Our balance of payments may be a problem for administration officials and for the citizens who will pay for both the cause and the "cure," but it is hardly a problem for United States–based multinational corporations. Profit seeking knows no national loyalties.

Those with such great expectations for soybean exports have also overlooked another problem. Currently the soybean has two major uses. The high protein meal pressed from the bean is used in feeding livestock, while its oil is used in cooking and manufacturing. The market for soybean oil, however, appears to be in even greater trouble than that for soybean meal. The trouble? Palm oil. As the headline in the March, 1976 issue of *Successful Farming* puts it: "THE WORLD PALM OIL BOOM: SCARE STORY THAT'S SHOCKING THE PANTS OFF AMERICAN SOYBEAN FARMERS."

An acre planted with palm oil trees can produce as much as seven to eight acres of soybeans. Now that's competition. The palm oil threat packs a one-two punch. First, by cutting into the market for U.S. soybean oil, palm oil will depress the prices American soybean growers get for their oil. Then, with lower returns from soybean oil, farmers will plant fewer soybeans. Because fewer soybeans will be grown in the United States, the price of the soybean *meal* will go up, making it less competitive with peanut and fish meals for livestock feed. Moreover, the price of livestock products will be forced up because of higher soybean meal prices.

As a result of all this competition, only a year after soybeans were called the American trump card to save the dollar, production in the United States dropped 19 percent. Thus in assessing the potential for Food Power on its own terms we would have to conclude that even in what the United States does best —growing soybeans — it might still get crowded out of the market.

So far, USDA officials refuse to limit palm oil imports, their allegiances being to the principle of free trade. This position, as we will soon document, puts the supposed protectors of American farming on the side of large farmers and multinational corporations, not on the side of the average American farmer.

The Backlash

Some high officials at USDA have publicly questioned the Flanigan strategy on other grounds. Two are Don Paarlberg, former chief economist for the Department of Agriculture, and his assistant, Patrick O'Brien. "Using food as a tool requires an extremely tight demand situation," says O'Brien. "If you happen to be sitting on a large supply in one short year, you're in good shape." But in the long run, he fears, high prices run the risks of creating a backlash as countries decide to grow their own. "You encourage every little producer to step up and do his duty." As examples, he cites Thailand's effort to increase its own production of corn and sorghum.[6]

What O'Brien implies to be the almost irrational response of "every little producer" is, of course, quite a realistic assessment by countries that do not want to make their survival dependent on a nation that has shown itself to be so ruthlessly willing to use food exports to serve its domestic interests and to grant political favors. Even European countries such as France are thinking twice now before becoming more dependent on American food imports.

Thus the Food Power strategy, aside from being unnecessary, is a risky operation; other countries, often with the help of U.S. corporations, can effectively compete with the United States, and more and more countries are perceiving that guaranteeing their own food supply is the basis for security. Yet there is an even greater risk.

The Long-Run Cost of Food Power

The view that, "well, at least Food Power works" is worse than shortsighted if it ignores the cost to America's agricultural base. What do we mean? Simply that reports now coming in from this country's richest agricultural states show that the pressure for "fence-to-fence" planting is leading to rapid soil deterioration that may be virtually irretrievable. The problem is manifold. The intense pressure to increase production has brought more easily eroded soils into production, has decreased or eliminated fallow periods that regenerate the soil, and has led to the continuous planting of corn or other row crops that expose the soil to erosion, as opposed to crops such as hay that make the soil more erosion resistant.

According to a Soil Conservation Service official in Iowa, that state is now losing an average of ten tons of top soil per acre each year. Expressed another way, on much of the sloping land in

Iowa, a farmer is losing two bushels of top soil for every one bushel of corn he produces! At this rate, all of the top soil in Iowa will be gone within less than a century.[7]

Moreover, now that Food Power has made agriculture the latest speculative industry, new irrigation technology is spreading to marginal soils. Former Nebraska pasturelands are being made into highly productive irrigated corn fields. But for how long and at what price? These are questions Nebraskans are asking about the rapid spread of center-pivot irrigation,[8] a method of tapping underground water, requiring a $60,000 investment but very little labor. Today there are 10,000 such units in Nebraska, over one-third owned by outside and even foreign investors. The farmers working the land often become mere sharecroppers, receiving only one fourth of their crop. In addition to the obvious shift in control of the land that accompanies such a capital-intensive investment as center-pivot irrigation, there is the question of the life of the soil itself. Center-pivot irrigation makes possible the irrigation and therefore the cultivation of sandy, marginal soils not possible with other types of irrigation. But sandy soils are erosion-prone and leach soil nutrients into the ground, causing pollution of waterways. Moreover, center-pivot irrigation, a push-button sprinkler system of two rotating pipes, each one-quarter mile long, cannot accommodate trees. The trees must go. And indeed they do. Precious "shelterbelts," rows of trees planted by conservation-conscious farmers years ago, are now being pulled up to make way for the center pivots.

The center-pivot system, in widespread use only for the last ten years has been associated with a ten-foot drop in the underground water table. The University of Nebraska has concluded that since water is being taken out of the ground faster than it is being naturally replenished, "groundwater mining is in progress." How long, then, will be the lifetime of center-pivot irrigation in Nebraska?

In 1973, state investigators in Montana reported another serious threat, exacerbated by the Food Power plant-it-all push. In Montana, North Dakota, South Dakota, and the Prairie provinces of Canada much land that has always served only as *grazing* land is now being planted every other year in grain. Even this moderate level of cultivation on these dry and vulnerable soils appears to have upset the soil's moisture balance. The result is that ground salts are being deposited on the soil surface, making it unusable for agriculture. Already by 1977, over 170,000 acres of land in Montana alone had been lost to saline seepage. And the investigators concluded that just in Montana 146 million acres may be threatened.[9] So what will be left of family-farm agriculture and of the top soil itself once the Food Power push for production at all costs has run its course? To say "at least Food Power works" might turn out to be the equivalent of claiming that a sane way to build an addition to your house is with bricks from the foundation.

32

Who Gains and Who Loses?

Question: Perhaps Food Power is not a necessity. Still, what is so evil in the current Food Power strategy? If we make money selling food to countries who want it, and if our farmers are helped, isn't the end result positive?

Our Response: If Food Power is so good, why, then, did Nixon, Flanigan, and Butz try to keep the Flanigan Report out of the hands of Congress? Why did they even try to deny that it was their report? The real reason for keeping the Food Power strategy under wraps was that its "free-market-all-the-way" prescription amounted to an invigorating tonic for larger farmers and for the big grain-exporting corporations — at the expense of a lot of belt tightening by American consumers and foreclosure for thousands of family farms. Obviously the report did not spell things out in these words. But the implications for this country of so-called free market agriculture were clear enough.

The label "free trade" is insidiously misleading when applied to a system in which six giant grain-trading corporations control 85 percent of all United States grain trade. While the administration boosts an export-oriented agriculture in the name of family farmers, the exports are implemented not by farmers, not even by the national government, but by a handful of private corporations. Family farmers do not wine and dine Kremlin bureaucrats and sign whopping sales contracts in Moscow, Tokyo, Bonn, and Cairo. Farmers sell to the likes of Cargill, Cook Industries, and Continental Grain. In 1974, Cargill alone controlled 29 percent of wheat exported from the United States, 16 percent of corn, 18 percent of soybeans, 22 percent of sorghum, 42 percent of barley, and 32 percent of oats. In the process the balance of payments position of the United States Treasury *is* improved, but most of the profits end up with these few corporations and not on the family farm.

It is only the farmer who has been put on the "free market." The corporations have sources of information to judge how on or off target government production estimates will probably wind up. They can rely on their insider information from their former executives now in government posts and their own efforts to drum up foreign sales commitments. And about what they learn, they can even keep the government in the dark. Moreover, they have their own intelligence networks constantly assessing the agricultural prospects and likely food purchasing of other countries. According to *Business Week*, Continental Grains' worldwide intelligence network is so effective that agents of the CIA "often wine and dine the company's traders to pick their brains."[1]

The Soviet Grain Deal: A Case Study of an "Unfree Market"

Extreme cold combined with inadequate snow cover during the Soviet winter of 1971–1972 killed 25 million acres of wheat — or the equivalent of half the entire United States crop. The lack of snow also meant low soil moisture, making spring planting difficult. Harvests were bound to be poor just at a time when Soviet policy makers had begun developing grain-fed livestock herds in order to increase the availability of meat.

Enter Clarence D. Palmby, Butz's assistant secretary with responsibility for foreign trade. In early April 1972, Palmby headed an American trade delegation to the Soviet Union. (Before his departure Continental Grain offered him a vice-presidency in their Manhattan headquarters. Although Palmby now says that he turned down the offer, the fact is that before leaving for Moscow he purchased a $100,000 Manhattan apartment, using the name of Continental's president as a reference.)[2] The Soviets obviously wanted to talk about grain sales, but they found American credit terms unsatisfactory. They were still interested, however, and continued to discuss possibilities, according to Palmby's later testimony.

Back in Washington, one month later, Soviet representatives showed up at Palmby's office. They discussed credit terms, the possibility of a barter agreement, and whether they could purchase directly from the government. Palmby flatly turned down the government-to-government proposal.³ Whatever credit might be arranged with the government, he told the Soviets, the purchases would have to be made through the grain companies. In June, the Soviets found Palmby in his new office at just such a grain company, Continental Grain.

What did all this mean for the American wheat farmer? Despite many clear indications that the Soviets were in the market to buy in a big way and the indisputable evidence that bad weather nearly everywhere in the world meant there would be an exceptional demand for American grain, the USDA, contrary to law, did not inform the farmers. In May, the USDA publication *Wheat Situation* warned farmers there would be a big surplus even after all foreseeable sales. Thus, only a few American government officials and grain company executives were in the know.

By early June 1972, Continental Grain, Cargill, and the other four members of the grain export club rushed out to the early-harvest Southwest to buy up wheat. The farmers knew that harvests were going to be big and since they did not know about the strong foreign market prospects, they were happy to unload their wheat. They got about $1.25 a bushel. A few weeks later the same wheat would have brought $2.25 to the farmer. (In early 1973, wheat would be hard to get at $5 a bushel.)

By July 5, Clarence Palmby, Continental Grain's vice-president, helped the firm to conclude the biggest grain sale in history — three days before the official announcement of the $750 million loan to the U.S.S.R. that made the deal possible and that had been negotiated by Palmby while still a USDA employee. Still at USDA in May Palmby had even attended meetings between Continental and the Russians and surely knew a big sale was in the offing. But Palmby and his bosses at USDA had still neglected to inform the farmers, despite their legal mandate to do so.

It was not until mid-July that the USDA informed the farmers. By then in the Southwest and the early harvest areas of the Midwest, one quarter of all the wheat had already been sold.⁴ In Oklahoma alone, the withholding of information by the Department of Agriculture cost wheat farmers about $47 million. Butz's rationalization? "Farmers didn't lose money because of early sales, they just didn't make the additional money they might have made."⁵

The Soviets kept buying and the grain companies kept selling. While huge commitments were being made, the August USDA

Wheat Situation did inform farmers that the Soviets were buying but said that the likely total figure would be just half what Continental Grain alone had in fact *already* sold to the Soviets in early July. While the Soviets continued to buy wheat, Secretary Butz toured the country talking about *corn* sales.

In addition to extra profits made because uninformed farmers were willing to sell cheaply, the grain companies had yet another guarantee for unprecedented gain. In order to encourage exports the government at that time subsidized the exporting companies by making up the difference between the domestic price at which they bought the wheat and the lower price at which they sold it abroad. These subsidies went as high as 47 cents a bushel. (Clearly there was no need for such an additional customer incentive: the Soviets needed the grain for their livestock and no other country besides the United States had it to sell.) As domestic prices finally began to rise, the companies claimed ever larger subsidies even though some of the wheat they were then selling in fact had been purchased earlier at lower prices.

A subsequent Senate investigation discovered that a grain export corporation sometimes collected the subsidy on sales to its wholly owned foreign subsidiary. The investigation documented sales by Cargill to its subsidiary in Panama. This subsidiary then sold to another Cargill subsidiary in Europe, which then sold the wheat at an unknown but doubtlessly higher price to a second party. In this way, headquarters collected a multimillion dollar subsidy not considered taxable income while the profits rung up by the foreign subsidiaries were sheltered from taxation as long as they stayed abroad (and that despite this country's drive to improve its balance of payments!). These transactions were in fact all on paper; the wheat never left the ship on which it was originally loaded.

Over a mere seven weeks taxpayers handed the six grain-exporting companies $300 million in subsidies. Food Power could indeed be profitable for some.

By contrast, the subsidies to farmers moved in the opposite direction. In 1972 subsidies were still paid to farmers to make up the difference between "parity," a price level considered fair in relation to the cost of machinery and supplies a farmer must purchase, and the average market price over a five-month period. The catch, in 1972, was that the government figured the period to begin in July, when most farmers in the Southwest and some in the Midwest had already sold out. As news of the big grain deal spread, wheat prices rose, narrowing the difference between average market prices and parity, thus cutting into the subsidies for the farmer. The farmers' lost subsidies have been estimated at $55 million.

Cook Industries, on the other hand, increased its annual profits fifteenfold between 1972 and 1974. Cook is the only firm with publicly held stock and therefore the only one required to disclose its earnings. Dan Morgan of the *Washington Post* reports, however, that privately held firms like Cargill and Bunge have doubled or tripled their net worth since 1972, according to reliable trade sources.[6] The General Accounting Office found the big traders had profits on those hundred of millions of bushels ranging from 2 cents to 53 cents a bushel[7] whereas normally a profit of 1.6 cents per bushel is considered good.[8]

So "free trade" and an all-out export drive worked well for the grain companies. Characteristically, Butz added insult to the farmers' injury by claiming that grain companies won and the farmers lost out in the 1972 grain sales simply because the farmers "weren't smart enough to take advantage of the situation." Some trading companies did make big money in the deal, he conceded, "but that's the name of the game."[9]

Butz is right. Big money is the name of the game. Under free trade export companies are able to extend their control and increase their profits. During the winter of 1972–1973, three of the large grain export corporations, Cargill, Continental, and Cook, were able to corner 90 percent of the soybean harvest for $4.00 a bushel, sending soybean prices up to $10.00 a bushel only a few months later.[10] What free trade really does is free private multibillion dollar corporations to manipulate prices and supply to their advantage.

When we say "private" we mean very private — with no room for public scrutiny. Five of the six largest grain conglomerates are closely held, private firms owned by a few individuals or families. None publish any detailed financial information. When Dan Morgan wondered why grain trade lobbyists are hard to find in Washington, one former grain trade lobbyist explained it to him this way: the grain companies "don't need to have powerful lobbyists — for they have no regulation."[11]

American consumers finally discovered that their wheat had been exported when they went to the grocery store that winter. Meat prices especially shot up because feedgrain prices rose so fast that many farmers cut back on their cattle and hog-raising operations. The House Agriculture Committee concluded that higher food prices, directly attributable to the grain exports and the way they were handled, amounted to about $3 billion.

Free trade allows speculators to drive up prices out of all relation to actual supply. Speaking of food prices in 1973, Donald Paarlberg, then USDA's chief economist, said that his staff could account for only one half to two thirds of the sudden price rise. "The rest is psychological and speculative activity and these are not in our models," he explained.[12] How real is any model of the free market that does not include speculation?

Free Market and the Small Farmer

The USDA has invariably tried to sell us the idea of leaving American farmers to the workings of the free market as "getting the government off the farmer's back." What farmer would be against that? But, in fact, American farmers need some kind of controls to ensure against price declines caused by overproduction in relation to the ability of people to buy. As Jim Hightower, well known for his in-depth investigations of the problems of American farmers, explained, without control of production, "American farmers regularly have the capacity to produce themselves out of business."[13]

The Department of Agriculture admits that putting farmers on the free market means that they will experience "worldwide fluctuations" in demand and that their prices will "become more volatile."[14] But a family farmer cannot adjust to such fluctuation the way a corporation can. If market indicators look poor for General Motors, it simply lays off workers or even shuts down a plant. Given just the unpredictability of weather, a farmer's view of market prospects is hardly clear. But can the farmer simply lay himself off and not plant if prospects are poor?

Hightower recounts the not atypical story of how one department official, who never has to worry about his salary, paid by taxpayers, explained to some farmers the "new horizons" opened to them by United States Food Power:

In one breath, an assistant secretary of agriculture told a farm group that in the new order of things each farmer must respond to signals of demand from world markets, that only their own forward-thinking management would protect them from the "ups and downs" of the market place. In the very next breath, this public servant told farmers that markets were changing on a daily basis, with doors opening and closing so fast that "what might happen next, no one can tell." Good luck, and good-bye.[15]

Often the case is made that small farmers should be forced to face the music. If they do not survive in the free market, it means they were not efficient enough to make it; therefore, it is all for the best for the country as a whole. Earl Butz described those farmers who have gone under in recent years as being either "unwilling to change or not wanting to compete."[16]

Only there is one big hitch. What makes it possible for the big producers to survive has nothing to do with their efficiency. Large amounts of capital and diversified investments allow big producers to survive an unstable market. In fact, an unstable market can work to the great advantage of the large producer, ready to buy out the small farmer who has nothing to fall back on during market busts. (This is the same shake-out process we have seen follow the introduction of modern commercial farming in underdeveloped countries.) In the eyes of one American farmer, government willingness to abandon farmers, as if they were all equal, to a boom and bust market, is equivalent to an elephant in a chicken coop declaring, "O.K., fellows, every one for himself."

The Food Power alternative looked good to many farmers in 1973—1974. But by 1975, net farm income had already dropped 15 percent.[17] By the fall of 1976, the price of wheat on the futures market had dropped to $3.18 a bushel, or 24 percent *below* the break-even point for a farmer — and farmers do not receive the full price quoted on the futures market.[18] (Even at $3.50, a bushel of wheat that makes $24.50 worth of bread brings only $1.00 to the farmer.)[19]

In 1975 and 1976 farmers are relatively worse off than under any previous period back to and including the Depression. Farm income level is usually stated as a "parity" ratio. Parity measures the prices farmers get in relation to the costs of production. A parity of 100 percent implies a satisfactory return. In 1975, farmers received only 76 percent of parity; by November 1976, parity had dropped to 66 percent. Even during the decade of the 1930s farmers fared better. The average then was 78 percent.[20]

Who has gained, then? Within the farming sector, gains in earnings over the past several years have accrued almost entirely to large farm operators, while hundreds of small farmers have gone out of business each week. The nation's largest farms, representing only 4 percent of all farms, increased their average annual net farm income two and one-third times between 1971 and 1974, from $36,000 to over $84,000.[21] This top 4 percent had gained control of 46 percent of all farm-produce sales even as early as 1973.[22] But the majority of all farmers, those with sales of $20,000 or less, were able to increase their average net farm income only about 20 percent — from about $2000 in 1971 to less than $2500 in 1974.[23] Increases in the incomes of small-farm families have come only through off-farm jobs. This alone says a lot about the impact of the Food Power strategy.

Defenders of the administration's policy point out that although the prices farmers are now getting have dropped, they are still above what they got before 1972. What this defense neglects is that the *cost* of farming has gone up much more — and stayed up higher — than the prices farmers receive. A typical tractor costs twice what it did in 1971. The price of fertilizer has tripled. Worse still, when overproduction or slumps in domestic and now international demand lead to price drops, farmers' costs remain high. The few large corporations monopolizing the sales of farm equipment and supplies are able to raise their prices to protect their profits from increasing costs. Farmers are thus at the mercy of both the market and the corporations. In 1972, the Federal Trade Commission found that the lack of competition in the farm machinery industry had cost farmers an extra $251 million in overcharges.[24]

Farm debt is also an indicator of the vulnerability of the small farmer to a less predictable free market price. Total debt of farmers in the United States has now reached $93.6 billion. It increased 12 percent in 1975 alone and has more than *doubled* in only one decade.[25] By 1974, the debt of an average farmer was equivalent to almost three years' income, compared to nine months' income in 1950.[26]

Finally, most Americans think of their country as one of mostly small farmers who own their own land. But that view leaves out the fact that 22 percent of production is now controlled directly or indirectly by giant corporations. Just as important, it leaves out the large amount of rented land. In the United States 38 percent of all farmland is rented, almost 90 percent of it from nonfarm landlords.[27] Just as we saw in underdeveloped countries, this in itself means considerable insecurity; if farm prices fall while costs rise so that farmers cannot pay the rent, they are evicted.

USDA's View of the Future

The Department of Agriculture knows full well what the impact of free trade policies will be on the structure of rural America. In 1975, the department initiated a study of what would happen to American farms under various trade and government-support policies.[28] The study concluded that if the American farmer were left to the vagaries of the market with no income protection, America would lose over one and one-half million more farms by 1985! Of those farmers left, only 9 percent would be full owners of their land, compared with the one-third who are today. These projections of the inevitable results of a Food Power–free trade strategy were so embarrassing to the department that the office within USDA that carried out the study was summarily abolished.

The USDA obviously does not seek to prevent this increasing concentration of farm ownership. In the eyes of USDA, the decline of the small farmer is a fait accompli. Speculating on what American agriculture will look like in the future, USDA's Director of Agricultural Economics predicts a "highly coordinated industry of large farms very likely . . . operat[ing] in much the same fashion as nonfarm manufacturing industries."[29] Never mind that USDA has shown in its own studies that there are no economies of scale above the one-or two-operator farm[30] and that the greatest value per acre is produced on family-size farms.[31]

The USDA recently sponsored research on the feasibility of a 3600-head computerized dairy farm. Is this the USDA dream for future dairy farmers? It certainly could not be a dream for many of them. Today the nation's average dairy herd is about 100 head. To transform the dairy industry into operations of 3600 head would mean the demise of 300,000 dairy farmers.[32]

Former Assistant Secretary of Agriculture Robert Long has

made the following incredible defense of the department's policy of neglecting the small farmer. He claimed that if the department were to help the small farmer, production would increase. And if production increased, prices would go down — which would then hurt the small farmer.[33] One can only conclude that USDA wants a few large, capital-intensive farms controlling United States agriculture, which are certain *not* to increase production so that prices can stay up!

What Are We Losing?

Often supporters of family farms are viewed as romantics who are yearning for the good old days that never really existed. Is it just nostalgia that makes many want to revitalize small-farm America? To answer that question we must know: What is the difference between a rural America dominated by a few large-holders and corporations and a rural America dominated by family farmers?

In 1944 a remarkable piece of sociological work was done in California. A researcher with the USDA selected two towns, Arvin and Dinuba, similar in the dollar value of production yet different in the average farm size — one with a few large farms and the other with many small farms. The differences between these two communities can tell us a lot about the future of America if the present direction toward concentration of control is not reversed.

By every measure the quality of life in the small farm community turned out to be significantly richer than in the large farm community. The "quality of life," generally a vague term, was quantified by this study. For example, Dinuba, the small-farm community, supported:

- about 20 percent more people and at a higher level of income;
- a working population that was mostly self-employed in contrast to the large-farm community where less than 20 percent were self-employed (and nearly two-thirds were agricultural wage laborers);
- many more democratic decision-making organizations and much broader representation in them;
- better schools, parks, newspapers, civic groups, churches, and public services;

• twice the number of small businesses and 61 percent more retail business.

Researcher Walter Goldschmidt had intended to continue the study by comparing other farm communities. He never got the chance. The implications of this study were so "hot" for the Department of Agriculture that Goldschmidt was ordered to stop his investigations. In recent testimony before a Senate committee on land monopoly in California, Goldschmidt was asked to reflect on the changes in American agriculture over the thirty years since his study of small-farm Dinuba and large-farm Arvin. He stated: "The vision of the future under increased corporate control of the land is the vision of Arvins rather than Dinubas — indeed of super-Arvins."[34]

Food Power and the American Consumer

We have focused on the decline of the small farmer. Often Americans believe that the farmer's loss is the consumer's gain. The American consumer is faring no better than the small farmer.

When farm prices are high, the giant processors and export companies are able to pass the costs right on to the consumer. When farm prices drop, consumer prices are miraculously insulated and the food companies' profits inflate. It is not surprising, then, that in 1975 farmers earned a 4.7 percent return on equity, whereas food chains earned a 12.6 percent return and food processors a 24.6 percent return.[35] The Internal Revenue Service has found that grocery chains average 48 percent higher profits than all other retailers.[36]

Moreover, in a highly concentrated economy, recession accompanied by a drop in food purchases, may not trigger a fall in food prices, as college economics classes led us to believe it would. In fact, a study of the Joint Economic Committee of Congress has found the opposite to be true. When a few corporations control a whole sector, a drop in consumption can lead to an *increase* in prices by corporations seeking to make up for lost sales.[37]

The repeated assertion that the American family needs to spend on average a mere 16 percent of its budget on food would be laughable if the reality were not so serious. But even higher averages hide the burden most Americans face. The bottom half of all

Americans must spend significantly more. Those families with incomes in the middle (the mid-10 percent) spend at least 20 percent of their income on food while those on the lowest rung spend 69 percent of their income to buy food.[38] Never figured in are such hidden costs as the budget of the USDA and those of other tax-funded programs that subsidize food production.

So much for the view of America as a nation of people who do not properly appreciate their "cheap" food. We can conclude that this view is valid only for the top 10 percent income group; they spend only 10 percent of their income on food.

From January 1972, just as Food Power got into full swing, to October 1975, the Consumer Price Index for food rose 48 percent.[39] Between early 1972 and mid-1975 the total *increase* in the nation's food bill averaged out to almost $20 billion *each year*.[40] Yet a top USDA Official tells us, "The fact is that the nation could not have a more effective anti-inflation agricultural policy."[41]

Food Power versus Food First

Does it make sense to have a national policy that pushes food exports (largely destined to satisfy the increasing taste for meat of the world's well-fed) when millions of Americans are under-nourished? The Select Committee on Nutrition and Human Needs of the United States Senate found that recently rising food costs have produced "statistically significant declines" in per capita consumption of protein and many essential vitamins and minerals.[42] Nutritionists testified before the same committee that it is not possible to obtain a balanced diet on food stamps — yet over 20 million Americans must rely on the Food Stamp Program.

Some suggest that the Household Food Consumption Survey that was scheduled to begin in January of 1976 was delayed in order not to embarrass the president in an election year with reports of the nutritional decline of millions of Americans. After the elections the USDA announced it would not be able to include a sample of 5000 low-income families in the survey "due to lack of funds." Finally, a recent *New York Times* op-editorial by an assistant professor of preventive medicine in Virginia estimated that one million Americans rely on pet food for a significant part of their diet.

The most serious criticism of Food Power, then, is that it moves the United States itself in the opposite direction from Food First. Just as in many underdeveloped countries, food is seen as just another commodity with which to earn foreign exchange.

Food Power is not a solution to a problem; it is a way to avoid the solution. Food Power is an escape hatch for presidents, a way to avoid taking "unthinkable" steps. Relying on Food Power to earn foreign exchange is a way out for a government unwilling to touch the power and profits of the large grain-trading and other corporations moving abroad in search of new markets and cheap land and labor. Indeed, a Food Power–free trade strategy reinforces the power of large corporations both directly and indirectly: by undercutting small farmers who cannot survive extreme market fluctuations; by increasing the price swings on which speculative companies thrive; and by using food exports to earn foreign exchange so that the United States can continue to pay for imports of agricultural and manufactured goods produced abroad often by American corporations — items that could have been produced at home. Finally, Food Power is a way to pay for a costly United States antipeople strategy that puts American military presence in every corner of the world to preserve "law and order."

We are now only beginning to pay the price of allowing our land, food processing, and distribution increasingly to be controlled by fewer and fewer people. Today 5.5 percent of all farms in the United States control more than 50 percent of all farmland;[43] six grain corporations control 85 percent of all grain exports,[44] 50 out of almost 30,000 food manufacturers control half of all the industry's assets.[45] We have already seen the results: almost $20 billion more spent each year for food, increasing poverty and malnutrition for many Americans, and the loss of livelihood for millions of rural people.

Clearly a program to reverse these trends must start with land reform in America — with legislation against the takeover of agriculture by corporations and limits on farm size. Small farmers should be protected if food prices fall below levels necessary to provide farmers with a decent livelihood.[46]

A natural concomitant of land reform in America would be the development of local and regional food self-reliance. In other words, work to redistribute control over our land and food must also initiate a movement to reinvolve more Americans on a local level in supplying basic needs. Through work to bring democracy to our food economy — control by the people who work the fields, process, and distribute our food — we will demonstrate that without economic democracy in every segment of our economy, our political "democracy" is meaningless.

The United States, like underdeveloped countries today, must become more self-reliant in food both for the good of our own people and to make the nation less of a burden on the rest of the world. Pushing our food exports abroad is also not in the interest of the majority of people in other countries. While it may be in the interests of foreign elites, it ultimately undercuts production in other countries, the livelihood of their people, and their self-determination. In a world of extreme power differentials between countries there is no such thing as food interdependence. Interdependence, as we have said, becomes a smokescreen for the control of food by a few.

The way to discredit a Food Power strategy is to show how it works against Americans and the majority abroad. How can we make America safe for the world? What would a self-reliant America look like? These are the most important questions.

We would be doing you a great disservice, however, if we left you with the impression that this redirection could be pursued by our present government. Indeed this chapter demonstrates that our government is beholden to the very interests that *benefit* by the increasing concentration of control over our food system. The necessary restructuring of United States agriculture is, therefore, not something the government will do for us. *We* must take the responsibility. Educating ourselves and other Americans about the struggle for control over farmland going on right now in America is the first step toward the fundamental restructuring that must take place.

On a research trip in northwest Mexico we approached a community of landless laborers who had recently occupied and planted land that was theirs legally but that for decades had been controlled by one of the region's largest landowners. As soon as they realized we were Americans, their first question was: "Don't you have land reform in America?" Yes, we too are at a national turning point. Will we allow the basic necessity of human survival, food, to be controlled by a few and treated as any other commodity on which profit is enhanced by the creation of "scarcity"?

*   *   *

Agriculture policy should be directed toward maintaining agriculture as a viable industry and not as a way of life. The number of farms or farm population size is irrelevant except as these influence performance of the agricultural industry.

U.S. Department of Agriculture, "New Directions for U.S. Agricultural Policy," (Report of the USDA's Young Executive Committee, 1972), p. 11

Every new regulation that hampers agricultural production — every new bit of legislation that interferes with the individual farmer's management decisions, every new economic control that erodes his profit incentive — drives another nail into the collective coffin of mankind.

Earl Butz, "A Policy of Plenty," p. 57

PART VIII

World Hunger as
Big Business

33

Don't They Need American Corporate Know-How?

Question: If underdeveloped countries are ever going to realize their food-growing potential, won't they need agricultural assistance from more advanced countries? Perhaps it is a mistake, however, to think that this assistance should come through government channels. There is too much politics, too many chances for bureaucratic red tape, too little business sense. Isn't what these countries need exactly what corporations have to offer: the know-how that comes out of the most successful agricultural system in the world?

Our Response: Agribusiness executives would certainly agree. If you ever weary of pessimistic assessments about world hunger, just listen to what corporate executives have to say. Hunger to them is clearly a "growth industry."

Charles Hall, a banker who chaired a 1974 conference entitled "Feeding the World's Hungry: The Challenge to Business," has proclaimed that the "diminishing self-sufficiency" of the underdeveloped countries can be reversed by applying a "systems approach" in which "multinational business concerns can play an essential role."[1] According to Hall, multinational corporations "either possess or have access to the organizational and management ability, the capital and the technology, to apply such systems right now." John H. Perkins, a bank president, described the challenge as one of bringing to the "hungry countries" the "technological revolution" that transformed "American agriculture into the most amazingly productive system on earth."

Zeal, then, indeed missionary zeal, is not what agribusiness lacks. Even firms we would not normally think of as part of agribusiness have jumped aboard the agribusiness-has-the-solution bandwagon. At a 1974 United Nations-sponsored conference an executive from the St. Regis Paper Company expounded eloquently on how improved paper packaging could be the key to the solution to world hunger (what could he mean — that the trick is to devise a dry cereal container that will survive the Indian monsoon?).[2] Another would-be savior for the world's hungry is World Food Systems, Inc., an institutional catering service. Its president reported to the same conference that "large meal delivery system[s]" could deliver to the world's hungry millions "a satisfying eating experience" and at the same time carry out an "on-the-job consumer market analysis." Yes, why hadn't anyone thought of it before? All the hungry need is an efficient catering service and a taste preference survey!

A Global Farm for the Global Supermarket

The question contends that agribusiness firms possess a unique expertise to share with the poor in underdeveloped countries. But we ask, expertise for growing *what* kind of food and for *whom*?

In Part V we discussed the mechanization and commercialization of agriculture in underdeveloped countries; in Part VI, the promotion of agriculture for export. Put the two together and we have the increasing worldwide penetration of agribusiness, the linking up of underdeveloped countries' farms with global food markets: a Global Farm supplying a Global Supermarket.

The world's hungry people are being thrown into ever more direct competition with the well-fed and the over-fed. The fact that something is grown near your home in abundance, or that your country's natural and financial resources were consumed in producing it, or even that you yourself toiled to grow it will no longer mean that you will be likely to eat it. Rather, it will go to an emerging Global Supermarket where the poorest must reach for it on the same shelf as hundreds of millions of others. Every item has a price and that price, in large part, is determined by what the world's better-off customers are willing to bid. None without money will be able to get through the check-out line. Even Fido and Felix in the United States can outbid most of the world's hungry people. This emerging Global Supermarket will be the culmination of food "interdependence" in a world of unequals.

As much as agribusiness firms talk of producing food in underdeveloped countries, they are not talking about the basic staples — beans, corn, rice, wheat, and millet — needed by the hungry. Instead they are referring to "luxury crops": asparagus, cucumbers, strawberries, tomatoes, pineapples, mangoes, beef, chicken, even flowers.

Furthermore, agribusiness "expertise" is not so much in producing as in marketing. They know who and where the world's affluent shoppers are — a small group in the underdeveloped world's urban centers such as Mexico City, Nairobi, Delhi, and Rio and a much larger group in New York, Tokyo, Zurich, and Stockholm. And agribusiness knows what they "demand."

Del Monte is but one example of agribusiness creating a Global Farm to service a Global Supermarket. Del Monte operates farms, fisheries, and processing plants in more than two dozen countries. Board Chairman Alfred Eames, Jr., wrote glowingly in a recent annual report: "Our business isn't just canning, it's feeding people." But which people? Del Monte is operating Philippine plantations to feed the banana-starved Japanese; contracting with Mexican growers to feed asparagus-cravers in France, Denmark, and Switzerland; and opening a new plantation in Kenya so that some Britishers might not go without their ration of jet-fresh pineapple. A pineapple that would bring only 8 cents on the Philippine plantation (still a significant portion of a worker's pay) can bring $1.50 in Tokyo. No wonder that Del Monte exports 90 percent of its Philippine production. Yet the average Filipino has virtually the same inadequate caloric intake as the average Bangladeshi and serious protein-calorie undernutrition affects an estimated half of all Filipino children under four — one of the highest rates in the world.

There is nothing really new in food being grown for those who can afford to buy it. What is new is the agribusiness notion that *all* the world can be its Global Farm. Production of many low-nutrition crops that can fetch premium prices for the seller is being shifted out of the countries where most of the buyers live. These overseas production sites, in many countries with vast undernourished populations, are becoming mere extensions of the agricultural systems of countries such as the United States and

Japan. In fact, the corporations themselves regularly refer to their farms and processing plants in underdeveloped countries as "offshore production units" — a revealing terminology.

This historic shift is occurring in our lifetime. A fundamental factor helping to create the agribusiness vision of One Global Farm has been the development of low-cost transportation technology. One Bank of America executive noted the shift of agribusiness production out of the United States: "With the welcome mat out in many underdeveloped countries and with the lure of cheap land, cheap labor and ready international markets there has been a rush to get in on the ground floor." Moreover, tax concessions and tax havens beckon, and 360 days of sunshine can make farming easy.

The Mexican Connection

In Mexico the rush to link up with the Global Supermarket is far advanced. Traditionally, the American sunbelt and more northern greenhouses have supplied the United States with vegetables during the winter and early spring. But now agribusiness giants such as Del Monte, General Foods, and Campbell's, as well as numerous southwest-based "food brokers" and contracting supermarket chains such as Safeway and Grand Union, are changing all that.

Take the asparagus industry. Up until a few years ago you could bet the asparagus that you ate or that was exported from the United States to Europe was grown in central California. But now a significant part of production has been shifted to Irapuato, 150 miles northwest of Mexico City.[3] Since 1975, for instance, white asparagus is no longer grown in California. In Mexico, two firms control over 90 percent of asparagus production. One of them is Del Monte. In 1973, Del Monte paid American asparagus farmers 23 cents a pound for their crop; Mexican Del Monte contractors got 10 cents a pound.[4] The Mexican contractors pay the seasonal workers a mere 23 cents an hour.[5] Since labor costs account for up to 70 percent of the cost of growing vegetables, Del Monte translates cheap labor into bigger profit margins.[6]

Mexican soil and labor are already supplying one half to two thirds of the United States market for many winter and early spring vegetables.[7] The rate of increase has been been phenomenal. One way of keeping tabs on it is the USDA's annual *U.S. Foreign Agricultural Trade Statistical Report*. (It is yours for the asking. The report is telephone-book size; but if you can get into it, your next trip to the supermarket will put you in touch with the Global Farm. Typical of United States government publications, however, it does not name the agribusiness firms that control the imported items.)

Here are a few examples of the shift in Mexico from cultivation for local consumption to production for the United States.[8] Most are operations contracted and financed by American firms. From 1960 to 1974, onion imports from Mexico to the United States increased over five times to 95 million pounds. From 1960 to 1974, cucumber imports soared from under 9 million to over 173 million pounds. From 1960 to 1972, eggplant imports multiplied ten times, and squash imports multiplied forty-three times. In 1972, over a half billion pounds of tomatoes were grown in Mexico for the United States. Frozen strawberries and cantaloupe from Mexico now supply a third of United States annual consumption. (The National Bank of Mexico notes that domestic strawberry consumption depends on "what's left over after exports.")[9] About half of all the tomatoes sold in the wintertime in the United States come from Mexico, or, more precisely, from some 50 growers in the state of Sinaloa who in 1976 sold $100 million of tomatoes to the U.S. West and Midwest.

The shift is so far advanced that Ray Goldberg, of the Harvard Business School, in his 1974 study *Agribusiness Management for Developing Countries* notes, "If the recent rates of growth of imports from Mexico continue, in a relatively short time Mexico will account for almost the entire winter supply of most of these fruits and vegetables." The same study goes so far as to recommend that Mexico "seek further expansion" of vegetable exports.[10]

Multinational agribusiness is radically altering the availability of food for Mexico's poor, but in the wrong direction. Only a few years ago the national production of many fruits and vegetables was sufficient to keep prices low enough for lower-income families to eat some of these local products, at least occasionally. But now luxury crops grown for the Global Supermarket often crowd out more nutritious crops for local consumption,[11] taking over land that previously had grown up to twelve local food crops.[12] The land that is now contracted by Del Monte once grew corn, wheat, and sunflower seeds for local consumption. (Most significantly, crops for the Global Supermarket monopolize the funds and services of government agriculture programs.) As obvious as it may sound, we must remind ourselves that land growing crops for the Global Supermarket is land the local people cannot use to grow nutritious food crops for themselves. Higher prices of basic staples due to distortion of production priorities are making even beans a luxury Mexico's poor can no longer afford.

A Cucumber Republic?

In order to play off both U.S. and Mexican producers, agribusiness has started contracting with Central American businessmen-farmers for alternative sources for a wide variety of fresh fruits and vegetables. While banana exports barely increased, the volume of other fresh fruits and vegetables (such as cucumber, cantaloupe, honeydew, and okra) entering the United States from Central America rose thirteenfold between 1964 and 1972. Focusing narrowly on gross production and revenue figures without asking who benefits and who loses, agricultural economists and international aid and lending agencies have applauded this diversification into "nontraditional" fruits and vegetables. ("Nontraditional" is in contrast to the great "tradition" of bananas, coffee, and cotton.)

Enthusiasts see this sharp increase as only the beginning for Central America. According to Goldberg, such nontraditional exports could jump from 18 million pounds in 1972 to over 100 million pounds per year by 1980. They could become a *new* tradition! Already by 1969 over 19 percent of the total crop area of Central America was planted with nontraditional fruits and vegetables.[13] If we combine this 19 percent with the 29 percent of the cropland devoted to coffee, cotton, and sugar exports[14] — not to mention untold acres for banana and cattle exports — we begin to understand why so many people in these countries are undernourished.

The utter inability of the Global Farm to meet the needs of the majority of the people — the absurdity of the whole scheme — came home to us in one fact, so calmly stated in a Harvard Business School study: At least 65 percent of the fruits and vegetables produced in Central America for export is "literally dumped or, where feasible, used as animal feed"[15] because it either confronts an oversupplied market in the United States or does not meet the "beauty" standards of consumers there, while at home, where it is produced, people are too poor to buy it.

Strawberry Fields Forever?

In only fifteen years whole areas of Mexico have been turned into strawberry fiefdoms by U.S.-based suppliers to the Global Market: Pet Milk, Ocean Garden, Imperial Frozen Foods, Griffin and Brand, and Better Food Sales. Already by 1970 over 150 million pounds, three-quarters frozen, were being exported to the United States annually.

For two years Dr. Ernest Feder, formerly an FAO specialist on peasants in Latin America, painstakingly investigated the strawberry industry in Mexico. He was not particularly fascinated with strawberries — in fact, he is allergic to them — but he believed the industry would show how agribusiness affects rural people in an underdeveloped country.[16]

Dr. Feder's research makes clear that, first of all, we should not speak of the *Mexican* strawberry industry but of the U. S. strawberry industry located in Mexico. Officially, Mexican growers produce the berries and even own some of the processing facilities. The real control, however, remains with the American investors and food wholesalers. Using production contracts and credit facilities, these American firms make all the important decisions: the quantity, quality, types, and prices of inputs; how and when the crop will be cultivated; the marketing processes, including prices for the producers; the transportation and the distribution; and the returns on capital investments. U.S. marketing control is so powerful that, despite efforts by the Mexican government to develop markets in Europe, all Mexican strawberries pass through American exporters even when ultimately retailed in a third country such as Canada or France.

Even more revealing of this control, all strawberry plants come from nurseries in the United States. After fifteen years of commercial strawberry growing, Mexico does not yet have its own source of high-grade strawberry seedlings based on varieties best adapted to conditions in Mexico. Only two varieties are sold to Mexican producers; and they are not necessarily those best adapted to Mexico but the ones that meet the preferences of American consumers.

Although competition among strawberry producers might appear as a war between Mexican and Californian producers, in fact the rivalry is between two American groups, with different production sites. And the only way the Mexican production site can compete with the Californian one (where inputs and careful management give high yields per worker and per acre) is by keeping production costs extremely low. First, wages *must* be kept miserably low. Wages average only one seventh of those in California, even taking into account the higher cost of living in the United States. Feder is convinced that the very enforcement of Mexican minimum wage laws would "tend to drive the U.S. strawberry industry located in Mexico back to the U.S. or into some other Latin American country."

Second, the U.S. strawberry industry's interest in Mexico is strongly linked to cheap land and water. Water is "cheap" to the investors since its cost is largely paid for by federally funded irrigation schemes.

Third, the investors, Feder observes, bring in only enough technology to keep production going without raising costs. If they were to put in the type of money that would give yields comparable to those in California, they might as well stay in the United States.

Finally, the attraction of Mexico is that land obtained cheaply can be treated cheaply. Rather than requiring careful farming and applying inputs to increase yields, more land is simply plowed. The land, according to Feder, is "plundered": bad plants, destructive use of irrigation, bad farming, and misuse of pesticides is in many places ruining the soils. But agribusiness knows that it can just move on to new land, eventually even into another country, where the whole process can be started again.

Because such an agricultural system is not oriented to the needs of the domestic population, it is, by that very fact, thrown into competition with production centers in other countries. To compete, commercial agriculture in Mexico must maintain underdevelopment (cheap wages and land) even at serious jeopardy to the longer term future. It is a vicious circle: this maintenance of underdevelopment ensures the continuing absence of a strong domestic market that alone could orient production toward local consumption.

The Desert May Bloom . . . but for Whom?

It takes a lot of freight to fill a DC-10 cargo jet. Yet three times a week from early December until May a DC-10 takes off from Senegal loaded with green beans, melons, tomatoes, eggplant, strawberries, and paprika. Its destination? Amsterdam or Paris or Stockholm. Ironically such airlifts began just as the drought in Senegal was beginning and they dramatically increased even as it was getting worse.[17]

In the late 1960s, certain agribusiness firms circled Africa's semiarid regions on their world maps. Were they concerned about hunger there? No. What they saw in the Sahel was not hunger but low-cost production sites from which they might profit, given the European demand for fresh winter produce.

In 1971, Fritz Marschall, an executive of the European affiliate of the world-ranging, California-based Bud Antle Inc., visited Senegal. Bud Antle, one of the world's largest iceberg lettuce growers, once filed a complaint, during a farmworkers organizing drive, that led to the jailing of Cesar Chavez for picketing. Marschall was struck by the similarity of the climate of Senegal to that of southern California, where only two generations ago United States government irrigation projects had made the desert bloom. Why couldn't Senegal, he mused, replace California as his company's source of vegetables for the high-priced European winter market? By February of the following year Marschall had set up Bud Senegal as an affiliate of Bud Antle's Brussels affiliate, the House of Bud.

Today, Bud Senegal operates giant garden plantations, using nothing but the latest technology. Israeli, Dutch, and American engineers have set up a drip irrigation system with miles of perforated plastic tubing. The water for this system comes over some distance from northern Senegal through pipelines installed at government expense. In order to make way for mechanized production, Bud uprooted scores of centuries-old baobob trees. To remove baobob, sometimes as much as thirty feet in diameter, required the power of two or even three Caterpillars. The local villagers explained to us the value of these unusual trees: Not only do they protect the soil, but they provide the local people with material for making everything from rope to houses.

Since the undertaking is billed as "development," Bud has had to come up with virtually none of its own capital. Major stockholders and soft-term creditors include the Senegalese government, the House of Bud, the World Bank, and the German Development Bank. The Senegalese government also helped by removing villagers from land that was to become Bud's plantations. Even four members of the Peace Corps are helping develop vegetable plantations for marketing through Bud.

Despite the rhetoric about development and the reality of widespread undernourishment in Senegal, all the production is geared to feeding consumers in the European Common Market. This, in spite of the fact that in 1974 alone European taxpayers spent $53 million to destroy ("withdraw from the market") European-produced vegetables in order to keep prices up. One year green bean prices in Europe went lower than the costs of picking, packing, and air freighting Bud's big crop in Senegal. Did that mean more food for hungry Senegalese? Hardly. As the director of Bud Holland, Paul van Pelt, admitted "since the Senegalese are not familiar with green beans and don't eat them, we had to destroy them."

From May to December, European tariffs make it unprofitable to export any vegetables. Does Bud Senegal let its plantations lie fallow or allow the local people to grow food for themselves during those months? Again, no. Bud's better idea is to grow feed for livestock.

The case of Bud Senegal reminds us of the enormous productive potential of Africa's semiarid regions that we discussed in our response to Question 14. Obviously no natural limitation of the region makes hunger inevitable.

The House of Bud is now multiplying its success with mangoes from Mali, eggplant from Martinique, and coconuts and pineapples from the Ivory Coast. Bud has achieved the multinational corporate ideal of vertical integration, controlling all stages from production through processing and transport right up to retailing.

American Foods Share Co., a multinational corporation owned by two Swedish shipping firms also has its eyes on Africa. President Robert F. Zwarthuis states "Anyone who says that 'we go to Ethiopia in order to help those poor things' is lying." The company is now "trying out" countries such as the Ivory Coast, Egypt, Kenya, and Ethiopia as production sites for supplying Europe. Investments in Africa, he estimates, can expect a yield on capital two to two-and-one-half times those in Sweden.[18]

Zwarthuis admits that the need for a "continuous supply" makes him favor countries like Ethiopia and Egypt "which do not have any local market for these products." He foresees that "Africa is going to become the world's biggest producer of vegetables, not only to Europe but also to America." Recent World Bank reports on Senegal and Mauritania also see the region's future in mango, eggplant, and avocado exports.

Why is Africa so attractive to agribusiness? Not only is it close to high-paying consumers in the Middle East and Western Europe but many African countries offer the prospect of unutilized land. Take the case of Ethiopia, where, notwithstanding the recent severe famines, *most* of the arable land is not utilized. The existence of large, uncultivated royal and church estates has been an open invitation to agribusiness looking for cheap production sites. One obstacle, a lack of adequate roads to transport the production out of the country, is being removed: Foreign aid projects and World Bank loans are beginning to "open the country up."

Ethiopia's climate makes possible several cuttings of alfalfa a year, compared to only two or three in the United States. In the early 1970s, the Ethiopian government granted a concession to the Italian firm MAESCO to produce alfalfa to feed livestock in Japan. MAESCO's plantation is in the area where thousands of people, evicted by such commercial plantations from their best grazing lands, starved to death in 1973 along with their herds of camels, sheep, cattle, and goats. That year MAESCO started to raise cattle and sheep for export.[19]

Exporting the Steak Religion

The question asserts that what the underdeveloped countries need is know-how. Certainly there is one activity in which a lot of American know-how is being applied abroad — cattle raising. United States firms have set out with missionary zeal to spread the American steak religion to the world. Yet, we ask, who benefits? Is the meat going to the hungry? Or does it merely mean low cost imports for fast-food chains in the United States?

From one third to one half of total meat production in Central

America and the Dominican Republic is exported — principally to the United States. Alan Berg, in his Brookings Institution study of world nutrition, notes that, despite dramatic gains in per capita meat production in Central America, the meat is "ending up not in Latin American stomachs but in franchised restaurant hamburgers in the United States."[20] Central America has become the chosen site for investment in meat export operations, first because it is so close to the United States and, second, because it is free from foot-and-mouth disease, not true of Argentina and Brazil whose fresh and chilled meat imports are not allowed into the United States. Should Central America consider itself fortunate?

In 1975, Costa Rica, with a population of 2 million, sent 60 million pounds of beef to the United States. Per capita beef consumption declined in Costa Rica from almost 49 pounds in 1950 to 33 pounds in 1971. If the 60 million pounds exported had stayed in Costa Rica, local meat consumption would have doubled.

Per capita consumption figures, however, are deceptive. Many Costa Ricans — those without land or jobs to earn money — can never afford meat no matter how much is available. One half of the country's children do not get enough food to eat, much less meat. True, however, to the Global Supermarket phenomenon, a few well-off Costa Ricans can afford to get some Costa Rican beef just like Americans — at one of the three McDonald's in San José. ("El Big Mac" is now in every Central American capital.)

The export market for beef has lured farmers, in countries like Costa Rica and Guatemala, away from raising dairy cows. The result has been sharp increases in the price of milk, putting it out of reach of most families.

We might think that, even though most of the meat gets exported because people are too poor to buy it, at least local folk are the ones who make money on these exports. But are we really talking about Central American small-time producers making good in the big-country market?

Not exactly. Those profiting in the meat export market are the traditional oligarchs as well as former United States diplomats (e.g., the ex-ambassadors to Nicaragua and British Honduras), a former Peace Corps director in Costa Rica, big western ranchers (including the lawyer for the country-sized King Ranch in Texas), and giant processors like United Brands' meat subsidiary John Morrell Co.[21] Even industrial multinational corporations like

Volkswagen are getting into the beef business. As one Volkswagen executive pointed out, "You get a lot more for a pound of sirloin than a pound of beetle in Tokyo."

The World Bank, regional banks, and agribusiness corporations, working in projects costing several billion dollars, seem as committed as ever to increasing cattle production for export from Latin America and Africa. Several studies indicate it may be only the beginning.[22] The growth rate for world demand for beef has been higher than that for any other agricultural item.

Those who demand meat with every meal are capable of being coaxed on to a higher and higher price to get it. The American steak religion has already caught on in Japan and Western Europe and is becoming the "in" thing in Eastern Europe, the Soviet Union, and the oil-producing Middle East. In many Asian countries, a taste for grain-fed meat is being developed. But why is cattle production shifting to the underdeveloped countries? First, big U.S. ranchers have turned away from the higher land and labor costs of the United States. As one rancher put it: "Here's what it boils down to — $95 per cow per year in Montana, $25 in Costa Rica."[23]

Second, to avoid the rising costs of feedgrains, the beef industry is searching for areas where grazing is economical. Moreover, multinational conglomerates have recently taken over the major meat-processing firms (Now Armour is really Greyhound, Wilson is L.T.V., Swift is Esmark, and Morrell is, as we just saw, another way of saying United Brands.) As meatcutters in the United States and Europe are just beginning to realize, these firms will now try to transfer labor-intensive meat preparation (boning, prepacking) right to the new production sites in cheap-labor countries. Finally, giant agribusiness firms do not want the bother of purchasing from several independent suppliers and competing among themselves for those supplies. Thus, United Brands is integrating backwards to ranching subsidiaries, especially attractive due to cheap labor, government incentives, and available development funds, in countries like Honduras. The Global Ranch is but a variant of the Global Farm.

Another impetus behind shifting the beef industry abroad is the U.S. government and corporate drive to build markets for American grain and soybean exports. Meat production may yet become the equivalent of the 1960s "screwdriver" industries for many

Third World countries. Just as in the sixties underdeveloped countries assembled consumer items that were machined in industrial countries for shipment *back* to industrial markets, cattle operations controlled by multinational corporations commonly import American grain to be fed to animals that then get shipped to the United States.

In their drive to increase exports to Western Europe, Japan, and the United States, many governments in underdeveloped countries have enacted a whole series of measures to *de*crease domestic beef consumption at home. Several Latin American countries, including even Argentina and Uruguay, have even decreed days and weeks of the year during which no beef can be sold. (The principal impact has been that the well-off suddenly decide it is time to buy a freezer!)

Africa has many of the same attractive features for livestock investors as Latin America. European corporations are reportedly considering numerous ranching projects in Kenya, the Sudan, and Ethiopia — some of the finest and cheapest grazing land near Europe. According to one FAO officer who is afraid to be quoted, the plan is to use Green Revolution inputs on fully mechanized farms to raise the feed grains. This feed would fatten the animals brought in from ranches. The goal is export.

A Chicken in Every Pot?

Americans tend to think of chickens as a true "people's food" compared to meat. Promoting chicken in the underdeveloped countries might sound like a good idea: Isn't a low-cost source of protein just what they need?

But that is not how Ralston Purina sees it. Ralston Purina considered creating a poultry industry in Colombia, not so that the poor would have more chicken in their diet, but to create a need for its chief product, concentrated feeds. Experience had taught multinational feed companies like Purina that promoting poultry production was the fastest way to create customers for concentrated feed. The poultry business requires less initial capital and land than the cattle-feeding operations. Moreover, poultry feeds are among the most profitable for the feed companies.

First, Purina offered credit to commercial farmers to buy baby chicks and feed. Soon there were more chicks than could be supplied by feedgrain. So the company offered credit to other commercial farmers to grow feed crops and encouraged the government and private creditors to do the same. Traditional food crops like corn gave way to sorghum for feed. A portion of the corn crop that had been for human consumption now brought a higher price as grist for Purina's mill. Beans, another staple of the poor, gave way to soybeans for feed. Between 1958 and 1968, the acreage planted with the traditional beans was halved while soybean plantings — all grown for animal feed — jumped sixfold.

The plight of the poor is compounded by the nature of the market. As livestock feed production takes up land that once grew beans and grain for human consumption, the prices of these staples go up.

Ralston Purina still likes to talk about how it was a prime mover in the production of new sources of protein: chicken and eggs. It is true that Colombia, an egg importer in 1957, was by 1961 no longer importing eggs. From 1966 to 1971, annual broiler production doubled from 11 million to 22 million. Yet, as the excellent Consumers' Union–sponsored study *Hungry for Profits* notes, "The displacement of cropland from pulses [beans] to feed crops did not simply replace a cheap source of protein with an expensive one. It also reduced the total availability of protein in the country, because animal sources of protein are less efficient to produce than are vegetable sources."[24]

A plot of land used to grow beans and corn can satisfy the protein requirements of significantly more people than when it is used for animal feed crops. Based on actual experience in the Valle region of Colombia, the Universidad del Valle arrived at the following estimates: One acre of land growing feed crops for chickens provides only one-third the amount of protein for people that the same land could provide if it grew corn or beans; if the acre grew soybeans for human consumption, it could provide sixteen times more protein than is produced by using that land to grow chicken feed.[25] Using the feed to produce eggs instead of chicken reduces these differences somewhat. But according to calculations based on Colombian government statistics for 1970, a dozen eggs would cost more than an entire week's earnings for over a quarter of the population.

Ralston Purina and the other feed companies in Colombia like to cite figures showing increases in per capita egg consumption.

But, as usual, per capita figures are misleading. Higher averages merely reflect the increased consumption of eggs by the small middle- and upper-income groups, directly or in processed items such as snack foods and mayonnaise. For all the additional eggs Ralston Purina can count on a national basis, there is evidence that Colombia's protein gap is growing eight times faster than the population.[26]

Thus what looked like just the way to create a needed source of cheap protein for Colombians turns out to undermine the only accessible protein sources of the people. Ralston Purina helps teach us, as discussed earlier in Part V, that "modern" techniques and production skills in themselves mean nothing. We must always ask: For what? For whom? At the cost of what alternatives? The answer to these questions will be determined by who is in charge of the production: the people themselves or multinational corporations.

Where Have All the Flowers Gone?

Another "know-how" that agribusiness is eager to bring to underdeveloped countries is the production of "ornamental crops" — the academic name for cut flowers and foliage.

If the local peasants cannot afford chicken or eggs, perhaps they can brighten their shacks with cut flowers. Since 1966 the value of cut flowers and foliage imported into the United States has increased over sixty times to over $20 million in 1975 — over 90 percent coming from Latin America.[27] Some experts feel that by 1980 it will no longer be "feasible" to produce cut flowers in many current production areas in the United States.

The favored country so far is Colombia, where cut flowers are now a $17-million-a-year business. In 1973, a Colombian government economist estimated for us that one hectare planted with carnations brings in a million pesos a year; planted with wheat or corn, the same hectare would bring only 12,500.[28] Given that at least 70 percent of Colombia's agricultural land is controlled by a small group of wealthy farmers who need not think of land in terms of growing food to live by, it is not at all surprising that ornamental crops join feedgrain and cattle on their list of priority crops.

Ecuador and Guatemala, and to a lesser extent Mexico, are also being transformed into major flower production sites for the Global Supermarket. Already in 1972, Guatemala was supplying the United States with 159,278,421 — the USDA counts them! — chrysanthemums, roses, pompoms, daisies, chamaedorea, and statice.

Agribusiness's shifting of flower production to underdeveloped countries to supply the Global Supermarket follows the twofold pattern we have seen with other crops.[29] First is the search for lower-cost production sites (land preparation costs for flower cultivation in Central America have been estimated to be less than 10 percent of comparable costs in Florida). Second is the corporate effort to integrate operations from the seed to the flower shop. The U.S. flower business has historically consisted of large numbers of independent enterprises: small growers, larger grower-shippers, and tens of thousands of retail shops. But certain agribusiness firms such as Sears, Green Giant, Pillsbury, and United Brands and the supermarket chains are beginning to eye the profits to be made by linking the retailing to low-cost foreign production sites[30] — an integration process that is a little out of the reach of your neighborhood florist. United Brands is known already to have production operations of several hundred acres in Central America and plans for major expansion. These corporations would seek to brand name flowers as United Brands did with Chiquita bananas in the 1960s. They will market the flowers through supermarket chains and franchised stores ("Flowers from Sears" and Backman's European Flower Markets, a subsidiary of Pillsbury). Neighborhood florist shops could well go the way of tens of thousands of other mom and pop stores — out of business.

So agribusiness firms are doing exactly what the question suggests: bringing their production know-how to the countries where many go without food. But what are they growing? Asparagus, cucumbers, strawberries, eggplant, beef, and flowers — "luxury crops." And for whom? For the well-fed to whom it is profitable to sell. More and more of the prime agricultural resources that the hungry people abroad need for their food get channeled into supplying Americans and other well-fed foreigners.

In answering this question we have not looked for the worst corporations. Those we use as illustrations are run by managers probably no better or more ill intentioned than any others. But there is one fundamental obstacle: corporations must sell for a profit. You say that agribusiness firms cannot afford not to be successful. You are right. "The bottom line is what counts," James McKee, chief executive of CPC International, told us in an interview. "If we lose sight of that, no matter how much good we were doing, we wouldn't be around long." But that is exactly the reason they cannot help the hungry. No matter how many hungry people there are, as long as they are being impoverished, hungry people just do not add up to a market.

*   *   *

We find ourselves in the right business at the right time. Agriculture and the food industry will have top priority in a world of shortages. Rises in population and income will create unprecedented demand. Food will be the growth industry for at least the remainder of the century.

Heinz management, 1975

We must encourage the developing nations of the world to establish more sophisticated systems of food distribution, in order to eliminate the unnecessary waste and spoilage of vital foodstuffs between production sites and needy people. Our basic feed and food operations are aimed at these crucial objectives.

The Restaurant Group is composed of fast service Jack in the Box . . . and a network of specialty dinner house restaurants. . . . Both operations posted record sales. . . .

A new program of developing color-keyed interiors, custom designed for local areas, has been implemented. The Foodmaker Architectural and Graphics Departments have developed many new concepts for pleasing visual impact, both inside and outside the restaurants. Such furnishings as hanging flower baskets, stained glass partitions, semi-concealed trash containers and colorful and comfortable seating, are designed to increase customer satisfaction. New bright orange and yellow miracle fabric uniforms for restaurant employees, introduced during the second half of the fiscal year, are another step to improve visual impact!

Ralston Purina Company, "Report to
Shareholders," 1974, p. 12

I was sitting at a table beside the swimming pool of the Biltmore Hotel in Guatemala City writing up my log of the day's interviews, when I became aware that six men at the next table were discussing development plans for Guatemala.

When I went over later and introduced myself, I learned that the advisor of the group was the former executive director of a foundation whose effectiveness in providing overseas assistance had been endorsed by Presidents Kennedy, Johnson, and Nixon. Two of the men in the group were wealthy businessmen from upstate New York who had generously decided to contribute money and time to set up their own program to help feed the people of at least one hungry nation.

The sincerity of the men in the group and their basic Christian goodwill are also typical, and I urge that their conversation not be interpreted as a caricature of naivete. On the contrary, they were too highly motivated for that.

"What are the crops they raise here?"

"Don't know, but we can ask AID or the (U.S.) Department of Agriculture."

"World's going to starve to death in 1976, so we don't have much time."

"How much time do we have?"

"Two years."

"Let's work on that basis."

"That means we've got to have a crash program."

"How do they plant corn? Anyone here ever planted corn?" (Silence)

"Hell, the Dept. of Agriculture can tell us that. What we need to know is how to change the system here. It's bound to be lousy."

"You mean we don't have a contract to do this yet? How do we get one?"

"That's what we're talking about now. We've got to get a plan first."

"Right. That's what we need, a contract and a plan. The plan, I guess, comes first."

"These people (the Guatemalans) don't even know how to use a screwdriver. You can't imagine how easy it would be to double their food production once you get them to accept our ideas."

"What ideas do you mean?"

"You know, modern machinery. That's what they need."

"Right. Think what a tractor would do here!"

"How about strawberries? Hell, they use a lot of strawberries in the states."

"That's a great idea!"

"Strawberries grow ten months of the year, and all you do is plant them and cultivate. Wonder why they don't raise them here."

"Personally, I think this coconut idea is worth looking into. Of course, you can't use them all, but how about 15 or 20 million coconuts?"

"There ought to be a market for that many."

"Why not go into the cattle business or raise pigs. We could feed the coconuts to the pigs. We'll get the natives to harvest the coconuts to feed to the pigs."

W. Paddock and E. Paddock,
We Don't Know How, pp. 61—64

34

Still, Don't the People Benefit?

Question: Agribusiness firms obviously go abroad, not to feed the hungry, but to take advantage of low-cost production sites in order to sell luxury crops to the well-fed around the globe. But surely this is not the whole picture. Don't multinational agribusiness firms create thousands of rural jobs and bring greater income to small farmers whose produce the companies buy for export? So while agribusiness may look irrelevant to the development process doesn't it in reality expand the local economy and further the development of the country?

Our Response: Traditionally foreign agricultural investment in an underdeveloped country meant owning and operating plantations. This is changing. Due to risk of "expropriation, revolution or insurrection" plantations are a "poor risk" says the Overseas Private Investment Corporation (OPIC),[1] the United States government agency insuring American firms against just such risks. Direct ownership of production, moreover, is not attractive to a corporation seeking to tie up as little capital as possible.

Contract Farming

It is not surprising, then, that by 1965 agribusiness investment in direct land ownership abroad was half the value of a decade earlier.[2] Nevertheless this decline has come at a time of a stepped up interest in investment in Third World agriculture. Is this a contradiction? Not really: Many agribusiness firms are shifting from the plantation mode to that of "contract farming." Exceptions are found where certain dictatorships make foreign corporations feel totally secure and when firms find that they must produce directly in order to control quality.

Instead of owning land and farming directly, contract farming means that the corporation gets local producers to sign a contract committing them to use certain inputs to produce a stipulated amount of specified products with the date of delivery to the corporation and the price fixed. The corporation obviously still maintains the control it requires, with little capital invested — and, best of all — there is nothing that can be nationalized.

United Brands (UB) pioneered the way to get out of direct ownership and still maintain control. It saw the light in 1960 when the Cuban government nationalized 271,000 acres.[3]

The company began to develop its "Associate Producer Program," which allowed it to sell much of its land. In Central America alone UB's direct ownership has fallen from close to two million acres in 1954 to a third of that by 1971. In Ecuador the company sold all its extensive holdings by the mid-sixties. But in every case UB maintained total control.

An associate producer is a local person who buys or leases land from the plantation company. Such an individual is hardly a struggling small farmer. In Guatemala Del Monte's one associate producer, formerly contracting with United Fruit, has over 3000 acres.[4] A United Nations study found that Del Monte's thirteen associate producers in Costa Rica own an average of 612 acres each.[5] The associate producers contract to buy their inputs and technical assistance from the company and to sell their entire production to it. If the company believes an associate is politically well placed, he or she might also receive a company loan to get started. The company splits the difference between the total cost of production and the purchase price *the company sets*. In addition, the company nets a further profit marketing the produce in what *Business Week* calls "the big, well-heeled market."[6] There are two additional bonuses to such contracting for the foreign companies: one economic and the other political. When the foreign market is booming, the companies rely on the associate producers to supplement their own direct plantation production. But when an oversupply might depress prices, the companies simply raise quality standards so as to reduce purchases from their associate producers. Politically, the system gives foreign companies an influential bloc of nationals who identify their welfare with that of the companies — the best insurance against nationalization of the remaining holdings or against national tax reforms, as the banana companies proved in 1974.

The corporation may not be called United Fruit anymore and soon there may be no more company plantations, yet little has changed for the ordinary people. The best lands still grow fruits like bananas and vegetables for the world's well-fed. Still the best that rural inhabitants can hope for are low-wage, seasonal jobs in an associate producer's field. Most of the value produced still goes to UB.

Former Secretary of Agriculture Orville Freeman, a leading agribusiness spokesperson, thinks this type of contract farming holds a bright future for Third World agriculture. He is now president of Business International and of a company called Multinational Agribusiness Systems, Inc. At a United Nations–organized conference on agribusiness and world hunger,[7] he shared his vision with other multinational executives of "a kind of contract farming" he prefers to call "satellite farming." He foresees "many agribusiness companies" — he named Del Monte, FMC, International Systems and Controls, the Hawaiian sugar companies, and Nestlé — with "the experience, technology and the management know-how" cultivating a "core-producing unit of optimum size, using the most modern technology," and providing "supervisory services" to "hundreds of adjacent small farmers" and contracting their production.

Such a vision is not new. Contract farming was not invented by agribusiness for underdeveloped countries. It is an already proven tool of agribusiness in gaining control over food production in the United States itself. To understand what contract farming now offers underdeveloped countries, we have to know what it has meant to American farmers.

The "New Slaves"

The food business in the United States is tightly controlled. Even though a food-industry lobbyist might argue that it is a highly competitive industry in that there are 28,656 food-manufacturing firms, just 50 brand-name giants own 60 percent of total food-manufacturing assets[8] and take 75 percent of the industry's total profits. Referring to them as giants, then, is hardly an exaggeration. But how does this affect life on the farm or the average consumer?

In this near-monopoly context the big processors like Del Monte, Campbell's Soup, General Foods, Heinz, and Coca-Cola aim at keeping the price they pay for farm goods at a minimum. Their principal tool is the contract. It is incredible to find that USDA does not categorize such processors as corporate farmers but as "subsistence" farmers — since they "consume" all of what they "produce." So much for statistics on corporate farming![9]

Del Monte directly owns fifty-five farms in the United States totaling 130,000 acres and, in addition, has hundreds of thousands of acres under production contracts with 10,000 farmers. Already over 22 percent of the total American food production is under direct corporate control, four fifths of that by contract.[10] Of the vegetables processed in the United States, 78 percent are produced by farmers under contract and 10 percent by the processors themselves. This means that corporations control 88 percent of the American vegetable crop.[11] There is therefore no competitive market to which the individual farmer can turn. He has little choice but to sign up with a corporation. Almost all of such basic favorites as sweet corn, green beans, tomatoes, and even popcorn are grown under production contract.[12] The process resembles the oil companies' control of oil from the wellhead to the service station. As we have seen in Part VII, it is a disastrous arrangement for the family farmer, as well as for the consumer.

The American Agricultural Marketing Association enthusiastically estimates that 50 percent of the American food supply will be produced under corporate contract at the end of this decade and that by 1985 the agribusiness giants will have their grip on 75 percent of United States food production.[13] Is this something we should feel good about? Is this the "successful" model that agribusiness has to offer the underdeveloped countries?

We can only answer these questions by first finding out how a typical production contract in the United States works.

Before planting time a farmer signs up with a corporation to produce a specified amount of a certain product and to deliver it by a fixed date. Many of the contracts specify exactly what kind of inputs must be used and some offer credit.

"Farmers sign contracts because they are hard-pressed," states Gene Potter of the National Farmers Organization.[14] There are many sellers and few buyers. Already deeply mortgaged, the farmer is hardly in a position to negotiate. The preprinted contract prepared by a corporate lawyer is presented to him on a take-it-or-leave-it basis.

If farmers organize to pressure the corporation, in all likelihood the corporation only speeds up its shift of production to "offshore" sites. This is already happening in part. Asparagus growers in California, Oregon, and Washington produce most of their crop under contract to Del Monte. A few years ago the growers organized into a bargaining association and won a price boost from Del Monte. That is when Del Monte began moving some of its asparagus operations to Mexico.[15]

The processor's superior power does not end with getting farmers to sign up. The contracts they sign, after all, are written by the corporations for the corporations. Jim Hightower reports the asparagus growers find that their contracts with Del Monte "allow the corporation to decide what part of the crop is 'acceptable.'" In 1972, 8 percent of the asparagus crop was rejected in this way. "With no open market to sell on," Hightower observes, "farmers literally had to eat that loss." He goes on to reveal how the farmers' loss is Del Monte's gain:

> In many cases, however, Del Monte will buy the rejected asparagus from the farmer — at cut-rate prices. In 1972, the price for "acceptable" canning asparagus was 23¢ a pound. The price for asparagus the corporation found unacceptable was .0005¢ a pound. Del Monte has sole power to decide whether a batch of asparagus is worth 23¢ or .0005¢, and the contract requires the farmer to offer any unacceptable asparagus to Del Monte. If the corporation does not want to buy it, then the farmer can take his rejects elsewhere. But there is nowhere else.
>
> Why would Del Monte want to write such a provision into its contract? Because there are windfall profits in those asparagus culls. The farmer may have to give the stuff away to Del Monte, but Del Monte certainly does not give it away to you. Del Monte packages and sells these rejects as asparagus soup, asparagus cuts and asparagus tips — all drawing a pretty penny at the supermarket.[16]

No examination of contract farming is complete without looking at the poultry industry: the first in the United States with contract operations on a large scale.

The production contract was the tool by which corporations like

Ralston Purina, Cargill, Pillsbury, and Continental Grain took control of chicken production in the United States beginning in the late 1950s. Since at that time prices were only a few pennies a pound, an offer of credit from the corporation was one a hard up independent farmer could hardly refuse. These same corporations controlled the feedgrain market and, sure enough, the contract required the farmer to use only his creditor's feed.

Within ten years the percentage of United States chicken production under contract went from 4 percent to 92 percent.[17] USDA nonetheless insists on calling these contracted farmers "family farmers." In reality they are little more than hired hands in a corporate factory. Only there is one big difference. It is they who must go into debt to build the "factory" and put in new equipment. As an official of the Mississippi Farm Bureau told USDA researchers, "Today a Mississippi farmer could not sell broilers in the market if he wanted to produce them. Farmers do not own the birds. They furnish only the labor and the houses. They do exactly what they are told."[18]

George Anthan, a first-rate investigative reporter for the *Des Moines Register*, described a recent visit to a poultry area in Northern Alabama after the "integrators" came in:

> For farmers to get a contract, certain "improvements" specified by the corporation had to be made on their farms. These investments were financed by the farmers through local banks. Failure to meet the specifications would result in the contract being withdrawn, leaving the farmer virtually without a market. The integrators did not offer long-term contracts in exchange for the farmers making the changes the companies insisted upon.
>
> The farmers I talked to said that every time it looked like they were going to get the loan paid off, the integrators would come up with a new "improvement" like gas heaters, insulated chicken houses, and automatic feeding equipment. Once in debt, the farmer had to stay in business, but to stay in business they had to get deeper in debt. One of the farmers described himself and other poultry farmers as the "new slaves."
>
> Most of the farmers had to take jobs in town to supplement their incomes and usually had a wife or daughter working in the local poultry processing plant for minimum wages. Farmers were getting about 2¢ a pound for their chicken. I didn't find a single farmer making more per pound than they made five to ten years ago, but their costs had doubled.[19]

According to Harrison Wellford in the chapter "Poultry Peonage" of his pioneering study *Sowing the Wind*,[20] a USDA economist found Alabama chicken growers making minus 36 cents an hour for their service to the corporations. The same USDA study in 1967 concluded chicken farmers were pauperized because of their lack of bargaining strength in dealing with the corporations. In 1962, some poultry growers in Arkansas under contract to processing companies tried to organize an association. The companies blacklisted the growers and ruined them by making certain that they could never again receive a contract.[21]

Growers do not dare speak out against the unfair trade practices for fear of being blacklisted. This fear was dramatized in an interview with a contracting chicken grower in Alabama on ABC-TV in 1973.[22] The woman so feared reprisals that she would not allow her face to be shown or any mention of the corporation for which she raised chickens. At the end, the interviewer asked, "Why do you stay in the business of chicken raising?" The reply: "We have to! We'll lose our house mortgaged to pay $29,600 for the chicken houses. Our farm. Everything we've worked for."

In 1958, Earl Butz, just having left the post of Assistant Secretary of Agriculture to become both Dean of Agriculture at Purdue and a director of Ralston Purina, wrote a widely disseminated article directed at American farmers titled, "Don't Be Afraid of Integration" (certainly an eye-catching title in the South in 1958). Today agribusiness, the United States government, and the World Bank would have farmers in underdeveloped countries trust the corporate hand, hoping they have not heard of the fate of small American chicken farmers.

Tens of thousands of American farmers, hardly naïve to the ways of the modern world and living in a country with an array of antimonopoly and fair trade laws as well as regulatory agencies, have not been able to protect their interests against a few powerful poultry supply and marketing corporations. What then is the likelihood that farmers, even the better off, in countries like Pakistan, Mexico, Colombia, and Thailand will fare any better?

A retired official of the FAO invited us to consider two alternative visions of the world, both of which can already be foreseen in different countries. In the one, tens of thousands of entrepreneurial "farmers" receive corporate credit to raise chickens, using hired laborers and all the latest feedgrain and chemical techniques designed to bloat chicks in the shortest time (regardless of how tasteless and watery they become), for a few giant worldwide marketers like Ralston Purina and the Rockefeller-owned Arbor Acres. In the alternative vision, hundreds of millions of farmers have a few chickens each in their backyards eating insects and scraps, with some occasional input such as inexpensive chicken cholera vaccine. "In which world," asked our friend, "do you think more people are likely to eat chicken? Or are agricultural resources less likely to be used raising feed for animals instead of food for people? Or is less foreign exchange likely to be lost to the country on imported supplies and through repatriated profits and fees?" The FAO itself may already be committed to one vision; both Ralston Purina and Arbor Acres are key members of the FAO's Integrated Meat Development Working Group. Yet to us it was reassuring to realize there *is* an alternative and it is not starvation.

Popeye City

Agribusiness giants can turn whole towns, even regions, into company operations. The Agribusiness Accountability Project, an independent research group, did an in-depth study[23] of the "Spinach Capital of the World," Crystal City, county seat of Zavala County, Texas, where Del Monte owns 3600 acres of irrigated farmland producing an annual $14 million worth of spinach. Canning all the spinach grown in Crystal City, Del Monte is by far Crystal City's biggest employer. There is no competition: Del Monte can buy the farmers' spinach without bidding against Green Giant, Bird's Eye, Libby — or anyone else. If farmers do not want to sell to Del Monte, they can, as Jim Hightower comments, "look forward to long days of eating lots of spinach."[24]

While billion-dollar-a-year Del Monte prospers, it refuses to contribute to Crystal City's welfare. Del Monte even built its plant outside the border of the town to avoid $11,987.61 in property taxes. The corporation argues that as the major employer it contributes sufficiently to community welfare. Del Monte has, it is only fair to note, donated to City Hall a statue of Popeye.

Even those who do find jobs with Del Monte can barely subsist. The 1970 census revealed half of the families in Zavala County had incomes below the official poverty level. Del Monte pays $2.12

to $3.09 an hour for processing spinach and $3.56 an hour in the can-manufacturing plant. If these wages were for *full-time* employment, yearly incomes would range from $4000 to $6800, somewhat below Del Monte's chief executive's $438,000. But most of Del Monte employees are not full-time but "seasonal" workers.

Del Monte has a long documented record of obstructing workers' legal rights not only to organize for decent wages and better working conditions but even to vote in municipal elections.

According to the study, Del Monte's plant is hellish in summer and bone-chilling in winter. It lacks adequate toilet and medical facilities. Conditions are no better in other Del Monte operations where the corporation houses its seasonal workers. George Ballis, a noted photographer, reported on workers' housing in Del Monte's "labor camp" in San Joaquin, California, the "Asparagus Capital of the World":

> The places — of cement blocks — don't look too bad . . . except for the whole prison camp feel: high wire fence topped with barbed wire (a Del Monte trademark), and huge "No Trespassing" signs at the gate.
>
> The grounds are one big mudhole in the winter rains. There is no hot water in the units.
>
> No baths. No toilets. No heat.
>
> When the workers complain, they are told the camp was made for summer use only, even though it has been used year round for 16 years.[25]

Is Crystal City or San Joaquin what Orville Freeman has in mind when he tells the world that Del Monte has "the experience, the technology and the management know-how to manage efficiently"? And what about Ray Vicker, of the *Wall Street Journal*, asserting in *This Hungry World* that Del Monte "has far more to gain through helping farmers in the developing countries to help themselves than through any exploitative method of operation"?[26]

Agribusiness Meets the Peasant

What is the real life condition of those who labor to supply the Global Supermarket? Has the coming of agribusiness meant decent jobs, income for adequate food and a secure foundation for development? Certainly not in the case of the thriving strawberry industry in Mexico studied in-depth by Ernest Feder in his book *Strawberry Imperialism: An Enquiry into the Mechanisms of Dependency in Mexican Agriculture* (see also Part VIII, Question 33).

As Feder relates, in the mid 1960s, before the strawberry boom hit the Zamora Valley, Zamora and the neighboring Jacona were small towns. Today Zamora has 100,000 inhabitants and Jacona 30,000. Thousands more come to the valley in search of work and return to their villages at night or sleep in the streets, since the cost of transportation for some represents 30 percent of their daily wage even if they find work. Over three quarters of the population lives in half-mile wide carton-shack slums that ring the towns. No sanitation, no running water, little electricity. All and all, a classic case of "overpopulation."

Yet in the Zamora valley you can also find the ranch-style houses of the new "strawberry millionaires." As employers, these few individuals and their American partners directly benefit from the desperate misery of the majority. Since the number seeking work far exceeds the number of jobs, the growers are able to hold wages down. Some growers, despite the large numbers of unemployed already in Zamora, send recruiter trucks to outlying villages because the peasants there are willing to work for still less.

In Zamora, during the four months of peak field work you can find over 5000 would-be workers gathering at 5:30 A.M. next to the railroad station. Guarded by the military armed with submachine guns, they wait for the growers or their agents to come in trucks. The largest growers come to pick up several hundred workers at a time. Still, many do not find a job. They must walk back to their villages only to return the next day hoping for better luck.

Those who do get hired get somewhat under the legal minimum wage of $3 per day. This is particularly true for women and children who, despite the law on equal wages for equal work, have to be content with two thirds of the wages paid to men. The employers say they prefer women and children "because they do not have to stoop so far," but fortunes have been made on such thoughtfulness. Like fieldhands in the fruit and vegetable industry in the United States (where the orange crate alone sells for more than the labor to fill it), a family must field every member including young children, if it is to survive.

When the trucks do come no worker dares to ask how much he

would be paid, for, according to Feder, he would simply be told: "There is no work for you." The workers climb on board the truck without the slightest idea of where they will be taken, how much they will be paid, or whether they will have work the next day. As one worker put it, "In order not to starve, we don't ask any questions."

Employers are known to use a variety of tactics to boost their profit on each worker such as shortening the lunch break and working the laborers overtime and seven days a week without extra pay. Everyday exposure to pesticides results in vomiting, fainting spells, severe headaches, and even death. Efforts to organize for better working conditions have always met with employer violence.

And what about the strawberry-processing and-freezing factories? Do they through their famed "transfer of technology" develop new skills and provide decent employment?

The strawberry factories are geared to just one thing — strawberries. Since strawberries are harvested less than half the year, the factories lie idle six to seven months, employing no one. Despite this wasteful use of capital equipment, owning a factory can be quite lucrative. Feder reports that some companies have recovered their capital investment in a single year. During a few peak weeks the freezing factories in Zamora (most with United States capital) employ 10,000 to 12,000 women and girls, mostly between fourteen and twenty-five years of age. But the work for most is very short-term since the factories operate way below capacity during the beginning and end of the harvest.

Although child labor is illegal, Feder reports that in plants controlled by American capital he found up to sixty children working. The work is monotonous and the conditions are unconscionable. The workers must stand all day even though, during the peak season, that means standing up to eighteen hours a day, at 40 to 50 cents an hour. In some plants supervisors make extra money selling the obligatory white uniforms that cost four to five days' wages.

What about the small farmers in the region — can't they at least profit from growing strawberries? Only in theory. First of all, government permits, aimed at preventing massive overproduction, regulate who can plant how many acres. Since there is money to be made, those with political and economic influence make sure they get the permits.

In one *ejido* land-reform community, 19 out of 220 families received permits. Each recipient had a clear power connection. None actually worked on the land.

The processing factories, according to Feder's research, further narrow down the number of growers. Production contracts favor the larger suppliers, giving them priority and better terms in distribution of inputs and the purchase of their output.

Some larger growers use their influence literally to pocket the key to the watergates of the irrigation system. They can then use water in excess of the legal limit while the small producers are left to fight over the remaining water that trickles down to them. The district's small farmers growing food crops find they have less and less water. Mainly because of the flooding of the strawberry fields, the area irrigated by the Zamora system has actually shrunk. Strawberries use up 75 percent of the water on only 20 to 30 percent of the total area under cultivation.

In contrast to the agribusiness-controlled monoculture of today's Zamora, a peasant-controlled agriculture would naturally build on mixed cropping. Mixed cropping is not only environmentally sound (as discussed in the response to Question 19), but also means year-round food supply and work. Furthermore, when the rural population individually or collectively owns and controls the agricultural resources, it is likely to use its spare time to improve the agricultural resources — drainage, irrigation, terracing, tree planting, storage, and so on. By contrast, in Zamora today, most of the population can obtain at best only part-time seasonal work. The control of the valley's agricultural resources by an export-oriented industry with a pronounced seasonal peak and unstable export markets results in mostly part-time, insecure jobs and a plundering approach to the land.

In Zamora a single system produces millionaires and paupers. It adds up to a stunning waste of human life, as well as agricultural resources and even the vast underutilization of investment capital. Hardly a foundation for development.

Counter Land Reform

Much of what we have learned points to one truth: People must control their agricultural resources if they are to free themselves from hunger. Yet supposed land redistribution programs in such countries as Brazil, Colombia, Central America, Iran, and the

Philippines have exempted agribusiness land, even though it is often the best land.

The Philippines, a country with an estimated 3,000,000 landless peasants, is a recent clear example. A "sweeping" land reform program — sometimes presented in the media as the justification for the martial law suspension of all human rights — exempted fully two thirds of the country's agricultural land because it has been put into production for the global Supermarket. Little wonder that after four years only 15,000 landless peasants have received any land.

In the Bukidnon region Del Monte is attempting to coerce self-provisioning smallholders to lease their land to the company. Armed company agents have fenced off and driven cattle onto the cultivated fields of those who refuse to lease.[27] An American priest, arrested for helping the peasants resist, described Del Monte's landgrabbing: "They bulldozed people right off the land. Now they're using aerial sprays, harming farm animals and giving people terrible rashes."[28]

A few years ago when we began mapping out our research on agribusiness in the underdeveloped world, we were not all that sure that agribusiness could do much harm to the people in a country like Iran with oil revenues of $20 billion, large quantities of arable land, and the world's highest GNP growth rate. We were wrong. Iran is a prime example: a country where equating agricultural development with agribusiness investment has spelled the *reversal* of land reform. Consequences for the rural population have been disastrous.

In 1962 the Shah of Iran declared a substantial land reform that irrevocably broke the political power of the large landowners. "Land to the tiller," however, was taken literally. If a family was not well-off enough to own a plow and a draft animal — and many were not — they could not qualify for the broken-up estates.[29]

Throughout Iran, farmers who did receive land began to produce food. In the Khuzestan province, bordering on Iraq and the Persian Gulf, the farmers' productivity was extraordinary, especially considering the lack of technical assistance and irrigation and the 98 percent illiteracy. Traditional farming methods provided ample work for all.

Also during the 1960s, the government began to construct several large dams under the supervision of David Lilienthal,

Roosevelt's designer of the Tennessee Valley Authority. The largest dam is on the Dez River in Khuzestan. It offered the prospect to the small farmers of over 200,000 acres of irrigated land. It sounded promising. Then, just when the dam was being completed, the shah and his elite advisors decided that what Khuzestan needed was foreign agribusiness corporations.

Today the farmers in Khuzestan no longer speak of land reform. Nor do they wait for the waters of the Dez to reach their parched lands. Irrigation channels, built for only *one fifth* of the potential irrigated area, take water to the "farms" managed by such firms as Hawaiian Agronomics, the Diamond A. Cattle Co., Mitsui, Chase Manhattan, Transworld Agricultural Development Corp, Bank of America, Dow Chemical, John Deere & Co., Shell, Mitchell Cotts, and Hashem Naraghi (an Iranian émigré who became a major Californian grower).[30] For most of these firms, Khuzestan is but the latest venture out there on the Global Farm. Hawaiian Agronomics, for instance, is a subsidiary of C. Brewer — known in most western states by its C and H brand line — which in 1974 netted $3.8 million from agribusiness operations in Iran, Indonesia, Ecuador, and Guadalcanal.

Khuzestan today, instead of being an area of many small family farms utilizing the new irrigation, is a province dominated by large-scale (12,000 to 50,000 acres), highly mechanized, capital-intensive, cash crop units. Some 17,000 Iranians have been pushed off their lands.[31] Hawaiian Agronomics has boasted, "Land Barren for 23 Centuries Now Producing Food, Supporting Livestock."[32] The fact that peasants produced food there before the coming of agribusiness is ignored. Even more significantly, it was the massive irrigation system installed at public expense *before* agribusiness moved in that really made the parched lands productive. As one agribusiness executive remarked, "they develop the water first and we come in and farm it. It's an attractive arrangement."[33]

What might have looked to the shah like a way to achieve efficient, "sophisticated" agricultural production is not even working by the standards of the agribusiness firms themselves. So far only one firm is making a profit; already three firms have opted to sell out to the government. Productivity on these fully modernized tracts is lower than that of medium-sized Iranian farms in irrigated areas.[34] Two economists report that the firms "overestimated their ability." As one explained, "You just can't walk in, do a few soil samples and say these 10,000 acres should be artichokes." Another economist has pointed to the operating costs "due to the high salaries to technical experts and expatriate managers." Ironically, a 1975 study by an American consulting firm cites "management problems related to the large sizes of the production units."[35]

But do these problems discourage agribusiness? Some firms such as Chase Manhattan, John Deere, and Bank of America have kept on with their fumbling agricultural projects because of a series of government incentives, such as rebates from taxes on other income, and a desire to keep the shah happy. Mitsui is doing all right back home on selling as livestock feed the dehydrated alfalfa it exports out from the Khuzestan. The foreign corporations marketing inputs to cattle operations are doing all right, too. The shah wants cattle to such an extent that the government is paying World Airways to airlift 250,000 pregnant cows to Iran by 1979. One British firm, Fowler, Ltd., is importing cattle so ill-suited to the climate that the government must provide air-conditioned stables!

And how are the people of rural Khuzestan doing? Most are landless and jobless. Some see no alternative but to flee to the already overcrowded urban slums. Many of these refugees are in their teens and twenties. They would gladly farm if they had their own plots; their real skills are those of small rice farmers. The government has not even sought to train them for semiskilled jobs as construction workers, truck drivers, and machinists in Iran's supposedly boom economy. While urban unemployment soars, the government *imports* workers — 80,000 South Koreans and innumerable Pakistanis for such jobs. Meanwhile the agribusiness refugees sit and wait around warehouses hoping for a few cents to lug a sack, sweep the floor, or shovel out the chicken droppings from the new British-owned ten-million-bird-a-year poultry factory in Teheran. Others who used to till fields have gone to the sparsely populated Arab states across the Gulf, proving to some that Iran is "overpopulated."

Those in Khuzestan forced to sell their land to agribusiness projects are winding up in one of the government's several "labor centers."[36] The purpose of these new labor centers is to provide the agribusiness projects with pools of labor — most of it on tap at $3 a day. As one foreign expert who out of fear wishes to remain anonymous wrote us, "You can see the government's theory that the agribusinesses will require much more labor than they displace documented in government and even World Bank reports but not in the streets and houses where the idle gather." He has observed villagers, previously capable of self-initiated collective projects like building new villages, mosques, and schools, now demoralized, passive, and individualistic. He also reports that those families forced to work on agribusiness projects after they lost their plots eat even less well than before.

Reading such descriptions, all we could think of is that Khuzestan, Iran, might not be so far removed from Crystal City, Texas.

Sweet Corn

Of course not all contract agribusiness projects are export-oriented. At a symposium on world hunger in September 1975, CPC International presented the history of its investment in Pakistan to show what a positive contribution a foreign enterprise can make to a country's food supply. CPC International (known to you by its Thomas' English muffins, Skippy Peanut Butter, and Mazola Corn Oil) is no newcomer in underdeveloped countries. It has sizable operations in three dozen underdeveloped countries and therefore can be taken as a significant example of what agribusiness has to offer.

There are two ways of reading the CPC case study the company presented. The intended victory-over-hunger version is roughly as follows: In 1962, CPC International purchased control of Rafhan Maize Products, the largest corn grinding and processing company in Pakistan. By the late 1960s, Rafhan had expanded with loans from U.S. AID and the Pakistani government. But its mills just could not get hold of enough corn. So in January 1970 Rafhan "launched a corn development program." CPC decided it would use the agricultural expertise of its associated companies and brought in its subsidiary from the United States, the Funk Seed Company, to design a high-yielding hybrid. CPC has, the company notes, "people with know-how."

Rafhan worked out a contract system with the leading farmers whereby the company would supply on credit the right seed, pesticides, and fertilizers to be deducted at harvest from the contract price. "The contract farmers obtained average yields of more than twice the national average." Furthermore, "The concept of a second crop started to gain acceptance." Rafhan also built "modern facilities to shell, dry, and store the grain." So successful was Rafhan that it decided to expand yet further its processing plant.

Sounds good. But let's give it a second, more careful reading. Why was CPC not getting enough corn to its mills? According to the company:

> Historically in Pakistan corn has been a food crop consumed by the underprivileged [*sic*] in the country and in the villages. It has been a popular food commodity because it was nearly always plentifully available during about six months of the year. . . . The price has been lower than the alternative food grains — wheat and rice. Corn has also been used for barter by farmers in the rural areas.[37]

It was the crop the farmers with the poorest lands depended on: "it was normally a secondary crop that was grown where more lucrative crops could not be grown." Little fertilizer, practically no pesticides, and traditional seeds from the previous year's crop were used, so yields were low.

In the 1960s, once CPC moved in, corn prices did increase and some better-off farms expanded total corn production. But still, according to the company, "the supply of corn available to the processors increased very little." The company sees three reasons for this: First, corn farmers "ate too much of their corn" or "bartered it for [other] food." Second, as the numbers of the poor grew rapidly they collectively "consumed increased quantities of corn as food." Third, the growing poultry industry was competing for the supply of corn. To get around these "problems" Rafhan in 1968 attempted to get more corn by purchasing *before* planting time all of the corn farmers could produce. But even "this approach did not appreciably increase Rafhan's supply of corn."

Rafhan's contract system is what made it work. Rafhan "completely changed the pattern of corn production." Corn farming is no longer the subsistence crop of the small farmer. CPC notes, "Corn had been cultivated on very small areas — not more than five acres for each farmer — now it was planted in larger fields."

As for storing the harvest, CPC states "there were two alternative methods." One was for the farmers to build narrow corn cribs where the air could circulate between the unshelled ears "preventing molding — *until the farmers wanted to sell"* [emphasis ours]. Rafhan, however, chose the other alternative: "Purchase the corn from farmers at the time of harvest, dry it in mechanical dryers and store it in [the company's] silos." Why? According to CPC, "the alternative of helping farmers obtain and own their corn cribs had two weaknesses." First, Rafhan "needs" corn, not cobs, and "the farmer-owned or community-owned shelling equipment is small, slow and inefficient." Second, when farmers store corn in their own cribs, there was always the chance that they might let family or friends consume the grain; or the farmers might sell or barter it to someone else!

Rafhan *will* have its corn. CPC indirectly notes an added advantage for the company, namely, that by buying up at harvest, rather than "when the farmers wanted to sell," the company is likely to get more and get it cheaper since the large supplies at harvest depress the price.

"Improved" corn farming has come to Pakistan. Once a subsistence crop, corn is now grown by large farmers as just one link in a process controlled from seed to bin by CPC's Rafhan.

And what is it all for? To make "corn sweetener" as a sugar substitute in the fast-growing market for soft drinks and other snack foods among Pakistan's urban better-off classes.

Foreign corporations in an underdeveloped country's agriculture, then, are no help to the hungry, the landless or the small farmers. Natural resources like land and water, human resources and great sums of capital are spent on making profits for the corporations and their few local partners. The hungry do not benefit. It is not they who eat the food (if indeed it is food that is grown). It is not they who sell the products. Their wages must remain miserably low if production is to compete in the Global Supermarket. Their jobs, relatively few and seasonal compared to what could be the alternatives, are fundamentally insecure. Foods once relatively inexpensive become commercialized at prices affordable only by the world's well-fed. Agribusiness, furthermore, reverses and dooms agrarian reform.

Once a country's elite has opted to make agribusiness the engine of development, government must cater to agribusiness. The government is increasingly deprived of the capacity for independent economic and social planning. The interest of the state becomes indistinguishable from the interests of the multinational agribusiness firms within its territory. "Fiscal encouragements" lead to more "fiscal encouragements." There is the corporation's ever-present threat of pulling up stakes or turning to another country's supply. While a national firm may be no more interested in the welfare of the local people than a multinational firm, it is more easily controlled. In practice an increasing number of national firms and landed entrepreneurs are mere partners of multinational agribusinesses. All are united in opposition to the peasant majority taking control of the agricultural resources.

Multinational agribusiness, often building on a colonial inheritance, is elite-controlled export agriculture under another name.

*   *   *

Among the most important reasons for the internationalization of the multinational corporation is to increase its utility in the developing world of Latin America, Asia and Africa. Its role in the development process becomes more urgently clear every day, as we witness the limitations and handicaps of local governments ... even if local governments were strong and assistance to them plentiful, the fact is that the enormous complexities of the development process require abilities and attributes which are as natural to the multinational corporation as they are unnatural to government.

Herbert C. Cornuelle, United Fruit Company
Annual Report, 1968, Boston

The poor countries, on the other hand, have to try to "denationalize" the subject of agribusiness investment and treat it for what it is: an amazingly efficient way of institutionalizing the transfer of technical knowledge in agriculture.

Lester Brown, *Seeds of Change*, 1970

35

Agribusiness Abroad: A Boon for Americans?

Question: Agribusiness's shifting the production of luxury crops to underdeveloped countries does seem to have a devastating impact on the majority of people there. No one likes that. But isn't it true that it does not hurt the United States and at least we Americans get cheaper food?

Our Response: To understand what is the impact on Americans let us start with a look at the big plantation companies like Del Monte and Castle and Cook (Dole).[1] They are spreading their production sites throughout the underdeveloped world. Most controversial is their shift of part of their pineapple production from Hawaii to the Philippines.

As recently as 1951 Hawaii produced three fourths of the global supply. For years the big plantation companies imported thousands of low-wage workers from the Philippines and elsewhere. But, just as in an underdeveloped country, a dependence on tourism and importing goods rather than growing basic foods fueled inflation. In the 1960s plantation-worker unions struck several times for wages sufficient to cover the minimum cost of living. They eventually won the highest agricultural wages in the world: $2.85 an hour. These "high" wages combined with rising land values (due to competition from resort land speculators) have made Hawaii less attractive then other sites such as the Philippines, where wages can be as low as 15 cents an hour.

Over the past several years the Hawaiian state government has tried all the usual incentives offered by a typical underdeveloped country to keep Del Monte and Dole "home": defeat of a proposed minimum wage, weakened environmental protection standards, real property taxes permanently sliced in half, and tax-funded agricultural research.

While the plantation companies have snapped up these subsidies in the past, they now claim that they are not enough. Del Monte has already cut its Hawaiian production by 40 percent, expanded its production and canning in the Philippines, opened a new plantation in Kenya, and drawn up plans for pineapple production in Guatemala in 1977. The company now claims it will keep some operations open in Hawaii to supply the fresh pineapple market — in case the lid is blown off in the potentially politically explosive situation in the Philippines, Kenya, or Guatemala. Dole, with 100 percent of its operations in Hawaii as late as 1959, had only 25 percent there in 1975. Dole now owns 19,000 acres in the Philippines and in 1972 it expanded into Thailand.

What about the workers whose livelihoods have been made to depend on exporting pineapple from Hawaii? Their strike in 1974 in protest against the companies' shift of production was ineffectual, largely because of the difficulty of coordinating with pineapple workers in other countries.

The corporations talk about trying to get them jobs in hotels on the other islands. Responds Tony Hodges of the Life of the Land public interest lobby, "You don't take a 45-year-old guy (the average age of the pineapple workers) who's been picking pineapples all his life and, presto, put him in a suit and make him a night club entertainer."

Has the control of pineapple growing by a few giant corporations now shifting production abroad been in the interests of the people of Hawaii and of the United States as a whole? What if, alternatively, the United States produced enough pineapples domestically, providing American workers — or even better, independent farmers — a decent income?

The shift by agribusiness of major segments of United States agriculture outside the United States, like the runaway manufacturing plants of the sixties and early seventies, will cost thousands of jobs. With Del Monte's shift of white asparagus production to Mexico that we already mentioned, over 6000 workers in California have lost their jobs. Moreover, as in manufacturing, the mere threat of such shifts acts as a check on the efforts of workers organizing for higher wages and better conditions here.

Displaced American agricultural workers and small farmers can no longer be conveniently thought of as being "absorbed" by a booming urban industrial economy. The unemployment and welfare roles show that even now the economy is unable to absorb those *already* outside the rural sector. The defenders of agribusiness will assure us that new jobs in the United States will be created in machinery and other agricultural export factories selling to the modernized sectors in foreign countries. But how many? And how easily can someone be transformed from a truck farmer into a tractor factory worker? A middle-aged, unschooled tomato picker into an ammonia plant engineer?

The question suggests that the one thing we Americans could gain from the Global Supermarket is lower prices for food grown more cheaply abroad. But, while their foreign-produced products do, in fact, cost less to produce, we are very likely to pay the *same* price we did for the domestic product. The companies, not the consumer, pocket the savings.

Mushrooms are a good example. Only a few years ago several hundred competitive, family-owned companies canned mushrooms they bought from Pennsylvania farmers. Now many are being bought out or squeezed out by large corporations like Clorox (Mr. Mushroom), Green Giant (Dawn Fresh), Ralston Purina (Steak Mate), and Castle and Cook (Shady Oak West). These agribusiness giants are turning their backs on American growers and instead contracting in low-wage South Korea and Taiwan.[2] As a result, mushroom imports have quadrupled. One out of three processed mushrooms is now an import. But does this loss of livelihood for American farmers and plant workers at least mean cheaper mushrooms for Americans? Not at all. Green Giant, which imports almost all of the mushrooms it sells in jars, admitted to the United States Tariff Commission that it could get plenty of high-quality mushrooms in this country but that the foreign imports mean greater profits for the Green Giant.[3] Now, as agribusiness watchdog Jim Hightower comments, "A few large food firms can fatten their profit margins on mushrooms, supposedly a low-calorie item."[4] Furthermore, the remaining American mushroom growers now give the excuse that they cannot pay decent wages to their workers because of competition from imports.

Similarly, in an investigation of pineapple profits, the federal Tariff Commission found that Del Monte and Dole "market the imported product at the same price that they ask for their domestically canned pineapple" despite the fact that wage costs at its foreign production sites are but a fraction of those in the United States. In fact, the small Maui Pineapple Co., which markets its entirely domestic-grown production through supermarket chain labels, sells for less than Del Monte and Dole foreign-grown imports.

The day might not be far off when multinational agribusiness firms will be able to manipulate prices as well as supply *on a global basis* through many of the "shared monopoly" practices corporations have already perfected in the United States. Once production has been shifted throughout the world, no national government would be able, even if it so desired, to know the truth about supply or costs.

United States Government Support of Agribusiness

Just because we ordinary Americans do not benefit from the expansion of U.S.-based agribusiness into underdeveloped countries does not mean that the American government is not doing everything possible to encourage it. In addition to military, law and order, and financial support that helps keep governments in power that are favorable to American investment, the United States government provides a whole package of fiscal incentives and other inducements to corporate investment abroad.

Chief among the incentives are U.S. tax laws themselves. As stated earlier, a corporation can defer income earned by its subsidiary abroad as long as that income remains overseas. Even when earnings are brought back into the United States, taxes paid to foreign governments can be deducted from the total taxes owed. The upshot of these two rules is that a corporation has every incentive to open up overseas subsidiaries and to maximize — often through creative accounting — the portion of its total earnings that show up on its off-shore subsidiary's books. Corporations find they can also minimize taxes paid to foreign governments by simply setting up a one-room "subsidiary" in a tax-haven, such as Panama or the Bahamas. A corporation contracting for the production of vegetables in Mexico might technically sell the production to its Panama "subsidiary" only to sell it in turn to its headquarters in San Francisco. An additional encouragement for investment in Latin America was created by Congress in 1942 when it authorized U.S. corporations to conduct business there through what are called Western Hemisphere Trade Corporations that the government taxes at a reduced rate — 34 percent instead of the usual 48 percent.[5]

Most significant, perhaps, is that the United States government puts itself, ultimately the American taxpayer, behind corporate investment abroad. The Overseas Private Investment Corporation (OPIC), a government initiated program backed by the United States Treasury, guarantees corporate investment abroad against losses incurred when a local currency cannot be converted into United States dollars, war damage, and expropriation. Through OPIC, the United States government has put a total of 3.2 billion tax dollars behind investment abroad by private companies. And it does so on easy terms: OPIC's rates average only 1.5 percent with terms as long as twenty years.

Nearly two thirds of all U.S. private investment in underdeveloped countries, not including petroleum, is insured by OPIC.[6] Beneficiaries include some of the largest American firms. In the early seventies, for example, OPIC insured both Del Monte's and CPC's agribusiness investments in Kenya. In addition, OPIC provides loans to help corporations get started in underdeveloped countries. A recent loan went to establish an export-oriented vegetable processing plant in Costa Rica.

But OPIC is not a mere passive agent; it helps seek out investment opportunities. OPIC conducts investment-research trips to underdeveloped countries for corporate officers. It describes its own role as "brokerage": seeking out the most promising investments and making a "concerted effort to interest American companies in them." And in agriculture, the most promising investments involve large landholdings. As OPIC official Pat Counts explains, "our OPIC policy . . . limits our assistance to projects involving large land holdings."[7]

The most pernicious aspect of OPIC is, however, that it puts the United States government in opposition to any movement or government in an underdeveloped country that might even potentially expropriate American businesses, even if such movements are working in the best interests of the majority of local people. One of the motivations for United States covert support for anti-

Allende forces in Chile in 1970–1973 was the belief that Allende's success would exhaust OPIC's reserves and be a drain on the United States Treasury, the final guarantor for OPIC-insured losses in cases of expropriation.

Legislation authorizing OPIC activities expires on September 30, 1977. For OPIC to continue to operate, Congress must pass new legislation. A number of members of Congress, including Senator Frank Church, have indicated a desire to end the program altogether.

Pitted Against the Hungry?

There is a more subtle but even graver problem for Americans. As multinational corporations expand into the underdeveloped world, American consumers are rapidly being made dependent on a whole range of imported agricultural products. Once this shift is made, there will no longer be hundreds of thousands of farms in the United States supplying the vegetables, fruit, meat, and even flowers Americans buy. *The food needs of American consumers will be made dependent on the active maintenance of a distorted land use system in underdeveloped countries.* We will be forced to translate our own legitimate food requirements into opposition to those of countries where hundreds of millions go hungry. Agribusiness, by putting American consumers at odds with the interests of the world's hungry, creates a type of interdependence no one needs.

The buying power of Americans — no longer able to find suppliers within the United States — will be a powerful suction force working against the land use changes that must be made now in underdeveloped countries if the hungry there are to eat. Already, of course, multinational agribusiness has made such changes more difficult, not only by giving the well-off a bigger stake in the *status quo*, but by encouraging governments' retreat on such basic issues as land reform, as we have seen in Mexico, the Philippines, and Iran to mention just a few countries.

This type of American food dependency fosters a certain foreign policy. American tax dollars are spent in both blatant and secret collaboration with regimes that repress efforts of the people to take control of the food resources they need to support themselves.

Once corporate interests put American farmers out of business, making America self-reliant in food will not be easy or accomplishable overnight. The implication, therefore, of an American food dependency created by corporate and government policies is that, when the oppressed in the underdeveloped countries do seize control and re-order their national priorities, we will be faced with shortages and higher prices — prices beyond the means of many of us.

The question therefore is: Will we continue to support policies of oppression to try to postpone that re-ordering or will we work now to put a halt to ever greater dependency both on monopolistic corporations and on the food resources that belong to other peoples?

In an earlier question (Question 33), it was suggested that agribusiness brought efficiency and production know-how to "backward" agricultural systems. In responding we have asked several key questions in an attempt to explain what agribusiness really offers:

- Which crops? They turned out to be luxury, nonessential items tying up valuable resources that could be producing staples.
- For whom? They turned out to be for the local and foreign elites.
- With what production model? It turned out to be contract farming — perhaps the very worst experience of American farmers with agribusiness.

For whose benefit? Neither that of the majority in underdeveloped countries nor most Americans. The undernourished — usually a full 40 percent of the population in underdeveloped countries — are paying the cost of this kind of "modern agriculture." Not only do they not benefit, they find their lot deteriorating. The irony is that alternatives are not only possible; they are the very ones that are most accessible – as we will see in Part X.

36

Better Than Beans and Rice?

Question: Perhaps an underdeveloped country faces a problem if an agribusiness firm comes in and controls production. But aren't you overlooking something? Are there not other types of agribusiness companies? What about the food processors and distributors that have perfected an efficient food delivery system in the United States? Aren't these firms bringing to underdeveloped countries more nutritious and varied food than their traditional, starchy diets?

Our Response: The beans and corn diet of Latin America, the lentils and rice of India, and the soybean and rice diet of China appear to most Americans as starchy and nutrient poor. In fact, they are not. Such diets evolved because they *work*. As basic dietetic staples, these combinations are, in fact, quite ingenious. In each case the two items together give more biologically usable protein than if each were eaten separately.[1] Therefore, when we consider the problem of world hunger, we should always keep in mind that the traditional diet is adequate — *when* you can get enough of it. The problem is usually not quality. The problem is quantity.

What, then, do the food companies have in mind for "improving" the food of the poor?

Until several years ago the involvement of foreign firms in food processing in the underdeveloped countries was insignificant. With markets burgeoning at home and with so few urbanized consumer markets in the underdeveloped countries, there seemed little reason to bother. But suddenly multinational food processors have begun to take another look. The top 10 to 20 percent of the population in the underdeveloped countries constitute an emerging consumer class — but one lacking the servants who once made "convenience foods" unnecessary. At the same time the market in industrial countries for highly processed, more expensive, convenience items has become "saturated."

A 1973 *Business Week* article, "Starving for Profits," published a survey indicating that U.S. food processing companies had reported the lowest annual rate of domestic sales growth (5 percent) of any industry surveyed.[2] Each new dollar invested in advertising to get you to buy this or that exciting new convenience food was meeting with fewer and fewer market results. Population growth had plummeted. The middle classes in the industrial countries were unlikely to ever consume more than their 1700 to 2000 pounds a year of grain per person.

But perhaps the "worse" sign for American food processors, according to Joseph Winski of the *Wall Street Journal*, is that "After years of looking for the quick and easy way, Americans are returning to the basics in their food consumption." With more brown-bagging of lunches, more home gardening and canning, more homebaking and cooking "from scratch," convenience food sales have been plummeting. According to one estimate, unit sales of canned goods are down from 25 percent to 60 percent depending on the item. One large supermarket chain reported its frozen prepared food volume fell by 16 percent in one year alone. As its chairman Donald S. Perkins commented, "Today's consumers are willing to do it themselves." Even more disheartening to food-processing executives is that their own surveys show that the slump in the highly profitable convenience foods is not just a passing phase attributable to the recession. A *Better Homes and Gardens* survey revealed that 63 percent of the respondents agreed with the proposition that they were making "important and lasting changes" in the way they shop and the foods they eat regularly.[3]

The giant food companies have responded to the depressed home market in three ways. First, by diversifying into nonfood consumer products (such as toys — General Mills acquired Parker Brothers, Quaker Oats took over Fisher-Price and Marx). Second, by seeking to control cheaper sources of supply from foreign countries, as we have already seen. And third, by expanding into the new urban markets of Latin America, Asia, and Africa.

We have emphasized markets because that is what the food companies themselves emphasize. For the executive of a world-ranging food company, underdeveloped countries are not to be thought of in terms of the number of inhabitants, let alone the number of the malnourished. Countries *are* markets.

Peter Drucker, prolific corporate theologian, advises executives not to be put off by India's obvious poverty but to keep in mind that "within the vast mass of poverty that is India" there is "a sizeable modern economy, comprising 10 percent of the Indian population, or 50,000,000 who can consume on the level with most Americans and Western Europeans."[4] When we discussed the future of Nabisco in the underdeveloped world with Lee Bickmore, then chief executive of the corporation, he told us of his enthusiasm for the initial surveys indicating that Brazil could mean 20 million potential Ritz munchers, even though an estimated half of its 100 million people are so poor that they *never* handle money. In Mexico, considered one of the largest and most dynamic markets for food processing companies, less than one third of the population has the means to buy some type of canned foods — as compared with 90 percent in the United States.[5]

André van Dam, who plans strategies for Hellmann's mayonnaise, Skippy's peanut butter, Knorr soup cubes, and other CPC products to "penetrate" Latin American markets, is quite aware what a large portion of the population is outside his industry's net. But he is not discouraged. With such large total populations van Dam is excited by the absolute numbers who could be made into customers. In a 1975 speech to top executives of food companies in Latin America he estimated the potential customers:

> Within ten years . . . Latin America will have 444 million inhabitants. . . . Of this number, a fifth will be able to buy, through their economic power, almost all the products which the gentlemen industrialists here presently manufacture, while a third will be able to buy some of these products only very infrequently. The rest of the population, about half of the total, are not customers except for the most simple and basic products and probably will continue on a subsistence basis. The potential market varies from country to country, from product to product, but those who have a continental vision realize that the potential market of 1985 in Latin America will double compared to today.[6]

No doubt Mr. van Dam would like to be concerned about the hungry. But with the "continental vision" of 89 million affluent Latin

Americans ready to buy, he hardly need worry about those 208 million so miserably poor they could never buy a jar of Hellmann's mayonnaise or Skippy peanut butter.

At Home Away from Home

The question implies that food companies are bringing in new products and greater efficiency — that is, a better food system. But are multinational food processors really bringing something new and are they successful because they are more efficient?

Corporations, like people, behave much the same away from home as they do at home.[7] If anything, away from home there are fewer inhibitions. At home, firms have become giants not by offering a better product and greater efficiency but by a one-two punch of local takeovers and advertising expertise. And that is exactly how the multinational food companies are expanding throughout the underdeveloped world.

Rather than starting from scratch, the food companies gain an initial foothold by buying out a local firm that is already in at least one of the same product lines. Nabisco has taken over local biscuit and cracker companies in countries like Venezuela, Mexico, Iraq, Brazil, Nicaragua, and Puerto Rico. Pepsico, big in the United States snack market since its acquisition of Frito-Lay, has taken over an established Venezuelan bakery company. Borden bought out the largest maker of pastas in Brazil. In 1966, W. R. Grace, a conglomerate with an historical base in guano (fertilizer from bird droppings) and shipping in Latin America, bought Alimentos Korn in Guatemala. Grace developed it into a frozen-foods line. By 1969, Grace claimed to control 60 percent of the Central American market for packaged processed foods with sales increasing at the rate of 70 percent a year.[8]

General Foods is a star acquisition operator. Former president C. W. Cook reflected on the lessons of the company's experience. "With the rapid progress we made in England through acquiring Alfred Bird and Sons, we concluded that where possible we would find an ongoing business with a management that knew the country, the trade, the banking facilities, the governments and the people." He observed that "starting from scratch" in Germany had proven a "difficult experience." So the question was — where could profitable takeovers still be made? "When we looked around,

Europe was pretty well combed over." Latin America, however, offered excellent prospects.[9]

In 1956, General Foods acquired La India, the largest chocolate processor and the best-known seafood processor in Venezuela. In 1960, it took over Kibon, the largest ice cream manufacturer in Brazil. Other acquisitions gave General Foods two thirds of Brazil's chewing gum market. General Foods already had the gum market wrapped up in Europe through takeovers there (Hollywood and Maple Leaf). In Mexico, in the 1960s, General Foods acquired several coffee and soup manufacturers.

Expanding through acquisitions has advantages. Starting costs are minimized. In addition General Foods requires each new subsidiary to finance itself through retained earnings and local loans. With such a low-cost-to-headquarters strategy, a big food company can enter several country markets almost simultaneously. Politically there is an advantage, too. The new subsidiary can be "low-profile" American. Most Brazilians think that Kibon is as Brazilian as the Mardi Gras. Yet in terms of the benefits of support from the U.S. government, from government investment insurance — OPIC — or diplomatic or moral support, Kibon is as American as can be.

What Is Agribusiness Offering?

The food companies expanding overseas are not a cross section of the United States food industry, according to such major studies as *At Home Abroad*, but those whose American operations are concentrated in high-advertising products. "In investing abroad, these firms have sought out the faster growing, convenience foods where advertising, rather than price cutting, is the instrument of competition."[10]

The underdeveloped countries are thus getting our worst, not our best. They are getting those corporations *least* likely to fill real needs or to be useful models. Underdeveloped countries are but the latest markets to conquer for those corporations that have made it big and are getting bigger because they have hit upon a formula for large profit margins, maximum processing, and advertising. Is this what either we or the underdeveloped countries need?

At least 92 percent of the "research and development" costs of these big food companies goes to develop quick preparation and consumer appeal or what the National Science Foundation calls "motivational research and product promotion."[11] "Quick preparation," "convenience" foods mean prewashed, prepeeled, precooked, premashed, premixed — almost preeaten foods! Take the common potato, a staple in human diets for centuries — and not just because it fills you up. It actually contains such a wide array of vitamins, minerals, and protein that you could practically live on the potato alone. This applies to the potato as it comes out of the ground: a cheap, nutritious food that you can eat for about 9 cents a pound. The more a potato gets processed, however, the more its price goes up and its nutritional value goes down (i.e., you get much more fat and chemicals per unit of real potato). Birds Eye (General Foods) frozen french fries are 66 cents a pound, Frenches' instant mashed potatoes are $1.30 a pound, regular potato chips are $1.18 to $1.58 a pound, and Pringle's New Fangled Potato Chips (Proctor and Gamble) is the winner at $2.10 a pound.[12] Each processing step offers a new opportunity for profits.

Of course, the potato is just one example of a basic, inexpensive, low-profit staple turned into an expensive, high-profit "modern" food. Big profits are made the same way in the breakfast cereals industry, which the Federal Trade Commission has called a "shared monopoly," with the Big Four dividing up 91 percent of sales![13] In October 1975, General Mills was getting $75.04 per bushel for corn in the form of Cocoa Puffs. Farmers were getting $2.95 a bushel for corn. Quaker Oats was charging $69.44 a bushel for corn (Cap'n Crunch) and $110.04 per bushel for wheat that has been "puffed." Food industry investigator Jim Hightower did similar checking and found there is only 2 cents worth of wheat in a regular-sized box of Wheaties (General Mills) selling for 53 cents. The box costs more than the wheat.[14] General Mills, in an effort not to lose the nutritionally conscious, also puts out Total. But, as Dr. Michael Jacobsen of the Center for Science in the Public Interest points out, Total is merely Wheaties sprayed with vitamins. The additional cost to General Mills is half a cent; to you, 22 cents.[15] Not surprisingly, the breakfast food market has averaged almost twice the profit level of the food industry in general.

In highly processed foods, freshness, color, shape, and texture are frequently chemically induced. This makes it possible for big processors to get by with cheaper grades of farm products. In 1971 Alfred Eames, Jr., chairman of Del Monte, cited its pudding cup desserts as an example of a "continuing shift" to "higher-profit formulated or 'manufactured' products." "What do they have to offer?" he asked. "Among other things, above-average profit margins and little or no dependence on agricultural commodity prices."[16]

Ironically, according to a Federal Trade Commission study, most of the processing technologies were developed with public funds — many through Pentagon contracts — reminiscent of Napoleon's awarding of the first contract for canned food in 1810 for his far-traveling army. Your tax dollars bought the research for frozen concentrated juices, prepared mixes, low-calorie foods and drinks, baby foods, dried milk products, instant beverages, frozen poultry, and refrigerated biscuits.[17]

Advertising is the other part of the growth formula of the giants. In product lines dominated by only three or four corporations, advertising allows each company to increase its sales volume without lowering its price below a competitor's — an unsporting act that would narrow the comfortable profit margins of all "club" members.

The food processing industry puts a greater share of its budget into advertising ($13 a year for every man, woman, and child in America) and less into research than any other industry. The National Commission on Food Marketing reported that in 1966 the U.S. food industry spent, for basic food and nutrition research, only one tenth of 1 percent of what it spent on advertising. Already by 1962 the food industry's advertising accounted for more than a fifth of all advertising and was second in size only to cosmetics and toiletries. To be a big food processor a company has to advertise tremendously, but to afford to do this it has to be already well-established. Of the almost 30,000 food firms, the twenty biggest accounted for over 70 percent of all food advertising. The fifty largest food companies account for 63 percent of all advertising on television.

It is precisely these giant food companies,which have succeeded by maximum processing and all-out advertising, that have been expanding abroad — first into Canada, Latin America, Western Europe, and South Africa, then into the Far East, and now even into Africa.

Branded Consciousness

The immediate goal of a food company is brand consciousness: making consumers conscious of supposed differences between its product and Brand X. You can be sure you have brand consciousness if you reach for the brand-name product even though it seems identical (and probably is) with the one having the private label of the supermarket chain. It is the development of this brand loyalty, not feeding people, that is the goal of multinational companies in underdeveloped countries. The former chairman of Nabisco, Lee Bickmore, told us that his yardstick for measuring success of his company in Brazil would be whether people no longer ask for crackers but instead ask for Ritz. "That's what I call consumer demand," he said.

What a global food company, then, has to offer underdeveloped countries is not good food but good advertising. And as a multinational operator, it can repeat the same performance with each new audience — recycling a successful advertising campaign based on research originally paid for by sales in the American market.

The costs of designing such a campaign could never be afforded by a local firm. As Robert Ledogar in his well-documented probe of American food and drug companies in Latin America observes, "Translating this success [of a U.S. advertising campaign] into another language is so much easier for a multinational firm than developing new products to meet specific local needs."[18]

General Foods brought in marketing and advertising experts when it acquired Kibon, its Brazilian ice cream subsidiary.[19] Why not, they reasoned, promote Kibon products in rural areas by offering toys made of popsicle sticks? But the real problem was how to get urban Brazilians to eat ice cream in the winter rainy season. One bright idea was "lucky visits": A Kibon representative might some evening call at your house and award you a gift certificate if you had a pint of Kibon's ice cream in the refrigerator. (The suspense was undercut for millions since they are too poor to have refrigerators.)

In Mexico, General Foods took over a dried-soup company to serve as its launching vehicle for Jell-O. It relied on a tried and true promotional gimmick: Put on the back of each three-pack carton a plastic Walt Disney figure (costing 6 cents each) and then saturate the media encouraging kids to aspire to be "the first to collect all 24." In one test market Jell-O sales jumped 1000 percent in one week. (Jell-O has virtually *no* nutritional value.)

Also in Mexico, General Foods masterminded a way to get Mexicans to pay more for one of their most traditional food items — chili powder. It added a few herbs like oregano and marjoram, figured out how small the packets had to be to get the cost within the reach of lower-income buyers (50 centavos each) and shaped the envelopes, called *triangulitos,* to imitate a locally popular stew flavoring. General Foods then topped it all off with a huge advertising campaign complete with a singing jingle, display signs in thousands of small shops throughout the countryside, and promotional gimmicks like a lottery and a TV contest.

Soft Drinks — Something for Everyone?

Although most multinational food processors aim their products at small upper-income groups, some are determined to market *something* to the poor — even to the very poor. But is it possible to find a product that the poor will want and that can be priced within the reach of millions while still producing a profit large enough to support the big advertising budget necessary to make the poor want it? Nothing fits this description better than soft drinks. The ingredients cost little — they're basically sugar and water. Yet the poor can be made to think of soft drinks as symbols of the good life.

The most extensive dietary impact of foreign corporations in the underdeveloped world is unquestionably coming from soft drinks. In many underdeveloped countries, as diverse culturally as Iran and Venezuela, the jump in sugar consumption is attributed largely to increased soft drink sales. Mexicans go through well over a staggering 14 billion bottles a year, or nearly five bottles per man, woman, and child *every week.*[20]

With such volume markets, even a small profit on each bottle translates into big advertising budgets and big profits. According to Albert Stridsberg, writing in *Advertising Age*, it is saturation advertising that makes the difference. He notes with satisfaction that "in the poorest regions of Mexico where soft drinks play a functional role in the diet [whatever that means!] it is the international brands — Coke and Pepsi — not local off-brands, which dominate." Coke, having taken over several local bottlers' brands, has "captured" 42 percent of the Mexican market. Stridsberg evidently thinks that Coca-Cola's advertisers should be commended that "a Palestinian refugee urchin, shining shoes in Beirut, saves his piastres for a real Coca-Cola, at twice the price of a local cola."[21]

To appreciate how deeply soft drinks can penetrate into the most remote regions of an underdeveloped country, we would like to quote from a letter written by a Mexican priest, Father Florencio, in June 1974:

> It seems that soft drinks are a very important factor in the development of villages. I have heard some people say they can't live one day without drinking a soft drink. Other people, in order to display social status, must have soft drinks with every meal, especially if there are guests. . . .
>
> Near the larger towns where daily salaries are a little higher, soft drinks are cheaper. But in the very remote villages where people earn much less, and where soft drinks have to be transported in by animals, soft drinks cost in many places up to twice as much. The typical family in Metlatonoc can't earn more than 1,200 to 2,000 pesos a year. But even the little they receive each year they spend drinking soft drinks. In the richest village in this area, Olinala, where the majority of people are artisans and earn from 25 to 70 pesos a day [$2.00 to $5.60], about 4,000 bottles of soft drinks are consumed each day. Olinala has 6,000 inhabitants.
>
> The great majority of people are convinced that soft drinks must be consumed every day. This is mainly due to extensive advertising, especially on the radio which is so widespread in the mountains. . . . In the meantime, in these same villages, natural products such as fruit are consumed less — in some families just once a week. Other families sell their own natural products in order to buy soft drinks. . . .[22]

Robert Ledogar found Coca-Cola has also been busy in Brazil. Coca-Cola's competition came from a local popular soft drink with stimulant properties, made from the guaraná fruit grown by small farmers in the Amazon basin. Unlike Coke, the caffeine in guaraná is a natural ingredient, extracted from the seeds of the guaraná tree. Because it is pasteurized it avoids several controversial additives used by Coca-Cola (and Pepsi Cola) products. In

1972, Coca-Cola decided to undercut the popular local drink once and for all. It began to produce Guaraná Fanta. It is entirely artificial, however; hardly the "real thing."

Fanta Orange is Coca Cola's biggest seller in Brazil after Coke itself. Despite its name Fanta Orange contains no orange juice. Yet Brazil is the world's largest exporter of orange juice. Brazil sells almost all of its orange crop to foreigners, mostly to the United States where Coca-Cola is one of the prime buyers for its Snow Crop and Minute Maid orange juice brands. Brazilian consumption of oranges is very low and many Brazilians suffer from a vitamin C deficiency. A study in 1969–1970 of working-class families in populous Sao Paulo found that poor working-class families obtained only about half of the minimum daily requirement of vitamin C.

Fanta-Uva ("Grape") has not a drop of grape juice. Yet in southern Brazil there is a chronic "surplus" of grapes — sometimes over 200,000 tons — that necessitates government-support programs.

Fruit growers recently have been pressing the government for a "Juice Law" that would require soft drinks with the image of a fruit juice drink to contain a specified amount of that juice. The soft drink companies are fighting this. As Ledogar comments in his study, the companies are "anxious to avoid adding costly nutritious [natural] ingredients to their products" that might force them out of an expanding "poor" market.

Another strategy is to reach a younger and younger market of new consumers. Brazilian Robert Orsi who is in charge of Pepsi's million-dollar advertising account adapted Pepsi's American advertising campaign to the "needs" of the Brazilian market. The "Pepsi Generation" became the "Pepsi Revolution." Orsi explains the choice:

> In this country the young don't have protest channels; the present generation didn't receive any political or social education. So we provide them with a mechanism for protest. It is protest through consumption; the teenager changes from the old-fashioned Coca-Cola and adopts Pepsi, the Pepsi with a young and new image, and he is happy, because he is young and young people drink Pepsi.

The seduction of the youth market begins right at school. The cola companies provide or finance refrigerators and other appliances and provide free soft drinks at school events in exchange for permission to sell in the schools. Dr. Anne Dias of the Nutrition Institute in Rio de Janeiro surveyed six- to fourteen-year-old school children. She found high levels of consumption of Coke, Fanta, and Pepsi (one to two bottles per day) by all but the very poor with family incomes under $80 monthly. Dr. Dias also found vitamin deficiencies even in the diets of the rich children (who were the highest soft-drink consumers). Middle-class children showed symptoms of protein malnutrition as well as vitamin deficiency. The children of poor families, of course, suffered from both protein-calorie malnutrition and vitamin-deficiencies. Virtually none of the children drank milk.

In Zambia babies have become malnourished because their mothers fed them Coke and Fanta, believing it is the best thing they can give their children. In the area of the country that produces much of the world's copper, Dr. Stevens, the only pediatrician, reports that 54 percent of the seriously malnourished children admitted to the Children's Hospital at Ndola have "Fanta Baby" written on the progress charts at the foot of their beds. The Zambian government now has reportedly banned Fanta advertisments "because of their influence on the poor."[23]

Canned Pineapple by the Slice

Besides soft drinks, some of the least nutritious foods the companies have been able to devise, are now reaching the poor. While frozen foods and aerosol cans clearly can never be sold to the poor, there are other products that can reach them by being divided up into smaller units. A smaller salable unit means a smaller price — but, of course, higher cost per volume.

Just visit many of the shacklike stores in poor neighborhoods and rural areas throughout the Third World. You will see chewing gum sold by the stick and even the half stick; Ritz crackers counted out one by one; Kellogg's Frosted Flakes scooped out of regular boxes and sold by the cup; popsicles split; a roll of Charms divided up; cigarettes sold singly; a pack of two ITT's Hostess Twinkies cupcakes split open to sell separately. In pineapple-rich Mexico, you even find stores selling Del Monte's canned pineapple by the slice.

As we have seen, the strength of the multinational food company is not food, but advertising and marketing strategies. Advertising reaches into the most remote villages of the underdeveloped world. Mr. V. G. Rajadhyaksha, former chairman of Unilever (Lever Brothers, Good Humor Ice Cream, Lipton's in the United States) in India is enthusiastic about the "new and exciting challenge" of "penetrating rural markets."[24] His goal is to sell Unilever's products in 565,000 Indian villages. Unilever has been persuading "dealers" in the larger towns to open branches, particularly in those villages where they have relatives. No promotional vehicle is beyond consideration, including cinema vans with advertising films, puppet shows, clowns, wall paintings, and sales personnel on stilts. Radio advertising is possible in the so-called well-to-do rural villages where 30 to 50 percent of the people have transistors. In any Third World country, go into the smallest shop in the most remote village and you will have a good chance of finding a placard for Nestlé or for Coca-Cola.

Lee Bickmore, the former Nabisco chairman quoted earlier, long ago saw the connection between media advertising and getting Ritz crackers into the smallest stores:

> Why, we plan someday to advertise all over the world. We might spend, say, $8 million for an advertisement on a communications satellite system. It might reach 359 million people. So what we are doing now is establishing the availability of our products in retail outlets all over the world.[25]

With this advertising effort, even those with very little money are reached. It persuades them that food in a package has special powers. Its subtle message is that their traditional diets of beans, corn, millet, and rice are worthless compared to what Americans eat.

Mexican nutritionist Joaquin Cravioto has studied the changing food habits in Mexican villages. He told us that the *compesinos* are switching from traditional corn tortillas to white breads like Pan Bimbo (ITT's name for Wonder Bread south of the border). ITT might argue that it has more vitamins ("enriched") but the reality is that a poor family's few pesos could buy much more nourishment if they were used to buy tortillas. As nutritionist Alan Berg notes, "Industrial processing inevitably elevates a product's cost beyond that of an equal quantity of the staple."[26] Berg, working for several years in India, found that "saturation food advertising convinced many low-income families they *must* buy certain high-priced nutritious products to keep their children well and alert." As a result, Berg found low-income families "seduced into spending a disproportionate amount of their income on canned baby foods and similar items *at the expense* of more needed staples."

If people in the United States insist on processed, branded food, they simply end up by spending more of the family income on food. Nobody starves, although nutrition suffers. But in underdeveloped countries where it is common for families to have to spend 80 percent of their income on food, the impact of shifting to more costly but less nutritious food is grave.

* * *

Lack of effective media in developing communities inhibits demand stimulation activities. Creative, adaptive applications of demand stimulating techniques are needed for the developing communities.

> Charles C. Slater, "Foreign Agribusiness
> Contribution to Marketing Agricultural
> Products," May 1972

What is it that GFC can contribute to a foreign subsidiary? Well, first we have more than 10 percent of all the food researchers in private industry in this country, and therefore we have a capability in food technology to contribute. Our Dream Whip and Gainoburger dog food products, for example, were technical achievements.

> President, General Foods

How often we see in developing countries that the poorer the economic outlook, the more important the small luxury of a flavored soft drink or smoke . . . to the dismay of may would-be benefactors, the poorer the malnourished are, the more likely they are to spend a disproportionate amount of whatever they have on some luxury rather than on what they need. . . . Observe, study, learn [how to sell in rapidly changing rural societies]. We try to do it at IFF. It seems to pay off for us. Perhaps it will for you too.

> H. Walter, Chairman of the Board, International
> Flavors and Fragrances, "Marketing in
> Developing Countries," *Columbia Journal
> of World Business*, Winter 1974

37
Do They Really Kill Babies?

Question: Some corporations have been criticized for marketing infant feeding formula in underdeveloped countries. And yet, isn't a high protein and vitamin-packed formula exactly what poor mothers need to get their babies started out on the right track?

Our Response: When the birth rate in industrial countries started to decline in the 1960s, articles in business magazines proclaimed the crisis: "The Baby Bust" and "The Bad News in Babyland."[1] One response of baby food corporations was to diversify into other products. Another was to market to the fast-growing population of infants in underdeveloped countries. Sales of infant formula in underdeveloped countries by Abbott Laboratories, American Home Products, and Bristol Myers (through its Mead Johnson Division) began to increase faster than sales at home. Nestlé, with 81 plants in 27 underdeveloped countries and 728 sales centers throughout the world, intensively promotes its Lactogen, Nan, and Cerelac. Borden and Carnation are also in on the growing business.

Most people would assume that sales of baby formula stand in dramatic contrast to the pushing of nonnutritious processed food. Why is it then that over five years ago international agencies such as the World Health Organization (WHO) began to look upon the increased sales of infant formula in underdeveloped countries as a serious health *problem*? Indeed, a public interest group in England, War on Want, in 1974 launched an international campaign claiming that the promotion of infant formula in underdeveloped countries was contributing to severe malnutrition and even to the death of infants.[2] When their pamphlet was translated into German as "Nestlé Kills Babies," Nestlé sought $5 million in damages in the Swiss courts. Nestlé charged that the accusations in the pamphlet — that its efforts were unethical and immoral, that its marketing techniques resulted in infant death, and that it disguised its representatives as medical personnel — were all defamatory. At the last minute Nestlé decided to drop these three claims of defamation. The only charge which Nestlé pressed was that the pamphlet's title "Nestlé Kills Babies" was defamatory. Although the judge ruled in favor of Nestlé on this count, he declared, "This verdict is no acquittal [of Nestlé]."

What did the judge mean? What is the evidence that links the marketing of bottled formula to increased infant death?

In underdeveloped countries the mortality rate for bottle-fed infants is about double that of breast-fed. A recent Inter-American Investigation of Mortality in Childhood, checking on the causes of 35,000 infant deaths, has determined that "nutritional deficiency" as an underlying or associated cause of death was "less frequent in infants breast fed and never weaned than in infants who were never breast fed or only for limited periods."[3] In rural Punjab, India, according to a 1974 report in the medical journal, *The Lancet,* "in the study population virtually all infants died who did not receive breast milk in the first months of life."[4] Two decades ago when breast-feeding was widespread among the poor, severe malnutrition was usually held off beyond the absolutely crucial first year of a child's life. But now, according to World Bank nutritionist Alan Berg, the rapid decline in breast-feeding over the past two decades has caused the average age of the onset of malnutrition to drop from eighteen months to a more critical eight months in several countries studied.[5]

Baby formula displaces mother's milk. But because, as scientific research indicates, mother's milk has changed and evolved along with the human race, it, like nothing else, can sustain the newborn. It contains not the "highest amounts" but the *proper* amounts of proteins and fats for the human baby. Human milk contains only 1.3 percent protein; cow's milk, 3.5 percent.[6] The protein, mineral and fat levels in mother's milk, notes Dr. Hugh Jolly, a prominent London pediatrician writing in the London *Times,*[7] suits the capacity of a human baby's kidney perfectly. Calves need and can handle more protein because they grow much faster. A six-week calf is, after all, already a small cow. These are just some of the reasons why pediatrics professor Paul Gyorgy of the University of Pennsylvania likes to say, "Cow's milk is best for baby cows and human breast milk is best for human babies."[8]

If you still need to be convinced that nature knows what it is doing, please note that human milk comes complete with infection immunizers for humans, especially critical in unsanitary living conditions. Scientists hypothesize that the immunity probably results from the initial dose of antibodies in the colostrum (the yellowish fluid that comes from the mother's breast a few days after birth). Apparently colostrum protects the child against locally common infections, particularly those of the intestinal tract, and against food allergies. "This might explain why allergies are more common in artifically fed babies," comments Dr. Alan Berg. "Gastroenteritis is almost unknown in breast-fed babies, whereas it may be lethal in those fed on cow's milk, especially where sterilization of bottles may be impossible," notes Dr. Jolly.[9] Diarrhea, which can prevent the absorption of any nutrients at all, is rare among breast-fed babies.[10] A mother can adequately feed her infant for at least six months. Even mothers who are themselves malnourished can adequately breast-feed — although partially at the expense of their own tissues. Physiologists agree that the first months of life are crucial for normal brain development. The negative effects of later malnutrition, though highly undesirable, are far more remediable.

Actually a child can be well nourished on breast milk for two years or more if a few other foods are added — and they certainly need not be from a can. In some cultures children are breast fed much longer. As recently as forty years ago, Chinese and Japanese mothers nursed their children as long as five and six years; Caroline Islanders up to ten years; and Eskimoes up to fifteen years.

Several multinational companies, however, have not been satisfied with nature — or at least, not satisfied that nature seemed to leave no room for commercial exploitation. But to create a market where none seemed to exist, multinational corporations found they could play upon another aspect of human nature — the natural desire of parents to ensure a healthy baby. Exposed to countless billboards, newspaper advertisements, and color posters, parents in underdeveloped countries come to equate a happy, healthy baby with a bottle or can of Lactogen. They learn that educated and upper-class families use feeding bottles. They, too, want the best for their baby. The tragic irony, however, is that for most parents in underdeveloped countries, formula feeding actually endangers their baby's life.

First, most families simply cannot afford to buy the necessary amount. To feed one four-month-old infant in Guatemala would require almost 80 percent of the per capita income. To feed such a baby in Lima, Peru, adequately by bottle would take almost 50 percent.[11]

These cost estimates do not include bottles, artificial nipples, cooking utensils, refrigeration, fuel, and medical care (often ten times more needed for the formula-fed than for the breast-fed child). How can a family devote over half or more of its income to food for their youngest and totally unproductive member? The answer is that it cannot.

The seeming solution is to "stretch" the formula with water. Reports of dilution are commonplace. A 1969 survey in Barbados found that 82 percent of the families using formula as the sole food for two- or three-month-old babies were making a four-day can last five days to three weeks.[12] Dr. Adewale Omololu, a professor of nutrition in Nigeria, reported treating a severely malnourished baby whose mother had switched from breast-feeding to a bottle. For a month the child had nothing but water from the bottle because there was only enough money for the *bottle;* it took a month to save up to buy the can of formula!

On diluted formula, a baby loses weight and deteriorates progressively into the malnourished condition called marasmus. The child becomes increasingly susceptible to infection, a problem compounded by bottle-feeding, as we will see.

Second, formula-feeding requires clean water and conditions for sanitary preparation that often do not exist even for the middle classes in underdeveloped countries. "Wash your hands thoroughly with soap each time you have to prepare a meal for baby," reads the Nestlé's *Mother Book* distributed by the company in Malawi.[13] But 66 percent of the households even in the capital city have no washing facilities. "Place bottle and lid in a saucepan of water with sufficient water to cover them. Bring to the boil and allow to boil for 10 minutes," is the counsel of the Cow and Gate Company in its Babycare Booklet for West Africa. The text is accompanied by a photo of a gleaming aluminum saucepan on an electric stove. But you have to go far to find an electric stove in West Africa. Most West African mothers have to cope with a "three-stone" kitchen, that is, three stones supporting a pot above a wood fire. There is only one pot. One pot for sterilizing the baby's bottle and for cooking the family meal. To the mother's eye, putting the bottle in boiling water doesn't seem to do much, anyway; so sterilizing is probably forgotten.

The bottle, the nipple, and the formula are invariably found in the context of illiteracy, a contaminated water supply and the lack of washing, refrigeration, or cooling facilities, and household hygiene. The combination, then, of malnutrition and exposure to bacteria sets up a vicious circle. The infant gets chronic diarrhea and therefore is unable to assimilate even the diluted formula. The infant's nutritional state worsens and it becomes even more vulnerable to respiratory infection and gastroenteritis. This is the state of millions of children who could have been adequately nourished by their mother's milk.

The companies like to argue that they are *fulfilling* and not creating a need. "Just think what the situation would be if we were to say, all right, we think these people [the critics] are right. What would the result be?" asks Ian Barter of Cow and Gate Company.[14] "It would be the death of thousands of children because there are tens of thousands of mothers in these countries who have got to have some substitute for their milk in order to feed their babies."

Let's look at the facts. Nutritionists recognize that there are some women who cannot feed for physiological reasons. But even the companies admit that at most such mothers are fewer than 5 percent.[15] Dr. David Morley surveyed a rural Nigerian village and found less than 1 percent of mothers had serious breast-feeding problems.[16] Moreover, many societies have devised "wet nurse" arrangements to meet the needs of a newborn whose mother could not nurse it.

Indeed, confidence — lack of anxiety — seems to be the key to breast-feeding without difficulties. Several doctors now believe that the typical company advertising does more than anything else to undermine the mother's confidence. By just mentioning "women who do not have milk" and "poor quality" milk, the companies place not so subtle doubts in a mother's mind about her ability to breast-feed.

The companies also stress that their products are needed by

women who work. In fact, the percentage of Third World women who work away from their families is very low. (Countries where there is far greater employment for women, such as the Soviet Union and Cuba, provide extensive paid maternity leaves and day care centers at the workplace, which allow working mothers to breast-feed several times a day.)

But even if there is a need for artificial feeding, does it follow that a country needs a half dozen profit-oriented multinational firms? Is this the only alternative that you, say, as a minister of health, could think of for your country? Is the technology of making an equivalent baby food really so difficult? The United Nations Protein Advisory Group has recommended that underdeveloped countries come up with a product *better* than the expensive, easily contaminated products of the world's largest companies.[17] Various nutritionists have designed, for mothers who cannot breast-feed, nourishing artificial feeding regimes suitable to low-income homes with minimum hygiene, no refrigeration, and limited cooking facilities — and several would cost only a quarter of the current high-priced formulas.[18]

Finally, the companies try to defend themselves by claiming that they really aim their products only at the rich. According to Ross Laboratories' president David O. Cox, only "coincidentally" do his company's promotional activities reach the poor.[19]

This claim again does not fit the facts. The companies have actually devised sophisticated and often ingenious promotion strategies specifically for expanding sales down the income ladder. To begin with, colored wall posters of a healthy baby clutching a feeding bottle greet women, both rich and poor, who enter hospitals and clinics. The companies also employ milk nurses, women who commonly are fully trained nurses. In Nigeria 96 percent of mothers who used bottle-feeding thought they had been so advised by impartial medical personnel, mainly nurses. In fact, these nurses were company representatives. Nestlé employs 4000 to 5000 such "mothercraft advisors" in underdeveloped countries. Dressed in crisp white uniforms, they visit new mothers, no matter what their income level is. In many countries these nurses are allowed to enter maternity wards. Often they receive a commission in addition to salary. Moreover, higher pay offered by the companies diverts nurses trained at public expense from basic full-time health work.

In addition, the companies provide free samples, often through the hospitals. Surveys have shown that just as many illiterate mothers as literate ones receive samples, indicating there was no attempt to select mothers who were able to afford the product.[20] Companies often supply hospitals with free formula supplies, hoping that mothers will feel they must keep on using the products. Abbott Laboratories recently sold $300,000 worth of Similac to the New York City hospitals for only $100,000. A city spokesperson said, "For the company, it's an investment. They hope to get the future business."[21]

Another device clearly aimed at the poor are "milk banks,"[22] usually in hospitals and clinics. They sell the commercial formulas at discount prices to mothers who can prove they are really poor. In this way they can expand sales among the really poor without lowering the price in the normal commercial market. Milk banks in their hospitals just serve to convince women that they need something that they really don't. But even at discount prices (usually 30 to 40 percent), the formulas are too expensive for parents to buy enough. In Guatemala City, fifty mothers buying at a milk bank were questioned. Despite the discount, they could not afford enough so they "prepared the bottles with less milk and more water and in this way the milk lasted longer." Tea or chocolate drink is often substituted.

Radio is also an advertising vehicle to reach the poor. A typical day in Sierra Leone sees fifteen 30-second radio advertisements for Nestlé: "Now Lactogen a better food cos it don get more protein and iron, all de important things dat go make pikin strong and will. . . . Lactogen and Love." The use of the common dialect of the poor makes it hard for Nestlé to convince us that they are directing their advertising at only those who can afford it.[23]

Under the pressure of unfavorable publicity, the companies say they have modified their advertisements.[24] Now the commercial product is pushed as "the next best thing to mother's milk," for cases in which "you find you need a substitute or a supplement to breast milk." Nestlé now recommends "an occasional bottle-feed — if you cannot breast-feed Baby entirely yourself."

The tactic is ingenious. As a Consumers' Union–funded study comments, "By openly recommending breast feeding, the companies can earn their public relations credits. At the same time, the companies can undermine breast feeding by implying repeatedly that a mother may not have enough milk and may need supplementary bottles of formula."[25] La Leche League International, an organization devoted to helping women breast-feed, comments, "The 'supplementary' formula is one of the greatest deterrents to establishing a good milk supply, and frequent nursing is one of the greatest helps."[26]

Such ingenious modification of tactics serves to emphasize how the solution to this grave situation is not simply another "code of conduct" for the companies. One such code, already drawn up, would have company milk nurses wear the company insignia on their uniform. The companies must really think their critics are simple-minded! All the codes condone the use of medical facilities to market their products.[27]

Not only is the decline in breast-feeding a personal tragedy for babies who suffer malnutrition and disease, but it can be calculated as a loss to the natural resources of the country. In Kenya, notes Alan Berg, "The estimated $11.5 million annual loss in breast milk is equivalent to two-thirds of the national health budget, or one-fifth of the average annual economic aid."[28] In the Philippines $17 million was wasted on imported milk in 1958; by 1968, the number of mothers breast-feeding their babies dropped by 31 percent, and the national dollar loss had doubled. As breast-feeding declined sharply in the 1960s, Colombian milk imports soared; in 1968 they were seven times greater than the 1964–1967 average. Berg concludes that "losses to the developing countries more likely are in the billions."

An attack on the bottle-baby tragedy is now underway in some underdeveloped countries. Here are only a few examples. In Papua, New Guinea, the director of public health is enlisting the support of all health workers to persuade storekeepers not to display formula company advertisements.[29] Dar es Salaam University in Tanzania has put out a new guide on baby care for paramedical workers warning of the dangers of formula feeding. In Segbwena, Sierra Leone, a Nutrition Rehabilitation Unit is feeding malnourished children on locally available foods and showing mothers how to prepare well-balanced and inexpensive meals for their families.[30] The Nairobi City Council, Kenya, has banned milk nurses. Some African governments have even instructed rural health workers to destroy formula ads wherever they find them.

In contrast to the private multinational companies, a state-owned company in Zambia announces on its can of milk: "BREAST FEED YOUR CHILD." The label goes on to persuade the potential buyer not to buy the product unless the purchaser can afford to buy enough for many months.

Public action in the industrial countries to halt the ongoing tragedy did not stop with the Nestlé trial in the summer of 1976. Later that summer groups from eight countries working on infant formula malnutrition met in Bern to plan and coordinate their efforts. That fall in New York the Sisters of the Precious Blood, working with the Interfaith Center for Corporate Responsibility (ICCR), brought suit against Bristol Myers. The involvement of the Sisters with Bristol Myers had actually begun a year earlier with a shareholders' resolution requesting information about the company's sales and promotion practices. Bristol Myers refused, however, even to disclose where it sells its products, the first question asked by the Sisters. In their suit against the company the Sisters are charging Bristol Myers with committing fraud in its proxy statement to shareholders. In its statement Bristol Myers claims to have been "totally responsive" to the concerns of the earlier stockholder resolution. Moreover, the company claims that it does not promote its products to people who cannot afford to use them safely, that it does not sell directly to the consumer at all but only through professional medical personnel. The Sisters, working with ICCR, have gathered over 1000 pages of testimony and other evidence from around the world that directly contradict these claims. This documentation demonstrates that Bristol Myers does use many techniques to reach the poor, including selling its products in poor peoples' stores, distributing free samples through health clinics, and using sales personnel dressed as nurses.

The news of the bottle-baby tragedy is spreading — through the press, through a congressional resolution and possible hearings, and through the action of local groups around the world. A film entitled "Bottle Babies" describing the crisis is available through the National Council of Churches in New York.

We hope that by now we have given you an understanding of what the judge in the Swiss trial meant when, after ruling in favor of Nestlé, he added: "This verdict is no acquittal [of Nestlé]."

In an interview on West German radio in 1975 a pediatrician on the staff of Nairobi's Kenyatta National Hospital, Dr. Elizabeth Hillman, told this story:

A short while ago . . . the Nestlé's representatives came to visit us at Nairobi's hospital to ask if we had any opinion about the publication "Nestlé Kills Babies." They really wanted us to say that Nestlé did not kill babies.

We discussed this at length with them and were not able to say of course that Nestlé either does kill or does not kill, statistically speaking. But, to illustrate the point, I mentioned that there was a child over in our emergency ward . . . who was very near to death, because the mother was bottle-feeding with the Nestlé's product (Lactogen, a milk preparation), and out of interest I asked whether they would like to see the baby. I took the two representatives over into our emergency ward and as we walked in the door the baby collapsed and died. I had to leave these two non-medical gentlemen for a moment . . . and help with the resuscitation procedure. It was unsuccessful. And, after the baby was pronounced dead, we all watched the mother turn away from the dead baby and put the can of Nestle's milk in her bag before she left the ward. . . . In a sense . . . it was a vivid demonstration of what bottle-feeding can do because this mother was perfectly capable of breast-feeding. The two gentlemen walked out of that room, very pale, shaken and quiet and there was no need to say anything more."[31]

*   *   *

Its broad geographical and product diviersification, its involvement with the population explosion in backward countries, where it makes cheap baby food, and finally, the fact that it keeps its cash in solid Swiss francs, make Nestlé *shares good insurance against depression, inflation, or revolution.*

Barrons, May 20, 1968

Part IX

The Helping Handout:
Aid for Whom?

38

Triage?

Question: Many people are talking about *triage*, the term coined on the battlefield to describe the sorting out of the wounded into three categories when it is clear that not everyone can be cared for. In order to save anyone at all, it is necessary to aid those with the greatest likelihood of survival. Those hopelessly wounded must be ignored for the sake of the survival of the others. Many experts are saying that we should apply the same principle in selecting countries that should receive our assistance. What is your opinion?

Our Response: In a very real sense our whole book is an answer to triage. The triage metaphor simply does not fit the reality of the world we have discovered through our research.

First, the triage concept is misleading because it implies that the United States has been giving aid according to some softhearted notion of need and that now we must be realistic, selecting recipients according to who is most likely to make it. But no one who has seriously looked at United States aid policies could accuse our country of being softhearted! As one member of the National Security Council put it, "To give food aid to countries just because people are starving is a pretty weak reason." No, as we will demonstrate in this Part, our aid is already highly selective, going to serve the narrow political and economic interests of certain groups in this country.

Second, triage assumes that the underdeveloped countries are on the receiving end only, when, in fact, many underdeveloped countries are net food exporters, particularly of high protein foods such as meat, seafood, and legumes. It reinforces the idea that these countries are the greatest burden because they have too many people. In fact, as we have shown in our response to Question 29, it is the industrial countries that are the major food importers. Between 1970 and 1974, four of the highest GNP countries — Japan, the United Kingdom, Italy, and West Germany — imported six times more grain than China and India, although these four countries have only one-fourth the population of China and India.[1]

Third, triage is built on the scare notion that we are entering an era of absolute scarcity. According to the theory, food must be allocated judiciously to ensure the survival of — let's face it — ourselves.

Another analogy is suggested by biologist Garrett Hardin: that of the lifeboat. If we let everyone on board our lifeboat, we will all drown. But as we have seen throughout this book, the world has hardly reached this point. We have discussed what we call the "inefficiency of inequality" — that the main constraint on food production is the gross inequities in control over the earth's food producing resources. The hungry have increasingly less control over the production process. The result? Tremendous waste: the underutilization of land, the expansion of nonfood and luxury crops to feed the already well-fed, and the feeding of over one third of all the world's grain and at least one quarter of the world's fish catch to livestock. As long as we have a system that is actively *creating* scarcity out of plenty, to say we are reaching natural limits is worse than merely misleading. The suggestion allows the present scarcity-generating system to go on unrecognized for what it is. Meanwhile people are manipulated with fear-evoking images of "shortages" and "overpopulation." Metaphors like triage thus work in the interests of those few who have seized power and wealth for themselves — forces that are steadily undermining the welfare of people both here and in underdeveloped countries.

39

Debt for Development?

Question: If agribusiness corporations cannot solve the problem of hunger, can the assistance given by the United States government do the job?

Our Response: One always hears about the United States "giving aid." In reality, however, more than half of American "aid" is not given at all but loaned with interest.[1] We all know a loan is not a gift even if the interest rates are low. Low interest rates have not prevented the debt obligation of the underdeveloped countries from becoming an increasingly unbearable burden. In just five years between 1967 and 1972 the collective debt burden of eighty-six underdeveloped countries *doubled.*[2] By 1972, the underdeveloped countries owed over $150 billion to banks, governments, and lending agencies in the industrial countries. Each year a greater and greater portion of aid coming in must go out again just to repay loans received in previous years. By 1973, almost 40 percent of all the official development assistance received by underdeveloped countries was spent on debt service payments on past "aid."[3]

Moreover the debt service payments are growing faster than the rate of increases in aid. (For many countries the level of aid is decreasing, not increasing.) Debt service payments are going up twice as fast as the export earnings that bring in foreign exchange to repay the loans. For example, between the mid-sixties and the end of the decade, the gross flows of external aid to Pakistan rose by 5 percent; but the debt service payments rose by 91 percent![4]

It is an obviously no-win situation for the underdeveloped countries. Many Americans, nevertheless, are made to go on believing that all we can do to help is to increase aid. Not only will more aid of this type only compound the debt burden (which is quickly catching up with loan disbursements); it will also force a destructive dependency on exports. As we discussed in Part VI, the only way to get the foreign exchange to repay debts is to sell in the international marketplace. Internal development (building sanitation facilities, schools, and clinics, for example) based on local production and local currency does not count; it does not earn foreign exchange. Thus, without anything else to sell to get the foreign exchange, debt obligations push countries down the dead-end street of heavy reliance on export agriculture.

In any discussion of development assistance these facts should never be forgotten: "Assistance" is largely loans and the debt they create can itself be the ultimate roadblock on the path to self-reliance. Debt takes an increasing bite out of development resources and ensures that a country's economic choices will be determined by foreign markets, hardly equivalent to the internal needs of the country. If development assistance were called "debt for development," the absurdity of thinking that this path could lead to self-reliant growth would be obvious.

40

Food Aid for Whom?

Question: Throughout the book you seem to be talking about an idealized future. What about the present? Food self-reliance *sounds* good, but to get to a state of self-reliance the underdeveloped countries need help *now*. The United States has been the most generous country in the world; since 1950, we have given $25 billion in food aid. Recently, when the need has been greatest, when the food import bill of most underdeveloped countries has doubled, our food assistance has dropped off. Isn't the urgency to help greater now than ever before?

Our Response: This question suggests that U.S. food aid has been an expression of the national concern of the American people. Indeed the intentions of most Americans supporting food aid have been genuine. But the first thing we ourselves have learned in trying to answer this question is that the intentions of the American people may be very different from the actual function of United States policy.

At different periods American food aid has served many purposes for diverse interest groups, but at no time has its primary aim been to feed the hungry. In fact, it was not until 1966 that humanitarian intent was even written into the food aid law. Food aid has been an extension of U.S. foreign policy and business interests, which in most cases are mutually supportive.

To understand how food aid got started you have to look no farther than an interview with the coordinator of United States food aid in the Ford administration, Robert R. Spitzer. After recounting how, in the early 1950s, farmers' groups were calling for something to be done with the mounting surpluses threatening their incomes and how "humanitarians" hated to see food wasted, Spitzer continues:

> There were other people who realized that there was a great potential for the products of the American agricultural community, and that perhaps by wisely placing some of these foods in certain countries, we would develop buyers for future commodities. Then we weren't thinking too much of oil, but I think some of our advanced thinkers were beginning to realize that we were not independent so far as many of the trace minerals are concerned. So someone had to do some thinking. Okay, what do we have to ship out? So the Public Law (480) [food aid] was passed.[1]

Spitzer touched on virtually all the motives for food aid: the farmers' interest in unloading potentially price-depressing surpluses, the interest of agribusiness corporations in creating markets, and the potential of food as a weapon in assuring access to strategic materials. The only motive he neglected to mention was the use of food aid in support of United States military intervention, one of its principal functions since the mid-1960s.

Spitzer labeled as "advanced thinkers" those who saw in food the power to obtain strategic raw materials. In fact, as early as the late 1940's, a special commission of the Truman administration concluded that the United States was dependent on foreign sources for several strategic raw materials.[2] In 1951, India made an emergency request to the United States for grain to stave off famine precipitated by monsoon failure. Since the end of World War II, India had embargoed exports of monazite sands that contain thorium, used in the production of atomic energy. Now the American government saw that food could give it the leverage to lift the embargo. Congressman Charles J. Kersten, Republican of Wisconsin, put it bluntly: "In return for the wheat we are asked to give to India, the very least we should ask of India is that it permit the United States to buy some of these strategic materials."[3] The result was the India Emergency Food Act of 1951, which is a direct predecessor of Public Law (P.L.) 480, passed in 1954 — later called "Food for Peace."

P.L. 480 itself resulted from an even more immediate crisis. A greater problem than how to acquire needed materials was how to get rid of unnecessary ones! America had too much food.

During the 1940s, grain production in the United States had

increased by about 50 percent, while domestic consumption lagged well behind, increasing only by about 30 percent. Productivity increases, based on more fertilizers and pesticides, plus better seeds, and price supports for farmers, created enormous surpluses that were costing taxpayers $1 million a day just for storage.

These surpluses represented a terrible dilemma. The farm lobby would not allow them to be put on the domestic market. And if dumped on the world market, grain prices would drop by a dollar a bushel. U.S. grain corporations were opposed to such a disruption of their international commercial market. In 1952, at their national convention, the American Farm Bureau, a group representing large- and medium-sized farmers, proposed a solution: Create a secondary foreign market by allowing food-deficit countries to pay for American food imports in their own currencies instead of in dollars. That is what P.L. 480 did. P.L. 480, then, was seen as a way to help low-income countries, which otherwise would not constitute a market at all, to buy surplus American food while keeping the commercial dollar price up for higher-income countries. P.L. 480 meant the United States could have its cake and eat it too.

Three fourths of all our "food aid" has gone under Title I of P.L. 480. Title I provided dollar credits (on a low-interest, long-term basis) to friendly governments to import food from the United States. The foreign government then sells the food on the local commercial market or, in exceptional cases, in government ration stores, to those who can pay. Until the end of 1971, the U.S. government accepted the local currencies generated by these food sales as repayment of the loans.

The fact that the food is sold in local commercial markets means, of course, that most food aid never reaches the people who most need it. As drought reports brought food aid to West Africa in the early seventies, most of the relief grains arriving in Upper Volta and the Ivory Coast were sold on credit to the peasants at usurious rates of interest. One observer familiar with the area contends that since the harvests would not be adequate to repay the debts, the peasants and their children would be forced to work for their creditors to pay back their debts. Thus food aid kept in motion the process of virtual enslavement of the rural people.[4]

Market Development

In the first five years after it was passed, P.L. 480 succeeded in unloading abroad over $5 billion worth of American grain or 28 percent of total American agricultural exports. But even this was not enough. The surpluses continued to mount. By 1959 the United States held its highest stocks in history. Merely responding to food-deficit countries was not enough to unload the surpluses. Policy makers decided they had to take an active role in *creating* markets. The goal spelled out in the preamble to P.L. 480 included these words: "to develop and expand export markets for United States agricultural commodities." The goal was clear; the question was how to achieve it.

The answer was "development." P.L. 480, by allowing countries to import food *without* using dollars, made it more likely that poor governments would have dollars available to import American capital goods for light industrialization. Assistant Secretary of State W. L. Clayton testified that the World Bank financing for such capital goods "would certainly be a very good one for U.S. agricultural exports, because as you help develop them industrially, you will shift their economy to an industrial economy, so that I think in the end you would create more markets for your agricultural products."[5]

To reinforce this direction, Congress in 1957 modified P.L. 480 so that up to 25 percent of the local currency accepted in exchange for food could be loaned at very low interest rates to U.S. corporations investing in those countries. Some companies, it was thought, could quite directly create demand for American agricultural exports. Eldridge Haynes, chairman of Business International, the service organization for multinational corporations, told the committee, chaired by Senator Humphrey, of the need for expanding the American food-processing industry into the underdeveloped world:

> We are not exporting bread, we are exporting wheat. Somebody has to convert it into bread. If they do not, if there are not more facilities to make bread, it will not be consumed.[6]

Haynes said the same is true of cotton and tobacco. He suggested, therefore, that American corporations get "Cooley loans" (named after a House Agricultural Committee chairman from North Carolina) in order to construct processing facilities for cloth and cigarettes.

Food surpluses in the United States were sold on credit to a foreign government that in turn sold the food for local currency. That local currency then in part financed American companies that would, it was hoped, generate the need to import yet more food. Under the Cooley loan provision, part of P.L.480 until 1971, 419 subsidiaries of American firms in thirty-one countries established or expanded their operations at very low cost. In India, alone, Cooley loans have gone to Wyeth Labs, Union Carbide, Otis Elevator, Sylvania, Rockwell International, Goodyear, CPC International, Sunshine Farms, First National City Bank, the Bank of America, and American Express, among others.

In addition, the Department of Agriculture uses food loan repayments (in 1975 alone to the tune of $12 million) to support private trade associations such as the United States Feed Grains Council, whose members are the major grain-exporting companies. It uses the money to promote feedgrain livestock and poultry industries throughout the underdeveloped world.[7]

Building a Feedgrain Market: The Case of Cargill, Inc.

In 1968, Cargill decided to set up a complete poultry operation in South Korea breeding chicks, producing chicken feed, and retailing chickens. The American government — that is, the American taxpayers — provided 95 percent of the financing for what looked like a very profitable operation. Almost $500,000 came as a Cooley loan.

Korea Cargill (whose local partner happened to be the dictator, President Park) picked up an additional $1.9 million loan from the U.S. government under the Private Trade Entity provision of P.L. 480. (This provision allows the Commodity Credit Corporation, part of the USDA, to loan to a private corporation the money to purchase American agricultural commodities. The corporation then sells them in a foreign market, using the proceeds to establish its operations there. So far over $120 million has gone to corporations under this P.L. 480 provision.)

All this help was not enough for Cargill. By 1972, the Cargill operation was in trouble. Cargill had used up all conceivable P.L.

480 credits for importing grain. Never known to be turned down, Cargill approached its friends in the United States government to persuade South Korea to relax domestic price controls and import restrictions that interfered with its feedgrain import operations. The State Department instructed the embassy in South Korea to see that the "poultry and livestock industries" receive special consideration from the government. Finally, when all else failed, Cargill sought and received a deferment of payment on its two P.L. 480 loans. Apparently, this giant corporation, which most loudly condemns government meddling in trade and business, cannot survive without its favors.

P.L. 480 credits also enabled Ralston Purina and the Peavey Corporation to establish poultry operations in South Korea. The net effect has been to make South Korea heavily dependent on imported feed. Whereas South Korea had earlier imported no feedgrain, by 1974 it imported about one million tons from the United States. Moreover, once having become dependent on American feedgrain imports, South Korea saw the United States raise the price three and a half times between 1970 and 1974. The intent of turning South Korea into a market for United States grain has been achieved.[8]

Building a Wheat Market

P.L. 480 has succeeded in creating markets for wheat among the world's original rice lovers. P.L. 480 "was the best thing that ever happened to the wheat industry," said one market development specialist, pointing to the tremendous increase in wheat consumption in such countries as Japan, Taiwan, and Korea. Wheat aid credits to the Taiwanese government allowed it to export the people's staple, rice, while it exhorted the population to embrace the new diet by such slogans as "eating wheat is patriotic."[9] South Korea now has 7000 bakeries, and Koreans eat Italian-style noodles made from wheat flour.[10] "We taught people to eat wheat who did not eat it before," brags an official of USDA.[11]

P.L. 480 has perhaps proved that people like what they eat rather than eat what they like. At any rate American corporations have taught them to eat what they have to sell. This achievement was lauded, in 1974, in testimony before the Senate

Foreign Relations Committee by former Secretary of Agriculture Orville Freeman, now president of Business International (the same organization whose chief, Eldridge Haynes, you will recall, seventeen years earlier had urged the use of P.L. 480 to create markets for American agricultural exports). Freeman noted that, "In the last seven years, our agricultural exports to Taiwan have climbed by 531 percent and those to [South] Korea by 643 percent because we created a market." P.L. 480 "makes very good sense," he added.

Yet does it make good sense for South Korea?

United States Food Aid and Local Production

South Korea has been the second largest recipient of American food aid and has purchased more U.S. agricultural goods than any other underdeveloped country. What has been the impact on South Korea's own agriculture? United States grain imported into Korea has helped American farmers and corporations but it has stifled the incomes of Korean farmers and farm workers. The neglect of food production has resulted in a notable decline in agricultural output and, according to a 1974 World Bank analysis, sharp deterioration in rural incomes in contrast to urban areas.[12] South Korea will soon need to import *half* of the food needed for domestic demand, but even then the jobless will not be able to eat. The real role of United States food aid has been to keep food prices down and thereby keep the urban classes less unhappy with the authoritarian regime of President Park that bans strikes and other forms of protest. Still former Assistant Secretary of Agriculture Clayton Yeutter recently claimed, "South Korea is the greatest success story worldwide of the Food for Peace [P.L. 480] program in terms of its contribution to the growth of the nation."[13]

Colombia is another dramatic case, showing the effects of P.L. 480 shipments. Between 1955 and 1971, Colombia imported over 1 million tons of wheat that could have been produced more cheaply at home.[14] The marketing agency of the Colombian government fixed the price of the imported grain so low that it undercut domestically produced wheat. This dumping resulted in 50 percent lower prices to Colombian farmers. From 1955, the first year of P.L. 480 shipments, to 1971, Colombia's wheat production dropped by 69 percent while its imports increased 800 percent to the point that imports came to account for 90 percent of domestic consumption.[15]

Moreover, two thirds of the 407,550 acres that were pushed out of wheat production by subsidized wheat imports have not been compensated for by increases in other crops for local consumption. The fertile Sabana de Bogotá Valley, for example, which once grew wheat, is now used for cattle grazing — primarily for export.[16] Such poultry and cattle feeding operations were abetted by P.L. 480 Cooley loans that went to subsidiaries of United States corporations such as Ralston Purina, Quaker Oats, Pfizer, and Abbott Laboratories to build plants for processing feed and producing drugs. Landlords, now making greater profits on beef, flowers, and vegetables for export, expand their operations, evict their tenants, and, in general, exclude more and more ordinary farmers from the land. Without land and without jobs, those needing food cannot buy the food aid. Already in Colombia this rural impoverishment is far advanced. The richest 10 percent of the rural population in 1970 received 35 percent of total income, while the poorest 20 percent received only 4 percent.[17] In this traditionally corn-eating country, the imported wheat is to meet the "demand" of the "Americanized" minority who can afford processed, brand-name foods.

The impact of American food aid to Bolivia has been similar. But an additional turn of the screw came when the United States stopped accepting payments in local currency and demanded dollars for food aid shipments, albeit on easy terms. Despite its rich agricultural potential and high rural underemployment, Bolivia had come to depend on United States imports, and local wheat production had stagnated. Millers had turned themselves primarily into flour-importing companies because importing was more profitable than milling. Thus, even after local currency was no longer accepted to repay P.L. 480 shipments (the final cutoff point being at the end of 1971), Bolivia had to continue to import flour. The big difference, however, was that Bolivia was forced to use up scarce foreign exchange to purchase the flour in dollars, foreign exchange that might have gone to purchase what it could *not* easily produce itself, such as productive industrial goods.

Even before we began out research for this book, we had long been familiar with the claims that United States food aid ship-ments depress the incentive of foreign farmers to grow their own food. We were tempted to reject the conclusion simply because it sounded like some "right-wing," unfounded critique of welfare ("If you feed 'em, they won't want to work").

We did not understand an important distinction. Many critics were saying that if you give people food, they will not *want* to grow food for themselves; whereas the fact is that dumping large quantities of low-priced American grain on underdeveloped coun-tries makes it economically *impossible* for the small domestic producers to compete — no matter how much they might want to. Unable to get a fair return for their grain, such producers are fre-quently forced to sell their land, becoming landless (and often job-less) laborers. A study published in an agricultural economics journal in 1969 concluded that for every pound of P.L. 480 cereals imported, there was a net decline in Indian domestic production over the following two years of almost one-half pound because of the reduced return to the farmer.[18]

Food Aid, Strings Attached

In a recent article entitled, "P.L. 480 — Humanitarian Effort Helps Build Markets," USDA congratulates itself for helping to stimulate food sales abroad. "Many countries," it says, "have 'graduated' from P.L. 480 status."[19] Besides helping American corporations build import-demanding industries abroad, P.L. 480 created yet another method for helping countries "graduate" to commercial purchases. In order to receive food aid, the potential recipient had to accept one condition: agreement to purchase in the future on commercial terms, American agricultural com-modities in the future. In 1973, our government made food credit to the Dominican Republic conditional upon much larger com-mercial purchases. In 1975, P.L. 480 loans to Egypt for wheat and to South Korea for rice were tied to additional commercial pur-chases of these commodities.

The United States applies this stipulation regularly for all commodities except wheat and reserves the right to apply it to wheat also. "The U.S. takes this seriously," emphasizes one American official. "If a country hasn't met its commercial re-quirements by the end of the year, the requirement is added on to the next year."[20] Apparently the compassion of the United States government is limited to future customers.

Now you can understand why the former Secretary of Agriculture Earl Butz said recently:

> It was my good fortune to be Assistant Secretary of Agriculture during the middle 1950's when Public Law 480 was enacted and the market development program got underway. Reflecting on that period, I think of it as quite historic and forward looking — a time in which some of the groundwork was laid for the successes of recent years in agricultural trade.[21]

Food as a Weapon

United States food aid as a political and military weapon in the sixties and seventies is not a new story. Immediately following World War I, future President Herbert Hoover put his support behind a food aid program for Germany to avert the danger of hungry Germans voting socialist (as well as to solve the American food surplus problem generated by the wartime agricultural effort).

In 1943, forty-three nations created what would become the United States–dominated United Nations Relief and Rehabilitation Administration (UNRRA) to give food aid to war victims. The aid was "not to be used as a political weapon and no discrimination was to be made in distribution for racial, religious or political reasons."[22] Despite this explicit provision, American food aid went to fascist forces in Greece and to Chiang Kai-shek in China. India received no help following the great famine of 1943 in which 4 million Indians died, nor in the 1946–1947 famine. Just as the Department of State might say about Africa today, India, at that time, did not qualify as a liberated war zone or as a priority anticommunist front zone, according to then Secretary of State Dean Acheson.

Following World War II, over one quarter of all United States funds spent on food aid was spent under the Marshall Plan. Enormous quantities of grain on credit flowed into Italy and France to help keep the impoverished working class from voting against capitalism. Marshall himself stated at the time: "Food is a vital factor in our foreign policy."

In 1959, Senator Humphrey criticized those who would have

food aid serve only as a surplus disposal mechanism. He saw food as a potent political weapon:

> We have been told repeatedly that this is a worldwide struggle between the forces of evil and the forces of decency. . . . We all know we are engaged in the struggle of men's minds, for their loyalties. There is a struggle between ways of life, a system of values. Our values are different from those of the totalitarians. If it is a worldwide struggle, it would seem to me we would want to mobilize all the resources we possibly can in order to win it. And in a world of want and hunger what is more powerful than food and fibre?[23]

Since we have been told China, North Vietnam, and North Korea are "the forces of evil," naturally most of our food aid has gone to the bordering countries: India, South Vietnam, during the Vietnam War, Cambodia, South Korea, and Taiwan. By 1973, almost *half* of all U.S. food aid was going to South Vietnam and Cambodia. Between 1968 and 1973, South Vietnam alone received twenty times the value of food aid that the five African countries most seriously affected by drought received during that same period.[24]

The withdrawal of food aid can also be a powerful political weapon. Aid to Chile was abruptly discontinued when a government was elected that threatened American corporate interests, as we will discuss later. This withdrawal of food to serve political ends is not unique. During the summer of 1974 the State Department refused low-interest loans for food to Bangladesh unless it stopped exporting gunny sacks to Cuba.[25]

It stands to reason that if the United States sees food as one way to make its political muscle felt, then it would hardly want to contribute its food to agencies where the direction and use of the aid would be outside its control. And such is the case. In October 1974, the *Washington Post* reported on an unreleased government document, part of the preparation for the World Food Conference the following month. In it the United States opposed expansion of the World Food Program (WFP), a United Nations program to aid in famine areas, to help vulnerable groups such as pregnant women and to supply food-for-work projects. The draft said that the United States has "not been able in recent years to influence appreciably the policies and procedures of the WFP or the distribution of aid to particular destinations. There would appear to

be no advantage to the U.S. favoring a greater role and more resources for WFP."²⁶ The administration clearly wanted to have
nothing to do with food aid projects it could not mold to its own
purposes.

Food Aid as the Perfect Guise

By 1973, with commercial sales booming, thanks to U.S. Food
Power export policies, the amount of agricultural products shipped under P.L. 480 dropped to 3.3 million tons, one fifth of the
level of the mid-sixties. The Department of Agriculture no longer
needed P.L. 480 to dispose of surpluses. But the National Security
Council and the State Department under Kissinger were there to
pick up the food aid baton.

Congress had begun to resist efforts by the administration to
continue to prop up the regimes in South Vietnam and Cambodia
as well as to aid the Chilean junta, which so flagrantly disregards
human rights. P.L. 480 provided the administration with just the
funding vehicle needed to skirt congressional controls.

First, the administration was confident that expanding food aid
expenditures would be hard for Congress to oppose since so many
well-meaning Americans think food aid is to feed hungry people.
Second, P.L. 480 country programs are not subject to annual congressional appropriations. The budget submitted is only an estimate that can change without congressional approval. For instance, in the fiscal year 1974, Cambodia was slated to receive $30
million in food aid but in fact received $194 million.²⁷ In addition,
the Commodity Credit Corporation (CCC), established in 1957 to
expand markets for American agricultural products, has its own
capacity to extend credits for agricultural purchases to favored
governments. Here, too, there is flexibility. During the course of
the fiscal year 1976, the actual CCC credit sales were double the
amount originally budgeted. All this gave the government quite a
bit of leeway.

Third, food aid can easily, yet discreetly, be turned into direct
support for foreign military efforts. The food can be sold locally by
foreign governments, thereby generating funds for that government's military budget. In the case of certain countries the administration does not require repayment of the food aid loan. It
simply authorizes the recipient government to use the proceeds

from the food resale as a grant for "common defense." In October 1973, an agreement signed with South Vietnam allowed all proceeds to the Saigon government from P.L. 480 sales to go to the military budget; in Cambodia the figure was 80 percent of food aid sales.

Between 1946 and 1975, $6 billion in local currencies generated by the sale of P.L. 480 food was spent for military purposes; over one third of this in South Korea and South Vietnam. [28] One study showed that in 1965 over 85 percent of South Korea's resale funds were used for "common defense and security."[29]

These three realities make food a handy tool indeed. In fiscal year 1974, for instance, Congress cut more than 20 percent out of the economic aid requested for Indochina by the administration. Undaunted, the White House more than doubled the P.L. 480 allocation to South Vietnam and Cambodia to $499 million, giving these two countries half of all food credits that year.[30] An American reporter in Cambodia documented a refugee camp where 70 percent of the small children were malnourished while nearby the bags of food aid were being sold to pay the troops.[31] In contrast to Indochina, all of Africa received less than 15 percent of the food aid total that year.

In 1973, Congress, pressured by outraged citizens, tried to stop America's food for war program. It prohibited the use of any P.L. 480 resale funds for military purposes. The effect, however, was almost meaningless. Since the proceeds from the reselling of United States food often go into the general treasuries of the receiving countries, it is impossible to check how they get spent.[32]

For fiscal year 1975, the administration was again budgeting half of all P.L. 480 credits for South Vietnam and Cambodia. In light of a growing image of America as indifferent to the plight of the hungry, Congress tried to balance the obvious military and political intent of U.S. food aid with some concern for the starving. It passed an amendment requiring that 70 percent of the food aid go to countries on the United Nations list of "most seriously affected" countries.

Here was a real challenge for the government: What steps should be taken? The first tack was to claim that the 70 percent rule applied only to food items — not to cotton and tobacco also shipped under P.L. 480. (The government was aware that these commodities could be turned into guns just as readily as food could.) Another strategy initiated by Kissinger, then secretary of state, was simply to get Vietnam put on the United Nations list of "most seriously affected" countries; that one failed.

Finally, in order to get the amount of military support it wanted for Cambodia and Vietnam and to give its vote of confidence to other repressive regimes in Chile, South Korea, and the Middle East, the administration merely increased the total amount of food aid available. It could then support its client regimes and still stay within the new ruling requiring 70 percent of our food aid to go to the neediest countries, claiming, all the while, to have generously acceded to the demands of the "humanitarians" by increasing food aid from $1 billion to $1.6 billion.

In 1975, in protest against the junta's repressive policies, Congress placed a $26 million limit on economic aid to Chile (still the second-highest amount granted by the United States to any country in Latin America) and cut off military aid altogether. All that meant little. By the end of the year, Chile's share of food aid was over $60 million.[33]

With the defeat of the United States in South Vietnam, South Korea has taken on a new strategic significance in East Asia. The familiar pattern is being repeated: Congress tries to phase out military aid and the administration brings in food aid to fill the gap. South Korea's food aid credits for the fiscal year 1975–1976 are twice what they were the previous year.

Food for Strategic Materials

In the mid-seventies we are exactly at the point where we came in twenty years ago. Promoters of Food Power allude to uses of food aid reminiscent of Congressman Kersten who, you will recall, suggested in the 1950s that food might be the way to secure strategic materials. Today our food is seen as a weapon of counter attack against those underdeveloped countries the U.S. government fears will model themselves on OPEC, seeking a better deal for their exports of raw materials. President Ford's warning to the underdeveloped countries that might entertain such notions was unmistakable. In a speech to the United Nations General Assembly in 1974, he said:

> The attempt by any nation to use one commodity for political purposes will inevitably tempt other countries to use their commodities for their

own purposes. . . . It would be tempting for the United States, beset by
inflation and soaring energy prices, to turn a deaf ear to external appeals for food assistance.[34]

In this not-so-veiled threat the uses of American food aid have
come full circle.

The "New" Food Aid?

In late 1975, Congress reacted to this long history of the misuse
of food aid by passing H.R. 9005, a new assistance bill in which
the humanitarians supposedly recaptured food aid for their purposes. We read the bill eagerly to see just how Congress was going
to redress at least twenty to thirty years of American history.
Perhaps we should not have been surprised to find that even the
bill's humanitarian tone is garbled by the familiar theme of food
aid to serve United States economic interests.

Under the heading of "Food Aid to Poor Countries" the new bill
reads:

In furnishing food aid under this Act, the President shall . . . assure
that allocation of commodities or concessional financing is based upon
the potential for expanding markets for America's abundance abroad.

The goal of expanding commercial markets for American commodities is once again clearly spelled out.

And in 1976 food aid continued to serve as a surplus disposal
program. ("Surplus disposal" is not a term we invented. A multilateral committee organized to smooth out snags in food aid
calls itself the Consultative Subcommittee on Surplus Disposal.)
America had "too much" rice so it tried to get rid of it through P.L.
480 agreements with India and Bangladesh. India and
Bangladesh did not want rice, however; they had a bumper rice
harvest, too. In fact, in 1976, Bangladesh did not have enough
storage room even for domestically produced rice. The minister of
agriculture was justifiably concerned that the imported rice
would reduce local rice prices and thus undermine farmer incentives for the next planting.[35]

The new food aid bill also specifies that 80 percent of all P.L.
480 commodities must go to countries with per capita incomes of
less than $250. But given all we know now about the budgetary

discretion and maneuvers of the administration, will it be enforced?

We do not claim to have all the answers about food aid. A few points have, however, become clear to us. First, hungry people should know that the United States can never be a source of food security. Indeed, food security is not something that can be given, even by a well-intentioned foreign government. Underdeveloped countries had better *assume* that the United States will use its food surpluses to help expand its commercial markets, to assist the penetration of agribusiness firms and to support the very regimes that work in direct opposition to the policies that would enable hungry people to feed themselves. Let anything else be a pleasant surprise.

Second, food aid reserves must be controlled by a multilateral institution in which all donor and recipient nations participate in order to lessen the opportunity for political and commercial manipulation. We have seen that the United States government has strongly and secretly resisted one step in this direction, the World Food Council.

Third, once controlled by a multilateral institution, food aid should be used as payment for work that directly contributes to creating the preconditions for food self-reliance. An example will illustrate what we mean. The United Nations WFP contributed sorghum to Senegal to be used to pay laborers. In one village a ton of the local staple, couscous, was made from this sorghum. That *one* ton of food was then used to mobilize 60 people to clear and plant 74 acres of bush that soon yielded 45 tons of rice.[36] Food aid, in this case, helped people to grow their own food.

Fourth, concerned Americans must stop thinking of food aid as the most direct way to help the hungry. Dwelling on the issue of American food aid — how much and who is getting it — diverts attention from the *process* of how hunger is created. It allows us to forget that the overriding impact of the United States on the ability of people to feed themselves is not through food aid, but through its corporate, military, and economic involvement.

*   *   *

America's agricultural strength, flowing steadily to other nations, as well as into our domestic markets, is probably the greatest contributor to world peace that we now have. Food crosses uncrossable borders; it skirts bamboo curtains and pierces iron curtains.

Secretary of Agriculture Earl Butz, 1976

I have heard . . . that people may become dependent on us for food. I know that was not supposed to be good news. To me, that was good news, because before people can do anything they have got to eat. And if you are looking for a way to get people to lean on you and to be dependent on you, in terms of their cooperation with you, it seems to me that food dependence would be terrific.

Senator Hubert H. Humphrey, 1957

During the last 10 years, the United States supplied 80 percent of the world's food aid. We did this, on the whole, without making the recipient nations deeply dependent upon our continued assistance — this danger has been, for the greater part, averted.

Don Paarlberg, USDA official

41

What About the "New" Aid?

Question: The major multilateral assistance organizations like the World Bank seem to have learned from their mistakes during the 1960s. They admit now that they have concentrated too much on industrialization. They admit also that they mistakenly focused on the large landowner, thinking that this was the path to rapid progress. These organizations have now focused on the small farmer, as the answer to the world food problem. For the American concerned about world hunger, isn't it best to support this more enlightened approach — called the new aid? Shouldn't we lobby our own representatives in Congress to increase U.S. support for the World Bank?

Our Response: There has been a dramatic shift in the rhetoric of the World Bank. Robert McNamara, once Secretary of Defense and now the Bank's president, has changed his career from making war in Southeast Asia to a worldwide war against "absolute poverty." Recently he stated:

> The object of development is the human being. In other words, it is not enough simply to build a road, or a dam, or a power station. It is necessary to do those things in such a way that they contribute most to creating a better, fuller, and more productive life for the people.[1]

How could anyone criticize this change of heart? World Bank literature is full of references to — "the small farmer," "improved income distribution," "the rural poor," "integrated rural development," and "labor-intensive techniques." All the words are right. But what do they mean?

Even assuming Robert McNamara might "like" the World Bank to focus its resources just on the small farmer, the Bank does not seem to be about to do it. Between the time that McNamara took over in the late sixties and 1973, only 25 percent of all agricultural credit financed by the Bank went to the small farmers (even generously defined to include those cultivating up to 12 acres) while 75 percent was awarded to medium and large farmers. The World Bank itself admits that its credit has been reaching *less* than 1 percent of all such small farmers in the underdeveloped countries. The Bank says that during the next five-year period it will allocate almost half of its rural credit to small farmers.[2] Read another way, this means that more than half the Bank's rural credit will still be going to medium and large farmers who constitute only about 20 percent of all landholders in the underdeveloped countries.[3] Furthermore, no Bank credit will reach the many millions of would-be farmers who have no holdings small or large.

The same is true, of course, of all the channels in the underdeveloped countries through which the Bank spreads its funds. In the period from 1969 to 1973, about 80 percent of all World Bank agricultural credit went through foreign governments to commercial banks, development banks, agricultural banks, or special project authorities. Only 20 percent went through cooperatives — and even "cooperative" does not necessarily mean small farmers.[4] The World Bank itself acknowledges that these specialized agricultural and development banks lend primarily to large farmers, even if their stated purpose is to benefit the small farmer.[5] For example, the World Bank made two loans in the Philippines to rural banks that were partially government-owned. Although the stated purpose was to help small farmers, actually smallholders with less than 7 acres (who comprise 73 percent of all farmers in the area) received less than 1 percent of the credit extended. This pattern appears all too typical. The World Bank itself does not seem optimistic about changing the policies of the agencies through which its funds flow.[6]

In his often cited 1973 speech in Nairobi McNamara defined the Bank's prime goal as increasing the production of the small farmer. Seeming to believe there is a conflict between a focus on the small farmer and increasing production, the Bank explains why it is not about to turn its back on the larger farmer.

> Recognizing the high priority of food production, the Bank looks upon the need to reduce poverty in rural areas as twin goals. Its emphasis on rural lending, therefore, includes lending not only for

those in the poverty target groups but also for the larger-scale farmers when it is necessary to raise their production in order to increase domestic food supplies and/or contribute to exports.[7]

The World Bank continues to support the large farmer despite evidence from every corner of the globe showing that the small farmer can be more productive than the large, as McNamara himself points out elsewhere in his Nairobi speech.

Can the Bank promote *both* the small farmer and the large farmer? Promoting the large farmer necessarily undermines the lot of the small farmer. The rich farmers can use their access to credit to expand their holdings and mechanize their production, thus displacing both farmers and laborers. In addition, increasing the availability of credit for large farmers who are more likely to grow export crops, further undercuts the local food supply. Finally, large landholders, finding that the World Bank credits make their operations more profitable than ever, will be even more adamant against land redistribution, as will the national government that guarantees repayment of the Bank's loans.

Marketable Surplus

If the Bank is so concerned about hunger, then why does it continue to support the largeholder? To understand the Bank's position we must keep in mind that while "feeding the hungry" might warm the heart of Mr. McNamara, there is no column headed "full stomachs" on his ledger sheets. Hungry people who grow food so that they can eat better do not produce much money and foreign exchange. Only if they grow enough to sell, that is, a marketable surplus, will loans get repaid with interest. And that is what the Bank has got to be concerned about.

The World Bank, like any other bank, is concerned with minimizing its risk. The Bank itself notes, "Lending only to those with investment opportunities sufficient to produce a significant marketable surplus is perhaps the best way to reduce the level of default."[8] "Those with investment opportunities" is a euphemism for the larger farmer. It is rough to try to be a bank and a savior of the world at the same time!

Besides betting on the large farmer, the Bank often carries its risk minimization one step further: Farmers are sure to come up with a marketable surplus, indeed all of their production will go to market, if they are "encouraged" to produce nonfood crops. After all, cotton and rubber can't possibly be eaten up by the producer. Furthermore, as the Bank notes, "Delinquencies [in loan repayments] have also been reduced when repayment has been coordinated with the marketing of crops that are centrally processed, for example, tobacco, cotton, cocoa, tea, and coffee."[9] Thus to limit its own risks the World Bank prefers not to lend for the basic food crops of the people. Actual agricultural loans overwhelmingly demonstrate this preference.

The World Bank and its affiliate, the International Development Association, are lending $26 million to Cameroon to expand oil palm, rubber, tea, and pepper plantations. Cocoa is their focus in Ghana and Nigeria; tea in Uganda and Mauritius; coffee in Burundi and Kenya; tobacco in Uganda and Tanzania; and cotton in Upper Volta.[10]

Livestock is another "cash crop" highly favored with World Bank credit. Livestock is the largest category of agricultural loans; nearly one third of all the Bank's agricultural credit is for livestock projects. The amount rises in some areas. In Latin America, for instance, over 70 percent goes to livestock projects.[11] A 1967 loan of $4 million for the first stage of a livestock project in Ecuador provided $16,000 credit on the average for 240 ranchers — who at that rate could hardly be considered the rural poor. None of the 60 percent of the people of Ecuador who earned less than $75 per year could possibly be so creditworthy. In 1971, the Bank made its very first loan to Guatemala for agricultural development. It provided $4 million to cover 52 percent of the costs of a beef project and promised a $15 million follow-up loan for expansion. The benefiting ranchers were to be "medium-sized." In fact, the subloans went to the country's 300 richest export ranchers.[12]

Besides focusing on the larger farmers and cash crops, still another way to ensure that the so-called marketable surplus does not get eaten is to send out supervisors to make sure it does not happen. Again we quote the Bank itself: "Supervision is designed to help the farmer but also to prevent loan funds from being misused for financing consumption and to ensure repayment. . . . *But supervision can never completely eliminate increases in consumption* following the receipt of loans, even when credit is provided in kind" [emphasis added].[13] Even the World Bank can't always prevent people from eating what they grow!

Steadying the Boat

In his Nairobi speech in 1973, Mr. McNamara asked, "What can the developing countries do to increase the productivity of the small farmers?" In answering his own question, McNamara put land reform first on the list of essential steps. But how does Mr. McNamara's stated priority fit in with a more recent major policy paper that explains how the Bank must deal with "the existing social system?" The paper states: "In many countries, avoiding opposition from powerful and influential sections of the rural community is essential if the program is not to be subverted from within."[14] Can the Bank promote land reform and also avoid opposition from the powerful and influential? Despite its public agonizing, the Bank would appear to be succeeding in keeping "the powerful and influential" content.

The large, export-oriented commercial farmers being helped by the Bank assuredly figure significantly among the "powerful and influential." The policy paper goes on to state explicitly that you cannot expect most of the project's benefits to accrue to the poor. In other words, do not rock the boat or you might not achieve "development."

The World Bank talks so much about helping the hungry that one forgets that three fourths of its loans do not go to agriculture at all but for commercial development. Most Bank projects are for what economists call infrastructure — electric power, railroads, highways, ports, telecommunications — all of the type required by foreign corporations to make their investment profitable and for which they are, needless to say, happy to have someone else foot the bill.[15] Such Bank loans aid the industrial countries by financing their capital goods exports — a principal objective of the Bank, according to its charter.

Indeed, the astonishing thing to us now is that the World Bank has been so successful in convincing so many that it has changed its focus from industry to agriculture, shifted its concern from the large to the smallholder and become in practice an aid agency. The World Bank is still a bank; its concern is with the stability of current elite-controlled economies; and its clientele will never be the world's hungry.

42

Has AID Seen the Light?

Question: The United States Agency for International Development (AID) is not a bank and is not bound by the same constraints. In fact it has a clear mandate from Congress to gear its programs to the needs of the rural poor. What is AID's impact?

Our Response: H.R. 9005, the latest legislation empowering AID to carry out programs in our name, reads as if it were composed by the most enlightened development expert. Once again, the right phrases tumble forth — "participation of the poor," "labor-intensive production," "more equitable and more secure land tenure," and "intermediate technology." Moreover, Congress has legislated that none of our development assistance money shall go to governments that use torture, prolonged detention without charges, or in other ways deny the right to "life, liberty and the security of person."[1]

Under the heading "Criteria to Measure Progress" the new legislation states that assistance programs should be increasingly concentrated in countries that meet certain criteria. The first is land reform to ensure that those who work the land also own the land. The second is that recipient countries must aim for a greater degree of self-sufficiency in food. Both criteria undoubtedly reflect the intent of certain members of Congress who are genuinely concerned about world hunger.

But can A.I.D. really help the hungry achieve self-determination? To answer this question we found that we had to ask a more fundamental one: What model does the United States have to offer the underdeveloped countries?

The new aid talks about alleviating hunger. Yet, after two

hundred years of "development" in our own country there are still over 20 million malnourished Americans. The new aid law talks about increasing the income of the poor abroad, yet the income of the poor in America is declining. According to the Department of Commerce, the number of poor Americans increased by 2.5 million in 1975 alone to total 26 million now.[2]

The new aid talks about generating greater equity in income in underdeveloped countries. Yet, are we achieving greater equity here? A 1972 Labor Department study reveals "a slow but persistent trend toward inequality" in the United States for the period 1958–1970.[3] The poorest 20 percent of the country receives only 7 percent of all income whereas the wealthiest 20 percent receives almost 60 percent of all income.[4] In fact the distribution of income in the United States today is about the same as that of India and is worse than that of Taiwan.[5]

The new aid talks about helping the small farmer. Yet in the United States over the last twenty years 1900 farms, most of them small, have gone out of business *each* week,[6] largely under the weight of the ever more pervasive big business control of our food system.

The new aid talks about land reform for the underdeveloped countries. Yet in the United States the largest 5.5 percent of all farms operate over half of all farmland while the bottom 40 percent of all farms operate only 4.5 percent.[7]

The new assistance law talks about the "participation of the poor." Yet the poor in our country are almost as marginal to economic and social decision making as in any underdeveloped country.

We are not saying that because the United States has failed fully to achieve its own goals it cannot help others. Rather the question is whether the United States has a model that could *ever* lead toward the noble ends that our aid agency sees as goals for the hungry countries. If the U.S. model of development is not achieving these ends at home, how can we expect it to work abroad? This is our first question.

Second, the government and even AID have assisted U.S.-based corporations to establish themselves profitably in the economies of underdeveloped countries. We must therefore ask: Can AID be serving both some of the world's most powerful corporations and the interests of powerless poor people at the same time? As we saw in Part VIII, if there were ever a case of conflict of interest, this would appear to be it!

Third, we ask whether the United States government can be concerned about maintaining alliances with the government elite in another country and about the needs of the poor majority of that country at the same time? Since in most countries the interests of the poor majority clash with the interests of the government elite, how can the United States government serve both?

Now let us take each of these fundamental questions one by one. First, what is the model of development AID is offering?

Does Commercialization Equal Development?

In its brochure designed to sell itself to Congress, AID lists five areas in which United States development assistance will focus. The first on the list is "to increase and diversify agricultural production through research and improved farm inputs." Tagged on the end of the list is "improved income distribution." AID's view of the world is that all you have to do is *improve* the existing situation. They use words like "increase," "strengthen," "integrate," "localize"; no basic *restructuring* is necessary: just build on what is there.

This is exactly the model of development most people accept for our own country. If we just keep going in the same direction *eventually* everyone will have enough. The common American view of poverty is that it can be eliminated by increased production and by better "management" — both done best by private enterprise — and AID has simply transferred this approach abroad.

For AID, just as for the World Bank, "rural development" is equivalent to the commercialization of agriculture. The majority of funds go to "production programs." Neither organization is concerned first with creating self-provisioning rural communities; both aim to create successful small farm businessmen. As one AID official has written, the focus of the new aid of AID and the World Bank "is on the rural poor plus their holdings, if any, *as income-producing units* rather than as farm producers" [emphasis added].[8] Not surprisingly, the first goal of the new aid according to an AID brochure, is to "Promote Profitable Production."[9]

The creation, of a new class of small-scale entrepreneurial

farmers *will not eradicate hunger*. It will leave out the hungry — the large number of landless and smallholders who were not at the right place at the right time to take advantage of an AID "project."

In AID's view of the poor world, what hampers production is lack of inputs, such as fertilizers or improved seeds. But as we have seen throughout this book, lack of inputs to the smallholder is only a symptom, not a cause, of poor production. The lack of inputs to the smallholder or an inadequate marketing system is only a symptom of an inequitable social power structure. Getting more fertilizer to the small farmer this year is not going to change that power structure. A more adequate marketing system in the context of sharp rural inequalities means farming will become a profitable business and the more powerful farmers, as we have repeatedly seen, will seek to enhance their profits by monopolizing credit, inputs, and government services as well as by acquiring their less powerful neighbors' lands.

We fear that, by dealing with symptoms and being limited by money and time to work with a small number of farmers in any one country, AID (in the name of all of us) will help create an "enclave" of prosperous commercial farmers who identify their prosperity with an export-oriented economy and with the multinational corporations who process and market their products. Instead of igniting a far-reaching movement for fundamental social change that would involve the poor majority, the new aid threatens to co-opt the potential leaders of such a movement into becoming supporters of the status quo. And the status quo for the majority will still be hunger.

Is This the New Aid?

AID irrigation projects in Morocco, approved in 1976, confirm that such a fear is well founded.[10]

The two projects will reach only about 1000 families, or less than one tenth of 1 percent of the farm families in Morocco. If the $11,000 expenditure per family were spent on every family in Morocco, the total cost would be double the present Moroccan GNP. Obviously these projects cannot possibly represent a viable development model.

Apart from their impracticality as models, what more can we

learn about the projects themselves? The project descriptions make it clear that AID officials *thought* they had built in special consideration for small farmers. Farmers with 12.5 acres or less pay nothing for the irrigation; larger farmers do pay. But the $141 per acre that the larger farmers must pay is a far cry from the actual cost of $1215 per acre. Thus the more land owned, the greater the actual subsidy. A farmer of 12.5 acres receives in effect a subsidy of $15,000; a farmer of 37 acres receives a $42,500 subsidy, and a farmer owning 62 acres, $66,250.

The greatly uneven distribution of benefits is proof that until the issue of control over the land is confronted, injecting large sums of development funds will only increase inequality by selectively enriching the larger farmers. The fact that one quarter of all landholders in the area own one half of all land did not, however, stop AID.

Unless it is willing to confront the local power structure, how can AID hope to do anything but reinforce the present inequities?

We then looked at a project that AID brags about in the July 1976 issue of its own magazine, *War on Hunger.* The title of the article proclaims: "More Coffee — More Income for Haiti's Small Farmer." The agency is granting $700,000 and loaning $6 million to Haiti to help increase the yields and therefore the income, they say, of one-third of Haiti's five million inhabitants. With high rates of malnutrition, is more coffee what Haitians need? In a special insert within this article AID explains the timeliness of the project: coffee prices, says AID, are going up due to the frost devastating Brazilian coffee production in 1975, a Colombian flood, and the Guatemalan earthquake. We were dumbfounded. AID leaves out the fact that many other coffee-producing countries will also be expanding their production to try to get in on the higher prices. What is to prevent them all from coming on the market at the same time? Wouldn't the three countries struck by natural disaster begun to recover by then? Yet in the eyes of AID it has fulfilled its mandate to focus on the small farmer. This case only proves to us that a small farmer focus per se is no solution for the world's hungry. What matters is whether that small farmer is part of a movement to transform the use of resources to serve first the needs of the local population.

We also looked carefully at the projects that AID mentions in its 1975 progress report to Congress.[11] We assumed these projects would be ones AID considers exemplary. We looked, for example, at a series of projects in the Philippines. In fiscal year 1976, almost two thirds of the budget for one of the projects and three fourths of the budget for another will go to pay the salaries of United States technicians. Clearly AID is defining development as a process of experts collecting data, making the correct diagnosis of the limits on production, and then supplying the "cure," that is, technical knowledge and inputs. But this process is *not* development.

Genuine development, by contrast, starts with the mobilization of the peasants themselves; only they can adequately identify the obstacles in their way; only they can remove them. In the Philippines, however, peasant-initiated organizations are illegal. Unions of agricultural laborers are also banned. The only peasant cooperatives recognized are those organized by the government itself. And the AID project does not even work within *these*! The coordination of the programs operates right out of the office of the president who rules by decree. It is explicitly an operation directed from the top.

This leads us to an inevitable question: Should our money lend power and credibility to a regime whose land reform measures are so weak that they can only be considered a distracting appeasement to a small group of peasants in order to protect the power of the landlord class?

The latest Philippine agrarian reform law, supposedly designed to turn tenants living on rice and corn lands into landowners, excludes those tenants of all landowners with holdings of less than 62 acres. This alone means that 80 percent of all tenants are not covered by the reform. Moreover, it excludes land growing crops other than corn and rice, already the equivalent of 38 percent of all cultivable land. Ironically, this exemption is a strong incentive to landlords to plant nonstaples and export crops. Nor does the reform benefit the largest rural group — over 3 million landless laborers — including the thousands of underpaid seasonal workers on plantations like Del Monte's and Dole's. And finally, the reform requires the tenant purchasing the land to pay for it with 6 percent interest over a fifteen-year period. For these years the tenant will, in reality, still be a tenant; he gains no equity through his payment. If the tenant is ever unable to pay his annual installment, he automatically forfeits his right to own any land.[12] Is this reform? Are the technical inputs of AID experts what the peasant majority in this country needs?

AID and U.S. Corporations: Partners in Progress?

The second question we had to ask ourselves was whether an agency that assists the world's most powerful corporations could also help the world's more powerless people, the poor majority in the underdeveloped countries. Recall Part VIII in which we discussed the devastating impact of agribusiness on the lives and livelihood of the rural poor. Yet, only recently, the then administrator of AID, Daniel Parker, openly promoted the expansion of agribusiness in order to bring the "unique reservoir" of talent of United States agribusiness to underdeveloped countries.

The director of AID is at the same time the chairman of OPIC, an insurance program that puts the U.S. government behind investments by multinational corporations abroad (see Part VIII, Question 35).

In addition, AID directly supports some of the world's largest corporations. One unmistakable case in point is the Latin American Agribusiness Development Corporation (LAAD), a holding company that numbers among its fifteen shareholders a Chase Manhattan agribusiness subsidiary, the Bank of America, Borden, Cargill, CPC International, John Deere, Gerber, Goodyear, Castle and Cooke, Ralston Purina, and ADELA (itself a multinational investment company whose 240 shareholders are some of the largest multinational corporations). By 1976, AID loans to LAAD totaled $17 million, at only a 3 to 4 percent rate of interest. (Let some small American business try to get loans on as favorable terms from the United States Government.) LAAD can even use AID's generous terms to turn a cool profit: Latin American partners that borrow from LAAD must pay back at rates up to 9 percent over a three-to-seven-year period.

LAAD's current portfolio includes sixty-six agribusiness projects in Latin America: processing and marketing beef, growing and exporting fresh and frozen vegetables, cut flowers, ferns, and tropical plants, wood products, seafood, and other specialty items.[13]

In 1975 alone LAAD's net profit after interest payments was

$519,765. Not bad, considering the total capital the corporate shareholders had invested was a mere $2 million. Profits hard to count, of course, come from sales by shareholders of their products to the 66 LAAD projects and the business experience they gain. Although American taxpayers contributed to LAAD, it pays no taxes to the United States: LAAD is incorporated in tax-haven Panama.

In 1974, AID hired a private consulting firm to evaluate LAAD. Although not unsympathetic to LAAD's purposes, the firm commented that LAAD's presence has not provided additional food for those who need it "because the bulk of the product lines handled are either destined for upper middle, upper class consumption, or for export." Nor, according to the evaluation, have small farmers and new small businessmen been helped: "LAAD's efforts have not, for the most part, been diluted by social motives to 'reach the small man.' " Instead, according to the report, LAAD has been "supporting businessmen whose success is predictable."[14] In other words, one safe way not to fail in helping someone is to pick someone who could probably succeed anyway.

Almost a quarter of LAAD's operations are in Nicaragua. Besides interests in export-oriented cattle ranches, ice production (now there's a pressing food need!), and American-style supermarkets, LAAD lent over $300,000, mostly from our AID tax money, to Industrias Amolonca. Industrias Amolonca now ties up prime agricultural lands to produce black-eyed peas for stews and soups and freezing vegetables like okra for its major contractors, Safeway Stores and Southland (Seven-Eleven).

Amolonca employs a grand total of twenty-six people, ten of whom are salaried managers and administrators. The capital invested per employee is a phenomenal $47,817. All this in a country where rural unemployment runs between 20 and 32 percent and over three quarters of the rural people earn less than $120 a year. LAAD probably considers the Amolonca project not only profitable but a form of political insurance; the Nicaraguan partners are related to the dictator, President Anastasio Somoza, a West Point graduate, whose father ruled Nicaragua for almost two decades in close collaboration with United States policy makers.

At this writing LAAD is expanding its operations into the Caribbean area. In the eyes of AID, LAAD has proved to be a suc-

cess — a success that should be copied in other parts of the world
to help agribusiness gain a foothold.

Aid for Whom?

In its most recent sales pitch to Congress, AID explains why
"we" have to help the underdeveloped countries. First of all, AID
says, American corporations increasingly depend on underdeveloped countries for raw materials. Second, these corporations
need the markets of the underdeveloped countries. And finally,
according to AID, these countries provide "opportunities for productive and profitable investment of U. S. capital and technology."[15]

To fight back against attacks on foreign aid in 1971, AID entered a report into the *Congressional Record*, specifying the value
of aid for the United States economy. According to AID, in fiscal
year 1971, the economic assistance portion of the aid program
financed purchases totaling $976 million from more than 4000
firms in all fifty states. In addition, U.S. companies and institutions benefited from $632 million in technical service contracts.[16]

What stimulates all these sales for American corporations? It
became clear to us that exporting an American model of commercial agriculture or, as AID would say, "promoting profitable production," means at the same time creating new customers for
United States agribusiness corporations and tying the agricultural potential of underdeveloped countries into the Global
Supermarket dominated by these companies. Whereas we have
found that rural development must be measured in terms of increasing food self-reliance — both the ability of the local population to grow food as well as to constitute a market for that food.
Development AID-style, even the "enlightened" AID focus on the
small farmer, moves agriculture in the Third World in the opposite direction — toward increasing dependence on foreign corporate suppliers of agricultural inputs and on export crops destined
for volatile international markets.

The Case of Chile

Nothing more clearly reveals how AID deals with the conflict of
interest between multinational corporations and the rural poor

than the case of Chile. If AID were able and willing to support the rural poor, it had its chance to prove it in Chile.

By July 1972, only 20 months after President Allende's inauguration, the Popular Unity government had incorporated into its agrarian reform program more than 13 million acres of land benefiting 40,000 to 45,000 farm workers and small peasants. This was nearly twice the number that had benefited under the *six years* of land reform carried out by the previous administration. In only 20 months the number of expropriations had doubled, and the area covered by the reform program had increased by 150 percent.[17] Even more important, the government encouraged development of participatory small farmer organizations so that the new holders could pool their work and resources, and for the first time the rural poor would have a strong voice in overall development policies.

What was the response of AID to a government doing exactly what the agency states to be its *own* primary goal — improving the lot of the rural poor? Within the first few months the United States drastically cut economic assistance, previously the highest amount to any Latin American country, to practically nothing. Those few programs kept open, as we now know from congressional investigations of the CIA, were in fact covers for subversive activity. In addition, the Nixon administration secretly organized a blockade of sales of parts for U.S.–made machines, including farm machinery. The United States wielded its virtual veto power in the World Bank and in the Inter-American Development Bank to block any loans to Chile, even for projects previously approved and despite the fact that the Chilean government continued to meet the sizable payments on loans taken out by previous administrations.[18]

These tactics, aimed at whipping up opposition to the government, were potent precisely because previous pro-American governments had not put Food First. They had allowed large landlords to underutilize much of the country's prime agricultural land. Many kept estates as country villas while they invested their capital in partnership with American firms manufacturing consumer goods for the middle and upper classes. Chile was no longer a country of high agricultural productivity; in fact, its food production had long since fallen to levels achieved at the turn of the century. Not only were many Chileans seriously underfed, but the country had also been made vulnerable to any embargo of concessional and commercial food imports from the United States.

The United States refused to send food aid to the Popular Unity government. It even refused to accept hard cash for food. After the Chilean military overthrew the constitutional government in September 1973, U.S. attitudes changed. Within hours of the bloody coup, ships loaded with American food set off from New Orleans for Chile. By 1975, Chile under the junta was receiving six times more food aid than the rest of Latin America put together. In its fiscal year 1976 report to Congress,[19] AID praises the economic measures of the junta — which have had a devastating impact on the poor and even on the middle class and small businesses. The military government not only halted but reversed land reform, driving small farmers and Indians off lands, which had in some cases been distributed to them even before the Popular Unity government came to power.

The junta's idea for development has been to increase its exports of luxury fruits, vegetables, and even beans to the industrial countries. (Agricultural exports now rank second, next to copper.) At the same time as we began to notice increased volumes of watermelon, grapes, and other fruits from Chile in our local supermarket, a member of the United Nations Protein Advisory Group told us of the worsening nutritional status of the Chilean people. He reported that after only one year of the junta's "belt tightening," so praised by AID, over one half of the Chilean people were eating less than the poorer half of the population of Bangladesh.[20]

The AID report on Chile repeats the rationalizations of the junta, given them by University of Chicago economists coached by Nobel Prize winner Milton Friedman: that draconian measures are necessary to halt the inflation caused by the Popular Unity government. AID does not, however, point out that rampant inflation has been a chronic problem of every government in Chile, so much so that during the six years of the earlier Christian Democrat government, so favored by the agency, the inflation rate was second highest in the world after South Vietnam, and the growth rate was the lowest in Latin America, just above Haiti.

Nor does AID point out that under authoritarian rule unemployment has risen from 3 percent to 19 percent, not counting of course the tens of thousands of Chileans murdered or forced into exile; the junta has only succeeded in reducing inflation from 400 to 340 percent annually. In praising the junta for its greater fiscal responsibility, the agency had to also overlook the fact that Chile's foreign debt increased almost fivefold since the fall of the Popular Unity government. As the *New York Times* concludes, "The military junta's management of Chile's economy has produced even worse results than occurred during the Allende regime it replaced, but the right-wing Government has been able to attract $2 billion in foreign assistance."[21]

Since the overthrow of the Popular Unity government, AID has raised its economic assistance twenty-fourfold from $3.8 million in 1973 to a planned $90 million for 1976.[22] Chile is receiving more economic assistance than any other Latin American country.

Thus, when we read in 1975 foreign assistance legislation that future assistance shall be concentrated in countries that institute land reform, we are forced to doubt. In view of what we know now about the case of Chile, is it realistic to expect this to happen?

A government that would undertake an authentic land reform program, mobilizing the rural poor, is hardly a government that would allow basic economic decisions to remain in the hands of large, private, especially foreign, corporations. AID then would again have to make a choice between its support for multinational corporations and its concern for the rural dispossessed.

AID in Context

Focusing the question on AID implies that it is the chief channel through which the United States government lends support to Third World countries. But we have learned, in part through the research of Jim Morrell at the Center for International Policy in Washington D. C., that the role of AID is increasingly overshadowed by the much greater impact of other channels through which funds flow without any congressional review or approval, channels such as the Export-Import Bank, the World Bank, the regional development banks, and the International Monetary Fund. In the last six years the share of the traditional aid outlets, those at least nominally reviewed and approved by Congress, has dropped from 46 percent to 31 percent of the total U.S. bilateral and U.S.–supported multilateral aid. In other words, *69 percent of such aid goes without any congressional review.*

This congressional impotence we have already witnessed in the case of food aid. Where the repressive policies of foreign governments have made those government's unpopular with Congress and the American people, administrators have only widened channels of support that escape congressional scrutiny. In his study, *Foreign Aid: The End Run Around Congress,* Morrell documents these examples: In fiscal year 1976 only 22 percent of the credits, guarantees, and insurance going to the authoritarian regime in South Korea came through outlets that are subject to prior congressional control. In Chile in the same year the figure was 21 percent. The Philippines, a nation governed by martial law, received $94 million, yet Congress specifically approved only 6 percent of that total. South Africa got $310 million from two United States programs and the International Monetary Fund in 1976 but Congress had not approved one cent.

Just as we found in regard to food aid, development assistance is an extension of United States foreign policy. In early 1976, former Secretary of State Henry Kissinger postponed agreements on development assistance to Tanzania and Guyana because he was angered by their voting in the United Nations against positions taken by the United States. Other nations, like Malawi and the Ivory Coast that voted with the United States, were told that they were to receive additional aid. Indeed, the *New York Times* reported that a special office had been set up in the State Department to monitor and analyze the vote in the United Nations by aid recipients. As long as development assistance is a tool of the administration to reward or to punish the ruling group in another country, how can it ever serve the needs of the local people?[23]

By the same token, can we reasonably expect the United States government simultaneously to maintain alliances with the propertied elites who rule most underdeveloped countries and help the poor in these same countries? How can AID address itself to the fundamental issue of hunger — the re-ordering of social relationships — when, as an arm of the United States government, its effective constituency is not the hungry majority?

All the talk in the world about concern for small farmers will not change one reality: AID's constituency in underdeveloped countries are the very privileged few who would have the most to lose by changes necessary to eradicate hunger. The agency is, therefore, at best left to deal only with such symptoms as the lack of technical inputs for increased production. But as we have shown throughout this book, increased production without structural re-ordering is worse than stagnation: it only further entrenches the powerful and weakens the poor.

We Americans, in genuine eagerness to do *something* about hunger, focus too narrowly on direct aid efforts. We therefore fail to grasp the overall impact of our government's role in other countries. We fail to ask in every case, whom is the United States government really supporting?

First we must weigh the impact of development assistance against the powerful and overriding influence of our military and intelligence programs that go directly to maintain the *status quo* of hunger abroad.

The Center for Defense Information estimates that the United States spends $62 billion each year to maintain military arrangements with 92 countries.[24] The Ford administration requested $4.3 billion for military assistance and military credit sales for fiscal year 1977. By contrast, what the administration requests for economic development aid, both bilateral and through international agencies, was only one third as much. Even if we include requests for funds for food aid and for contributions to international banks like the World Bank, the total was still less than the request for military support.

Between 1970 and 1975, U.S. military assistance, trained officers from the Dominican Republic in "urban counter insurgency," Nicaraguans in "military intelligence interrogation," and Panamanian officers in "jungle operations."[25] It is worth noting that the largest number of Latin American military "students" — over 1000 — trained under these military assistance programs have been Chilean. Altogether, since 1950, the United States has trained 350,000 military officers from Asia, Africa, and Latin America.[26]

In addition, our military sales program has tripled since 1970 to $9 billion in 1975 — making the United States by far the largest weapons merchant in the world. The *Defense Monitor*, published by the Center for Defense Information, includes a colored map showing the extent of American military sales and military aid around the world. We pinned it up on our wall so that it would really sink in. Except for the Soviet Union, China, Greenland, and a handful of African countries there is virtually no place on the globe that the United States does not have either troops, a military aid program, or a market for growing sales of American military hardware.[27]

Covert intelligence activities do not show up on this map. In 1976, the House Select Committee on Intelligence discovered the federal intelligence budget to be on the order of $10 billion — three to four times higher than officially reported. The committee estimated that "nearly one-third" of covert intelligence operations in the last decade "involved secret financial support to foreign political parties and government leaders."[28]

These facts about United States military expenditures begin to give us some idea of whose side our government is on. But nothing is more revealing than an excerpt from secret instructional material designed for use in the AID Program of the Foreign Intelligence Service. It begins with this warning: "This material should be burned or destroyed when it is no longer useful for instruction." It proceeds to explain to the "student" how to detect signs that rural "insurgents" are gaining support from the rural people.

> The refusal of *campesinos* [peasants] to pay rents, taxes or agricultural loans or any difficulty in collecting these will indicate the existence of an active insurrection that has succeeded in convincing the campesinos of the injustices of the present system, and is directing or instigating them to disobey its precepts.
>
> Hostility on the part of the local population to the government forces, in contrast to their amiable or neutral attitude in the past. This can indicate a change of loyalty or of behavior inspired by fear, often manifested by children refusing to fraternize with members of the internal security forces.[29]

Clearly, the very process of peasant resistance to injustice is, in the eyes of American officials, something to fear and something to suppress. What meaning does our economic assistance have with all the right words about participation and self-determination for the poor, when our government is actively suppressing such change?

We asked three questions and got three very clear answers. We found that the development model the United States is exporting cannot move the poor in underdeveloped countries toward greater self-reliance but can only increase the dependency and powerlessness of the poor.

Second, we found that the United States cannot be both a friend to American corporations and an advocate of the interests of the rural poor in the recipient countries at the same time. In the case of Chile we saw American aid withdrawn just at the moment the rural poor were gaining control over their land.

Third, we were forced to conclude that AID's identification with the governing class in any country makes it impossible for the agency to encourage changes that would threaten their power. We saw that the aid effort is overwhelmingly overshadowed by the impact of United States military and intelligence efforts.

It has been very hard for us to come to these realizations because we probably have the same instincts as most of you — that we should be able to *help*. We *want* to help.

We still do. Only now we have redefined what that means, as you will see in our final response in Part X.

*   *   *

Democracy and communism are engaged in a struggle for objectives of worldwide significance. . . . The maintenance of military bases and the network of alliances that surround the communist world is not enough to stop revolutionary war, and, unfortunately, its field of battle is widening every day. Economic aid, another form of subtle penetration, is a particular phase of this struggle, in that the major powers try to obtain dominant influence over developing nations.

> Lecture at the United States Army
> School of the Americas

Security Supporting and Development Assistance Programs are both directed toward the same ends, the providing of economic and social benefits to the less developed countries. . . . [Security Supporting Assistance] is designed to promote security, stability and economic growth for countries facing severe political and/or economic distress.

> Daniel Parker, Administrator, AID, 1976

We should immediately pay greater attention to agribusiness aspects of our food and nutrition programs. . . . AID will place priority emphasis on this sector. . . . Agribusiness also seems to be the most promising area in which to begin a comprehensive across the board effort to involve the talents and resources of local and developed country private sectors in the development process.

> Memorandum from Daniel Parker, Administrator,
> AID, to Mission Directors, October 27, 1976

43

Can Voluntary Agencies Play a Constructive Role?

Question: You have talked about aid as if it only comes through governments. That is just not true. America has a very long history of generous aid by voluntary agencies, particularly church groups who are trying to work directly with the hungry in many parts of the world. Can't small, nongovernmental organizations be more effective exactly because they are not constrained in all the ways you mention in regard to official aid?

Our Response: As we studied voluntary aid projects around the world, we felt ourselves in a quandary: Which organization or project should we recommend to our readers? Soon we realized that the most useful contribution we might make would not be to provide you with lengthy critiques of voluntary aid organizations but to provide you with the questions we found ourselves asking of *all* aid projects.

Seven Questions to Ask an Aid Project

1. Whose project *is* it? Is it the donor agency's?
   or
   Does it originate with the people involved?
2. Does the project diagnose the problem to be tackled as a technical or physical deficiency (e.g., poor farming methods or depleted soils) that can be overcome with the right technique and skills?
   or
   Is the physical or technical problem seen as only a reflection of social and political relationships that need to be altered?
3. Does it reinforce the economic and political power of a cer-

tain group which then becomes more resistant to change
that might abolish its privileges?
>   or
>   Does it generate a shift in power to the powerless?

4. Does it, through the intervention of outside experts, take
   away local initiative?
>   or
>   Does it generate a process of democratic decision making
>   and a thrust toward self-reliance that can carry over to fu-
>   ture projects?

5. Does it reinforce dependence on outside sources of material
   and skills?
>   or
>   Does it use local ingenuity, local labor, and local materials,
>   and can it be maintained with local skills?

6. Does it merely help individuals adjust to their exploitation
   by such external forces as the national government or the international market?
>   or
>   Does it encourage an understanding of that exploitation and
>   a resistance to it?

7. Will success only be measured by the achievement of the
   pre-set plans of outsiders?
>   or
>   Is the project open-ended, with success measured by the local
>   people as the project progresses?

Are there any groups that could meet the implied requirements? We have discovered a few, small groups who have the
combination of experience in underdeveloped countries, understanding of political contexts, and ingenuity necessary to be possibly of genuine assistance.

One organization, the Economic Development Bureau (EDB), is
the brainchild of a former academic. While working in Tanzania's
Ministry of Planning, American economist Idrian Resnick was
struck by the Tanzanians' own capacity to do much of what they
were asking foreigners to do. In 1975, he established an "alternative consulting service." It is not an ordinary consulting service by
any means. The more than 200 technical experts from over
thirty-five countries associated with the EDB do not see the problem of development as merely a technical one. They understand
that their knowledge can be a constructive one only after the local

community has begun building a truly democratic and collective decision-making process.

The contrast between the EDB approach and that of a typical consulting agency is most revealing. In Tanzania, a country with one of the lowest nutritional levels in the world, 50 to 75 percent of the grain is lost each year due to mildew, vermin, and insect infestation. At the request of the Tanzanian government, the Swedish International Development Agency hired several consulting firms to examine the grain storage problem. In three years, the consultants produced four reports — all recommending highly mechanized, extremely expensive silos and all requiring foreign technicians to run them. An additional three quarters of a million dollars was recommended for further designs by consultants! Six years after the first report, no silos had been built.

Enter the EDB. Invited by the Community Development Trust Fund of Tanzania, the EDB decided to attack the problem at the village level and in such a way as to ensure the direct control by the villagers throughout the project. The EDB team, including a Tanzanian trained in the adult education techniques of exiled Brazilian learning theorist Paulo Freire, entered the village. The villagers formed a storage committee. The team initiated a discussion in which the participants worked together to gain an understanding of the forces that were oppressing villagers, preventing them from adequately handling and storing their grains. The problem was not simply a matter of rats, mildew, and bugs, or of drying, spraying, and rebuilding. Uncovering and understanding the social and economic relations in the village were necessary before effective action was possible.

Through the dialogue and the work on modifying storage structures, the villagers came to realize that they had knowledge where they had thought they had none; and they experienced the collective power they have to change their own lives. A great deal of effective technology already existed with the people. But because the village is composed of many ethnic groups, neighbors were often unaware of each other's structures and methods. Through sharing experiences, the people became conscious of the richness of their varied knowledge and experience. As one of the EDB consultants put it, "It was necessary to convince the villagers that we did not have a preconceived idea ... 'up our sleeve' all the time just waiting for the little drama of village democracy to play itself out." The credibility of the EDB technicians was established only after they dropped a design that they had put forward in the discussions in response to serious criticism of it by the villagers. Only then did the villagers believe that they had not come "with an answer."

Rather than the introduction of any foreign technology, the successful storage system that evolved through this process turned out to be a recombination of the best elements in the traditional storage methods of the village. The people were part of a dynamic unfolding of events rather than on the receiving end of a technical exercise. They also generated something that even the best outside designers could never accomplish: an ongoing process of redesign.

The grain storage problem was approached as a social problem that could be solved by the villagers. A technical solution was only part of the project as conceived by the EDB. Integrated into, and more important than a technical solution, was the facilitation of a process of problem definition, exploration of local material resources and limitations, and the design of effective action that could be used by the villagers to attack future obstacles. Indeed, this project that succeeded in initiating twenty rat-proofed, elevated sorghum storage structures in one harvest season also resulted in the creation of a team of villagers highly skilled in problem solving — the storage committee. Representatives have now been asked by a neighboring village to hold public discussions to demonstrate the process of change. At the end of eight weeks the village storage committee conducted a seminar for the staff and students of the University of Dar es Salaam's Faculty of Agriculture!

This project reflects the EDB's underlying philosophy about economic development in the Third World: In order for development to liberate people from the causes and substance of their poverty, it must involve a *process* over which they have control. Multinational corporations like to decry the food lost to pests in underdeveloped countries, claiming that it takes the commercial packaging or chemicals that only they (conveniently) produce to solve the problem. The story of the EDB in Tanzania is evidence that not only can storage problems be solved using local materials and skills but that the initiation of the *collective problem-solving process* is as important as the product.

Oxfam, originally an international relief organization founded in England, is also trying to escape the pitfalls that we highlighted in our Seven Questions. One of many Oxfam projects is in Guatemala where it tackled the problem of helping earthquake victims. To most people, relief means simply handouts; success means achieving some semblance of what existed before. But not to Oxfam. In response to the stated desires of the peasants themselves, Oxfam is teaching a simple hut construction that will withstand future earthquakes. It is a design the Guatemalan villagers can themselves build with local materials. The villages can teach each other through their cooperative that Oxfam had already helped start.

CARE, by contrast, looked at the housing problems in Guatemala and was more concerned with speed than anything else. Turning out 26,000 houses in six months was their goal. Asked if the villagers would be involved in the design or construction, the CARE representative explained,

> There will be plenty of opportunity for people to participate when they fill in their walls. This project is too big to allow it to be held up by details. If the people lag behind, hold up the project, we may go in if we have to, dig the postholes ourselves, boom-boom-boom, and move to the next town.[1]

The contrast between Oxfam's approach and CARE's approach is the contrast between the view that development is the process of people taking charge of their lives and the view that development is a job to be done.

We have found another example of a private voluntary agency's willingness to take the risk of confronting the real causes of hunger. For several years the Unitarian-Universalist Service Committee has supported a newspaper in El Salvador, *Justice and Peace*. It is the sole vehicle of dissent against the injustices and atrocities inflicted upon peasants struggling for survival. During 1975, for example, army units in El Salvador massacred unarmed peasants. In two cases the attacks were reported in the Salvadorian press as guerrilla attacks on army patrols. Only *Justice and Peace* published the peasants' side of the story.

We are not saying, of course, that we endorse every project of these organizations. But they have demonstrated that they do not believe that development problems require merely technical assistance. Rather, development assistance is the facilitation of a process by which the people empower themselves through an awakening to their own collective potential. Technical knowledge becomes constructive *only* when it is offered in response to needs identified by the people themselves and only when it can be used to further the possibilities for self-determination.

Contrast this view with what one leader in the field of voluntary aid for rural development said recently before a congressional subcommittee. In praise of what his agency could do he stated:

> By remaining apolitical and by fostering projects whose primary goal is to make it possible for low-income people to attain dignity, a subtle depolarizing process seems to take place — alienation between rich and poor, governments and the people, tribal groups, and even between countries can be reduced.[2]

Remaining apolitical means not being involved in the shift of power from an elite propertied class to the majority. Concentrating on "apolitical" projects can only mean choosing projects that reinforce the present distribution of power, creating perhaps a new class of entrepreneurs. But such a choice will inevitably only serve the interests of those already in power by providing yet another layer of comparatively well-off individuals who then also have a stake in the status quo.

Assuming that aid is the only way to help the hungry reveals a lack of the fundamental understanding that we have tried to convey in this book — the view that people want to *feed themselves*. If they are not, it means that somebody is keeping them from doing so. We do not have to "help" them, teach them, or force them. If the obstacles are removed, they will feed themselves. But how can we contribute to removing those obstacles? We shall answer this question in our final response.

*   *   *

> We saw these young [Ivory Coast] volunteers at work this summer at Yakassé and Abengourou. They showed exemplary courage and tenacity and it has to be admitted that they deserved a better reception by the population. The peasants have acquired the habit of not being associated with decisions. Why then should we be astonished that they do not join in the work? Because decisions have been made for them, they thought the young people had come to work for them. Rumours had even circulated in Yakassé village to the effect that the young volunteers were there as a punishment for failure at school!

> M. Rafransoa, United Nations Development
> Program, Freedom From Hunger Campaign, 1974

Part X

Food First

44

What Does Food Self-Reliance Mean?

Question: Throughout this book you have mentioned food self-reliance. What does food self-reliance mean and how can it be achieved?

Our Response: Achieving food self-reliance involves at least seven fundamentals. These fundamentals are not speculative points but elements already proved to be necessary in countries that have achieved or are well on the way toward achieving food self-reliance — countries, we should not forget, that contain over 40 percent of all people living in the underdeveloped world.

Fundamentals of Food Self-Reliance

1. *Food self-reliance requires the allocation of control over agricultural resources to local, self-provisioning units, democratically organized.*

Only then will increased agricultural production benefit the local majority instead of local and foreign elites. A narrow focus on production results in greater hunger. This is not a theoretical point, as we documented in Part V. Recent in-depth studies by the International Labor Organization of seven Asian countries (containing 70 percent of the rural population living in the underdeveloped world) reveal that where a narrow production focus has succeeded in raising GNP per capita and production totals the well-being of the bottom 20 to 80 percent of the population has actually worsened.[1]

Many so-called land reforms in the last twenty years have claimed to reallocate control over agricultural resources. But most have not. Land reform laws in countries like Pakistan, the Philippines, India, and Egypt have neglected the landless — who comprise 30 to 40 percent of the rural population. Moreover, often only a small fraction of the land is affected; in the Philippines two years after the land reform decree, only 2 percent of the cropped land had been redistributed. In some cases, the largeholders are the real beneficiaries of these "reforms." In 1959, land reform in Pakistan compensated landlords handsomely for poor, unirrigated land that had previously yielded them no income.[2] Such fake reforms have obscured an appreciation of what the effects of real redistribution could mean.

Production advances have not been sacrificed in countries that have authentically redistributed the land and other food-producing resources, countries as different as Japan, Cuba, Taiwan, China, and North Vietnam. People who own their own land, either privately or collectively, naturally invest more time, labor, and money in it than do nonowners. Only the redistribution of control of the land can create a new kind of farmer, one willing to face up to difficult challenges, no longer afraid of bosses, moneylenders, and landlords. In Japan, in 1940, only about 31 percent of the landholdings were worked by people who owned the land. By 1960, over 75 percent of the holdings were operated by owner farmers.[3] This shift goes a long way in explaining why recent yields per acre of foodgrains in Japan were as much as 60 percent greater than in the United States.[4]

History suggests that the reallocation of control over production cannot succeed, however, if it is approached as a gradual reform. It must be a rapid and total reconstruction. In 1959 during the first phase of Cuba's agrarian reform, 50 to 60 percent of Cuba's farmlands, owned by only 5 percent of the landowners, was designated for redistribution. When the large landowners tried to subvert the reform by refusing to plant and withholding production, the National Institute of Agrarian Reform had to speed up the takeover to safeguard production. Thus, a land redistribution that Prime Minister Castro himself thought would take three years had to be completed in only months.[5]

As the Soviet Union has tragically demonstrated, public ownership does not in itself guarantee control by the people. Production stagnation on the state farms, as compared to the obvious productivity of private garden plots, can be seen as peasant resistance to a system in which they are mere employees — and underpaid at that.

2. *Food self-reliance depends on mass initiative, not on government directives.*

Self-reliance means not only mass participation but mass initiative, the initiative of people freed psychologically from dependence on authorities, whether they be landlords or government officials. Mass initiative is the opposite of individual self-seeking. It rests in awakening the confidence of the people that only through cooperative work in which all partake and benefit equally can genuine development occur. People have proved themselves willing to sacrifice and work hard for future reward, when they can see that all are sacrificing equally. Thus equality is a necessary prerequisite for mass initiative. In countries with great inequalities in wealth and income, appeals for national sacrifice are correctly perceived by the poor majority as a way for the controlling elite to extract yet more wealth through the extra exertion of the masses.

Since self-reliance presupposes equality, government programs that help only a segment of the poor should not be confused with self-reliant policies. They often only increase inequality. Between 1957 and 1970, about one quarter of all smallholders in Malaysia were settled through a government land development scheme. Their income rose several times higher than the average peasant household. Yet all other smallholders saw their incomes halved. Self-reliance is not the "project approach" to hunger.

Mass initiative, moreover, is the opposite of government managed "development." If food self-reliance is managed from above, people feel they are working "for the government," not for themselves. People become "clients," not the motive force.

A government policy of simply parceling out land to small farmers is not, for example, self-reliant development. Land reform must involve the people themselves who deliberate to decide how the resources are to be used and how disputes are to be resolved. Land reform must not only redistribute land but must be the first step in the creation of a mass democracy. The *process* of land reform is as important as the reform itself.

Sri Lanka, by contrast, has attempted to administer development from the top through a series of welfare programs, like free health care and the price subsidization of staples like rice and sugar, that amount to half of all government expenditures.[6] No fundamental redistribution of control over resources has taken place, no dependency patterns have been shaken up. Although the distribution of income figures obscures the fact, the standard of consumption in Sri Lanka has declined for all but the top 10 to 20 percent.

Even progressive Tanzania has, in part, fallen into the trap of trying to "manage" self-reliance. Political economist P. L. Raikes, in his detailed study of *ujamma* villages in Tanzania,[7] finds that bureaucratic, external interventions have thwarted release of the enthusiasm and productive energy of the peasants. Under urban- and foreign-oriented administrators, the peasants treat the communal lands as if they were government farms. The use of coercion leads to passive resistance. Raikes notes, for example, that all too often administrators present villagers with a plan that is primarily a set of production targets. The allocation of needed farming inputs and social services is made to depend upon acceptance of this plan. The villagers know that to question its merits will probably displease the bureaucrat, thus reducing the likelihood of their getting any assistance. Such "self-reliance by government order" is not what we mean by self-reliance — in part because it just does not work!

3. *With food self-reliance, trade becomes an organic outgrowth of development, not the fragile hinge on which survival hangs.*

Agricultural exports should come only after the agricultural resources are in the hands of people first meeting their own food needs. Only after food production has been diversified and people are feeding themselves can food trade play a positive role. Clearly no country can hope to "win" in the game of international trade, as we saw in Part VI, as long as its very survival depends on selling its one or two products every year. A country simply cannot hold out for just prices for its exports if it is desperate for foreign exchange with which to import food. Once the basic needs are met, however, trade can become a healthy extension of *domestic need* instead of being determined strictly by *foreign demand*.

After the Cuban people overthrew the Batista dictatorship, they diversified into food crops and livestock for local consumption. In addition, new land was cleared and fallow land was reduced so that the area under cultivation rose substantially. Between 1958 and 1962, the production of rice and corn almost doubled and bean production more than doubled.[8] Furthermore, guaranteed employment and the right to adequate basic foods put an end to hunger. The exporting of sugar was then no longer at the expense of the health of the Cuban people but rather one way of purchasing productive goods useful for further development. How different is the fate of the people of the Dominican Republic whose food needs are being sacrificed to the country's "sugarization": A rapidly expanding amount of the best land is planted with sugar to enhance the profits of such multinational conglomerates as Gulf and Western,[9] while food production per person declines. About 90 percent of the sugar produced is exported to the United States to make soft drinks, candy, cakes, and cookies. As Robert Ledogar's Consumers' Union–funded study observes, "To the undernourished small farmers, subsistence farmers and landless laborers — who together comprise about 75 percent of the rural population — the endless vista of canefields looks like a great green plague slowly destroying their land."

Self-reliance, then, aims at local self-sufficiency in the basic staples of life. On this there can be no equivocation. Apart from the basic food necessities, however, self-reliant development need not bar trade, even at the early stages. For certain useful items, like pumps, it should not be necessary to wait until the industrial base is built to produce them locally. Trade can help; the question is what *kind* of trade. If we think of beneficial trade as cooperation, a clear principle emerges: Choose a partner at a comparable level of power but with complementary needs. In this way the chances of manipulation are greatly diminished. The search for a trading partner should begin only after all avenues for local production have been tested.

When underdeveloped countries look to the industrial countries as *the* model, uniformity will inevitably result; self-reliance, on the other hand, will bring about diversity. There is no technological model nor agricultural practice that can be applied universally. Self-reliance means accepting the challenge to human ingenuity of originating unique models for unique localities. As development analyst Johan Galtung notes, any loss in efficiency that might result from reinventing something already invented somewhere else "is more than offset by the gain in self-confidence in accepting the challenge of being the innovator."[10]

4. *Food self-reliance means reuniting agriculture and nutrition*.

If colonialism's plantations first converted food into a mere commodity, production contracted by multinational agribusiness for the Global Supermarket completes the divorce of agriculture and nutrition. Self-reliance would make the central question not "What crop might have a few cents edge on the world market months or even years hence?" but "How can the people best feed themselves with this piece of land?"

As obvious as it may seem, the policy basing land use on nutritional output is practiced in only a few countries today. For these countries food is no longer just a commodity. As a necessity of life, it is considered as precious as life itself.

With Food First self-reliance, industrial crops (like cotton and rubber), livestock feed crops, and luxury fruits and vegetables are planted *after* meeting the basic needs of all the people. In the United States, by contrast, as pointed out in *Diet for a Small Planet*, livestock production is, in fact, antithetical to getting maximum nutritional output from our land. Livestock is used instead to get rid of "overproduction" in a world where most people do not have the money to buy the grain they need. Livestock thus consumes the production from over *half* of the harvested acreage in the United States. At the same time beans and grain products, competing with feed crops for land use, soar out of the price range of the really poor who rely on these staples.

A self-reliant policy in this country would use the land to supply Americans with all our necessary grain and other plant food staples before land was diverted to crops destined for livestock. With new attention to the development of improved forages and waste products to replace grain in livestock feeding, the United States, according to a USDA official's estimate, could reduce the amount of grain fed to livestock by 50 percent and still produce roughly the same amount of meat.[11]

In a Food First country like China people do not compete with livestock. Grain is not diverted from people to animals; in fact, very little grain is fed to animals at all. Most are raised by individual households primarily on farm and household wastes. The pigs also make a contribution to the farmland. *Each* pig produces four to five tons of manure a year,[12] a key source of organic fertilizer. When American wheat-breeder Norman Borlaug heard that China had about 250 million pigs (about four times the number in the United States), he could hardly believe it. What could they possibly eat? He went to China and observed, as he put it, "pretty scrawny pigs." Their growth was slow, but he admitted, in awe, that by the time they reached maturity they were decent-looking hogs. And all on cotton leaves, corn stalks, rice husks, water hyacinths, and peanut shells! It *is* hard for us Americans, brought up on corn-fed beef and milk-fed veal, to get the idea that livestock's unique role is to make food fit for humans out of things we *cannot* eat.

5. *Food self-reliance makes agriculture an end, not a means.*

In countries where so much of the population today is hungry, agriculture has been seen, since the onslaught of colonialism, as the sector from which to extract wealth to serve urban, industrial, and foreign interests. Theoretically things have changed. But have they really? In most underdeveloped countries agriculture continues to contribute much more to the national income than it receives in investment. Although agricultural production ordinarily generates most of the national product and foreign exchange, a recent survey found that, on the average, agriculture in underdeveloped countries receives only 11 percent of all investment. On the other hand, mining and manufacturing receive over one quarter of all investment.[13] A United Nations study of Africa notes that although agriculture contributes 20 to 50 percent of the GNP, it receives only 10 to 30 percent of the public investment.[14]

The Chinese people have chosen a different path. They have decided quite deliberately to reject the Soviet approach of squeezing farmers through low prices for their products and high prices for consumer goods and farm inputs. They have chosen a policy of relatively high and slowly increasing prices for agricultural commodities along with low prices for farm supplies.[15] In addition, the farm taxation rate has been effectively cut in half.[16] Rather than extracting a surplus from agriculture, the rest of the society contributes 23 percent in excess of what it receives from agriculture.[17]

With food self-reliance, rural development becomes an end in itself. We have seen in Part V that food production can be increased through an *agricultural modernization* that can hardly be considered *rural development*, since it results in many or even most of the rural people eating less. Since by food self-reliance we mean not only adequate food production but adequate food consumption by all, it cannot be achieved without a genuine rural development in which all participate. Indeed food self-reliance and true development must be seen as one and the same.

6. *With Food First self-reliance, industry will serve agriculture; town and country will meet.*

If the masses of people are in command, invention and production will be based on the *need* for a product. A rural, dispersed, small-scale industrial network will grow to fill the need for fertilizer, farming equipment, and other simple manufactures. We are not talking about plopping factories producing for urban markets in the middle of a rice field just for the sake of "decentralization," but of developing industry as an organic outgrowth of the needs of labor-intensive agriculture and those of the local population.

India made "decentralization" of industry official policy but didn't understand the process. Clock and radio factories were established in rural areas. But since both the production materials and the market for the finished product were in the cities, a lot of money was spent shipping springs to the country and clocks to the city. The problem was that a clock factory did nothing to stimulate the growth of agriculture and that agricultural growth did not give impetus to the clock factory.

Moreover, Food First self-reliance will halt, even reverse, the flow of landless refugees who daily migrate to cities in hope of work. The wide gap in income between rural and urban workers will begin to close. Rural life will no longer be looked upon as backward. The Cuban people, for example, understood the need to bring to rural areas the health, educational, and cultural facilities — dance, film, library, theater — invariably associated, especially by the young , with city life. Over the past several years more than 500 boarding high schools have been constructed in the countryside for students from both rural and urban areas. These schools are among the country's finest and offer not only a regular high school education but also daily work in food production. Through such schools in the countryside tens of thousands of young people come to appreciate the difficulties and rewards of rural work and to realize that they too can contribute to their country's development.

Sending students to the countryside, as is the policy in countries like Cuba, Somalia, and China, has often appeared to Western observers as a form of anti-intellectualism. Rather it is the recognition that the entire population, and especially the young, must appreciate the importance of agriculture. If not, rural development will likely be sacrificed by urbanized, white-collar bureaucrats who go on believing that agriculture should be the handmaiden to other sectors and to the needs of an elite (including themselves).

7. *Food self-reliance requires coordinated social planning.*

When Westerners look at China most are overwhelmed by the enormity of the organizational problems that have been tackled in the literal transformation of the countryside. When we see mammoth dams completed by human labor and whole landscapes transformed, it is hard for us to conceive of anything but people mindlessly following plans handed down to them. But social planning need not mean authoritarian rule from the top. Indeed, effective social planning of the scope necessary perhaps can only result from the decentralization of authority that allows each region to work out appropriate solutions.

The reconstruction of society involves "bottom up/top down" social planning on a grand scale. For instance, Food First self-reliance starts with the nutritional needs of all the people and translates them into a national agricultural plan. A Canadian report on agriculture and nutrition in Cuba describes how local farmers participate in this translation: "Meetings take place with all the farm workers and small farmers at the local level to discuss the plan and the production quotas allocated to their area. Suggestions for revisions or changes are made. This feedback process is very important because it is the local farmers and workers who know best what crops will grow in their area."[18]

The Food Self-Reliance Bandwagon

The devastating impact of export agriculture on the majority of the people will become more and more undeniable, and food dependency will continue to translate into food shortages and rising prices for the politically volatile urban centers. Predictably, national politicians will increasingly call, and some have already begun, for food self-reliance. They will claim that their new agricultural policies will make their countries independent. But the food self-reliant policies we have described simply cannot be implemented by the present governments of most underdeveloped countries. Why not? Simply because these policies directly counter the self-interest of the propertied elite now in power. Food First, then, is not a simple call to put food into hungry mouths. It is the recognition that, if enabling people to feed themselves is to be the priority, then all social relationships must be reconstructed.

If present governments will not implement Food First policies, what, then, is the value of this prescription for food self-reliance? Its value, we think, lies in showing what is possible — in giving evidence to groups struggling for self-determination that food self-reliance is a *viable* alternative. A prescription for food self-reliance and a continuing effort to garner the proof of experience that it is possible will serve to discredit all governments that now rationalize continuing dependency as necessary for survival. Indeed the strongest weapon of oppression is the belief, by oppressor and oppressed alike, that while dependency may not be desirable, it is better than starvation. Food self-reliance is the cornerstone of genuine self-determination and it is possible for every country in the world.

Food Self-Reliance and the Industrial Countries

How would food self-reliance in the underdeveloped countries affect those of us in the industrial countries? Many might assume that the citizens of the industrial countries benefit by the continued dependency of the underdeveloped countries.

The answer, we have seen, is an emphatic no. Self-reliance for the now dependent countries would strike at the heart of the Global Supermarket phenomenon, that is, the collaboration of elites in both industrial and underdeveloped countries to profit from the land and people of underdeveloped countries by supplying those locally and abroad who can afford to pay the most. Although citizens of the industrial countries might be told by the apologists of agribusiness that the Global Supermarket exists to serve them, it does not. We have already seen, in Part VIII, that it serves only its creators.

But would Food First self-reliance in the underdeveloped countries close important markets for the agricultural exports of countries such as the United States and Canada? Obviously it would. Does that mean, then, that every means must be used to keep other countries food-dependent, or otherwise American family farmers will be unable to make a decent and secure living? We think not. In Part VII we began to sketch the rebalancing of the structures in the American agriculture and food industry. (Not the least significant thing we pointed to is that the United States is importing enormous quantities of agricultural products that could easily and profitably be grown by American farmers without boosting prices to consumers.) Furthermore, the proper goal of the family farmer is not maximum volume but earning a satisfactory and steady income. It is urgent to work now to understand and implement those policies that would make farming a good, reliable livelihood without having to push our "abundance" onto others who could and would provide for themselves.

The prescription for food self-reliance presented here is not simply what "those poor, hungry countries" should do. Redistribution of control over food-producing resources is the only path toward true self-reliance for the industrial countries as well. By understanding the parallels, the majority in the industrial countries will come to see that the hungry masses they are often made to fear are, in reality, their natural allies. We are all in a common struggle for control over the most basic human need — food.

45

But Where Would Development Capital Come From?

Question: Your prescription for self-reliance sounds good, but where do you think underdeveloped countries would get the capital they need? Where would underdeveloped countries get foreign exchange to buy building materials, fertilizers, farm machinery, fuel, and so on. Not only do they need foreign exchange, but they need the wealth of their upper classes to invest in growth. If underdeveloped countries cut themselves off or redistribute their wealth, I'm afraid they will be resigning themselves to a state of miserable stagnation.

Our Response: The question implies that the Food First alternative we have just outlined would make accumulating capital for development more difficult than it is today. But shouldn't we evaluate any proposal for change first by comparing it to what exists? We think if you truly examine the "what is" now in underdeveloped countries, you will soon realize that no one could devise a system with *less* chance for accumulating capital.

Capital is not simply money in the bank. Most workers in every underdeveloped country, no matter how poor and undernourished the majority of its population, produce more than they consume. This surplus generated by their work is the root of capital. Thus the surplus to be converted into capital exists; the real question is who controls the accumulated goods and the means to produce more.

In most underdeveloped countries the surplus is not available to the majority of the people who produce it, for it is controlled by landlords, moneylenders, merchants, industrialists, state bureaucrats, and foreign corporations. Traditionally it is argued that unequal control over the surplus is "good" for a society because only the rich will save the surplus and invest in a society's future. Recently, however, respected economists studying underdeveloped countries have independently concluded that in reality such a rationalization of unequal control simply does not hold up.[1] They find that in the countryside, the landlords, moneylenders, and merchants who appropriate so much of the surplus generally do *not* reinvest it; rather, they tend to spend it on imported luxury goods and expensive consumer items manufactured in foreign-style factories that use up large amounts of capital and provide little employment. Even when they do invest, as we noted in Part V, it is invariably abroad or nonproductively, for instance, in hotels, bars, restaurants, rental property, taxis and the like.

One of us lived for several months in a village in the remote southern Yucatan jungle of Mexico. The Indians were poor farmers — former chicle gatherers for Wrigley's chewing gum until Wrigley came up with a synthetic gum — who were gravely exploited by the village's general storeowner and moneylender, whom we will call Don Eziquiel. One day Don Eziquiel used his accumulated profits to import what had been his heart's desire since the day he saw an ad in a newspaper — a Ford Galaxie — and there wasn't even a single paved road in the jungle!

What About Foreign Investment Capital?

Foreign corporations like to claim that underdeveloped countries need them because they need capital. But numerous studies[2] now have demonstrated that a multinational corporation usually brings in precious little initial capital to those countries. Why should a corporation bother when it finds it can tap the local savings since everyone wants to lend to, say, General Foods. Often a large part of the equity contribution by a foreign corporation to a joint venture with a local partner or the state consists not of capital, but of technical and marketing "know-how." In addition, all or part of the profit is frequently not reinvested but is "repatriated," that is, returned to the home country.

We have seen that agribusiness corporations, whether operating plantations or through contracts, appropriate the lion's share of the value of produce through their monopoly hold on foreign marketing. All types of foreign corporations regularly siphon off capital (in addition to declared profits) through untaxed royalties, debt payments, and inflated charges by headquarters for management advice, research, and the like. All the devices open to them rely on the marvels of modern corporate accounting (recently defined by one accountant as a subdivision of creative writing).

It is debatable whether even a country like the United States has enough skilled civil servants to monitor the accounting alchemies of the multinational corporations operating across its borders. Certainly no underdeveloped country can even come close to doing so. The chief accounting alchemies are overpricing imports from headquarters (including depreciated machinery) and underpricing exports to another subsidiary of the same company. These devices enable the local subsidiary to claim it is losing money. It can then threaten to pull up stakes if it does not receive even more subsidies, "tax holidays," no-strike guarantees, free roads, water, and so on.

Some governments are finally realizing therefore that a foreign "investor" is often a net exporter of capital. Ironically, one such government is that of Brazil. We say "ironically" because the military government of Brazil since 1964 has sought above all to provide the proper "climate" for foreign investment. An official study late in 1975 showed that the eleven most important foreign firms have remitted more capital out of Brazil than they have brought in. Since 1965, the giant agribusiness firm, Anderson Clayton, for example, has brought $1.6 million in capital into Brazil. By 1975, it had generated a surplus 32 times greater, $16.8 million of which was sent abroad in the form of profits and dividends.[3]

Plastic Shoes for Development?

Nonagribusiness firms also can appropriate the capital of the peasants and perpetuate a distortion of the country's potential food resources. A good example of this was sent to us by a missionary in the Cameroon. The Bata Shoe Company, a ubiquitous Canadian-based multinational corporation, a few years ago started manufacturing plastic shoes in the coastal town of Douala. The shoes are heavily advertised throughout the predominantly rural country and they have become one of those symbols of status that poor people buy. Tourists in Douala seek out traditional handcrafted shoes while the peasants save up money from the export of their cocoa, peanuts, and cotton to buy plastic shoes. With such "incentives" the peasants expand their production of export crops (thereby often lowering market prices) on land well suited for food crops, despite serious rural undernutrition. The Bata Shoe Company (and similar multinationals) therefore are in fact recouping part of the foreign exchange paid to the Cameroon for its agricultural exports — foreign exchange that theoretically goes for development needs. At the same time several thousand village shoemakers, perfectly capable of meeting the country's needs are being put out of work and will likely go hungry. The plastic shoe factory itself, the missionary noted, employs all of thirty workers.

Over the past few years European textile firms, like their New England counterparts years ago, are moving south, but, in their case, to central Africa to avoid labor unions and higher labor costs. The first impact, already dramatic in countries like Mali and Chad, is an increased push for cotton production at the expense of food staples. In addition, through the firms' repatriations and remittances for machinery, loans and service fees, much of the foreign exchange earned by the export of agricultural products and textiles leaves the country. In other words, foreign exchange is not being spent on the type of development that decreases poverty, unemployment, inequality, and hunger. Tens of thousands of local craftspeople, formerly tailors, makers of cotton and wool thread and cloth, are being put out of work. Such companies perpetuate underdevelopment by sopping up, displacing, and mischanneling the country's actual and potential capital.

So that is something of "what is." When we say Food First policies could scarcely run the risk of being a worse way to accumulate local capital and even foreign exchange, you now see why.

Capital Formation Begins with Land and People

In a Food First economy people would mobilize the potential capital of their labor power and of underutilized land. Vast tracts of underused land exist on large estates, monocultural plantations, and mechanized farms that employ capital to displace people.

Moreover, the redistribution of income that is the product of the Food First economy we described in our response to Question 44 can mean greater savings for investment, not less. We have seen, in Part VI, that even under present conditions poor farmers, especially if they have some land, often turn out to be better savers than the rich. And if poor peasants are given reason to believe that their savings will benefit them, they can save at impressive rates. After the Chinese revolution the net savings ratio in China rose from 1 to 2 percent in 1949 to 20 percent in 1953.[4]

The Chinese people have learned through their own struggle to overcome hunger that neither money capital nor the natural geographic endowment of an area are the determining factors. The village of Tachai illustrates this lesson for us as well as for six million Chinese peasants who have already visited it as part of an agrarian education effort.

In the 1950s, Tachai and Wu Chai-Ping were two neighboring villages with very disparate natural qualities. Wu Chai-Ping wanted to separate itself from Tachai because it felt that the potential of its superior natural endowment would be held back by its neighbor, the resource-poor Tachai. They did split up. But, Tachai, through intensive collective work has more than made up for its inferior natural resources. Tachai now produces better harvests and enjoys a considerably higher income than the other village. The people of Tachai overcame an extremely hostile environment *without outside material support*.[5]

The Chinese now point to Tachai to teach the lesson that capital to buy equipment and pay experts or even a favorable natural environment is not necessary for development. What is necessary is that the people truly believe that they themselves can overcome hunger and poverty through collective work. No amount of aid money, no amount of machinery, no amount of well-organized administration can generate that belief.

The early stages of Food First will rely on the mobilization of the unemployed and underemployed labor force for improving the productivity of the land. But it will not be long before the accumulated surplus, especially on a collective basis, can be used to purchase capital goods to increase production and lighten the work load. In Chinese communes farmer cooperatives vote what percentage of the surplus should be accumulated (generally they have chosen to save at a faster rate than that recommended by the government) and how it should be used. Since state policy has gradually but systematically reduced the prices of manufactured farm supplies compared to those of agricultural produce, the communes have been able to purchase considerable farm improvements. A report of the FAO gave us some idea:

> What a commune of modest means does with its accumulation fund is illustrated by the example of Yuechi Commune in Wuxien Hsien, Kiangxu province, one of the less prosperous communes. Within the five years of the Third Plan, the collective bought two 35-HP tractors and 67 8-, 10-, and 12-HP hand tractors, set up 11 irrigation drainage stations, purchased 12 heavy transformers, 15 electric engines totalling 284 kw, 71 electric pumps, 18 harvesters, 183 small threshers, 193 sprayers, 11 milling sets, 56 rice transplanters, 19 4-ton ferro-cement transport barges, 520 other sampans, 12 road trailers and 43 large handcarts.[6]

The development of a commune like Yuechi did not begin with the infusion of outside capital. Rather the people mobilized their local capital, mainly in the form of their labor power applied to the natural resource base.

The question asked whether underdeveloped countries do not need foreign exchange to import fertilizers, farm equipment, building materials, and fuel. Certainly basic farm equipment and building material can be locally produced, but what about fertilizer?

First of all, most of the fertilizers imported by many underdeveloped countries go to two or three export crops. We have already discussed how planting single commercial crops over large areas depletes the soil, leading to a notable dependence on costly chemical fertilizers. Shifting to crop rotation and mixing different crops in the same fields, even as first steps, would greatly reduce the need for fertilizer.

Most important, however, is the utilization of the vast untapped potential for production of organic fertilizer using indigenous waste materials. It has been estimated that the annual local potential in underdeveloped countries represented *six to eight* times the amount of nutrients used by underdeveloped countries in the form of costly chemical fertilizers in 1970–1971.[7] Fortunately, this energy and fertilizer potential can be tapped right at the village level, using materials that are often wasted. Biogasification is a simple method of fermenting organic raw material such as crop residues and manure to produce methane (for fuel) and a nutrient-rich effluent (for fertilizer). The fertilizer produced through the biogas technique is many times richer in nutrients than the waste products that went into it. By fermenting the village wastes of 500 human beings and 250 cattle, a biogas "plant" can supply the average cropped land of a typical Indian village with two and one half times the present nitrogen applied in the form of chemical fertilizers. Moreover, it can supply almost double the present daily energy needs of the village for cooking, water, pumping, electricity, and industries.

Producing fertilizer through the biogasification technique actually *generates* energy out of waste; whereas a typical coal-based fertilizer plant *consumes* the energy equivalent of the needs of about 550 Indian villages. Perhaps most important, biogas fermenters can be built by the villagers themselves using local materials. Does all this sound dreamy? It is not. Biogas fermenters are already working effectively in some Indian villages.[8]

The Chinese in order to achieve food self-reliance mobilized their organic fertilizer potential. Livestock and human excrement and other waste products are turned into high-grade plant nutrients. Mixed cropping and other farming methods that improve soil fertility are now universally practiced. During a recent visit to China technical experts from the FAO observed that China's soils appeared to be *improving*; of few other countries in the world could this be said.

Now that Food First for all has been achieved, China is seeking to boost still further its agricultural output by the application of chemical fertilizers to be manufactured regionally, taking advantage of the country's vast mineral deposits. Some would argue that since "China's doing it," that is, constructing chemical fertilizer plants using foreign technology, that all underdeveloped countries should too. They overlook the crucial point that in China each village *first* maximized the use of local organic materials and only then did regional collectives begin to invest part of their surplus in chemical fertilizer as a supplement to organic fertilizer. Moreover, while China has purchased some foreign technology there are no strings attached: No foreign fertilizer corporation will own the plants nor supply the raw materials.

Genuine collective action may seem distant in a culture like ours — or in most underdeveloped countries, for that matter. People sense intuitively and correctly that in a highly unequal society a call for national "sacrifice" is usually a convenient way for the rich to blind the nonrich to the fact that only *they* are being made to give up something. Only when people have enough to eat, have security, and have hope is it possible to appeal to them to eschew selfishness for collective work. Such appeals "would not make much sense," comments economist Joan Robinson," to the workers and peasants, say, in Mexico or Pakistan."[9] Justice, therefore, is an absolute prerequisite to the mobilization of human labor, which is the basis of all capital formation.

The next time you hear or read a discussion on the lack of aid, poor terms of trade or the poor natural endowment of the underdeveloped countries, don't conclude that such are the causes of underdevelopment. Lack of capital is not the problem. The problem is the powerful constraints we have talked about throughout this book that prevent the poor majority from realizing their collective strength.

46

Aren't Poor Peasants Too Oppressed Ever to Change?

Question: But aren't the peasants in the underdeveloped countries so oppressed, malnourished, and conditioned into a state of dependency that they are beyond the point of being able to mobilize themselves? Even if you are right that real change can only start at the bottom, isn't this just plain unrealistic?

Our Response: Perhaps this question reflects as much our own feelings of frustration with the social problems in this country as it does with those of peasants in underdeveloped countries. It may reflect a view of human nature we learn almost by osmosis in our culture, a view that people are basically passive and that they are incapable of assuming responsibility for their own lives. It derives, moreover, from a deep-rooted view about poor people in general — that they lack "get up and go," that they have somehow lagged behind due to personal deficiencies or due to the culture of poverty in which they are fated to be born and doomed to die.

Because we view our own society this way, we view others this way too. If small farmers can't make it in this country, how can they make it "over there"? If the majority here haven't taken back power from corporate interests, how could we think that some poor, illiterate peasants could take power from the landlord or bureaucrat they have been taught to fear?

Well-placed Americans decry the fact that we just don't know how to solve the problem of hunger (in fact, there is a book by that title). Seldom, however, do they seek to learn from the examples of peasant societies that *have* in fact overcome hunger.

Even during the worst years of the war, the North Vietnamese were not starving. In fact they were improving their agriculture. According to an FAO report yields were going up, and irrigation was extended from 20 percent of the cultivated area in the mid-fifties to nearly 60 percent in the mid-sixties.[1]

But do Americans have any notion of what the North Vietnamese had to overcome? Writing in 1945, Ho Chi Minh appealed to the people to overcome famine with these words:

> Owing to the barbarous policies of the French colonialists, who among other things requisitioned paddy and forced our peasants to grow jute instead of rice, over two million people starved to death in Bac Bo in the early part of this year. Then came floods and drought.

> Famine is even more dangerous than war. . . . In war, all the forces of the country must be mobilized and organized to fight the enemy. In our struggle against famine, we must also mobilize and organize our entire people.[2]

During the war much of Vietnam's cultivable land was bombed. In the village of Xuan Hoa in North Vietnam, 80 percent of the cultivable land was destroyed by B-52 bombing raids. Having waited one month after what turned out to be the last raid, the villagers filled in many of the bomb craters. Today rice is once again growing, giving the highest yields ever (one ton per acre). Xuan Hoa is not only self-sufficient but also is able to pay its taxes with rice. Fish cultivated in ponds made out of other bomb craters provide the villagers with several tons of high quality protein each year.[3]

Other countries offer similar examples but our ordinary sources of information about the world tell us little of how Vietnam, North Korea, China, Cuba, Guinea-Bissau, Mozambique, and other countries are achieving food security for all their populations. It is striking that so many who would question what peasants can do for themselves, seem unaware that, since only the early fifties, over 40 percent of the population of the underdeveloped world have completely freed themselves from hunger through their own efforts.

We can also look to Africa to learn that poor people can mobilize themselves effectively. Few realize, for example, that the movement for the liberation of Angola was ignited in 1961 when 15,000 men, women, and children were killed because they protested the Portuguese-enforced cotton cash-cropping. Even more telling is that many Westerners view the liberation of the Portuguese colonies — Guinea-Bissau, Mozambique, and Angola — as the result of the 1974 movement of young Portuguese army officers. Not many are aware that, on the contrary, it was the fifteen-year struggle of the colonized people in Africa that led to the overthrow of fascism in Portugal. As one Swiss report put it, "The everyday heroism of the Guinean people was at the root of the young [Portuguese] officers' slow process of political awareness."[4] Over long years of resistance, the African people demonstrated the absurdity of the colonial war.

What does hard-fought-for independence mean in terms of people and food? In Mozambique, to cite one example, the liberation movement, now in power, is successfully restoring a peasant food economy that had been destroyed by Portuguese colonialism. Since the 1928 Native Labor Code the peasants of Mozambique were compelled to provide their quota of such cash crops as rice, sugar, cotton, coffee, and copra because the law did not recognize subsistence farming as "living by one's own work." In 1961, the International Labor Organization studied the code and noted the exhaustion of the country's soil, largely because of the heavy demands of colonial monocultural cash cropping.

The peasant-based FRELIMO (Front for the Liberation of Mozambique), having early on won control of the northern provinces, was able to establish a vital and innovative food economy there despite bombardment and defoliation. In the southern regions the liberation movement inherited a more desperate situation. In 1973, the Portuguese, supported by the United States, engaged in last ditch terrorism. They rounded up the population into strategic hamlets, often in the most infertile areas, burned huts and fields as they were vacated, and confiscated all field tools for fear they might be used as weapons. The result was widespread malnutrition, destitution, and disease, including a cholera epidemic.

With victory, FRELIMO has had to mobilize the people for total reconstruction. FRELIMO has become known for its experimentation with new crops, for diffusing innovations, and for learning from the peasants' own examples. It has organized peoples' stores where basic goods like cloth, soap, or salt are exchanged for food. It has used its "food aid" to set up revolving funds to build or purchase basic agricultural equipment. Thus the independent Mozambique government has made the reconstruction of agriculture the foundation for the reconstruction of society.[5]

Are Americans aware of struggles for control over food production in underdeveloped countries where hunger has not yet been eliminated? In Honduras only 667 families and two banana companies, United Brands and Standard Fruit, own over 85 percent of the cultivated land. Much of the prime land of the large family estates either lies idle or is used for cattle raising. Three quarters of the population of almost three million must struggle for survival on the remaining land, much of it mountainous and rocky. Official statistics show that 90 percent of children under the age of five are undernourished; typhoid, malaria, and tuberculosis are endemic.

But recently there has been hope. In the early seventies, 140,000 peasants organized themselves into the National Peasant Union. Their goals are land to be cooperatively worked by all the peasants (easily possible if the large estates were broken up) and the self-teaching of better farming techniques.

By 1975, the peasants began occupying large uncultivated estates. The landlords' hired gunmen murdered dozens of them. In June, 1975, the peasants organized a "hunger march" on the capital. The cattlemen of the National Cattle Farmers Association and soldiers attacked them, killing six peasants and kidnapping nine others, including two foreign priests who were later summarily executed. In 1975 over fifty peasants were killed.[6]

Such united movement and bravery should clash with our notion of the hopeless, downtrodden, passive peasant.

What is left out of the American newspaper accounts of this struggle in Honduras is that the cattlemen fighting and killing to prevent this land redistribution make their money by supplying American meat-packing companies with imported meat. If the land reform the peasants demand were carried out it would directly cut into the profits of certain segments of the American meat industry that benefit from cheap Central American meat, not to mention the profits of American banana companies.

Nor do we read a single hint of the existence of United States military and police support and CIA operations in Honduras. During the 1970s, hundreds of Honduran military officers have studied "military intelligence interrogation," "jungle operations," and "counter insurgency operations" at the United States Army School of the Americas. Since 1950, United States military schools have trained over 2600 military officers from Honduras.[7] Are our taxes being spent to maintain a system that generates hunger?

Nor do we read that in Honduras AID is promoting a showcase

land reform aimed at creating private small farms to diffuse the peasant movement. The fear is that the peasants will move further in the direction of demanding the nationalization and elimination of individual ownership of all the country's productive resources.

We have seen how, in the state of Sonora in Mexico, the concentrated efforts at "modernization" have benefited a few large landowners while undermining the earlier land reform. Today, although the maximum legal irrigated smallholding is 250 acres, some estates, by subterfuge, have now accumulated as much as 25,000 acres. In one area a single landowning family possesses over 60 water holes, while 1500 nearby families have none. In one case a peasant has been waiting for twenty-five years for the government's promise of land to be fulfilled. Another group of peasants has been waiting for one official signature authorizing a land reform cooperative since 1942! Most Americans would assume that after such a long period of disappointment the peasants would simply give up.

No. This is not the case. The desperate landless peasants in the state of Sonora are now moving to seize the land that rightfully belongs to them. They have been machine-gunned by the army and police. Many are in jail. The national government, sensing the growing power of the peasant movement, dismissed the state governor. The police chief fled the state. At first the large Sonoran landowners threatened to strike back by withholding production and food supplies to the cities and sabotaging the irrigation canals. The new governor charged that the large landowners had sent two million dollars abroad. During a recent visit to Sonora, we found that the peasants have not been intimidated. They are stepping up their mobilization of other peasants and are waging a vigorous publicity attack on the landowners who have now backed away from their threats. As of this writing, the open battle is still raging.[8]

Another example of the mobilization of peasants comes from the African Sahel. The events of the famine-stricken Sahel are brought to us through a filtered lens. Events are often tinted in such a way as to change their meaning altogether. We read one news account stating that the economy of Senegal was ruined because of a fall-off in the production of export crops. Phrased that way, one's natural response would be to ask: What can be done to spur the lagging production of these crops? How can we get the economy rolling again? We thus identify with the *export economy* of Senegal, not the *people*.

In fact, production of export crops was down primarily because the peasants stopped growing peanuts, protesting that the government did not pay them fairly for their production. Indeed, with what they received for their peanuts, the Senegalese peasants could not buy enough food to feed their families. The peasants thus spurned the cash cropping to grow basic food for themselves, particularly millet and sorghum. This shift is interpreted by some as the reaction of tradition-bound peasants. On the contrary, however, this example of peasant resistance must be seen as a break away from tradition, if being traditional means doing what your superiors in the political and social hierarchy have always expected of you. Looked at this way, then, a *positive* step had been taken. For the first time the peasants broke the pattern that colonialism had imposed upon them. What we are saying is that these positive lessons are seldom, if ever, drawn. This is the power of selective news that reinforces the beliefs Americans have about the immobility of the world's oppressed.

Perhaps no other country so represents to Americans the utter passivity of the poor peasant than Bangladesh. Yet in the Rangpur district of Bangladesh a remarkable movement for self-reliance is underway in the village of Kunjipukur.[9] By developing a collective decision-making process the village has succeeded in

- repaying outstanding loans to credit agencies and replacing them with a common community fund.
- guaranteeing work to all the landless.
- planting fruit trees on all the idle village land to be cultivated collectively.
- constructing roads and irrigation canals using unoccupied village workers.
- establishing a literacy program.
- settling disputes through a village people's court.
- moving women toward economic independence from men by allowing the women to take over responsibility for and proceeds from poultry raising.

Encouraged by such progress in only two years, other villages, now numbering over sixty, have taken up this movement for self-reliance. Their true test came during the 1974 famine. In the

Rangpur district, one of the hardest hit in Bangladesh, 80,000 to 100,000 people died of starvation in only a few months. But in the self-reliant villages of Rangpur no one died of hunger. These villages *refused* government assistance and instead collectively arranged for food contributions from anyone with a surplus. The food collected went to those without food, in exchange for work or other repayment collectively agreed upon.

Even in Crystal City, Texas, a counterforce is emerging. Crystal City is the Spinach Capital of the world that we described, in Question 34, as an example of the worst conditions facing U.S. farm workers. Yet today, farm workers organized by the Raza Unida party are laying the groundwork for a 1000-acre cooperative farm. The farm will provide jobs to a community in which 30 to 40 percent of the adult population is unemployed during the summer. But Jesús Salas, executive of the nonprofit organization planning the cooperative, is enthusiastic about more than just providing jobs. Workers will be involved in directing farm operations. They will receive hot meals in the fields and have day care and sanitation facilities provided. Salas says that the reason that farm work has been demeaning is that workers have been oppressed, underpaid, and forced to live in horrible conditions. In his view, "the cooperative farm has to be involved in putting dignity back into the work of raising food."

Asking whether or not poor peasants are too oppressed ever to change ignores the reality that in every country in the world there is a struggle going on right now over who controls food-producing resources. Those involved are the very people who are perceived by so many as "too oppressed ever to change." Part of the reason we fail to appreciate the ongoing work of ordinary people for food self-reliance is the fault of the selective news we receive through our normal news channels. A major part of overcoming the "myth of the passive poor," then, is to seek out other regular sources of information that will help us, not only to understand what others are doing, but to see how our own work can support their efforts. At the end of the book we recommend some of the organizations and publications that can help us make these connections.

47

Food versus Freedom?

Question: Aren't the only successful peasant movements those that have ended up creating extremely restrictive societies? You talk about China; but, in order to overcome hunger, the Chinese have had to accept such regimented lives. Have we really reached the point where countries will have to become like China if they want to eliminate hunger?

Our Response: Most Americans who have anything good to say about China do see it as an example of the "lesser evil" — better to live a regimented and dull life than to die of starvation. What intrigued us, however, is China's success in overcoming agrarian problems that have plagued the rest of the world. Since at least the early 1960s it has had no inflation, no shortages of essential food, no beggars, no starvation, and no hunger. In addition, China is giving food aid and agricultural assistance to several other countries: This in a country where not so long ago famine was an annual occurrence. This in a country with one of the highest people-to-farmland ratios in the whole world. The Chinese, formerly plagued by droughts and floods, have worked to multiply their irrigated land in the last fifteen years so that they have one third of all the irrigated land in the world. They have doubled their yields of major grains in two decades. Their birth rate is dropping as rapidly as almost any country in history.

Now, to some this success in overcoming the perennial threat of famine means little — merely that the authorities were able to indoctrinate and control the masses, thereby getting them to accomplish a remarkably difficult undertaking. But to be successful on this scale is not just a matter of lining up bodies to heave shovelsful of earth out of an irrigation ditch. Accomplishing the fundamental reconstruction of agriculture requires imagination and initiative to overcome novel difficulties. The leaders of the Chinese Revolution had, after all, never tackled them before! What makes us think that they had a master plan that could simply be imposed by fiat? In fact, the most striking thing about the agrarian revolution in China is its *experimental* approach. People cannot be forced at the end of a bayonet or by threat of starvation to experiment. The basic living and working unit in China has evolved through several stages since the Revolution. And, according to the Chinese, it will continue to evolve. When asked whether the people's communes were regarded as the lasting solution to the problem of agrarian organization, one commune member replied: "Not at all. The people's communes are the fifth form of organization after the Revolution . . . But they are by no means the final answer — nothing is the final answer to anything."[1] The evolution of Chinese rural organization has been, and will continue to be, a product of the satisfactions and dissatisfactions of the people themselves.

When we speak of an experimental approach in China, we mean it in the literal sense also. In two communes, for example, ordinary farmers worked together to solve the problem of what the optimal density for rice planting is. For four years the question of optimal density remained controversial. Various work teams and brigades carried out mass experiments, pitting the various theories and techniques against each other. This plant research was designed by the peasants themselves. We would find it hard to believe that such experimentation could result from coercion. In fact, *the* most striking feature of Chinese agricultural development compared to that of other underdeveloped countries is that there is *less* centralized control and less control from above. In most underdeveloped countries development plans are formulated by national bureaucracies working with international lending agencies. Only at the final stages are the peasants *told* how they fit in. By contrast, Chinese planning is governed by an often repeated phrase, "From the bottom up/from the top down."

The planning process begins in every commune with an evaluation of the previous year's performance. The commune draws up its proposal for the following year with its own needs and priorities spelled out, including how it will use its labor and financial resources, and what it needs in terms of fertilizer and machinery. The plans then go to the province level where a provincial commission submits them to a central planning commission. After this commission has made sure that adequate production of all the essentials — grains, sugar, and cotton — has been planned on a national basis, the adjusted targets are passed back down through the province and to the commune levels where a second round of meetings takes place to firm up the plans. Two principles are said to govern the entire process: "leaving leeway," or the need for maximum flexibility and "combatting egotism," or taking into account the needs of others, whether that "other" is another person, another commune, or another province.[2]

Many agriculturalists studying China have concluded that the only way to explain the success is that maximum participation has been encouraged at every level of decision making. The effect of this participation is seen by a recent American visitor:

> To me, as a visitor to China, the most impressive and revolutionary aspect of the country was the attitude Chinese workers hold toward their work.
> They liked their work.
> Chinese workers identified with their jobs. They believed in what they were doing. They saw their work in overall social terms. And if you've ever worked in an American factory, you'll agree that such attitudes are, by comparison, nothing short of revolutionary."[3]

The Chinese people consider that to allow hoarding and speculation in food, practices that ensure that some individuals are victimized while others profit, is just as unthinkable as to allow a person to bodily injure another. Thus, as early as 1953 the Chinese introduced a uniform price for each commodity in each province and a nationwide ceiling price for each commodity. The price fixed was year-round, thus eliminating seasonal fluctuations. The result is that farmers feel safe to make their stocks immediately available rather than hold out in anticipation of higher prices later, as farmers often do in countries like the United States. Also, the uniform nationwide ceiling price means that there are no speculative and destabilizing shifts in production from one crop to another, as is so common throughout much of the rest of the world.

The question implies that the peasants in China have to be indoctrinated to make them accept regimentation and work — and that, moreover, we are *not* indoctrinated. Yes, the Chinese are being indoctrinated to believe in the "new man" (or, rather, the "new person"). They are being indoctrinated to believe that people *can* work together for the success of the whole, not just for themselves. In every society choices are made about who gets to eat. Everyone? Some people? And by what criteria? In our society are these decisions really made more democratically than in China?

Certainly there are limitations on people's choices in China. The individual cannot take any job he or she wants or move anywhere at will. These decisions are often made by groups of peers on the basis of the person's interests, performance, and what the society needs. But do most Americans have real choices? A very small percentage do, or at least appear to. But are *most* Americans able to choose the work they *really* want? Where they want to live? And the quality of the environment they want to live in?

Finally, this question presupposes that we must take a stand for or against the Chinese model in toto. It presupposes that in order to apply any of the insights gained from the Chinese experience, we must duplicate their culture. *We disagree heartily*. The real value of studying in-depth what is happening in a country like China is that by so doing we are able to reflect back on our own culture, seeing more clearly its values and modes of operation. We find that the Chinese clearly provide the most positive evidence in modern times of what great achievements are possible when agricultural development is defined as a social problem as opposed to a technical one. They have demonstrated what can be accomplished by believing in the human potential for local self-reliance and by local, democratic decision making in both social and economic areas. We also have learned much from the Chinese view that development is a continual evolution, kept in motion through self-criticism and the criticism of others from which no one can be exempt. Development is not a state to which one aspires but an ongoing struggle by individuals for ever greater self-determination and responsibility for how their actions affect all.

Nevertheless, while we can gain certain insights through examining the Chinese experience, we cannot model ourselves after any other culture in the world. Working to make our economy more democratic and more humane will create a society like none other in the world. It will be unique because our historical experience is unique. What will a people-centered society in America look like? We do not yet know. No one does.

48

What Can We Do?

Question: If you say that it is all up to the underdeveloped countries themselves, then what role is left for us?

The basic message of *Diet for a Small Planet* is that all fundamental social change has to begin with the individual. Do you still feel that way? Aren't individual acts no more than symbolic gestures against the enormity of the economic and political reality of hunger?

Our Response: Saying that self-reliance means self-help and therefore there is no role for Americans could be the most convenient way of escaping our responsibilities. Or, it could be the concept that will free us for the first time to perceive clearly an effective path of work and action.

When *Diet for a Small Planet* was first published there was no movement grounded in the issues of food and hunger. At that time it seemed necessary to focus on what the individual could do. But today it is no longer necessary only to speak of the individual. Now we can also talk about a movement. We are in touch with hundreds of groups all over the country who have emerged spontaneously in the last few years. In this very short time, a national movement has taken form. On college campuses, in religious organizations, among certain state and national legislators, in coop movements, and among ecology and natural food groups there is a feeling that food is the right place to start to focus attention and energy for change. At a recent national "hunger" convention we attended, there was a palpable level of positive energy generating hundreds of ideas for local campus and community action. This is definitely not a movement only of young people. It includes farmers' groups that have been fighting many of the battles we have just discovered for decades. Now they have new allies.

Wherever you are in the country it is possible to make your impact felt within this growing movement. But what should the impact be? What are the most important issues to focus on? What are the pitfalls? These questions we ask continually. We hope some of our answers to ourselves will be helpful to you.

Grasp the Root Causes — Don't Assume We Already Know Enough

It is important to to keep in mind where most Americans are starting, how deeply imbedded the myths are in all our psyches. Do not assume there is a common understanding even among "food activists." There is wide divergence of views, many of them rooted in the old myths we have tried to dispel in this book.

Most of what you read in the future will not reflect the reality that we have tried to convey here. Most of what you read will still frame the questions in the "old" way. You will be hearing that the United States is the world's only remaining "breadbasket," that the problem is simply "population pressure," "severe droughts," or "lack of openness to foreign investment."

One of the most important lessons learned in writing this book has been that acting out of ignorance can strengthen the very forces we must counter. Focus on the small farmer sounds good until we recall that in many countries up to 60 percent of the people in the countryside have no land. Focus on increasing the production sounds good until we ask how the hungry can partake of it if they are excluded from participating in the production process. Introducing mechanization sounds like progress until we ask whose jobs are being eliminated. Sending food abroad sounds good until we look at the impact on local producers and ask what is being done with the proceeds of the sales of food we send as aid. The role of the United States government as helper of the poor abroad sounds noble until we remind ourselves of the overriding impact of U.S. economic and counterinsurgency activities that support the very forces most oppressing the hungry. The desire of American corporations to feed the hungry sounds admirable until we recall that corporations trying to make a profit can only utilize resources, by which the hungry could feed themselves, to grow food for the already well-fed.

A Redefinition of "Help"

The question suggests that there may be a contradiction between self-reliance as the first goal of the hungry and our ability to help. First, keep in mind that *people will feed themselves*. If they are not doing so, you can be sure that mighty obstacles are in the way. These obstacles are not, as we have seen, the "hunger myths" — insufficient production, poor climate, inappropriate technology, discriminatory trade practices, or insufficient capital. The real obstacle in the way of people feeding themselves is that the majority of citizens in every market economy are increasingly cut out from control over productive resources. Thus the real lessons for us are these:

First: We cannot solve the problem of world hunger for other people. They must do that for themselves. We can, however, work to remove the obstacles that make it increasingly difficult for people everywhere to take control of food production and feed themselves.

Second: We should focus on removing those obstacles that are being reinforced today by forces originating in our country, often in our name and with our tax money.

Third: We must support people everywhere already resisting forced food dependency and now building new self-reliant societies in which the majority of people directly control food-producing resources. Direct financial assistance is important as is communicating their very existence to Americans still believing that "people are too oppressed ever to change."

Fourth: Working for self-reliance, both on a personal and national level, benefits everyone. Making America less dependent on importing its food and less dependent on pushing our food on others will be a step toward making America "safe for the world." Local self-reliance will make it more difficult for elites, both in the industrial countries and the underdeveloped countries, to manipulate prices, wages, and people for their own profit. Self-reliance for America means wholesome food available to *all*, supplied by a healthy domestic agriculture of widely dispersed control.

The forms that our energies will take in acting on these four lessons will of course be the outgrowth of our labors together in the coming years. They will differ depending on where you are, who you are, and whom you are trying to reach. Let us welcome a multiplicity of approaches at this stage. Here are some possibilities:

Hunger Re-Education

- Find out how "hunger" is being taught in your school or in the school in your community. Are your peers or your children being taught to fear scarcity and hungry people? Examine textbooks and classroom materials. Then develop alternative curricula and special events that present another view — a positive view that the problem is firmly in *our* hands.
- Form a counter-media group to provide an ongoing answer to your local media's interpretation of hunger here and abroad — through letters to the editor, a regular column, or radio shows sponsored by your group. In the future we ourselves will be developing curricula, study guides, films, cassettes, suggestions for radio program formats, and so on.
- Our own re-education work will continue in the form of in-the-field research and the publication of articles, pamphlets, class curriculum, and study guides. If you would like to be on our mailing list, please write to:

> Institute for Food and Development Policy
> 2588 Mission St.
> San Francisco, California 94110

In addition, at the end of the book, you will find a list of helpful organizations and publications.

Work for Self-Reliance Here

- Work now to open a national debate on the issue of democratic, national planning in the selection and production of food crops to ensure that America's abundance is available to all its people.
- Organize a food cooperative and grow your own food so you can opt out of "food-as-a-profit-commodity" system that creates scarcity. Get behind a network to link directly farmers to consumers in your area. It is a sure way to learn about

farmers' problems. Worker-managed food systems are evolving in cities as different as Minneapolis, and San Francisco.

- Work for regional food self-reliance policies within the United States that will carry with it a message for all Americans: We do not have to import food from hungry countries or waste our fossil fuel transporting food thousands of miles. Energy use for food transportation has *tripled* in the last thirty years. Four states have begun at least to study a move in this direction — Massachusetts, Vermont, Pennsylvania, and West Virginia. (A special state commission on food policy recently found that Massachusetts imports 84 percent of its food. Since 1945 farm acreage in Massachusetts has been cut by more than half.)

Democratize the U.S. Food Economy

- Introduce land reform in the United States, including a ceiling on the amount of land one person or one family can hold. In 1969, the largest 5.5 percent of all farms operated 54 percent of all farmland, while the bottom 40 percent operated only 4.5 percent.[1] The proportion of farmland rented was 38 percent, mostly from nonfarm landlords.
- Work for a national agricultural policy that ensures a reliable and decent income to all family farmers.
- Prohibit corporations with significant nonfarm investments from entering agriculture. Today 22 percent of all farm production is controlled directly or indirectly by large corporations. Minnesota and North Dakota are two states with significant laws to keep corporations out of farming. National anticorporate farming legislation was first introduced in Congress in 1973.
- Remove tax laws that encourage farm investment by nonfarmers seeking to lessen their taxable income.
- Alter inheritance tax laws that force surviving farm families to sell their farms to pay an inheritance tax on highly inflated farmland. (The average farm today is valued at $170,000; farmland is assessed at its real estate value, as if subdivision is intended, rather than at its value as food-producing land.)
- Require all food products to carry the name of corporations

owning the brand line. This would end the myth of a competitive food industry, a myth perpetuated by a handful of corporations selling under hundreds of different names.
* Work to end the monopoly control of advertising by a handful of food corporations — starting with the prohibition of commercials for low-nutrition foods during children's television programming.

Make America "Safe for the World"

* Outlaw government assistance through AID and OPIC and, indirectly, through the World Bank to U.S. private corporations investing in underdeveloped countries.
* Remove all tax laws that encourage American corporations to be abroad to escape environmental and wage laws and taxes here.
* Outlaw the export or sale abroad by a U.S.-based corporation of any additive, pesticide, or drug that is prohibited in the United States.
* Outlaw the importation for food from those countries in which the priority is not food for local people. At least 40 percent of all imported food that directly competes with United States farm production comes from underdeveloped countries.[2]
* End economic assistance to any country that is not actively redistributing control over food-producing resources to the people (includes in-rhetoric-only land-reform countries like the Philippines and Pakistan).
* Promote foreign assistance to countries where steps are being taken to democratize control over agricultural resources.
* Supply food aid only where it directly contributes to creating the preconditions for food self-reliance.

Each of these efforts requires serious back-up research and long-term commitments to study and organize. They will be the result of the combined energy of a movement that is only now becoming aware of itself. Many of these goals sound completely unrealizable in light of today's political climate. The grip of the hunger myths remains firm on most Americans. Still, working toward ends that seem unachievable today can serve as invaluable educational tools, as it reveals more starkly for all of us the concentrated power controlling our food economy.

Don't be afraid to be controversial. It is in controversy that people begin to learn that something new is being said.

Remember also that we are not alone — that within virtually every underdeveloped country there are individuals and groups working to establish Food First policies. Anything that we can do to reveal how corporations and government policies are interfering with their efforts will help to give strength and credibility to these helpful forces. We should never underestimate our unique position in this regard.

The Significance of Individual
Life Choices

The question asked if changes in personal life patterns were not mere token gestures and how we now feel about the steps outlined in *Diet for a Small Planet*. How valuable is it to alter our own eating patterns if we are really saying that the problem is rooted in the economic and political system? Let us explain what we feel is the real significance of such individual acts.

The message of *Diet for a Small Planet* got converted by some into the view that "if each of us only ate one less hamburger a week, the hungry could be fed." This is not what was meant. The change in eating habits that the book embodies is a way to take one step out of the make-believe world we live in. By "make-believe" we mean that we are *made* to believe that the way things are is the way they should be. For instance, we are made to believe that scarcity is a natural phenomenon about which people can do little. We are made to believe that a grain-fed meat diet is both necessary and a sound use of our food resources.

The American meat-centered diet came to represent to us, however, an extreme example of how profit criteria reduce our potential food supply, creating scarcity to ensure profit. Over half of our harvested acreage goes to livestock that only return a small fraction to us. Eating less meat and less processed food — eating in a way that reflects our bodies' real needs — is thus one way of saying no to a system that looks at food like any other profitable commodity — totally divorcing it from human need. A change in diet has been, moreover, a good place to start realizing that we can make real choices — based on our bodies' needs and the best use of the earth rather than on what our profit-oriented system dictates.

What Motivates Us?

After a talk we gave recently students asked: But what makes you think people can change — that anything can change? You say that your position counters the fatalistic overpopulation and weather theories of hunger; that it puts control of our fate back into the hands of the people. But aren't the forces of concentrated wealth and power just as hard to confront or more so?

First, the very phrasing of their question reflects the students' sense that the elite class dominating the food economy both here and in underdeveloped countries is now completely in charge. Yet, we have seen over and over again that the ruling groups are constantly on the defensive, trying to protect their power as more and more of us become aware of our worsening position. The Green Revolution, for example, with its commercialization and mechanization of agriculture, can be seen, in part, as a defensive move. This commercial transformation of agriculture is making people superfluous to production so that landowners no longer have to deal with the legitimate demands of workers and tenants. (Yet, as we see today in clashes between peasants and landlords in the Green Revolution's birthplace — Mexico — the people will not acquiesce.)

The phenomenon of the Global Supermarket can also be seen in part as a reflection of the effort of multinational firms to deal with the strength of farm labor movements in the industrial countries demanding decent wages for their work. Even the vast sums spent by corporations on advertisements portraying themselves as helping to solve world hunger mean that they themselves recognize that Americans are beginning to question the role of corporations. Perhaps those who control the food economy appreciate the power of the awakening people more than we ourselves do.

Second, and just as fundamentally, our answer to these students' question involves a very personal view of ours regarding our own life choices. We believe that anyone who is privileged enough to become aware must make a choice. We either choose to be observers of history, thereby lending our weight to the forces now in control or we choose to be participants, actively building a new culture based on human values. Put this way, do we really have a choice at all?

Human society is, after all, only a product of the collective struggle of all people. If we say that *we* have no power to change things, who does?

If we answer that the power is in the hands of an elite who alone are making the decisions, we will be doing exactly what the established forces of power want of us. We will have folded our arms in defeat, saying that we prefer to build defensive shells to protect ourselves from reality, to keep out the bad news.

Based on our own experience we have come to believe that people prefer a protective shell only because they are overwhelmed with negative information that they cannot integrate. They cannot integrate facts into useful action because they are made to feel guilty about and fearful of the hungry. Too often, the problem of hunger gets turned into a contest between them and us — all of us in the rich world versus all of them in the poor. In fact, the majority of the American people are *not* pitted against the hungry people; these are not the battle lines of the hunger struggle. The struggle is against a system that increasingly concentrates wealth and power. The struggle is against a system profiting on hunger in the Philippines or Brazil just as it is in the United States. The real forces creating hunger span almost all nations in the world. Once the lines of struggle are clear we can no longer be manipulated by profferers of guilt and fear.

Once we have an understanding of how hunger is created and how we fit in, then protective shells are no longer necessary. We won't want to go on shutting out the truth for we will have a framework in which to integrate what was previously overwhelming. The more isolated, negative information we receive, the more defeated we feel, while the more we understand, the more energy we have. That is what we ourselves have learned in the process of writing this book.

But some would say that our choices, if we do indeed have them, are limited — that since people are basically self-centered, all we can do is build on that trait. What we are saying is that this belief in human selfishness directly serves the interests of the already powerful. It is a view of human nature that neatly fits with the status quo. But the economic system we have today is not God-given; it represents a choice to build on certain human traits — to play on human insecurities. It in no way tells us what is *possible*.

New systems of human organization *are* being dared, systems that assume people can cooperate and work to provide opportunities for everyone to have a fulfilling life. There is no more important work today than explaining this to those in the industrial countries. Before they will be open to change they have to believe that change is possible, that a culture fixated on individual profit seeking is not "natural." The tragedy is that we have had to reach the point where millions of people are hungry, including millions here at home, before we can begin to see that our system — a system built on the vulnerabilities of the human personality instead of its strengths — can never create a humane society.

Impatience, however, can only lead to frustration and despair. It took centuries to create the worldwide deprivation we now witness. It will take time to construct a human world. That does not belittle our task; that makes it all the more important. Our personal time frames have changed. We must come to understand today's struggle in light of the entire scope of human history. We must not limit our vision by what we see around us today. What we see today may tell us little about what our children and their children are capable of creating.

When we say that we are learning through studying hunger where our own self-interest really lies, we are not saying simply that we are learning how our lives are limited by the same forces exploiting the hungry peasant in Africa or India. We are also saying that this work is in our own self-interest because, through it, we are made freer. We want you to join us, not simply because of the necessary struggle to construct a just and life-giving society, but because through our own experience we have become certain that none of us can live fully today as long as we are overwhelmed by a false view of the world and a false view of human nature to buttress it. Learning about world hunger then becomes, not a lesson in misery and deprivation, but a vehicle for a great awakening in our own lives.

Notes

Recommended for Further Study

Organizations and Publications

Index

Notes

Part II The Scarcity Scare

1. Standing Room Only?

1. Calculated from Food and Agriculture Organization, *Trade Yearbook*, vol. 28; *Production Yearbook*, vol. 28-1; and *Yearbook of International Trade Statistics*, 1974.
2. Helen Ware, "The Sahelian Drought: Some Thoughts on the Future," Special Sahelian Office, Food and Agriculture Organization, March 1975, p. 16.
3. Theodore W. Schultz, quoted by D. Gale Johnson, *World Food Problems and Prospects*, Foreign Affairs Study 20 (Washington, D.C.: American Enterprise Institute for Public Policy Research, 1975), p. 46.
4. Keith Griffin, *Land Concentration and Rural Poverty* (New York: Macmillan, 1976), p. 134.
5. Calculated from *Trade Yearbook*, vol. 28; *Production Yearbook*, vol. 28-1; *Yearbook of International Trade Statistics*, 1974; and Jose M. Bengo and Gonzalo Donoso, "Prevalence of Protein-Calorie Malnutrition, 1963-1973," *Protein Advisory Group Bulletin*, 4, 1 (1974).
6. *New Internationalist* (April, 1976): 4, citing a World Bank report.
7. Ray Goldberg, *Agribusiness Management for the Developing Countries — Latin America* (Cambridge, Mass.: Ballinger, 1974), p. 70.
8. Ibid, pp. 147, 150.
9. "Perspectives para el Desarollo y la Integracion de la Agricultura en Centro America," SIECA y FAO (Secretaria del Trajado General de Integracion Economica Centro Americana), Guatemala, May 1974.
10. Griffin, *Land Concentration and Rural Poverty*, p. 135.
11. *Mercado Commún Internacional*, Barcelona, Fasc., 91/1973.
12. *The World Food Problem: A Report of the President's Science Advisory Committee* (Washington, D. C.: Government Printing Office, 1967), Tables 7-9, p. 434; see also Leroy L. Blakeslee, Earl O. Heady, and Charles F. Framingham, "World Food Production, Demand and Trade," Iowa State University, 1973.

2. But What About the Real Basketcases?

1. Calculated from Food and Agriculture Organization, *Production Yearbook*, vol. 28-1, 1974.
2. Edgar Owens, U.S. AID, personal communication, 1976.

3. Dr. Benedict Stavis, Cornell University, personal communication, December 23, 1976.
4. Samir Amin, "L'Afrique sous-peuplée," *Développement et Civilisations*, nos. 47–48 (March/June 1972): 60–61.
5. Food and Agriculture Organization, *The State of Food and Agriculture — 1974*, p. 145.
6. Calculated from *Production Yearbook*.
7. Nick Eberstadt, "Myths of the Food Crisis," *The New York Review of Books* (February 19, 1976): 34–35.
8. Steve Raymer, "The Nightmare of Famine," *National Geographic* July 1975.
9. Food and Agriculture Organization, *Bangladesh: Country Development Brief*, 1973, pp. 7, 31–32.
10. United Nations Report (confidential), "Some Notes on Agriculture in Bangladesh," Dacca, Nov. 18, 1974, p. 4.
11. *Famine Risk and Famine Prevention in the Modern World* (UNRISD, 1976), p. 28.
12. Swadesh R. Bose, "The Strategy of Agricultural Development in Bangladesh," in *The Economic Development of Bangladesh: Proceedings of a Conference of the International Economic Association at Dacca*, eds. E. A. G. Robinson and Keith Griffin (New York: Macmillan, 1974), p. 14.
13. Ibid., p. 140.
14. Anisur Rahman, "The Famine," University of Dacca, November 7, 1974, mimeographed, cited by Susan George, *How the Other Half Dies* (London: Penguin, 1976), p. 46.
15. Food and Agriculture Organization, *Progress in Land Reform*, p. III-82 (emphasis added).
16. *Famine Risk*, p. 29.

3. The Price Scare?

1. U.S., Department of Agriculture, *Agricultural Statistics — 1972* (Washington, D.C.: Government Printing Office), Tables 650, 755, and 759.
2. Lester Brown with Erik Eckholm, *By Bread Alone* (New York: Praeger, 1974), p. 60.
3. *Wall Street Journal*, September 2, 1975.
4. Helen Bryant, *Fertilizer: Part of the Solution, or Part of the Problem?* (War on Want, 467 Caledonian Rd., London N7 9BE, 1975) Quoting Edwin Weheler, President of the Fertilizer Institute, at its annual meeting, February 3, 1975.
5. U.S., Department of Agriculture, *Foreign Agricultural Trade of the U.S. (FATUS)* (Washington, D.C.: Government Printing Office, April 1975), p. 30.

4. More People: A Thinner Slice for Everyone?

1. Reported by Colin G. Clark, "More People, More Dynamism," *Ceres* 6 (November/December 1973): 27ff.

5. Are People a Liability or a Resource?

1. Robert d'A. Shaw, *Jobs and Agricultural Development* (Washington, D.C.: Overseas Development Council, 1970), Table 2, p. 10.
2. World Bank, *The Assault on World Poverty* (Baltimore: Johns Hopkins University Press, 1975), pp. 242–243.
3. Charles Elliot, *Patterns of Poverty in the Third World* (New York: Praeger, 1975), p. 50.

4. Wolfgang Hein, "Over-unemployment or Marginality," a review of *Urban Unemployment in Developing Countries, The Nature of the Problem and Proposals for Its Solution* by Paul Bairoch (Geneva: ILO, 1973), in *Ceres* (May-June 1976): 61.
5. Edgar Owens and Robert Shaw, *Development Reconsidered* (Lexington, Mass: Heath, 1972), p. 54.
6. Richard Barnet and Ronald Mueller, *Global Reach* (New York: Simon & Schuster, 1974), p. 169.
7. Colin Tudge, manuscript, 1976, Chapter 1.
8. Robert Maurer, "Work: Cuba," in *Cuba: People — Questions*, ed. W. L. Kaiser (New York: Friendship Press/IDOC/North America, 1975), p. 22.
9. *New York Times*, November 1, 1970.
10. International Labor Organization, "Agricultural Mechanisation and Employment in Latin America," prepared by K. C. Abercrombie, in *Mechanisation and Employment in Agriculture*, 1973, pp. 61–63.
11. Steve Hellinger and Doug Hellinger, Overseas Development Council, unpublished manuscript, 1975, Part II-D, p. 46.
12. Gordon Gemmill and Carl K. Eicher, "A Framework for Research on the Economics of Farm Mechanization in Developing Countries," African Rural Employment Research Network, paper no. 6, p. 2., 1973, Department of Agricultural Economics, Michigan State University, East Lansing, Michigan.

6. People Pressure on the Ecosystem?

1. Lester Brown with Erik Eckholm, *By Bread Alone* (New York: Praeger, 1974), p. 87.
2. Howard E. Daugherty, *Man-Induced Ecologic Change in El Salvador* (Ph.D. dissertation, University of California, Los Angeles, 1969).
3. *El Salvador Zonificacion Agricola* (Fase I), Organization of American States, Washington, D.C., 1974, cited by Erik Eckholm, *Losing Ground* (New York: Norton, for Worldwatch Institute, 1976), p. 167.
4. Georg Borgstrom, "Ecological Aspects of Protein Feeding — the Case of Peru," in eds. M. Taghi Farvar and John P. Milton, *The Careless Technology: Ecology and International Development* (Garden City, N.J.: The Natural History Press, 1972), p. 901.
5. Food and Agriculture Organization, *Production Yearbook*, vol. 28-1, 1974.
6. Erik Eckholm, *Losing Ground* (New York: Norton, for Worldwatch Institute, 1976).
7. *The Economic Development of Colombia* (Baltimore: Johns Hopkins University Press, 1950), pp. 63 and 360, cited in Michael Hudson, *Super Imperialism* (New York: Holt, Rinehart and Winston, 1972), pp. 103–104.
8. Ibid.
9. René Dumont, *False Start in Africa* (New York: Praeger, 1966), p. 69; originally, *L'Afrique est mal partie*, (Paris: Seuil, 1962).
10. Jeremy Swift, "Disaster and a Sahelian Nomad Economy," in *Drought in Africa* eds. David Dalby and R. J. Harrison (London: Centre for African Studies, 1973), pp. 71–79; Douglas L. Johnson, "The Response of Pastoral Nomads to Drought in the Absence of Outside Intervention," paper commissioned by the United Nations Special Sahelian Office, December 19, 1973; F. Fraser Darling and M. T. Farvar, "Ecological Consequences of Sedentarization of Nomads," in *The Careless Technology*; D. J. Stenning, *Savannah Nomads* (London: Oxford University Press, 1959).
11. Ibid., especially Stenning.
12. Helen Ware, "The Sahelian Drought: Some Thoughts on the Future," Special

Sahelian Office, Food and Agriculture Organization, March 26, 1975, especially 3ff.

13. Claire Sterling, "The Making of the Sub-Saharan Wasteland," *Atlantic Monthly* (May 1974): 98–105.
14. Ibid.
15. Eduardo Cruz de Carvalho, " 'Traditional' and 'Modern' Patterns of Cattle Raising: A Critical Evaluation of Change from Pastoralism to Ranching," *The Journal of Developing Areas* 8 (January 1974).
16. Frank L. Lambrecht, "The Tsetse Fly: A Blessing or a Curse?" in *The Careless Technology*, 72ff. and 775ff.
17. Frances M. Foland, "A Profile of Amazonia," *Journal of Inter-American Studies and World Affairs*, (January 1971): 72ff.
18. Cited in Vic Cox, "Brazil: The Amazon Gamble," *The Nation* (October 11, 1975): 328.
19. Dr. Nelson Chaves, Head of the Nutrition Institute at the University of Pernambuco.
20. *World Environment Report*, Center for Environmental Information, New York, 1, no. 8, (May 12, 1975).
21. José S. Da Veiga, "Quand les multinationales font du ranching," *Le Monde Diplomatique* (September 1975): 12.
22. Ibid., p. 13.
23. See Erik P. Eckholm, *Losing Ground*, pp. 136–141.

7. The Food versus Poison Trade-off?

1. *New York Times*, February 14, 1975, citing Dr. G. M. Woodwell, Marine Biological Laboratory, Woods Hole, Mass.
2. Kevin Shea, "Nerve Damage," *Environment* 16 (November 1974): 6ff.
3. "Man's Impact on the Global Environment," Report of the Study of Critical Environment Problems (Cambridge, Mass.: Massachusetts Institute of Technology, 1970), cited by Erik Eckholm, *Losing Ground*, (New York: Norton, 1976), p. 162.
4. Harold M. Schmeck, Jr., "Pesticides' Control of Insects Is Found to Decline Sharply," *New York Times*, February 6, 1976, p. 1.
5. Shea, "Nerve Damage," p. 8.
6. Eckholm, *Losing Ground*, pp. IX–13.
7. See James S. Turner, *A Chemical Feast: Report on the Food and Drug Administration* (Ralph Nader Study Group Reports) (New York: Grossman, 1970) for a study of the influence in government of the chemical and drug companies; David Pimentel, "Realities of a Pesticide Ban," *Environment* 15 (March 1973) gives extensive reference notes.
8. Fred Willman, "Biodegradable Pesticides," *R. F. Illustrated* (Rockefeller Foundation) 2, 1 (March 1975): 5.
9. David Pimentel, "Extent of Pesticide Use, Food Supply and Pollution," *Journal of the New York Entomological Society* 81 (1973): 3–33.
10. Ibid.
11. Ibid.
12. *The AgBiz Tiller* (San Francisco Study Center, P.O. Box 5646, San Francisco, CA 94101) 3 (November 1976): 1.
13. David Pimentel, "Realities of a Pesticide Ban."
14. J. P. Hrabovszky, Senior Policy and Planning Coordinator, Agriculture Department, FAO, Rome, letter dated March 18, 1976, quoting Dr. W. R. Furtick, Chief, Plant Protection Service.

15. Teodoro Boza Barducci, "Ecological Consequences of Pesticides Used for the Control of Cotton Insects in Cañete Valley, Peru," in *Careless Technology, Ecology and International Development*, eds. M. Taghi Farvar and John P. Milton (Garden City, N.J.: Natural History Press, 1972), 423ff.
16. M. Taghi Farvar, "Relationship Between Ecological and Social Systems," speech delivered to EARTHCARE conference, New York, June 6, 1975, p. 4.
17. M. Taghi Farvar, "Ecological Implications of Insect Control," Center for the Study of Biological Systems, Research Report, February 6, 1970, pp. 6–8.
18. Farvar, "Ecological Implications of Insect Control," 1970, p. 11.
19. Ibid., p. 15
20. "Toward a Self-Sustaining Agriculture," *The Journal of the New Alchemists*, The New Alchemy Institute, P.O. Box 432, Woods Hole, Mass., 02543, 1975, p. 49.
21. *New York Times*, December 5, 1976, p. 39.
22. Farvar, "Relationship Between Ecological and Social Systems," 1975, p. 4.
23. Farvar, "Ecological Implications of Insect Control," 1970, p. 10.
24. *Environment* 17 (April/May 1975): 22.
25. *New York Times*, February 6, 1976, p. 12.
26. Richard Franke, "The Green Revolution in a Javanese Village" (Ph.D. dissertation, Department of Anthropology, Harvard University, 1972), 39ff.
27. *Pesticides* (The Journal of the Indian Pesticides Industry) February 1968, see entire issue.
28. Personal communication of L. More and T. F. Watson with Dr. Robert van den Bosch, Division of Biological Control, University of California, Berkeley, cited in Dr. van den Bosch's "The Politics of Pesticides," speech.
29. Richard Norgaard, "Evaluation of Pest Management Programs for Cotton in California and Arizona," Appendix C in *Evaluation of Pest Management Programs for Cotton, Peanuts and Tobacco*, Rosemarie von Rumker, consultant, RVR Project 66, Contract #EQ4AC036, Environmental Protection Agency and the Council on Environmental Quality, October, 1975; see also D. C. Hall, R. B. Norgaard, and P. K. True, "The Performance of Independent Pest Management Consultants in San Joaquin Cotton and Citrus," in *California Agriculture*, Division of Agricultural Sciences, University of California, 29 (October 1975).
30. John S. Steinhart and Carol E. Steinhart, "Energy Use in the U.S. Food System," *Science* (April 1974): 3–4.
31. Ray F. Smith and Harold T. Reynolds, "Effects of Manipulation of Cotton Agro-Systems on Insect Pest Populations," in *Careless Technology*, p. 389.
32. Martin Brown, "An Orange Is an Orange," *Environment* 17 (July/August 1975): 6ff.
33. *New York Times*, February 6, 1976, p. 12.
34. Ibid., citing National Academy of Sciences 1976 study.
35. Smith and Reynolds, "Effects of Manipulation of Cotton Agro-Systems on Insect Pest Populations," p. 389.
36. Farvar, "Ecological Implications of Insect Control," 1970, p. 5.
37. Ibid., p. 15.
38. David Pimentel, "Realities of a Pesticide Ban," p. 28.
39. Barducci, "Ecological Consequences of Pesticides Used for the Control of Cotton Insects in Cañete Valley, Peru," p. 431.
40. Erich H. Jacoby, *The Green Revolution in China* (Geneva: UNRISD, December 18, 1973), pp. 11–12.
41. A. Ayanaba and B. N. Okigbo, "Mulching for Improved Soil Fertility and Crop Production," *Organic Materials as Fertilizers*, Soils Bulletin 27, Swedish International Development Authority and FAO, Rome, 1975, p. 101.

42. Peter Feldman and David Lawrence, "Social and Economic Implications of the Large-Scale Introduction of New Varieties of Foodgrains," *Africa Report*, Preliminary draft (Geneva: UNRISD, 1975), pp. 198 ff.

8. Does Ignorance Breed Babies?

1. Mahmood Mamdani, *The Myth of Population Control: Family, Class and Caste in an Indian Village* (New York and London: Monthly Review Press, 1972), pp. 78, 113.
2. Helen Ware, "The Sahelian Drought: Some Thoughts on the Future," Special Sahelian Office, Food and Agriculture Organization, March 1975, p. 13.
3. S. Hassan, "Influence of Child Mortality on Fertility," paper presented at the annual meeting of The Population Association of America, New York, April 1966, cited in William Rich, *Smaller Families Through Social and Economic Progress* (Washington, D. C.: Overseas Development Council, 1973), p. 13.
4. David Heer and David May, "Son Survivorship Motivation and Family Size in India: A Computer Simulation," *Population Studies* 22 (1968): 206, cited in Rich, *Smaller Families*.
5. Roy E. Brown and J. D. Wray, "The Starving Roots of Population Growth," *Natural History* 83 (January 1974): 47ff.
6. W. Ahmed, "Population Policy and the Peasant," *The Bulletin of Atomic Scientists* (June 1974): 29 ff.

9. Sophisticated Fatalism?

1. Roger Revelle, Center for Population Studies, Harvard University, Letters, *Science* 187 (March 21, 1975).
2. James Howe and John Sewell, "What Is Morally Right?" *War on Hunger* 9 (June 1975): 4.
3. Lester R. Brown, "World Population Trends: Signs of Hope, Signs of Stress," Worldwatch Paper 8, Worldwatch Institute, Washington, D. C., October, 1976, pp. 7–8.
4. William Rich, *Smaller Families Through Social and Economic Progress* (Washington, D. C.: Overseas Development Council, 1973), Chapter 1.
5. Ibid., p. 24.
6. James Kocher, *Rural Development, Income Distribution, and Fertility Decline* (New York: The Population Council, 1973), p. 75ff.
7. Howe and Sewell, "What Is Morally Right?" p. 4.
8. Alan Berg, "The Trouble with Triage," *New York Times Magazine* (June 15, 1975): 26ff.
9. Leo Orleans, "China's Experience in Population Control: The Elusive Model," *World Development* 3 (July-August 1975): 507.
10. Brown, "World Population Trends," Appendix B. Our estimate is also based on discussions with Leo Orleans, China scholar at the Library of Congress.

10. Controlling Births or Controlling the Population?

1. Peter Adamson, *The New Internationalist*, (October 1974): 23–24.
2. James Kocher, *Rural Development, Income Distribution, and Fertility Decline* (New York: The Population Council, 1973), p. x.
3. Barry Commoner, *The Closing Circle* (New York: Knopf, 1971), p. 249.

Part III   Colonial Inheritance

11. Why Can't People Feed Themselves?

1. Radha Sinha, *Food and Poverty* (New York: Holmes and Meier, 1976) p. 26.
2. John Stuart Mill, *Political Economy*, Book 3, Chapter 25 (emphasis added).
3. Peter Feldman and David Lawrence, "Social and Economic Implications of the Large-Scale Introduction of New Varieties of Foodgrains," Africa Report, preliminary draft (Geneva: UNRISD, 1975), pp. 107–108.
4. Edgar Owens, *The Right Side of History*, unpublished manuscript, 1976.
5. Walter Rodney, *How Europe Underdeveloped Africa* (London: Bogle-L'Ouverture Publications, 1972), pp. 171–172.
6. Ferdinand Ossendowski, *Slaves of the Sun* (New York: Dutton, 1928), p. 276.
7. Rodney, *How Europe Underdeveloped Africa*, pp. 171–172.
8. Ibid., p. 181.
9. Clifford Geertz, *Agricultural Involution* (Berkeley and Los Angeles: University of California Press, 1963), pp. 52–53.
10. Rodney, *How Europe Underdeveloped Africa*, p. 185.
11. Ibid., p. 184.
12. Ibid., p. 186.
13. George L. Beckford, *Persistent Poverty: Underdevelopment in Plantation Economies of the Third World* (New York: Oxford University Press, 1972), p. 99.
14. Ibid., p. 99, quoting from Erich Jacoby, *Agrarian Unrest in Southeast Asia* (New York: Asia Publishing House, 1961), p. 66.
15. Pat Flynn and Roger Burbach, North American Congress on Latin America, Berkeley, California, recent investigation.
16. Feldman and Lawrence, "Social and Economic Implications," p. 103.
17. Special Sahelian Office Report, Food and Agriculture Organization, March 28, 1974, pp. 88–89.
18. Alan Adamson, *Sugar Without Slaves: The Political Economy of British Guiana, 1838–1904* (New Haven and London: Yale University Press, 1972).
19. Ibid., p. 41.
20. Eric Williams, *Capitalism and Slavery* (New York: Putnam, 1966), p. 110.
21. Ibid., p. 121.
22. Gunnar Myrdal, *Asian Drama*, vol. 1 (New York: Pantheon, 1966), pp. 448–449.
23. Feldman and Lawrence, "Social and Economic Implications," p. 189.

12. Isn't Colonialism Dead?

1. Eduardo Galeano, *Open Veins in Latin America: Five Centuries of the Pillage of a Continent* (New York: Monthly Review, 1973), p. 282.
2. Walter Rodney, *How Europe Underdeveloped Africa* (London: Bogle-L'Ouverture Publications, 1972), p. 240.
3. Peter Feldman and David Lawrence, "Social and Economic Implications of the Large-Scale Introduction of New Varieties of Foodgrains," Africa Report, preliminary draft (Geneva: UNRISD, 1975), p. 107.
4. Rodney, *How Europe Underdeveloped Africa*, p. 106.
5. George Beckford, *Persistent Poverty: Underdevelopment in Plantation Economies of the Third World* (New York: Oxford University Press, 1972), p. 82.

6. Robert E. Gamer, *The Developing Nations, A Comparative Perspective* (Boston: Allyn and Bacon, 1976), Chapter 2.
7. Edgar Owens and Robert Shaw, *Development Reconsidered* (Lexington, Mass.: Heath, 1972), p. 150; also see Gunnar Myrdal, *Asian Drama*, vol. 1 (New York: Pantheon, 1966), part III, Chapter 10.
8. Francine R. Frankel, "The Politics of the Green Revolution: Shifting Patterns of Peasant Participation in India and Pakistan," in *Food, Population and Employment*, eds., Thomas T. Poleman and Donald K. Freebairn, (New York: Praeger, 1973), p. 124.
9. Thomas P. Melady and R. B. Suhartono, *Development: Lessons for the Future* (Maryknoll, New York: Orbis, 1973), p. 209.

Part IV   Blaming Nature

13. Haven't There Always Been Famines?

1. M. Ganzin, "Pour entrer dans une ère de justice alimentaire," UNESCO *Courrier* May 1975, cited by Susan George, *How the Other Half Dies* (London: Penguin, 1976), p. 139.
2. "Famine-Risk and Famine Prevention in the Modern World: Studies of food systems under conditions of recurrent scarcity" (Geneva: UNRISD, June 1976), p. 36.
3. Famine Inquiry Commission, *Report on Bengal* (Delhi: Government of India Publication, 1945), p. 28.
4. Famine Inquiry Commission, *Report*, pp. 106, 198.
5. George Blyn, *Agricultural Trends in India, 1891–1947* (Philadelphia: University of Pennsylvania Press, 1966), p. 102, cited by Gail Omvedt in "The Political Economy of Starvation," unpublished manuscript, 1974.
6. ———. *The Agricultural Crops of India, 1893–94 to 1945–46* (Philadelphia: University of Pennsylvania Press, 1951).
7. Lester Brown and Gail Finsterbusch, *Man and His Environment: Food* (New York: Harper and Row, 1972), p. 7, cited by Omvedt, "Political Economy of Starvation."
8. Special Publication of the American Geographical Society, No. 6, p. 1.
9. *The Report of the American Red Cross Commission to China*, ARC 270, October 1929.
10. Joseph Needham, "The Nature of Chinese Society: A Technical Interpretation," a public lecture published in University of Hong Kong *Gazette*, May 15, 1974, cited by Harry Magdoff, "China: Contrasts with the U.S.S.R.," in "China's Economic Strategy," *Monthly Review* 27 (July-August 1975): 15–16.
11. *China Reconstructs*, 23, no. 2, 2ff.
12. Richard Greenhill, "Coping," *New Internationalist* (June 1973): 14–15.
13. *China Reconstructs*, 23, no. 2, 2ff.
14. A. de Vajda, Senior Advisor, FAO, Rome.
15. Greenhill, "Coping."
16. Ibid.

14. Can We Hold Back the Desert?

1. U. S. Agency for International Development, Office of Science and Technology, *Desert Encroachment on Arable Lands: Significance, Causes and Control* (TA/OST 72-10) (Washington, D. C.: Government Printing Office, August 1972).

2. Helen Ware, "The Sahelian Drought: Some Thoughts on the Future," paper commissioned by the United Nations Special Sahelian Office, March 26, 1975, especially pp. 2–5.
3. Douglas L. Johnson, "The Response of Pastoral Nomads to Drought in the Absence of Outside Intervention," paper commissioned by the United Nations Special Sahelian Office, December 19, 1973, p. 3.
4. Ware, "The Sahelian Drought," 2f.
5. A. T. Grove, "Desertification in the African Environment," in David Dalby and R. J. Harrison, *Drought in Africa* (London: Centre for African Studies, 1973), pp. 33–45.
6. *Christian Science Monitor*, quoted in *Environment* 1 (December 1974).
7. "Deserts," *China Reconstructs*, 23 (October 1974): 46ff.
8. D. Stamp, "Some Conclusions," in *A History of Land Use in Arid Regions* (Paris: UNESCO, 1961).
9. "Les ravages de la culture du coton," *Le Monde Diplomatique* (May 1976): 11.
10. Claude Raynaut, "Le Cas de la region de Maradi (Niger), in *Sécheresses et Famines du Sahel* (Paris: François Maspero, 1975), especially pp. 8–18.
11. Ware, "The Sahelian Drought," p. 21 citing a personal communication from S. Lallemand, "A Yatenga Village in the Course of the 1973 Drought." See also René Dumont, *False Start in Africa* (New York: Praeger, 1966).
12. Gert Spittler, "Migrations rurales et développement economique: Example du Canton de Tibiri," an unpublished paper discussed in "Social Institutions," a study commissioned by the United Nations Special Sahelian Office, March 28, 1974, p. 93.
13. Calculations based on Food and Agriculture Organization, *Yearbook of International Trade Statistics*, 1974.
14. Food and Agriculture Organization, *Production Yearbook* vol. 28–1, 117f.
15. Michael F. Lofchie, "Political and Economic Origins of African Hunger," *The Journal of Modern African Studies*, 13, 4, (1975): 555f. Also *Sécheresses et Famines du Sahel*, p. 70.
16. Personal communication from Dr. Thierry Brun, Institut National de la Santé Paris, Hopital Bichat, November 17, 1975.
17. Lofchie, "Political and Economic Origins of African Hunger," p. 554 and 561ff.
18. "Social Institutions," a study commissioned by the Special Sahelian Office, March 28, 1974, pp. 79f.
19. International Bank for Reconstruction and Development, *Senegal: Tradition, Diversification, and Economic Development*, 1974, 62ff.
20. "Social Institutions," p. 80.
21. Calculations based on the Food and Agriculture Organization, *Yearbook of International Trade Statistics*, 1974.
22. Interview with Dr. Marcel Ganzin, Director, Food Policy and Nutrition Division, FAO, April 20, 1976.
23. Letter from Dr. Marcel Ganzin, Director, Food Policy and Nutrition Division, FAO, dated December 18, 1975, emphasis added.
24. Food and Agriculture Organization, *Progress in Land Reform — Sixth Report*, 1976, especially p. 24. Also Grigori Lazarev, "Rural Development in the African Countries of the Sudano-Sahelian Africa," paper commissioned by the United Nations Special Sahelian Office, July 23, 1974, p. 5.
25. Claude Meillassoux, "Development or Exploitation: Is the Sahel Famine Good Business?" *The Review of African Political Economy* 1 (August-November 1974): 27–34.

Part V   Modernizing Hunger

15. Isn't Production the Problem?

1. Radha Sinha, *Food and Poverty* (New York: Holmes and Meier, 1976), p. 7.
2. Cynthia Hewitt de Alcántara, "A Commentary on the Satisfaction of Basic Needs in Mexico, 1917–1975," Prepared by the Dag Hammerskjold Foundation, May 7, 1975, pp. 1 and 9.
3. Cynthia Hewitt de Alcántara, "The Green Revolution as History," *Development and Change*, 5, 2 (1973–1974): 25–26.
4. Hewitt de Alcántara, "Commentary on the Satisfaction of Basic Needs," p. 10.
5. Hewitt de Alcántara, "The Social and Economic Implications of the Large-Scale Introduction of New Varieties of Foodgrains," *Country Report — Mexico* (Geneva: UNDP/UNRISD, 1974), p. 30.
6. Ibid., p. 19.
7. Ibid., p. 129.
8. Ibid., p. 156.
9. "Mexico: Roosting Chickens," *Latin America* (Nov. 28, 1975): 375.
10. Andrew Pearse, "Social and Economic Implications of the Large-Scale Introduction of New Varieties of Foodgrains," Part 4, (UNDP/UNRISD), pp. XI–19, XI–20.
11. Cited in Keith Griffin, *The Political Economy of Agrarian Change* (Cambridge, Mass.: Harvard University Press, 1974), p. 55.

16. But Isn't Nature Neutral?

1. Ingrid Palmer, *Science and Agricultural Production* (Geneva: UNRISD, 1972), pp. 6–7.
2. World Bank, *The Assault on World Poverty — Problems of Rural Development, Education, and Health* (Baltimore: Johns Hopkins University Press, 1975), pp. 132–133.
3. Andrew Pearse, "Social and Economic Implications of the Large-Scale Introduction of the New Varieties of Foodgrains, Part 2 (Geneva: UNDP/UNRISD, 1975), p. II–7.
4. S. Ahmed and S. Abu Khalid, "Why did Mexican Dwarf Wheat Decline in Pakistan?" *World Crops* 23: 211–215.
5. Charles Elliott, *Patterns of Poverty in the Third World — A Study of Social and Economic Stratification* (New York: Praeger, 1975), pp. 47–48.
6. Cynthia Hewitt de Alcántara, "The Social and Economic Implications of the Large-Scale Introduction of the New Varieties of Foodgrains," *Country Report—Mexico* (Geneva: UNDP/UNRISD, 1974), p. 181.
7. North London Haslemere, *The Death of the Green Revolution* (London: Haslemere Declaration Group; Oxford: Third World First), p. 4.
8. Victor McElheny, "Nations Demand Agricultural Aid," *New York Times*, Aug. 3, 1975, p. 20.
9. Keith Griffin, *The Political Economy of Agrarian Change* (Cambridge, Mass.: Harvard University Press, 1974), p. 205.
10. Pearse, "Social and Economic Implications," Part 1, pp. 111–118.
11. Nicholas Wade, "Green Revolution I: A Just Technology Often Unjust in Use," *Science* (Dec. 1974): 1093–1096.
12. Hewitt de Alcántara, *Country Report — Mexico*, p. 87.
13. Pearse, "Social and Economic Implications," Part 4, pp. XI–52, XI–53.

14. Pearse, "Social and Economic Implications," Part 3, pp. IX–23, IX–24.
15. Palmer, *Science and Agricultural Production*, p. 47.
16. Food and Agricultural Organization, *Report on China's Agriculture*, prepared by H. V. Henle, 1974, pp. 144–145.
17. Erich M. Jacoby, *The "Green Revolution" in China* (Geneva: UNRISD, 1974), p. 6.

17. Hasn't the Green Revolution "Bought Us Time"?

1. Erna Bennett, Department of Plant Genetics, FAO, Rome, personal communication, April 1976.
2. Francine R. Frankel, "The Politics of the Green Revolution: Shifting Patterns of Peasant Participation in India and Pakistan," in *Food, Population, and Employment — The Impact of the Green Revolution*, eds., Thomas T. Poleman and Donald K. Freebairn (New York: Praeger, 1973), p. 133.
3. Joan Mencher, "Conflicts and Contradictions in the 'Green Revolution': The Case of Tamil Nadu," *Economic and Political Weekly* 9, nos. 6, 7, 8 (February 1974): especially 315.
4. Andrew Pearse, "Social and Economic Implications of the Large-Scale Introduction of New Varieties of Foodgrains," Part 2 (Geneva: UNDP/UNRISD, 1975), pp. VI–14, VI–15.
5. "Tamil Nadu — Starvation Deaths in a Surplus State," *Economic and Political Weekly* 10 (February 22, 1975): 348.
6. H. P. Singh, "Plight of Agricultural Labourers. II, A Review," *Economic Affairs* 16 (June 1971): 283.
7. Wolf Ladejinsky, "Ironies of India's Green Revolution," *Foreign Affairs* (July 1970): 762.
8. Robert d'A. Shaw, "The Employment Implications of the Green Revolution," (Washington, D.C.: Overseas Development Council, 1970), pp. 3–20.
9. A. Eugene Havens and William Flinn, *Green Revolution Technology — Structural Aspects of its Adoption and Consequences* (Geneva: UNRISD, 1975), p. 25.
10. Ibid., p. 35.
11. Keith Griffin, *Land Concentration and Rural Poverty* (New York: Macmillan, 1976), p. 74.
12. A. Rudra, A. Majid, and B. D. Talib, "Big Farmers of the Punjab: Some Preliminary Findings of a Sample Survey," *Economic and Political Weekly*, Review of Agriculture, 4 (Sept. 27, 1969).
13. A. R. Khan, "Poverty and Inequality in Bangladesh," in *Poverty and Landlessness in Rural Asia*, eds., Keith Griffin and Azizur Rahman Khan, A Study by the World Employment Programme (Geneva: ILO, 1976), pp. 7–41, manuscript.
14. Cynthia Hewitt de Alcántara, "Social and Economic Implications of the Large-Scale Introduction of New Varieties of Foodgrains," *Country Report — Mexico* (Geneva: UNDP/UNRISD, 1974), p. 148.
15. Gordon Gemmill and Carl K. Eicher, "A Framework for Research on the Economics of Farm Mechanization in Developing Countries," African Rural Employment Paper no. 6, African Rural Employment Research Network, Department of Agricultural Economics, Michigan State University, East Lansing, Michigan, 1973, pp. 32–33.
16. Susan George, *How the Other Half Dies* (London: Penguin, 1976).
17. Edgar Owens and Robert Shaw, *Development Reconsidered: Bridging the Gap Between Government and People* (Lexington, Massachusetts: Heath, 1972), p. 74.
18. Hewitt de Alcántara, *Country Report — Mexico*, p. 215.
19. Food and Agriculture Organization, *Agricultural Development and Employ-*

ment Performance and Planning: A Comparative Analysis (Agricultural Planning Studies, no. 18), 1974, pp. 100, 102.

20. A. R. Khan, "Poverty and Inequality in Bangladesh," pp. 7–36.
21. Pearse, "Social and Economic Implications," Part 3, p. IX–25.
22. Ingrid Palmer, *Food and the New Agricultural Technology* (Geneva: UNRISD, 1972), pp. 64–65.
23. T. J. Byres, "The Dialectic of India's Green Revolution," *South Asian Review* 5 (January 1972): 109.
24. Donald K. Freebairn, "Income Disparities in the Agricultural Sector: Regional and Institutional Stresses," in *Food, Population, and Employment — The Impact of the Green Revolution*, eds. Thomas Poleman and Donald Freebairn (New York: Praeger, 1973), p. 108.
25. Rodger D. Hansen, *The Politics of Mexican Development* (Baltimore: Johns Hopkins University Press, 1971), p. 81.
26. Hewitt de Alcántara, *Country Report — Mexico*, p. 267.
27. A. R. Khan, "Growth and Inequality in the Rural Philippines," in *Poverty and Landlessness in Rural Asia*, pp. 11–13, 11–24.
28. ———. "Poverty and Inequality in Bangladesh," in *Poverty and Landlessness in Rural Asia*, pp. 7–21, 7–22.
29. E. Lee, "Rural Poverty in West Malaysia," in *Poverty and Landlessness*, pp. 9–6.
30. ———. "Rural Poverty In Sri Lanka, 1963–1973," in *Poverty and Landlessness in Rural Asia*, pp. 8–13.
31. *New York Times*, March 3, 1976, p. 2.

18. Where Has All the Production Gone?

1. Robert J. Ledogar, *Hungry for Profits: U.S. Food and Drug Multinationals in Latin America* (New York: IDOC/North America Inc., 1975), p. 96.
2. *Ceres* (May-June 1976): 8.
3. Ray Goldberg, *Agribusiness Management for the Developing Countries — Latin America* (Cambridge, Mass.: Ballinger, 1974), p. 87.

19. Wasn't the Green Revolution a Vital Scientific Breakthrough?

1. Andrew Pearse, "Social and Economic Implications of the Large-Scale Introduction of New Varieties of Foodgrains," Part 1 (Geneva: UNDP/UNRISD, 1975), pp. III–9, III–10.
2. Pearse, "Social and Economic Implications," Part 4, p. XI–29.
3. Pearse, "Social and Economic Implications," Part 1, p. III–12.
4. Edgar Owens, U.S. AID, personal communication, June 1976.
5. Pearse, "Social and Economic Implications," Part 1, pp. III–6, III–7.
6. Ingrid Palmer, *Food and the New Agricultural Technology* (Geneva: UNRISD, 1972), p. 43.
7. Roger Blobaum, "Why China Doesn't Starve," *Ramparts* (July 1975): 42.
8. Pearse, "Social and Economic Implications," Part 1, p. III–17.
9. *New York Times*, August 22, 1975, p. 4.
10. Ingrid Palmer, *Science and Agricultural Production* (Geneva: UNRISD, 1972), pp. 37–38.
11. Cynthia Hewitt de Alcántara, "Social and Economic Implications of the Large-Scale Introduction of New Varieties of Foodgrains," *Country Report — Mexico* (Geneva: UNDP/UNRISD, 1974), pp. 115–116.
12. Pearse, "Social and Economic Implications," Part 1, p. III–14.
13. Palmer, *Food and the New Agricultural Technology*, pp. 59–62.

20. Don't They Need Our Machines?

1. Cited by Wilson Clark, "U.S. Agriculture Is Growing Trouble as well as Crops," *Smithsonian Magazine* (January 1975): 63, 64.
2. Georg Borgstrom, "The Price of a Tractor," *Ceres* (November-December 1974): 17, 18.
3. Calculated from Eric C. Howe et al., "Measuring Labor Productivity in Production of Food for Personal Consumption, *Agricultural Economics Research*, USDA, Economic Research Service (ERS) 28, no. 4, (October 1976): 126–127; *1975 Handbook of Agricultural Charts*, Agriculture Handbook no. 491, USDA, p. 21; and Don Durost, USDA/ERS, personal communication, Sept. 30, 1976.
4. Robert d'A. Shaw, *Jobs and Agricultural Development* (Washington, D.C.: Overseas Development Council, monograph no. 3, 1970), pp. 34–35.
5. Andrew Pearse, "Social and Economic Implications of the Large-Scale Introduction of New Varieties of Foodgrains," Part 3 (Geneva: UNDP/UNRISD, 1975), p. IX–12.
6. Jennifer E. Miller, "Automatic Harvesters Mechanize North Carolina's Tobacco Industry: The Effect on the Tobacco Farmer," February 25, University of North Carolina, 1975, p. 11.
7. USDA study, quoted in *CNI Weekly Report* (Community Nutrition Institute) (February 21, 1974), p. 4.
8. International Labor Office, *Mechanization and Employment in Agriculture,* (Geneva, 1974), p. 8.
9. S. R. Bose and E. H. Clark, "Some Basic Considerations on Agricultural Mechanization in West Pakistan," *Pakistan Development Review* 9, 3 (Autumn 1969), cited by Owens and Shaw, *Development Reconsidered: Bridging the Gap Between Government and People* (Lexington, Massachusetts: Heath, 1972), p. 62.
10. Randolph Barker et al., "Employment and Technological Change in Philippine Agriculture," *International Labour Review* 106, 2–3 (August-September 1972): 130.
11. Frank C. Child, and Hiromitsu Kaneda, "Links to the Green Revolution: A Study of Small-Scale, Agriculturally-Related Industry in the Punjab," *Economic Development and Cultural Change* 23 (1974): 5.
12. Roger Blobaum, "Why China Doesn't Starve," *Ramparts* (July 1975): 41.
13. Amir U. Khan and Bart Duff, "Development of Agricultural Mechanization Technologies at the IRRI (Manila)," paper no. 72-02, mimeographed (International Rice Research Institute), cited in *Mechanization and Employment in Agriculture*, p. 11.
14. Lester Brown, *Seeds of Change* (New York: Praeger, 1970), p. 59.
15. "Companies — Massey-Ferguson's Success Story," *Business Week*, February 2, 1976, pp. 44.
16. *Mechanization and Employment in Agriculture*, p. 11.
17. Keith Griffin, *The Political Economy of Agrarian Change* (Cambridge, Mass.: Harvard University Press, 1974), p. 54.
18. Francine R. Frankel, "The Politics of the Green Revolution: Shifting Patterns of Peasant Participation in India and Pakistan," in *Food, Population, and Employment — The Impact of the Green Revolution*, eds., Thomas T. Poleman and Donald K. Freebairn (New York: Praeger, 1973), pp. 132–133.
19. M. Taghi Farvar, "The Relationship Between Ecological and Social Systems," Speech delivered to EARTHCARE conference, New York, June 6, 1975, p. 9.
20. Ray Vicker, *This Hungry World* (New York: Scribner's, 1975).
21. Food and Agriculture Organization, *Report on China's Agriculture*, prepared by H. V. Henle, 1974, p. 148.

21. Isn't the Backwardness of the Small Farmer to Blame?

1. Edgar Owens and Robert Shaw, *Development Reconsidered: Bridging the Gap Between Government and People* (Lexington, Mass.: Heath, 1972), p. 60.
2. World Bank, *The Assault on World Poverty — Problems of Rural Development, Education, and Health* (Baltimore: Johns Hopkins University Press, 1975), p. 215.
3. Owens and Shaw, *Development Reconsidered*, p. 60.
4. World Bank, *Assault on World Poverty*, pp. 215–216.
5. Ibid., p. 244.
6. U.S., Department of Agriculture, "The One-Man Farm," prepared by Warren Bailey (USDA/ERS-519) (Washington, D.C.: Government Printing Office, August 1973).
7. Calculated from U.S., Department of Agriculture, *Statistical Bulletin* no. 547, *Farm Income Statistics*, Table 3D, USDA/ERS (Washington, D.C.: Government Printing Office, July 1975), p. 60; and "The Balance Sheet of the Farming Sector, by Value of Sales Class, 1960–1973," suppl. no. 1, *Agricultural Information Bulletin* no. 376, Table 2, USDA/ERS (Washington, D.C.: Government Printing Office, April 1975), p. 30.
8. *New York Times*, November 5, 1974, p. 14.
9. Keith Griffin, *The Political Economy of Agrarian Change* (Cambridge, Mass.: Harvard University Press, 1974), p. 27.
10. World Bank, *Assault on World Poverty*, p. 105.
11. Sudhir Sen, *Reaping the Green Revolution* (Maryknoll, New York: Orbis), p. 11.
12. Andrew Pearse, "Social and Economic Implications of the Large-Scale Introduction of the New Varieties of Foodgrains," Part 2 (Geneva: UNDP/UNRISD, 1975), pp. 8–9.
13. Griffin, *Political Economy*, p. 28.
14. Keith Griffin, *Land Concentration and Rural Poverty* (New York: Macmillan, 1976), p. 122.
15. International Labor Office, *Poverty and Landlessness in Rural Asia*, A Study by the World Employment Programme, edited by Keith Griffin and Azizur Rahman Khan, 1976, pp. I–31.
16. Erich Jacoby and Charlotte Jacoby, *Man and Land* (New York: Knopf, 1971), p. 79.
17. C. H. Gotsch, "Technological Change and The Distribution of Income in Rural Areas," *American Journal of Agricultural Economics* 54 (May 2, 1972): 326–341.
18. Cynthia Hewitt de Alcántara, "Social and Economic Implications of the Large-Scale Introduction of New Varieties of Foodgrains," *Country Report — Mexico*, (Geneva: UNDP/UNRISD, 1974), p. 146.
19. Ibid., p. 90.
20. Jacoby and Jacoby, *Man and Land*, pp. 48–49.
21. Hewitt de Alcántara, *Country Report — Mexico*, p. 146.
22. Ibid., p. 260.
23. Ibid., p. 160.
24. World Bank, *Assault on World Poverty*, p. 142.
25. Don Paarlberg of USDA, speech before the 55th Annual Convention of Milk Producers, November 30, 1971.
26. Food and Agriculture Organization, *Agricultural Development and Employment Performance: A Comparative Analysis* (Agricultural Planning Studies no. 18), 1974, p. 124.

27. Keith Griffin, *Land Concentration and Rural Poverty* (New York: Macmillan, 1976), p. 190.
28. Ingrid Palmer, personal communication, May 1976.
29. Roger Blobaum, "Why China Doesn't Starve," *Ramparts* (July 1975): 42.
30. Food and Agriculture Organization, *Report on China's Agriculture*, prepared by H. V. Henle, 1974, p. 259.
31. Benedict Stavis, Cornell University, personal communication, December 22, 1976.
32. Food and Agriculture Organization, *Progress in Land Reform — Sixth Report*, April 1975.
33. Ibid.
34. U.N., Asian Development Institute, "Toward a Theory of Rural Development," prepared by Wahidul Haque et al., December 1975, 66ff.

22. Hasn't the Green Revolution Strengthened Food Security?

1. Jon Tinker, "How the Boran Wereng Did a Red Khmer on the Green Revolution," *New Scientist* (August 7, 1975): 316.
2. Nicholas Wade, "Green Revolution (II): Problems of Adapting a Western Technology," *Science* 186 (December 27, 1974): 1186–1187.
3. John Prester, "The Green Revolution Turns Sour," *Reports* (December 7, 1974).
4. Andrew Pearse, "Social and Economic Implications of the Large-Scale Introduction of the New Varieties of Foodgrains," Part 1 (Geneva: UNDP/ UNRISD, 1975), pp. II–8, II–9.
5. *Des Moines Register*, April 17, 1974.
6. Ibid.
7. D. H. Timothy and M. M. Goodman, "Plant Germ Plasm Resources — Future Feast or Famine?" paper (Journal Series of the North Carolina State University Agricultural Experiment Station), cites P. C. Mangelsdorf, *Proceedings of the National Academy of Science* (1966): 56, 370; and H. Garrison Wilkes, "Too Little Gene Exchange," letter to the editor of *Science* 171 (March 12, 1971): 955.
8. H. Garrison Wilkes and Susan Wilkes, "The Green Revolution," *Environment* 14 (October 1972): 33.
9. Robert A. Ginskey, "Sowing the Seeds of Disaster?" *The Plain Truth* 61 (June 1976): 35, quoting Wilkes.
10. Ibid.
11. Wade, "Green Revolution" p. 1191.
12. Bettina Conner, "Seed Monopoly," *Elements* (Washington, D.C.: Transnational Institute for Policy Studies, February 1975).
13. Ibid.
14. Frank B. Viets, Jr., and Samuel R. Aldrich, "The Sources of Nitrogen for Food and Meat Production," in *Sources of Nitrogenous Compounds and Methods of Control*, Environmental Protection Agency Monograph, p. 67, 73ff.
15. William Brune, State Conservationist, Soil Conservation Service, 823 Federal Building, Des Moines, Iowa, 50309, testimony before the Senate Committee on Agriculture and Forestry, July 1976.
16. Ramon Garcia, "Some Aspects on World Fertilizer Production, Consumption and Usage," paper, University of Iowa, 1975.
17. Swedish International Development Agency and Food and Agriculture Organization, "Organic Materials as Fertilizers," Soils Bulletin 27, 1975.

Part VI   The Trade Trap

23. What About Their Natural Advantage?

1. Cheryl Payer, "Coffee," in Cheryl Payer, ed. *Commodity Trade in the Third World* (New York: Wiley, 1975), p. 159.
2. Frederick Clairmonte, "Bananas," in Payer, *Commodity Trade*, p. 131.
3. Payer, "Coffee" in *Commodity Trade*, 156ff.
4. W. Green and Anne Siedman, *Africa: Unity or Poverty* (London: Penguin, 1968).
5. UNDP, "Changing Factors in World Development," prepared by Don Casey, (Development Issue Paper 5, Global I), UNDP, August 1975, p. 2.
6. Payer, "Coffee" in *Commodity Trade*, p. 158.
7. UNCTAD, "Marketing and Distribution System for Cocoa," (Report by the Secretariat), January 1975, p. 9.
8. Ibid., p. 6.
9. Payer, *Commodity Trade*, p. 185.
10. David Andelman, "Malaysian Land Plan Thriving, but Snags Arise," *New York Times*, September 4, 1976.
11. Susan deMarco and Susan Sechler, *The Fields Have Turned Brown — Four Essays on World Hunger* (Agribusiness Accountability Project, 1000 Wisconsin Ave., N.W., Washington, D.C.), 1975, p. 8.
12. Food and Agriculture Organization, *The State of Food and Agriculture*, 1974, p. 101.
13. ———. *Commodity Review, 1973–1974*, p. 6.

24. Don't the Rich Countries Need Their Products?

1. G. K. Helleiner, *International Trade and Economic Development* (London: Penguin, 1972), pp. 38–39.
2. Marion Gallis, *Trade for Justice: Myth or Mandate?* (Geneva: World Council of Churches), p. 35.
3. Ibid., p. 52.
4. William C. Bowser, "World Jute Industry Sees Little Joy in Future Years," *Foreign Agriculture* 13, (September 1975): 8.
5. Gallis, *Trade for Justice*, p. 50.
6. U.S., Department of Commerce, "Import Preferences Readied for World's Developing Lands: Public Hearings Underway," prepared by Rozanne D. Oliver, Office of International Trade Policy, 1974, p. 1.
7. Ibid.

25. Don't They Have Cartels Now?

1. UNCTAD, "Marketing and Distribution System for Cocoa" (Report by the Secretariat, January 1975), p. 89.
2. John Freivalds, "Futures Market — A New Way to Price Stability," *African Development* 9 (September 1975): 27.
3. Carl Widstrand, ed., *Multinational Firms in Africa* (African Institute for Economic Development and Planning, Dakar; and Scandinavian Institute of African Studies, Uppsala, 1975), p. 308.
4. Keith Griffin, *Land Concentration and Rural Poverty* (New York: Macmillan, 1976), p. 153.

5. Eduardo Galeano, *Open Veins in Latin America: Five Centuries of the Pillage of a Continent* (New York: Monthly Review, 1973), pp. 113–114.
6. Ibid., pp. 114–115.
7. Frederick Clairmonte, "Bananas," in Cheryl Payer, ed. *Commodity Trade in the Third World* (New York: Wiley, 1975), pp. 138–139.
8. Ibid., p. 136.
9. UNDP, "Changing Factors in World Development," prepared by Don Casey (Development issue Paper 5, Global I), August 1975, p. 5.
10. *Newsweek*, "Cartels: Just Bananas," August 26, 1974, p. 38; see also "Multinationals: A Banana Brouhaha over Higher Prices," *Business Week*, July 6, 1974, p. 42.

26. Doesn't Export Income Help the Hungry?

1. Andre Gunder Frank, *Capitalism and Underdevelopment in Latin America* (New York: Monthly Review Press, 1969; London: Penguin, 1971), pp. 286–287.
2. Susanne Jonas and David Tobis, eds., *Guatemala* (New York and Berkeley: North American Congress on Latin America, 1974), pp. 9, 16.
3. Gamini Navaratne, "Tea," *New Internationalist* (April 1976): 11.
4. Thierry Brun, "Demystifier la famine," *Cahiers de Nutrition et de Dietique* 9(2): 115.
5. UNCTAD, "Report of Intergovermental Group on Least Developed Countries," Geneva, 1975, p. 43.
6. Donal B. Cruise O'Brien, "Cooperators and Bureaucrats: Class Formation in a Senegalese Society," *Africa* (Journal of the International African Institute) 61 (October 1972): 273.
7. UNCTAD, "Marketing and Distribution System for Cocoa," (Report of the Secretariat, January 1975), p.34.
8. Derek Byerlee and Carl K. Eicher, "Rural Employment, Migration and Economic Development: Theoretical Issues and Empirical Evidence from Africa," African Rural Employment Study, paper no. 1, Department of Agricultural Economics, State University, East Lansing, Michigan, September 1972, pp. 13–14.
9. Ingrid Palmer, *Food and the New Agricultural Technology* (Geneva: UNRISD, 1972), p. 53.
10. Uma Lele, "A Conceptual Framework for Rural Development," Paper presented to the Development from Below Workshop, the Association for the Advancement of Agricultural Sciences in Africa (AAASA), Oct. 1973, pp. 8–9.
11. *Latin America* 10 (October 22, 1976): 326.
12. Roger Wertling, Jr., *Organic Gardening and Farming*, Emmaus, Penn., September 1972, p. 76.

27. If It's So Bad, Why Does It Continue?

1. Keith Griffin, *Land Concentration and Rural Poverty* (New York: Macmillan), p. 161.
2. Walter Hink, "Mobutu on Tightrope as Crisis Hits Zaire," *African Development* (September 1975): 48.
3. United Nations Economic and Social Council, Preparatory Committee for the Special Session of the General Assembly Devoted to Development and International Cooperation, Second Session, 16–27 June 1975 (E/AC. 621/8) May 5, 1975, p. 7.
4. Cheryl Payer, ed., *Commodity Trade in the Third World* (New York: Wiley, 1975), pp. 180, 184.

5. Gamini Navaratne, "Tea," *New Internationalist* (April 1976); 11.
6. Robert Shaplen, Letter from Manila, *The New Yorker*, May 3, 1976, p. 92.
7. William Paddock and Elizabeth Paddock, *We Don't Know How* (Ames, Iowa: Iowa University Press, 1973), p. 229.
8. David Feldman and Peter Lawrence, "Global II Project on the Economic and Social Implications of Large-Scale Introduction of New Varieties of Food-grains," Africa Report (Geneva: UNDP/UNRISD, 1975), p. 52.
9. Peter Dorner, "Export Agriculture and Economic Development," Land Tenure Center, University of Wisconsin, Madison, statement before the Interfaith Center on Corporate Responsibility, New York, September 14, 1976, p. 6.
10. Keith Griffin, *Land Concentration and Rural Poverty* (New York: Macmillan, 1976), p. 162.
11. Keith Griffin, *The Political Economy of Agrarian Change* (Cambridge, Mass.: Harvard University Press, 1974), p. 105.
12. R. L. Raikes, "Ujamaa and Rural Socialism," *Review of African Political Economy* (May-October, 1974): 36.
13. Cheryl Payer, *The Debt Trap — The IMF and the Third World* (London: Penguin, 1974).

28. Isolationism or Self-Reliance?

1. *Progress in Land Reform — Sixth Report*, Food and Agricultural Organization and International Labor Organization, New York, 1975, p. 104.
2. Pedro Alvarez Tabio, ed., *The Overall Situation of the Cuban Economy* (Havana: Instituto Cubano de Deportes, September 1975), 39ff.
3. Ibid., 26ff
4. Ibid., p. 39.
5. Interview, U.S. AID Mission, Santo Domingo, November 26, 1976.
6. Tabio, *The Overall Situation*, 34ff.

Part VII   The Myth of Food Power

29. Don't They Need Our Food?

1. The following comparisons regarding MSA countries are calculated from U.S., Department of Agriculture, *Foreign Agricultural Trade Statistical Report*, Calendar Year 1974, May 1975.
2. Calculated from Food and Agriculture Organization, *Production Yearbook, 1974*, and *Yearbook of International Trade Statistics*, 1974.
3. Calculated from U.S., Department of Agriculture, *U.S. Foreign Agricultural Trade Statistical Report*, Calendar Year 1974.
4. Calculated from *Yearbook of International Trade Statistics*, 1974.
5. Food and Agricultural Organization, *The State of Food and Agriculture*, 1972, pp. 182–186.
6. "Commodities," *Ceres* 7 (January-February 1974): 21.

30. Food Power to Save the Economy?

1. Richard Bell, Assistant Secretary for International Affairs and Commodity Programs, USDA, cited by Norman Faramelli, "A Primer for Church Groups on Agribusiness and the World Food Crisis," Boston Industrial Mission, Boston, Mass., 1975.

2. *New York Times*, August 19, 1975, p. 16.
3. *Feedstuffs* 47 (September 8, 1975): 4.
4. *Time*, November 11, 1974, p. 84.
5. "U.S. Grain Arsenal," *Latin America and Empire Report*, North American Congress on Latin America (New York and Berkeley) 10 (October 1975): 4.
6. Richard Barnet and Ronald Mueller, *Global Reach* (New York: Simon and Schuster, 1973), p. 266.
7. "U.S. Grain Arsenal," p. 4.
8. Barry Commoner, *The Poverty of Power* (New York: Knopf, 1976), p. 54.
9. *Future Petroleum Provinces of the United States — Their Geology and Potential*, 2 vols. (Washington, D.C.: National Petroleum Council, July 1970), cited by Commoner, pp. 53–54.
10. Barry Commoner, "Reporter at Large (Energy-1)," *The New Yorker*, February 2, 1976, p. 56.
11. Barnet and Mueller, *Global Reach*, p. 220.
12. Commoner, "Reporter at Large," p. 52.
13. U.S., Department of Agriculture, *Foreign Agricultural Trade Statistical Report*, Fiscal Year 1971 and Fiscal Year 1974, Table 10.
14. Jimmy Minyard, "Market Development Looks Ahead to New Markets and Programs"; also Darwin Stolte, "Team Effort Boosts U.S. Farm Exports," *Foreign Agriculture* 13 (May 26, 1975): 6, 9.
15. C. W. McMillan, "Meat Export Federation to be Newest Cooperator," *Foreign Agriculture* 13 (May 26, 1975): 14.
16. Philip B. Dwoskin and Nick Havas, "Fast Foods in Japan — A Billion-Dollar Industry?" *Foreign Agriculture* 13 (May 26, 1975): 33.
17. Elizabeth Jaeger, economist for the AFL-CIO, personal communication, June 18, 1976, citing U.S., Department of Commerce, *Survey of Current Business*, 1975.
18. U.S., Department of Agriculture, *Foreign Agricultural Trade of the United States*, Economic Research Service, April 1976, pp. 26–27.

31. At Least Food Power Works?

1. *New York Times*, November 3, 1974, p. 30.
2. "Can Agriculture Save the Dollar?" *Forbes*, March 15, 1973, pp. 38–39.
3. Ibid.
4. *Latin America Economic Report* 4 (January 23, 1976): 16.
5. Dan Morgan, *Washington Post*, January 2, 3, 1976.
6. "U.S. Food Power: Ultimate Power in World Politics?" *Business Week*, December 15, 1975, p. 58.
7. William Brune, State Conservationist, Soil Conservation Service, Des Moines, Iowa, testimony before Senate Committee on Agriculture and Forestry, July 6, 1976; see also Seth King, "Iowa Rain and Wind Deplete Farmlands," *New York Times*, December 5, 1976, p. 61.
8. "Wheels of Fortune: A Report on the Impact of Center Pivot Irrigation on the Ownership of Land in Nebraska," Center for Rural Affairs, P.O. Box 405, Walthill, Nebraska, 68067. See also "No One Knows the Value of Water Until the Well Runs Dry," *New Land Review* (Spring 1976): 3 (also published by the Center for Rural Affairs).
9. Report to the 1977 state legislature on the State Saline Seep Control Program funded by the 1974 and 1975 state legislatures, available from Department of State Lands, State of Montana, Helena, Montana, 59601.

32. Who Gains and Who Loses?

1. "The Incredible Empire of Michael Fribourg," *Business Week*, March 11, 1972, p. 84.
2. James Trager, *The Great Grain Robbery* (New York: Ballantine, 1975), p. 27.
3. William Robbins, *The American Food Scandal — Why You Can't Eat Well on What You Earn* (New York: Morrow, 1974), p. 185.
4. A. V. Krebs, "Of the Grain Trade, by the Grain Trade, and for the Grain Trade," in *The Great American Grain Robbery and Other Stories*, ed. Martha Hamilton (Washington, D.C.: Agribusiness Accountability Project, 1972), p. 289.
5. Jim Hightower, *Eat Your Heart Out: How Food Profiteers Victimize the Consumer* (New York: Crown, 1975), p. 194.
6. Dan Morgan, *Washington Post*, January 2, 3, 1976, p. A5.
7. U.S., General Accounting Office, *Exporters' Profits on Sales of U.S. Wheat to Russia* (B-176943, February 12, 1974), 15ff.
8. Hightower, *Eat Your Heart Out*, p. 194.
9. Steven Bennett, "U.S. Food Policy for Whom?" *Center Survey* 4(1): 6.
10. Cliff Connor, "U.S. Agribusiness and World Famine," *International Socialist Review* (September 1974), quoting James McHale, Secretary of Agriculture for the State of Pennsylvania.
11. Morgan, *Washington Post*, January 2, 1976.
12. Lawrence A. Mayer, "We Can't Take Food for Granted Anymore," *Fortune*, February 1974, p. 86.
13. Hightower, *Eat Your Heart Out*, p. 197.
14. Don Paarlberg, Director of Agricultural Economics, USDA, "Agricultural Trade and Domestic Adjustments in Agriculture," speech, March 21, 1974, p. 4.
15. Hightower, *Eat Your Heart Out*, pp. 198–199.
16. Earl Butz, "A Policy of Plenty," *Skeptic* no. 10 (November/December 1975): 57.
17. *NFO Reporter*, National Farmers Organization 4 (April 1976): 4.
18. Phyllis Berman, "Bursting Cupboards," *Forbes*, September 15, 1976; and National Farmers Union *Washington Newsletter*, November 29, 1976.
19. Roy D. Laird et al., "America's Agricultural Illiteracy," *Ag World* (December 1975): 19; and *New York Times*, October 8, 1976, p. D4.
20. Parity figures from Jim Thorp, USDA/ERS, telephone conversation, Dec. 9, 1976.
21. Calculated from U.S., Department of Agriculture, *Farm Income Statistics*, Annual Statistical Bulletin 557, Table 3D, July 1976, p. 60.
22. Ibid., Table 4D, p. 61.
23. Ibid., Tables 1D – 4D.
24. Hightower, *Eat Your Heart Out*, p. 144.
25. *NFO Reporter*, p. 4.
26. Peter J. Barry and Donald R. Fraser, "Risk Management in Primary Agricultural Production: Methods, Distribution, Rewards, and Structural Implications," Texas Agricultural Experiment Station, no date.
27. U.S., Department of Agriculture, *Farmland Tenure Patterns in the United States*, (USDA/ERS, February 1974), p. 3.
28. U.S., Department of Agriculture, *Alternative Futures for U.S. Agriculture — Part I* (USDA, Office for Planning and Evaluation for the Committee on Agriculture and Forestry United States Senate, September 25, 1975).
29. Don Paarlberg quoted in *Feedstuffs* August 16, 1976, p. 10.
30. U.S., Department of Agriculture, *The One-Man Farm*, prepared by Warren Bailey (USDA/ERS-519), August, 1973.
31. Calculated from *Farm Income Statistics*, Statistical Bulletin No. 547, Table 3D

(USDA/ERS), July 1975, p. 60; and *The Balance Sheet of the Farming Sector, by Value of Sales Class, 1960–1973*, supplement no. 1, Agricultural Information Bulletin No. 376, Table 2 (USDA/ERS) April 1975, p. 3.

32. *NFO Reporter*, p. 3.
33. *Alternative Futures for U.S. Agriculture*, Appendix.
34. Walter Goldschmidt, "A Tale of Two Towns," in *The Peoples' Land*, ed. Peter Barnes (Emmaus, Pa.: Rodale, 1975), 171ff.
35. National Farmers Union *Washington Newsletter*, November 29, 1976.
36. U.S., Internal Revenue Service, *Source Book, Statistics of Income, Corporate Income Tax Returns*, quoted in Economic Report on Food Chain Profits, Staff Report to the Federal Trade Commission, 1975, p. 16, cited in Belden, see below. (Supermarkets often claim low profits — only 1% profit on sales. What is neglected here is that the supermarket makes that 1% each time it turns over its stock which may be 12 or more times a year. Thus a 1% profit on sales may become an actual profit of 12% annually, or what economists call "return on investment.")
37. "Achieving the Goals of the Employment Act of 1946 — Thirtieth Anniversary Review," vol. 3, Inflation and Market Structure, paper No. 1. "The Inflationary Impact of Unemployment: Price Markups During Postwar Recessions, 1947-70," Joint Economic Committee, Congress of the U.S. (Washington, D.C.: Government Printing Office, November 3, 1976), 2ff.
38. U.S., Department of Labor, *Bureau of Labor Statistical Report 448-2* (Consumer Expenditure Survey Series: Diary Survey 1973).
39. U.S., Department of Agriculture, *1975 Handbook of Agricultural Charts* Handbook 491, (Washington, D.C.: Government Printing Office, 1975), p. 65.
40. U.S., Department of Agriculture, *National Food Situation* (USDA/ERS), November 1975, p. 11.
41. Clayton Yeutter, "Market-Oriented Farm Policies after Four Years," speech to the National Grange, November 15, 1974.
42. U.S., Congress, Senate Select Committee on Nutrition and Human Needs, *Food Price Changes, 1973-74 and Nutritional Status*, Part 1, 93rd Cong., 2d sess. (Washington, D.C.: Government Printing Office, 1974) pp. 12, 14.
43. U.S., Department of Agriculture, *Our Land and Water Resources* Economic Research Service, (Miscellaneous Publication no. 1290, 1974), p. 32.
44. For excellent discussions of the concentration of power in the grain trade see *The Great Grain Robbery and Other Stories*, ed. Martha Hamilton (Washington, D.C.: Agribusiness Accountability Project, 1972).
45. *The Structure of Food Manufacturing*. A report by the staff of the Federal Trade Commission (Technical Study No. 8) National Commission on Food Marketing, June 1966, p. 19., for figures on concentration in food industry see Dr. Russell C. Parker, testimony before U.S., Congress, Senate, Consumer Economics Subcommittee of the Joint Economic Committee, May 21, 1974, p. 4.
46. For an excellent discussion of these issues see Joe Belden, "New Directions For United States Agricultural Policy," Exploratory Project for Economic Alternatives (1519 Conn. Ave. N.W., Washington, D.C. 20036), Chapters 2 and 4.

Part VIII   World Hunger as Big Business

33. Don't They Need American Corporate Know-How?

1. "Feeding the World's Hungry: The Challenge to Business." Transcript of the Proceedings of an International Conference sponsored by the Continental Bank, Chicago, May 20, 1974.

2. Consultation with agroindustrial leaders in preparation for U.N. World Food Conference, September 10–11, 1974, Toronto, Canada.
3. George L. Baker, "Good Climate for Agribusiness," *The Nation*, November 5, 1973, p. 460; NACLA, *Bitter Fruits*, September 1976, *Latin America and Empire Report*, 12ff.
4. Baker, "Good Climate for Agribusiness," p. 460.
5. "Poverty in American Democracy: A Study of Social Power," U.S. Catholic Conference, November 1974, cited by *CNI Weekly Report*, Community Nutrition Institute, Washington, D.C., September 2, 1976, p. 8.
6. Baker, *"Good Climate for Agribusiness."*
7. Ernest Feder, "The Penetration of the Agricultures of the Underdeveloped Countries by the Industrial Nations and Their Multinational Corporations," Institute of Social Studies, The Hague, 1975, p. 8.
8. For commodity breakdowns see Ray Goldberg, *Agribusiness Management for Developing Countries — Latin America* (Cambridge, Mass.: Ballinger, 1974), 69ff. Calculations based on Goldberg, *Agribusiness Management*, Chapter 2; and U.S., Department of Agriculture, *U. S. Foreign Agricultural Trade Statistical Report Fiscal Year 1975* (Washington, D.C.: Government Printing Office).
9. Cited in Goldberg, *Agribusiness Management*, p. 70.
10. Ibid., p. 70.
11. Ibid., 150ff. gives some figures; see also Food and Agricultural Organization, *Production Yearbooks*.
12. Ernest Feder, *Strawberry Imperialism: An Enquiry into the Mechanisms of Dependency in Mexican Agriculture* (The Hague: Institute of Social Studies, in press).
13. Goldberg, *Agribusiness Management*, p. 147.
14. Ibid., p. 150.
15. Ibid., p. 87.
16. Ernest Feder, *Strawberry Imperialism*; unless otherwise noted, the facts on the strawberry industry in Mexico are drawn from Dr. Feder's comprehensive documentation.
17. Unless otherwise noted, the sources for the analysis of Bud Senegal are: Kees Pels, "Stijgende invoer van Afrikaanse groenten," 1975; Jan Bunnik, "Bud maakt Senegal groen," *Vakblad voor groothandel in aardappelen, groeten en fruit* February 6 and 13, 1975, pp. 11–15 and pp. 13–16; Transcript of KRO (Netherlands) televised documentary March 3, 1975; "Une remarquable reussite," *Senegal 1960–1973: 14 ans de développement*; "De situatie in Senegal," *Landbouw Wereldnieuws*, October 15, 1974; "Liefermoeglichkeiten Senegals," *Mitteilungen der Bundesstelle fuer Aussenhandelsinformation*, July 1974, 1ff.; and personal communication from Maureen M. Mackintosh, The Institute of Development Studies, completing a study of Bud Senegal, dated October 5, 1976.
18. Lars Bondestam, "Notes on Foreign Investments in Ethiopia," in *Multinational Firms in Africa*, eds. Carl Widstrand and Samir Amin (Uppsala: Scandinavian Institute for African Studies, 1975), 139ff. The interview referred to is in *SIDA-rapport*, no. 8, Stockholm, 1972.
19. Bondestam, "Notes on Foreign Investments."
20. Alan Berg, *The Nutrition Factor: Its Role in National Development* (Washington, D.C.: The Brookings Institution, 1973), p. 65.
21. *Wall Street Journal*, July 27, 1972 and January 7, 1970.
22. José da Veiga, "Quand les multinationales font du Ranching," *Le Monde Diplomatique*, September 1975, p. 13.
23. *New York Times*, July 4, 1972.

24. We are greatly indebted to the excellent study of Ralston Purina in Colombia researched by Rick Edwards and largely forming Chapter 6 in Robert J. Ledogar, *Hungry for Profits: U.S. Food and Drug Multinationals in Latin America* (New York: IDOC, 1976). Unless otherwise noted, data on Ralston Purina in Colombia comes from this study.
25. Giovanni Acciarri et al., "Produccion Agropecuaria y Desnutricion en Colombia," (Cali: Universidad del Valle, Division de Ingenicria, 1973).
26. Ibid.
27. Calculations are based on figures in the U.S., Department of Agriculture, *U.S. Foreign Agricultural Trade Statistical Report, Fiscal Year, 1975*.
28. Interview with Gabriel Misas, D.A.N.E. (National Department of Statistics) Bogata, Colombia, April 30, 1973, confirmed as "more or less correct" by the Embassy of Colombia in Washington, D.C., January 14, 1974.
29. A helpful source of data, largely compiled from U.S. government statistics, can be found in Appendix J in Ray A. Goldberg, *Agribusiness Management*, pp. 359–374.
30. Ibid.

34. Still, Don't the People Benefit?

1. Overseas Private Investment Corporation, Annual Report, 1973.
2. Calculation taken from Henry Frundt, *American Agribusiness and U.S. Foreign Agricultural Policy* (Ph.D. dissertation, Rutgers University, May 1975).
3. Unless otherwise noted, the data in this section is from Susanne Jonas and David Tobis, *Guatemala* (NACLA, P.O. Box 226, Berkeley, CA 94701), pp. 127–131.
4. "Bitter Fruits," *Latin America and Empire Report*, NACLA, 10 (September 1976): 30.
5. UNCTAD, *The Marketing and Distribution System for Bananas*, December 24, 1974, p. 24.
6. *Business Week*, January 18, 1969, p. 54.
7. Consultation with agroindustrial leaders in preparation for the U.N. World Food Conference, September 10–11, 1974, Toronto, Canada.
8. Dr. Russell C. Parker, testimony before U.S., Congress, Senate, Consumer Economics Subcommittee of the Joint Economic Committee, May 21, 1974, p. 4.
9. Jim Hightower, *Eat Your Heart Out: How Food Profiteers Victimize the Consumer* (New York: Crown, 1975), p. 163.
10. U.S., Department of Agriculture, prepared by Ronald L. Mighell and William S. Hoofnagle, *Contract Production and Vertical Integration in Farming, 1960 and 1970* (Economic Research Service), p. 4.
11. U.S., Department of Agriculture, *Interrelationships in Our Food System*, prepared by William T. Manley and Donn. A. Reimund (Economic Research Service) February 21, 1973, p. 6.
12. U.S., Congress, Senate, House Antitrust Subcommittee Hearings. "Family Farm Act." Testimony of Undersecretary J. Phil Campbell. March 22, 1972, 28ff.
13. *Feedstuffs*. December 12, 1970, p. 4, cited in Jim Hightower, *Eat Your Heart Out*, p. 165.
14. Cited in Hightower, *Eat Your Heart Out*, p. 164.
15. Ibid., 149ff.
16. Ibid., p. 170.
17. Ibid., p. 165.

18. U.S., Department of Agriculture, *Packers and Stockyards Administration*, prepared by Marvin L. McLain, May 14, 1974, p. 28.
19. Cited in Susan DeMarco and Susan Sechler, *The Fields Have Turned Brown — Four Essays on World Hunger* (Washington, D.C.: The Agribusiness Accountability Project, 1975), 73ff.
20. Harrison Wellford, *Sowing the Wind* (New York: Grossman, 1972), 101ff.
21. Hightower, *Eat Your Heart Out*, p. 168; see also U.S., Department of Agriculture, "The Broiler Industry," *Packers and Stockyards Administration* (August 1967).
22. ABC-Television News. "Food: Green Grow the Profits," documentary, December 21, 1973, transcript, 46ff.
23. The Food Action Campaign Papers. "Crystal City, Texas — A Del Monte Company Town" (Agribusiness Accountability Project. 1000 Wisconsin Avenue, N.W. Washington, D.C. 20007; $1). Unless otherwise noted, data on Crystal City are from this valuable study.
24. Hightower, *Eat Your Heart Out*, p. 149.
25. San Francisco *Consumer Action News*, October, 1975.
26. Ray Vicker, *This Hungry World* (New York: Scribner's, 1975), p. 224.
27. Vincent G. Cullen, "Sour Pineapples," *America* (November 6, 1976): 300ff.
28. Liberation News Service, June 22, 1974.
29. Ismail A. Jami, "Land Reform and Modernization of Farming Structure in Iran," *Institute of Agricultural Economy* (No. 2, December 1973): 118–121. Also Julian Bharier, *Economic Development of Iran, 1900–1970* (London: Oxford University Press, 1971), especially p. 138.
30. *Agriculture and Agribusiness in Iran: Investment Opportunities* (New York: Paul R. Walter & Associates, Inc., March 1975), p. 39. Also much information was obtained through correspondence with two Iranian economists who, for reasons of their personal safety, have asked to remain anonymous. Also helpful was an interview with John Tobey, a senior investment officer of the Chase Manhattan Bank, July 16, 1975.
31. Frances FitzGerald, "Giving the Shah Everything He Wants," *Harper's*, November, 1974, p. 55.
32. *International Agribusiness*, published by Hawaiian Agronomics (a subsidiary of C. Brewer and Company), Winter 1975, p. 3.
33. "How Iran Spends Its New Found Riches," *Business Week*, June 22, 1974.
34. FitzGerald, "Giving the Shah Everything he Wants."
35. *Agriculture and Agribusiness in Iran: Investment Opportunities*, p. 4.
36. While our information was gathered from correspondence, these "labor centers" are discussed at some length in FitzGerald, "Giving the Shah Everything He Wants," 74ff.
37. Presentation by CPC International at the World Food System Symposium, University of California, Berkeley, September 17–19, 1975. All quotes in this section are from this case presentation by CPC International.

35. Agribusiness Abroad: A Boon for Americans?

1. The information and data for this section are derived from Mary Alice Kellogg, "Hawaii Without the Pineapple," *The Nation*, March 16, 1974; "Hawaii: Pineapples or Parking Lots?" *Newsweek*, February 25, 1974; "Plantation Decline in Hawaii Spurs Exodus," *New York Times*, November 11, 1975; "Bitter Fruits," *Latin America and Empire Report*, NACLA, 10 (September 1976): 21ff.
2. Jim Hightower, *Eat Your Heart Out: How Food Profiteers Victimize the Consumer* (New York: Crown, 1975), 151ff.

3. Mushroom Processors Association. "Memorandum to Trade Staff Committee of the U.S. Tariff Commission." June 26, 1973. Investigation 332-72, p. 15, cited in Hightower, *Eat Your Heart Out*, p. 152.
4. Hightower, *Eat Your Heart Out*, p. 152.
5. Robert J. Ledogar, *Hungry for Profits: U.S. Food and Drug Multinationals in Latin America* (New York: IDOC, 1976), 150ff.
6. OPIC, Country List, brochure of OPIC, 1975.
7. OPIC, *Topics* (June 1975): 4a.

36. Better Than Beans and Rice?

1. See Frances Moore Lappé, *Diet for a Small Planet* (New York: Ballantine Books, revised edition, 1975).
2. *Business Week*, December 1, 1973, p. 89.
3. Joseph M. Winski, "Back-to-Basics Trend," *Wall Street Journal*, May 29, 1975, pp. 1 and 25; see also Peter T. Kilborn, "Food Industry Finds Shoppers' Tastes Are Changing," *New York Times*, April 28, 1975, pp. 45 and 49.
4. Peter Drucker, *The Age of Discontinuity* (New York: Harper and Row, 1969), p. 107.
5. *Food Processing and Packing Machinery and Equipment: Mexico*. Office of International Trade Promotion, April, 1971.
6. Andre van Dam, "El Futuro de la Industria Alimenticia en America Latina," Speech delivered in Porto Alegre, May 14, 1975.
7. Thomas Horst, *At Home Abroad* (Cambridge, Mass.: Ballinger, 1974).
8. W. R. Grace and Co. *Annual Report*, 1969.
9. Quotations are from David F. Hawkins and Derek A. Newton, *Case Study on General Foods Corporation* (Harvard Business School course materials, 1964).
10. Horst, *At Home Abroad*, p. 127.
11. Federal Trade Commission, "Structure of Food Manufacturing," Technical Study no. 8 (Washington, D.C.: Government Printing Office, June 1966), p. 80.
12. Research carried out in October, 1976, New York State, suburban supermarket.
13. Federal Trade Commission, "Structure of Food Manufacturing," June 1966.
14. Hightower, *Eat Your Heart Out: How Food Profiteers Victimize the Consumer* (New York: Crown, 1975), p. 52.
15. Michael F. Jacobson, *Nutrition Scoreboard* (Washington, D.C.; Center for Science in the Public Interest, July, 1973), p. 88.
16. Cited in Hightower, *Eat Your Heart Out*, p. 52.
17. Federal Trade Commission, "Structure of Food Manufacturing," p. 81, n. 33.
18. Robert J. Ledogar, *Hungry for Profits: U.S. Food and Drug Multinationals in Latin America* (New York: IDOC, 1976), 111ff.
19. We gratefully acknowledge the research on General Foods as coming from Henry Frundt, *American Agribusiness and U.S. Foreign Policy* (Ph.D. dissertation, Rutgers University, 1975), especially pp. 194–198.
20. We gratefully acknowledge much of the research for this section as that of Bernardo Kucinski, carried out for Robert Ledogar, *Hungry for Profits*, pp. 111–127. While the analysis may differ, the facts, unless otherwise noted, are from this source.
21. Cited in Richard Barnet and Ronald Mueller, *Global Reach* (New York: Simon and Schuster, 1974), 183ff.
22. Letter to Robert Ledogar from Rev. Crisoforo Florencio, parish priest of Olinala, Guerrero, Mexico, June 1974, cited in Robert Ledogar, *Hungry for Profits*, p. 113.
23. *Economic and Political Weekly* 4 (May 24, 1969): 890ff.
24. Ibid.

25. Quoted in *Forbes*, November 15, 1968.
26. Alan Berg, "Industry's Struggle with World Malnutrition," *Harvard Business Review* 50 (January-February 1972): 135.

37. Do They Really Kill Babies?

1. Roy J. Harris, Jr., "The Baby Bust," *Wall Street Journal*, January 4, 1972; "The Bad News in Babyland," *Dun's Review* 100 (December 1972): 104.
2. Mike Muller, *The Baby Killer*. Pamphlet (London: War on Want, 1975; 467 Caledonian Road). Contains extensive references and bibliography.
3. Ruth Rice Puffer and Carlos V. Serrano, *Patterns of Mortality in Childhood*, Scientific Publication no. 262. (Washington, D.C.: Pan American Health Organization, 1973), p. 161.
4. William A. M. Cutting, *The Lancet* 7870 (June 29, 1974): 1340 citing J. B. Wyon and J. E. Gordon, *The Khanna Study* (Cambridge, Mass.: Harvard University Press, 1971), p. 187.
5. Alan Berg, *The Nutrition Factor* (Washington, D.C.: The Brookings Institution, 1973), p. 95 citing D. S. McLaren, in *The Lancet* 7461 (August 27, 1966): 485.
6. Derrick B. Jelliffe and E. F. Patrice Jelliffe, "An Overview," in *The Uniqueness of Human Milk*, symposium reprinted from *The American Journal of Clinical Nutrition* 24 (August 1971).
7. London *Times*, June 29, 1974.
8. Paul Gyorgy, "Biochemical Aspects of Human Milk," *The American Journal of Clinical Nutrition* 24 (August 1971): 970.
9. Hugh Jolly, "Why Breast Feeding Is Food for Mother and Baby," London *Times*, March 26, 1975.
10. Michael C. Latham, "Introduction," in *The Promotion of Bottle Feeding by Multinational Corporations: How Advertising and the Health Professions Have Contributed*, ed. Ted Greiner (Ithaca: Cornell University Monograph Series. No. 2, 1975), iiff.
11. Data from affidavit submitted for *Sisters of the Precious Blood, Inc.* vs. *Bristol Myers Co.*, U.S. District Court, Southern District of New York, 1976; see also V. G. James, "Household Expenditure on Food and Drink by Income Groups," paper delivered at Seminar on National Food and Nutrition Policy of Jamaica, Kingston, May 27–31, 1974 and Latham, "Introduction," p. ii.
12. The National Food and Nutrition Survey of Barbados, Scientific Publication no. 237 (Washington, D.C.: Pan American Health Organization, 1972), cited in Robert J. Ledogar, *Hungry for Profits: U.S. Food and Drug Multinationals in Latin America* (New York: IDOC, 1976), 130ff.
13. This and the next example are from Muller, *The Baby Killer*, p. 7.
14. Ibid., p. 6.
15. Ibid.
16. Ibid.
17. *Report of an Ad-Hoc Committee on Young Child Feeding* (New York: United Nations Protein Advisory Group, 1971).
18. Ledogar, *Hungry for Profits*, p. 132. He cites M. D. Samsudin et al., "Rational Use of Skim Milk in a Complete Infant Formula," *The American Journal of Clinical Nutrition* 20 (1967): 1304; and John McKigney, "Economic Aspects," in *The Uniqueness of Human Milk*, p. 1009.
19. David O. Cox, "Economics of Feeding Infants and Young Children in Developing Countries," paper presented at the U.N. Protein Advisory Group Ad-Hoc Working Group meeting, Geneva, December 11–13, 1972.

20. Muller, *The Baby Killer*, 11ff.
21. *New York Times*, September 14, 1975.
22. This and more extensive information on milk banks can be found in Ledogar, *Hungry for Profits*, 138ff.
23. *The New Internationalist*, March 1975, p. 2.
24. From various company promotion, all books cited and noted in Ledogar, *Hungry for Profits*, 133ff.
25. Ibid., p. 135.
26. *The Womanly Art of Breast Feeding* (Franklin Park, Illinois: La Leche League International, 1963), p. 54.
27. Information obtained from Leah Margulies, Interfaith Center on Corporate Responsibility, New York, N.Y.
28. Alan Berg, "The Economics of Breast-Feeding," *The Saturday Review of the Sciences* 1 (May 1973): 30.
29. *The New Internationalist,* March 1975.
30. Ibid.
31. *Development Forum*, July-August 1976. Geneva: United Nations, Council for Economic and Social Information.

Part IX   The Helping Hand-Out: Aid for Whom?

38. Triage?

1. Radha Sinha, *Food and Poverty* (New York: Holmes & Meier, 1976), p. 8.

39. Debt for Development?

1. Food Policy Notes, Interreligious Taskforce on U.S. Food Policy (110 Maryland Avenue, NE, Washington, D.C. 20002) October 1976, p. 4.
2. UNCTAD, *Debt Problems in the Context of Development* (Report, by the Secretariat) 1974, p. 5.
3. UNCTAD, *Money and Finance and Transfer of Real Resources for Development*, International Financial Co-operation for Development (Report by the UNCTAD Secretariat, TD/188/Suppl.) February 1976, p. 32.
4. *Debt Problems*, pp. 1, 16.

40. Food Aid for Whom?

1. John McClung, "Dr. Spitzer Views Food Resources as Tool in Defending Nation's System," *Feedstuffs* (December 8, 1975): 7.
2. Richard Barnet and Ronald Mueller, *Global Reach* (New York: Simon and Schuster, 1974).
3. John Reibel, "Food Aid to India" (Mt. Airy Rd., Croton-on-Hudson, New York 10520, 1975), p. 1
4. Pascal de Pury, Agricultural Engineer, World Council of Churches, Geneva, Switzerland, personal communication, November 14, 1975.
5. W. L. Clayton, Assistant Secretary of State, U.S., Congress, House of Representatives, *Hearings on H.R. 2211, Bretton Woods Agreement Act,* Committee on Banking and Currency, 79th Cong. Ist. sess. March 9, 1945, pp. 275, 282; cited by Michael Hudson in *Super-Imperialism — The Economic Strategy of American Empire* (New York: Holt, Rinehart and Winston, 1972), pp. 92–93.
6. Eldridge Haynes, editor and publisher, *Business International* and testimony

before the Senate Committee on Agriculture and Forestry, *Policies and Operations under P.L. 480* (Washington, D.C.: Government Printing Office, 1957), p. 395.

7. "U.S. Grain Arsenal," Latin America and Empire Report, North American Congress on Latin America (NACLA) 9,7 (October 1975), p. 9.
8. Ibid.
9. Dan Morgan, "Opening Markets: Program Pushes U.S. Food," *Washington Post.*, March 10, 1975.
10. Dan Morgan, "Impact of U.S. Food Heavy on South Korea," *Washington Post*, March 12, 1975.
11. North American Congress on Latin America, Interview with George Shanklin, Assistant Administrator, Commercial Export Programs, p. 23.
12. Morgan, "Impact of U.S. Food on South Korea."
13. Ibid.
14. Leonard Dudley and Roger Sandilands, "The Side Effects of Foreign Aid: The Case of P.L. 480 Wheat in Colombia," *Economic Development and Cultural Change* (January 1975): 321.
15. Ibid., pp. 331, 332.
16. Ibid.
17. Melvin Burke, "Does 'Food for Peace' Assistance Damage the Bolivian Economy?" *Inter-American Economic Affairs* 25, (1971): 9 and 17.
18. J. S. Mann, "The Impact of Public Law 480 on Prices and Domestic Supply of Cereals in India," *Journal of Farm Economics* 49 (February 1969): 143.
19. Arthur Mead, "P.L. 480 — Humanitarian Effort Helps Develop Markets," *Foreign Agriculture* (USDA) 13 (May 26, 1975): 29.
20. Dan Morgan, "Self-Interest, Markets Bedevil World Food Aid," *Washington Post*, July 5, 1975.
21. U.S., Department of Agriculture, *Foreign Agriculture* 13 (May 26, 1975): 2.
22. Jacques Chonchol et al., *World Hunger: Causes and Remedies* (Washington, D.C.: Transnational Institute Report, Institute for Policy Studies, 1974), pp. 39–40.
23. Hubert Humphrey, testimony before the Senate Committee on Foreign Relations, 1959.
24. U.S. AID, *U.S. Overseas Loans and Grants and Obligations from International Organizations: Obligations and Loan Authorizations, July 1, 1945–June 30, 1973*, Office of Financial Management.
25. William Ryan and Peter Henriot, "Message from Bucharest for Washington and Rome," *America* (November 2, 1974): 251.
26. *Washington Post*, October 26, 1974, p. 7.
27. North American Congress on Latin America, p. 13.
28. Ibid., p. 14.
29. Morgan, "Impact of U.S. Food on South Korea."
30. North American Congress on Latin America, p. 14.
31. Editorial, *The New Republic*, December 7, 1974.
32. North American Congress on Latin America, p. 14.
33. Ibid., p. 15.
34. President Ford, speech before the U.N. General Assembly, *New York Times*, September 19, 1974, quoted in North American Congress on Latin America, p. 17.
35. *Washington Post*, December 18, 1975, pp. A1 and A16.
36. Food and Agriculture Organization, *The World Food Programme*, 3d. edition, 1973, p. 19.

41. What About the "New" Aid?

1. World Bank and IDA, *The World Bank in Africa* (Washington, D.C., January 1973), p. 7.
2. The World Bank, *Assault on World Poverty* (Baltimore: Johns Hopkins University Press, 1975), pp. 106, 118.
3. Ibid., p. 194.
4. Ibid., p. 185.
5. Ibid., pp. 154–155.
6. Ibid., pp. 159–160.
7. World Bank, *The World Bank Annual Report* (Washington, D.C., 1974), p. 75.
8. World Bank, *Assault on World Poverty*, p. 143.
9. Ibid.
10. World Bank and IDA, *The World Bank in Africa*, January 1973, p. 14.
11. World Bank, *Assault on World Poverty*, p. 125.
12. World Bank, *The World Bank Group in the Americas* (Washington, D.C., May 1974), pp. 43, 51.
13. World Bank, *Assault on World Poverty*, pp. 139–140.
14. World Bank, "Rural Development," (Sector Policy Paper) February 1975, p. 40.
15. *World Bank Annual Report–1974* Fact Sheet, (fold out page) and *The World Bank Group in the Americas*, May 1974.

42. Has AID Seen the Light?

1. H.R. 9005 passed by the Senate, November 1975, p. 35.
2. U.S., Department of Commerce, *Money Income and Poverty Status of Families and Persons in the United States: 1975 and 1974 Revisions* (Advance Report) (Series P-60, no. 103), September 1976.
3. Peter Henle, "Explaining the Distribution of Earned Income," *Monthly Labor Review*, U.S., Department of Labor, December 1972.
4. Lester C. Thurow, "Tax Wealth, Not Income," *New York Times Magazine*, April 11, 1976, p. 33.
5. World Bank, *Size Distribution of Income: A Compilation of Data*, prepared by Shail Jain, 1975, pp. 51, 108.
6. U.S., Department of Agriculture, *Farm Income Statistics*, Statistical Bulletin No. 547, July 1975; and U.S., Department of Agriculture, *Agricultural Statistics 1972*.
7. U.S., Department of Agriculture, *Our Land and Water Resources* (Miscellaneous Publication No. 1290) (USDA/ERS), May 1974, p. 23.
8. U.S. AID, "A Practical Agency Approach to Rural Development," prepared by S. H. Butterfield, mimeographed, February 1975, p. 4.
9. U.S. AID, *Food and Nutrition*, adapted from summary presented to Congress, July 1975, p. 16.
10. Triffa/Dukkala Irrigation Projects.
11. U.S. AID, "Implementation of 'New Directions' in Development Assistance," (Washington, D.C.: Government Printing Office, July 22, 1975), p. 12. Fiscal 1976, Submission to Congress, pp. 53–54.
12. Benedict J. Kerkvliet, "Land Reform in the Philippines Since the Marcos Coup," Twenty-sixth Annual Meeting of the Association of Asian Studies, Boston, Massachusetts, April 1–2, 1973.
13. *LAAD Annual Report* 1974.
14. Jack C. Corbett and Ronald J. Ivey, *Evaluation of the Latin American Agribus-*

iness Development Corporation, Checchi and Co., Washington, D.C., July 31, 1974.

15. U.S. AID, *AID in an Interdependent World*, A Summary of the Presentation to the Congress, FY 1976.
16. Steve Weissman, *Trojan Horse — A Radical Look at Foreign Aid* (San Francisco: Ramparts Press, 1974), p. 238 quoting the *Congressional Record*, November 9, 1971 and November 19, 1971.
17. COFFLA, Special Correspondent's Report from Santiago, November 24, 1972.
18. Joseph D. Collins, "Tightening the Financial Knot," in *Chile: The Allende Years* (New York: IDOC, 1973), 70ff.
19. U.S. AID, *Submission to Congress, Latin American Programs*, FY 1976, May 1975, pp. 43–57.
20. Jacobo Shatan, interview 1976.
21. The Week in Review, *New York Times*, February 22, 1976, p. 2.
22. U.S. AID, *Submission to Congress Latin American Programs*.
23. *New York Times*, January 9, 1976, pp. 1, 5.
24. *Defense Monitor* 4 (August 1975).
25. U.S. Army School of the Americas Catalogue and Tables submitted to NACLA.
26. U.S., Department of Defense Tables, 1975, submitted to NACLA.
27. *Defense Monitor*, 4 (August 1975).
28. *New York Times*, January 26, 1976, pp. 1, 14.
29. U.S. Army School of the Americas, Course 0-47, Curriculum, "Urban Counter-Insurgency Operations," p. 22.

43. Can Voluntary Agencies Play a Constructive Role?

1. Gerry Nadel, "Guatemala after the Terremoto," *The Atlantic Monthly*, July 1976.
2. Edward Bullard, President of Technoserve, testimony before the Subcommittee on Foreign Assistance and Economic Policy of the Senate Committee on Foreign Relations, July 21, 1975.

Part X   Food First!

44. What Does Food Self-Reliance Mean?

1. International Labor Office, *Rural Poverty: Trends and Explanations*, prepared by Keith Griffin and Azizur Rahman Khan, Working Papers, World Employment Programme Research, forthcoming, 1977.
2. International Labor Office, *Land Reform in Asia*, edited by Zubeda Ahmad, World Employment Programme Research, Working Papers, 1976.
3. Takedazu Ogura, ed., *Agricultural Development in Modern Japan* (Tokyo: Japan FAO Association, 1963), p. 25.
4. Edgar Owens and Robert Shaw, *Development Reconsidered* (Lexington, Mass.: Heath, 1972), p. 73.
5. Donald W. Bray and Timothy F. Harding, "Cuba," in *Latin America: The Struggle with Dependency and Beyond*, eds., Ronald Chilcote and Joel Edelstein (Cambridge, Mass.: Schenkman; New York: Wiley, 1974), p. 629.
6. U.N., Asian Development Institute, "Toward a Theory of Rural Development," prepared by Wahidul Haque et al., December, 1975, 60 ff.
7. P.L. Raikes, "Ujamaa and Rural Socialism," *Review of African Political Economy*," No. 3, May/June 1975.

8. Leo Huberman and Paul Sweezy, *Socialism in Cuba* (New York: Monthly Review Press, 1969), p. 67. Figures from the National Bank of Cuba.
9. Robert Ledogar, *Hungry for Profits* (New York: IDOC/North America, 1975), Chapter 5.
10. Johan Galtung, "Self-Reliance: Concepts, Practice, and Rationale," Ecumenical Institute, Chateau de Bossey, CH-1298, Celigny, Switzerland, April 1976.
11. Harlow Hodgson, "We Don't Need to Eliminate Beef Cattle," *Crops and Soils Magazine* (November 1974): 9–11.
12. Food and Agriculture Organization, *Report on China's Agriculture*, prepared by H.V. Henle, 1974, p. 114.
13. Dudley Jackson, "Third World Food Crisis," *New Society* (May 16, 1974): 380.
14. David Feldman and Peter Lawrence, "The Social and Economic Implications of the Large Scale Introduction of New Varieties of Foodgrains," *Africa Report*, UNRISD, Geneva, 1975, p. 215.
15. Food and Agriculture Organization, *Report on China's Agriculture*, 37ff.
16. "The Chinese Approach to Rural Development," *International Development Review* 15 (1973): 4.
17. Food and Agriculture Organization, "First FAO Professional Study Mission to China: Some Preliminary Observations," October 1975, p. 7.
18. Latin America Working Group Letter, vol. 2, 7 (February/March 1975): 18–19.

45. But Where Would Development Capital Come From?

1. See Dudley Seers, "The Meaning of Development," in *The Political Economy of Development*, eds. Norman T. Uphoff and Warren F. Ilchman, (Berkeley: University of California Press, 1972).
2. Richard J. Barnet and Ronald Mueller, *Global Reach: The Power of the Multinational Corporation* (New York: Simon and Schuster, 1974).
3. Banco Central, cited in *Latin America Economic Report*, January 9, 1976,4 no. 2, p. 6.
4. J. Gurley, "Rural Development in China," in *Employment in Developing Nations*, ed. E. D. Edwards (New York: Columbia University Press, 1974), p. 385.
5. Food and Agriculture Organization, *Progress in Land Reform — Sixth Report*, Rural Institutions Division, Rome, April, 1975, pp. III-69, III-70.
6. Food and Agriculture Organization, "Report on China's Agriculture," prepared by H. V. Henle, 1974, p. 200.
7. Swedish International Development Authority and Food and Agriculture Organization, "Use of Organic Materials and Green Manures as Fertilizers in Developing Countries" prepared by Ambika Singh, in *Organic Materials as Fertilizers*, Rome, 1975, p. 29.
8. Amulya Kumar and N. Reddy, "The Trojan Horse," *Ceres* (March/April 1976): 43; for greater detail see Arjun Makhijani with Alan Poole, *Energy and Agriculture in the Third World* (Cambridge, Mass.: Ballinger, 1976), Chapter 4.
9. Joan Robinson, *Economic Management in China*, Modern China Series, no. 4, p. 14.

46. Aren't Poor Peasants Too Oppressed Ever to Change?

1. Food and Agriculture Organization, *Progress in Land Reform — Sixth Report*, Rural Institutions Division, Rome, April 1975, p. III-88.
2. Ben Wisner, "Famine Relief and People's War," *Review of African Political Economy* no. 2, 77ff.

3. *Jeunesse du Vietnam*, May 1974, p. 14.
4. "Guinea-Bissau, Reinventing Education," IDAC Document 11/12, Winter 1975, Spring 1976, (27 Chemin des Crets, 1218 Grand Saconnex, Geneva, Switzerland), p. 6.
5. See Wisner, "Famine Relief."
6. *New York Times*, Nov. 14, 1975, p. 6, and Nov. 30, 1975, p. 3 of the News of the Week in Review.
7. Army School of the Americas Catalogue and other official sources.
8. *Latin America* (a weekly, Latin American Newsletter Ltd., 6 & 7 New Bridge Street, London EC4V 6HR) 9, 49 (December 12, 1975): 391.
9. U.N. Asian Development Institute, "Towards a Theory of Rural Development," prepared by Wahidul Haque et al., December 1975.

47. Food versus Freedom?

1. Johan Galtung and Fumiko Nishimura, "Learning from the Chinese People," unpublished manuscript.
2. "The Chinese Approach to Rural Development," *International Development Review* 15 (1973): 6.
3. Stuart Dowty, "Work: China," *China — People and Questions*, ed. Ward L. Kaiser (New York: Friendship Press and IDOC/North America), p. 22.

48. What Can We Do?

1. U.S., Department of Agriculture, *Our Land and Water Resources* (USDA/ERS, Misc. Publication No. 1290, 1974), p. 32.
2. U.S., Department of Agriculture, *Foreign Agricultural Trade of the United States (FATUS)* (USDA/ERS, April, 1976), p. 25.

Recommended for Further Study

Part II   The Scarcity Scare

Bryan, Helen. *Fertilizer: Part of the Solution, or Part of the Problem?* War on Want, 467 Caledonian Road, London N7 9BE.

Farvar, M. Taghi, and Milton, John P., eds. *Careless Technology.* Garden City, New Jersey: The Natural History Press, 1972.

Food and Agriculture Organization. *Progress in Land Reform — Sixth Report,* 1975.

Kocher, James. "Rural Development, Income Distribution, and Fertility Decline." An occasional paper of the Population Council, New York, 1973.

Mamdani, Mahmood. *The Myth of Population Control — Family, Class, and Caste in an Indian Village.* New York and London: Monthly Review Press, 1972.

Pimentel, David. "Realities of a Pesticide Ban," *Environment* 15 (March 1973): 18–31.

Shea, Kevin P. "Nerve Damage," *Environment* 16, 9 (November 1974).

Swedish International Development Authority and Food and Agriculture Organization. *Organic Materials as Fertilizers.* Soils Bulletin 27, 1975.

Turner, James S. *A Chemical Feast: Report on the Food and Drug Administration* (Ralph Nader Study Group Reports). New York: Grossman, 1970.

United Nations Research Institute for Social Development (UNRISD). *Famine Risk and Famine Prevention in the Modern World,* 1976.

Ware, Helen. "The Sahelian Drought: Some Thoughts on the Future," Research Fellow, Dept. of Demography, Australian National University, March 26, 1975.

Part III   Colonial Inheritance

Beckford, George L. *Persistent Poverty — Underdevelopment in Plantation Economies of the Third World.* New York: Oxford University Press, 1972.

Feldman, David, and Lawrence, Peter. *Africa Report,* Global II Project on the Social and Economic Implications Of Large-Scale Introduction of New Varieties of Foodgrains, UNDP/UNRISD, Geneva, 1975.

Rodney, Walter. *How Europe Underdeveloped Africa.* Bogle–L'Ouverture Publications, 141 Coldershaw Road, London, W. 13, 1972.

Williams, Eric. *Capitalism and Slavery.* New York: Putnam, 1966.

Part V   Modernizing Hunger

George, Susan. *How the Other Half Dies.* London: Penguin, 1976.
Griffin, Keith. *Land Concentration and Rural Poverty.* New York: Macmillan, 1976.
————. *The Political Economy of Agrarian Change.* Cambridge, Mass.: Harvard University Press, 1974.
Griffin, Keith, and Khan, Azizur Rahman, eds. *Poverty and Landlessness in Rural Asia.* A Study by the World Employment Programme, International Labor Office, Geneva (in press, 1976).
Hewitt de Alcántara, Cynthia. Global II Project on the Social and Economic Implications of the Introduction of New Varieties of Foodgrain *Country Report — Mexico,* Geneva: UNDP/UNRISD, 1974.
————. "The Green Revolution as History," *Development and Change* 5, 2 (1973–1974).
International Labor Office. *Mechanization and Employment in Agriculture,* 1974.
Owens, Edgar, and Shaw, Robert. *Development Reconsidered: Bridging the Gap Between Government and People.* Lexington, Mass.: Heath, 1972.
Palmer, Ingrid. *Science and Agricultural Production,* UNRISD, 1972.
Pearse, Andrew. Global II Project on the Social and Economic Implications of the Introduction of New Varieties of Foodgrains, Parts I–IV, Geneva: UNDP/UNRISD, April–July, 1975.
Swedish International Development Authority and Food and Agriculture Organization. *Organic Materials as Fertilizers.* Soils Bulletin 27, 1975.

Part VI   The Trade Trap

Galeano, Eduardo. *Open Veins in Latin America: Five Centuries of the Pillage of a Continent.* New York: Monthly Review, 1973.
Gallis, Marion. *Trade for Justice: Myth or Mandate?* Geneva: World Council of Churches, 1972.
Jonas, Susanne, and David Tobis, eds. *Guatemala.* New York and Berkeley: North American Congress on Latin America (NACLA), 1974.
Palmer, Ingrid. *Food and the New Agricultural Technology,* UNRISD, 1972.
Payer, Cheryl, ed. *Commodity Trade in the Third World.* New York: John Wiley and Son, 1975.

Part VII   The Myth of Food Power

Barnes, Peter, ed. *The Peoples' Land.* A reader on land reform in the United States. Emmaus, Pa.: Rodale, 1975.
Commoner, Barry. *The Poverty of Power.* New York: Knopf, 1976.
deMarco, Susan, and Sechler, Susan. *The Fields Turn Brown — Four Essays on World Hunger.* Washington, D.C.: Agribusiness Accountability Project, 1975.
Hamilton, Martha. *The Great Grain Robbery and Other Stories.* Washington, D.C.: Agribusiness Accountability Project, 1972.
Hightower, Jim. *Eat Your Heart Out: How Food Profiteers Victimize the Consumer,* New York: Crown, 1975.
North American Congress on Latin America (NACLA), "U.S. Grain Arsenal," *Latin America and Empire Report* 9, 7 (October 1975).

Part VIII World Hunger as Big Business

Berg, Alan. *The Nutrition Factor*. Washington, D.C.: The Brookings Institution, 1973.

Cullen, Vincent C. "Sour Pineapples," *America* (November 6, 1976).

DeMarco, Susan, and Susan Sechler. *The Fields Have Turned Brown — Four Essays on World Hunger*. Washington, D.C.: The Agribusiness Accountability Project, 1975.

The Food Action Campaign Papers, "Crystal City, Texas — A Del Monte Company Town." Washington, D.C.: Agribusiness Accountability Project.

Hightower, Jim. *Eat Your Heart Out: How Food Profiteers Victimize the Consumer*. New York: Crown, 1975.

Jonas, Susanne, and David Tobis, eds. *Guatemala*. New York and Berkeley: North American Congress on Latin America (NACLA) 1974.

Latham, Michael C. "Introduction," *The Promotion of Bottle Feeding by Multinational Corporations: How Advertising and the Health Professions Have Contributed*, ed. Ted Greiner. Ithaca: Cornell University Monograph Series, no. 2, 1975.

Ledogar, Robert J. *Hungry for Profits: U.S. Food and Drug Multinationals in Latin America*. New York: IDOC, 1976.

Muller, Mike. *The Baby Killer*. London: War on Want, 1975; 467 Caledonian Road.

North American Congress on Latin America (NACLA), "Bitter Fruits," *Latin America and Empire Report*. Berkeley, CA.: September 1976.

Wellford, Harrison. *Sowing the Wind*. New York: Grossman. 1972.

Part IX The Helping Hand-Out: Aid for Whom?

Chonchol, Jacques, et al. *World Hunger: Causes and Remedies*. Washington, D.C.: Transnational Institute Report, Institute for Policy Studies, 1974.

"Foreign Aid: Evading the Control of Congress," *International Policy Report*, Center for International Policy, Washington, D.C., January 1977.

Hayter, Theresa. *Aid as Imperialism*. Magnolia: Mass.: Peter Smith Publishing, Inc., 6 Lexington Ave., Mass. 01938.

North American Congress on Latin America (NACLA), "U.S. Grain Arsenal," *Latin American and Empire Report*, 9, 7 (October 1975).

National Action/Research on the Military-Industrial Complex (NARMIC). *Food as a Weapon — The Food for Peace Program*. 112 South 16th Street, Philadelphia, Pa., 1975.

Payer, Cheryl. *The Debt Trap: The IMF and the Third World*. London: Penguin, 1974.

Weissman, Steve. *The Trojan Horse: A Radical Look at Foreign Aid*. San Francisco: Ramparts, 1974.

Yost, Israel. "The Food for Peace Arsenal," *NACLA Newsletter* 5, 3 (May-June 1971): 1–13.

Part X Food First!

Ahmad, Zubeda. "The Chinese Approach to Rural Development," *International Development Review* 15, 4, 1973.

Food and Agriculture Organization. *Progress in Land Reform — Sixth Report*, 1975.

Food and Agriculture Organization. *Report on China's Agriculture*, prepared by H. V. Henle, 1974.

Galtung, Johan. "Self-Reliance: Concepts, Practice, and Rationale," Ecumenical Institute, Château de Bossey, CH-1298, Celigny, Switzerland, April 1976.

International Labor Office. *Land Reform in Asia*, edited by Zubeda Ahmad. World Employment Programme Research, Working Papers, 1976.

U.N. Asian Development Institute. "Towards a Theory of Rural Development," prepared by Wahidul Haque, December 1975.

Organizations and Publications

To link up with the food network, why not write to any of these research and action groups for more information or sample copies of their publications:

In the United States

Agribusiness Accountability Project-East, 1000 Wisconsin Ave., N.W., Washington, D.C. 20007; research studies are available and book on U.S. agriculture forthcoming.

Agribusiness Accountability Project-West, 1095 Market Street, Rm. 620, San Francisco, CA 94103. Publication: *The Agbiz Tiller*, P.O. Box 5646, San Francisco, CA 94101.

Agricultural Resources Center, P.O. Box 646, Chapel Hill, NC 27514. Speakers available; cofounded by Cary Fowler.

Bread for the World, 207 E. 16th St., New York, N.Y. 10003. Publication: Newsletter, focuses on hunger-related legislation.

Center for Rural Affairs, P.O. Box 405, Walthill, NB. 68087. Publications: Newsletter, *New Land Review* and research studies.

Center for Science in the Public Interest, 1757 S Street, N.W., Washington, D.C. 20009. Publication: *Nutrition Action*. Sponsors of Food Day.

Community Land Trust Center, % C.C.E.D., 639 Mass Ave., Cambridge, MA 02139. Publication: *Community Land Trusts*

Community Nutrition Institute, 1910 K Street, N.W., Washington, D.C. 20006. Publication: *Community Nutrition Institute Weekly Report*

Corporate Data Exchange, 198 Broadway, Room 707, New York, NY 10038. Initiating study of ownership of agribusiness corporations.

Earthwork — Center for Rural Studies, 1499 Potrero Ave., San Francisco, CA 94110. Bibliography available of educational material that they distribute.

Economic Development Bureau, 234 Colony Rd., New Haven, CT 06511. An alternative consulting service putting people with technical skills in touch with progressive Third World groups.

Food Action Center, 1028 Connecticut Avenue, N.W., Washington, D.C. 20036. Publication: *Food Action Exchange*

Institute for Food and Development Policy, 2588 Mission St., San Francisco, CA 94110. See coupon at end of book.

Institute for Local Self-Reliance, 1717 18th Street, N.W., Washington, D.C. 20009. Publication: *Self-Reliance*

Interfaith Center for Corporate Responsibility, 475 Riverside Dr., Rm. 566, New York, NY 10027. Film: *Bottle Babies* (See Question 37).

452   *Organizations and Publications*

National Catholic Rural Life Conference, 3801 Grand Ave., Des Moines, IA 50312. Publication: *Catholic Rural Life*
National Land for People, 1759 Fulton, Fresno, CA 93701. Publications: *People, Land, Food* (monthly), *Who Owns the Land* (monograph)
North American Congress on Latin America (NACLA), Box 57, Cathedral Sta., New York, NY 10025 or P.O. Box 226, Berkeley, CA 94701. Publication: *Latin America and Empire Report*
Oxfam America, P.O. Box 288, Boston, Mass. 02116. Sponsors self-help projects domestically and in the Third World. Write for resource guide, *Cross-world Food Puzzle*.
World Hunger Year (W.H.Y.), P.O. Box 1975, Garden City, Long Island, NY 11530. Publication (with the Institute for Food and Development Policy): *Food Monitor*, P.O. Box 1975, Garden City, NY 11530.

In Canada

Canadian Council for International Cooperation (National), 75 Sparks Street, Ottawa, Canada KIP 5A5.
Development Education Center, 121 Avenue Road, Toronto, Ontario.
DEVERIC, 1539 Birmingham Street, Halifax, Nova Scotia.
GATT-fly (National), 11 Madison Avenue, Toronto, Ontario M52 252.
IDEA Center, Box 32, Station C, Winnipeg, Manitoba.
IDERA, 2524 Cypress Avenue, Vancouver, B.C.
National Farmers Union (National), 250-C Second Avenue, Saskatoon, Saskatchewan, Canada S7K 2M1.
One Sky Center, 134 Avenue F South, Sasketoon, Saskatchewan.
Ontarion Public Interest Research Group (OPIRG), Room 226–Physics Bldg., University of Waterloo, Waterloo, Ontario.

Other Important Publications

Action for Development, FAO, 00100 Rome, Italy.
Asian Action, Newsletter of the Asian Cultural Forum on Development, Room 201; 399/1 Soi Siri, off Silom Road, Bangkok–5, Thailand.
Ceres, FAO Review on Development, UNIPUB, 650 First Avenue, P.O. Box 433, Murray Hill Station, New York, N.Y. 10016.
International Bulletin, P.O. Box 4400, Berkeley, CA 94704.
Latin America and *Latin America Economic Report*, Latin American Newsletters Ltd., 90-93 Cowcross Street, London EC1M 6BL, England.
New Internationalist, 113 Atlantic Ave., Brooklyn, N.Y. 11201.

Films

For an annotated guide to films on food and land issues as well as ideas for using film as an organizing tool, write to Earthwork, 1499 Potrero Ave., San Francisco, CA 94110.

Index

THE INSTITUTE FOR FOOD AND DEVELOPMENT POLICY
is an independent, not-for-profit research, documentation, and
education center for issues that link together U.S. agriculture,
hunger in America, world hunger, and underdevelopment.

Through a monthly publication, pamphlets, and articles, the
Institute provides material suited to individual study, church
groups, schools, and universities. Speakers are also available.

To receive information about publications of the Institute, please
fill out and send us this coupon.

Name _____

Street _____

City / State _____ Zip _____

Comments about your needs or our work _____

Send to: Institute for Food and Development Policy
           2588 Mission Street
           San Francisco, California 94110